Methods for Studying Language Production

Figure drawn by Diane Bond Hunt for *Language Development* by Peter Reich. Reprinted from Reich (1986) by kind permission of the artist, the author, and Prentice-Hall Publishers.

METHODS FOR STUDYING LANGUAGE PRODUCTION

Edited by

Lise Menn
University of Colorado

Nan Bernstein Ratner
University of Maryland

LEA LAWRENCE ERLBAUM ASSOCIATES, PUBLISHERS
2000   Mahwah, New Jersey   London

Lawrence Erlbaum Associates, Inc., Publishers
10 Industrial Avenue
Mahwah, New Jersey 07430-2262

Library of Congress Cataloging-in-Publication Data
Methods for studying language production / edited by Lise Menn, Nan
Bernstein Ratner
    p.   cm.
Includes bibliographical references and index.
ISBN 0–8058–3033–2 (c : alk. paper). — ISBN 0–8058–3034–0
(p : alk. paper)
    1. Language acquisition—Research—Methodology. 2. Language
disorders—Research—Methodology. I. Menn, Lise. II. Ratner, Nan
Bernstein.
P118.M47   1999
401'.43'072—dc21   99-12768
CIP

Printed in the United States of America
10 9 8 7 6 5 4 3 2 1

Contents

II.   GATHERING PRODUCTION DATA IN NATURALISTIC SETTINGS

III. DEVELOPMENTAL DISORDERS

IV. ADULT DISORDERS

1

In the Beginning Was the Wug: Forty Years of Language-Elicitation Studies

Nan Bernstein Ratner
University of Maryland

Lise Menn
University of Colorado

All fundamental scientific innovation must marry new ways of thinking with better styles of seeing. Neither abstract theorizing nor meticulous observation can provoke a change of such magnitude all by itself.
—Gould (1998, p. 18)

This book represents some major approaches to collecting language production data from children and young adults, but it is not intended as a complete handbook, which would require a much larger volume. The use of elicited narrative in cross-linguistic comparative developmental study, for example, has been richly elaborated elsewhere, especially by Berman and Slobin (1994), and is not covered here; for narrative in cross-linguistic aphasiology, Menn and Obler (1990) may be useful. Other aspects of production and methods of eliciting specific syntactic forms have been covered in the first several chapters of McDaniel, McKee, and Cairns (1998). For priming studies, see Bock, Lobell, & Morey (1992) and other

1

papers cited in Bock and Levelt (1994). The CHILDES data analysis (see also Sokolov & Snow, 1994) and the CHILDES Bib database can be searched for more information on how database corpora have been used (www//childes.psy.cmu.edu).

This book also is limited in its treatment of cross-cultural issues in data collection: The way people talk to children in front of strangers or while they are being recorded may differ a great deal across cultures, and even more when the stranger is a foreigner. This said, we are delighted to present a wider range of topics in language elicitation than has ever been brought together. All the contributors speak from experience, and we have all learned the art of elicitation by apprenticeship and by trial and error. We have created this book in the hopes of reducing the number of trials that you, the reader, will have to endure.

LOOKING BACKWARD: IN THE BEGINNING WAS THE WUG

Before the late 1950s language production was studied naturalistically, with rare efforts to elicit language knowledge through experimental paradigms. This was particularly true for the study of child language (Bar-Adon & Leopold, 1971). We begin our book on methods of studying language production, begins with a review of the paradigm that changed the nature of developmental psycholinguistic research: Berko Gleason's (1958)[1] wug test. Through the use of hand-drawn figures of whimsical creatures performing odd acts, Berko elicited plurals, past tenses, and diminutives, among other morphological affixes, by presenting the now classic task: "This is a picture of a wug. Now I have two of them. I have two ____."

The responses of Berko Gleason's subjects' provided the first experimental evidence that young children had productive knowledge of the morphological patterns of their language, generalizable to novel word forms. Prideaux (1985) noted:

---

[1] For comprehension of spoken language, Brown's (1957) article on children's comprehension of the morphological markers of syntactic category ("some niss," "a niss," "nissing") seems to be the first experimental study.

Bogoyavlenskiy (1957/1973), translated and reprinted in Ferguson & Slobin (1973), independently developed a production paradigm with three stimuli that he used to test eight children. However, this research was not available to most students of child language acquisition until 15 years after Berko's study made its mark on the field.

Jean Berko, in her pioneering work in language acquisition, set the stage for a great deal of experimental work by providing both conceptual and methodological orientations which have proven very valuable and productive . . . [this] work constitute[d] a landmark in language acquisition research. It set the stage for a series of studies employing her basic methodology, or variations of it, which have reaped rich rewards over the . . . years. (pp. 8–9)

Other researchers called the paradigm "ingenious" (Clark & Clark, 1977; Maratsos, 1979) and "a great methodological contribution" (Slobin, 1973) to child language acquisition research. Uniquely, the wug was both a controlled and naturalistic method for eliciting language behavior, at least for children who are used to playing utterance-completion games with their caregivers.

The wug has been used in many ways over the years. A citation search of published research that has utilized "wug like tasks," as they are sometimes called, reveals extensions of the technique almost immediately following its original publication. Many researchers sought to replicate Berko's findings of morphological knowledge by young children, extending the original scope of inquiry to speakers of other languages and bilinguals,[2] children with varying diagnoses of specific language impairment or delay,[3] children and adults with mental retardation,[4] reading-impaired children,[5] and children from differing socioeconomic and dialect communities.[6] Even a cursory listing of such efforts reveals their scope and remarkable frequency.

Subsequent work with English-speaking children was able to detail more finely the progress that children make toward mastery of the individual morphemes targeted by the wug task (Anisfeld & Tucker, 1967; Derwing & Baker, 1979; Ervin, 1964; Menn & MacWhinney, 1984; see also Prideaux, 1985, for discussion of unpublished research using the wug technique). Refinement of the design also allowed researchers to evaluate the adequacy of competing accounts of how regular affixation is mastered (see Derwing & Baker, 1986).

---

[2] For example, a representative listing would include the following: French: Hiriartborde & de la Bouillerie (1973); Spanish: Perez Pereira (1989); Russian: Zakharova (1973); Hungarian and German: MacWhinney (1978); Finnish: Lyytinen (1987); Quechua: Isbell (1972); and Bilinguals: Gray and Cameron (1980).

[3] For example, Wiig, Semel, & Crouse (1967), and Bellaire, Plante, & Swisher (1994).

[4] For example, Dever (1972) and Dever & Gardner (1970.

[5] For example, Wood (1985) and Mahoney (1994).

[6] For example, Ramer & Rees (1973).

Almost immediately following publication of Berko Gleason's research, clinicians noted the possible extension of the wug paradigm to formal assessment of language performance in children with suspected disorder. The Berry–Talbott Test was but one of many attempts to adapt the wug task as a tool for assessment (see Berry, 1969; more recently, Channell & Ford, 1991; Rubin, Patterson, & Kantor, 1991). However, clinical use of the wug task has been sporadic because of concerns about its relation to spontaneous language performance and the appropriateness of its normative expectations. More recently, as researchers focus attention on familial forms of specific language impairment (SLI; e.g., Gopnik & Crago, 1991), the "wug test" has been used to assess the nature of the underlying deficit in this population (Goad & Rebellati, 1994). Not only has nonsense-word affixation been tested, but the very ability of SLI children to associate the novel word *wug* with a variety of concepts has been appraised under varying levels of support (see Ellis Weismer & Hesketh, 1993). Similarly, the wug test has been used to assess conceptual generalization in Down syndrome children (Duffy & Wishart, 1994).

A review of citation lists of Berko Gleason's (1958) *Word* article over the years gives an interesting mini-view of the evolution of developmental psycholinguistics. References to the wug task appear among the first issues of many seminal journals of our time, such as *Applied Psycholinguistics* and the *Journal of Child Language*. In the first 15 years following publication, the article was extensively cited by researchers attempting to validate its utility and extend its findings to nontypical populations. Over time, however, it became apparent that children from infinitely varied backgrounds can in fact generate appropriate morphological inflections for words they have never encountered before; thus, the fact that almost any human being can do the task (albeit some more successfully than others) became much less interesting than the question of how it is accomplished.

A number of alternative hypotheses can explain how children perform on wuglike tasks (see Prideaux, 1985, for a particularly thorough discussion). The nonsense-word paradigm continues to feed active debate on the adequacy of competing models in explaining morphological acquisition and the potential role of modularity in language learning and use (cf. Prasada & Pinker, 1993); thus, after a period of relative quiet, citations of the article burgeoned in the 1990s. The wug has become a sort of rallying point for theories and simulations of how networks learn to generalize to novel events (e.g., Rumelhart & McClelland, 1986) and whether, for instance, the ability of children to inflect is best interpreted by connectionist models or by symbolic, rule-based architectures. The original interpretation of the wug studies, that children do not learn to inflect by rote or mimicry, has been tempered over the years by proposals that some language learning may indeed occur by rote, as well as by analogy and rule (MacWhinney, 1978). As theory now grapples with the results of functional brain imaging tasks, the wug task surfaces in discussions of how best to interpret neuro-imaging data on past tense processing (e.g., the debate between Jaeger et al., 1996, and Seidenberg & Hoeffner, 1998).

Because this is a book about language-elicitation techniques, some analysis of the strengths and weaknesses of the historic technique is appropriate. Extended application of the paradigm brought with it meta-analysis of its utility, including thoughtful discussion of the role that Berko Gleason's clever original pictured stimuli (or any pictured prompts) played in supporting children's performance on morphological tasks, as well as the inevitable discussion of whether nonsense-word affixation tasks were legitimate windows into the process by which children learn morphology or are able to demonstrate their competence (cf. Levy, 1987; Lewis & Windsor, 1996). It has become increasingly clear that subjects of all ages and degrees of linguistic sophistication tend, for the most part, to do more poorly on nonsense-word affixation tasks than on those that utilize real words of the language (e.g., Miller & Ervin, 1964; Perez Pereira, 1989); in fact, Berko herself noted this discrepancy in comparing the responses of her young subjects to the nonsense words and selected real-word stimuli. As thesis advisor to the original study, Brown (1973) provided a careful analysis of how to relate Berko Gleason's data to patterns of affixation in spontaneous language. He suggested important differences between controlled elicitation of grammatical affixes and spontaneous language use, including the child's need to understand cue words in the experimental carrier phrases (e.g., "yesterday" and "whose") and ability to focus on relevant aspects of the supporting pictorial stimuli.

Brown noted that Adam, Eve and Sarah's spontaneous language performance did not pattern exactly like performance by older children in the original wug study. His 1973 text spends more than 10 pages considering whether these differences can be accounted for by differing criteria for judging morpheme productivity. An immediate observation was that Brown's famous "14 morphemes" list collapsed all allomorphic variations into single morpheme classes (such as plural or past tense), whereas Berko Gleason's careful sampling of the varying morphophonemic contexts elicited a wide range of performance from children that seemed to depress accurate production of a supposedly early acquired morpheme seen in spontaneous language. In an analysis similar to one that motivated Bryant and Anisfeld's (1969) experimental inquiry into morphological perform-ance, Brown noted that there are probably at least three levels of difficulty in the original wug-set stimuli: those stem + affix pairs that only require the child to know a basic form of affix and to automatically apply voicing assimilation (dogs, cats; tagged, walked); those that pose an additional burden of specifying the voicing (days; played); and those that are phono-logically context and morpheme specific (houses; patted). Although oblig-atory contexts for the more difficult forms are less frequent in children's spontaneous speech samples than are those for the first group of affixes, Berko Gleason sampled broadly and somewhat evenly across the allo-morphs, thereby depressing the children's apparent level of competence—as well as producing differences in patterns of acquisition between her data and Brown's subsequent data. In a discussion that foreshadowed later con-cern over the roles that imitation and rule abstraction might play in lan-guage development (cf. MacWhinney, 1978; Pinker, 1991), Brown also speculated that some real-word plurals might, after all, be stored as wholes, whereas others might not.

Brown also noted another important methodological difference between spontaneous language sampling and elicitation tasks that is relevant to many concepts discussed later in this volume. Language sampling tends to isolate patterns in language from large amounts of data produced by small numbers of subjects, whereas Berko Gleason's study paved the way for eliciting data from large numbers of subjects. Cross-sectional patterns of failure or success of individual children may thus fail to duplicate patterns of mastery that emerge during the development of a single child. Finally, the novelty of the task itself may induce changes in children's tactics for language use that do not mirror their tendencies in natural conversation. This has also been a chronic concern of researchers over the years in comparing structured vs. naturalistic means of data collection, and numerous contributors to this vol-ume address the concept. After analyzing the data in a number of ways, Brown (1973) was confident that Berko Gleason's data could be reconciled with the order of acquisition data that flowed from analysis of his own Harvard children. He closed his discussion with the observation that natura-listic and elicited methods "together give us the best chance of discovering the truth" (p. 293). Many of the chapters in this volume agree with his assess-ment, and they show how researchers have tried to marry structured ques-tions about language with more naturalistic contexts for their exploration.

Other researchers noted limitations in extrapolating children's produc-tive knowledge of inflectional morphology from wuglike tasks. Levy (1987) suggested that older children may handle the task differently from younger children, who are still acquiring the basics of their language system; her youngest subjects showed closest parallels between the nonsense-word task and affixation of real nouns. Dever (1973) noted a poor correlation between the characteristics of spontaneous speech and performance on wuglike tasks by children with mental retardation, suggesting that the technique has less utility as a predictor of spontaneous language performance in this population. Indeed, the fact that many children with cognitive impairment find the task immensely difficult sheds interesting light on the nature of their generalization difficulties (Ratner, 1998).

The wug task is most often referenced in discussions of the acquisition of inflectional morphology. However, the 1958 nonsense-word task was also used to study the abilities of children to use derivational morphemes. Children in the original study found these morphemes surprisingly difficult to use, and this observation paved the way for numerous other studies in the same area (cf. Derwing & Baker, 1986). It is also sometimes easy to forget that the wug paradigm was only part of the original set of tasks that Berko used to explore children's morphological development. In the 1958 study, children were also asked to speculate on the origins of common English compound words; interest in children's capacity to coin and de-compose such terms continues to be of interest to researchers today (see Clark, chap. 4, this volume).

The passage of time has left its mark on the wug. During the 1970s, the genderless wug found itself included in a critique that found too few female characters and role models in speech and language tests (Rabe & Matlin, 1978). Like many visual icons that have endured (e.g., cartoon characters or corporate logos), the wug has undergone some minor facelifts over time (see Fig. 1.1). Although (like many of us) it seems to have put on a little weight over the years, it seems to be busily teaching future generations of students of psycholinguistics. Perusal of textbooks and a web search of psycholinguistics and language acquisition syllabi show an almost universal use of assignments designed to encourage (or require) that students test the paradigm for themselves. (In one interesting

Fig. 1.1. The wug parade. From left to right: Berko Gleason (1958); reprint of the article in Saporta (1961); Berko Gleason & Ratner (1998).

version, the instructor has "morphed" the wug into Henry Moore–like statuary, a tribute to the artistry of the original.) As an enduring concept in psycholinguistic research, the wug has become a generic, like Kleenex or Xerox, a concept so basic to what we know and do that increasingly it appears in the popular literature without attribution to its origins (cf. Pinker, 1994; and press discussion by Allman, 1991, and Safire, 1994).

In any field, the discovery of facts is of paramount importance in moving knowledge forward. However, the discovery of techniques is no less important: We can only find keys where there is light to search by. Perhaps no innovation other than the invention of the tape recorder has had such an indelible effect on the field of child language research.

Theories come and go, including those that account for how a child knows that more than one *wug* is *wugs*. Although, we are still learning from Berko's insight that children can be asked to count cats or dogs, we can learn even more, and be challenged much more, if we also ask them to count wugs—these oddly charming little birds and their whimsical friends.

METHOD, DATA, AND THEORY: FORTY YEARS ON THE ROAD

What method should one use to investigate a particular problem? There is, of course, the issue of whether to study production at all; many psycholinguists privately admit that they prefer to study comprehension, because production data are "too messy." Well, yes, they are messy. But messes can yield surprises, which pose challenges, which can lead to reformulations of issues and whole new ways of looking at things. That's the kind of excitement some of us live for.

How do methods of data collection shape researchers' view of language knowledge and behavior? Of many possible examples, the following are two recent findings for consideration.

1. Verb-argument structures: Roland and Jurafsky (1998) showed that the frequency of occurrence of particular verb-argument structures is systematically different depending on whether one analyzes a corpus of connected text or requests subjects to make individual sentences using specified verbs.
2. Lexicon, syntax, pragmatics: As people who study child language corpora have known for years, after children's mean length of utterance (MLU) reaches about 3.5, it no longer is much of an

index of syntactic development; instead, it is highly dependent on what the children are talking about and what role the children are playing in the conversation. An extreme example is provided by research at the University of Colorado (Biasca, 1999): Narratives elicited when a language-delayed pre-reader pretended to read a story book yielded low-frequency vocabulary ("queen," "witch") and longer formulaic elements ("they have to save Snow White because you have to go on your hat top of your head") appropriate to the genre, linked together syntactically and paratactically but with virtually no semantic or pragmatic coherence.

The list of such interactions between task and performance is endless, because the experimenter's (or observer's) method itself inevitably generates unintended effects, a type of noise that is called *experimental artifact*. Such noise can be so overwhelming as to invalidate the argument; the entire data set may then turn out to be as deeply flawed as the idea that the earth is flat.

As researchers, we all (at least secretly) hope that our data—if not our conclusions—will be able to stand throughout our own lifetimes, if not longer. If we have done a good enough job of controlling for interfering factors, this may be the case; later researchers may be able to use what we have done, and the field as a whole may show an orderly progression of successive approximations to understanding—that is, an early researcher's conclusions will still stand as roughly correct, and the "noise" in their data will become the data for later, more refined work. In that case, we have the delicious paradox of scientific research: The wilderness apparently resolves into the promised land, which, on closer examination, turns out to be full of new doubts and questions, and so on, world without end.

What can one do to make this happy spiral toward truth more likely to occur in one's own work? Take method seriously. Consider how theory shapes method. It is theory, explicit or implicit, that determines what observed events are to be regarded as data (the "good stuff" from which legitimate conclusions can be drawn) and what observed events are to be discarded as noise (random, irrelevant, and interfering with the good stuff). Method is a third and equal partner with theory and data; they are mutually dependent and deserve equal scrutiny. Theory is implicit in method, like it or not; and whether your data are really capable of supporting your theory depends on the validity of the procedure you used to obtain them. This does not make theory a villain: On the contrary, it is not really possible to recognize experimental (or observational) artifacts for what they are until a theory that will make them visible has started to emerge!

In this volume, chapters by Johnson (chap. 9) and Donahue (chap. 17) raise the issue of how method affects the kind of data that are available for analysis (see the following section of this chapter). Johnson's chapter deals with the ways that orthographic transcription can distort early morphological data; Donahue's chapter shows that children's longer-term social agendas affect their pragmatic behavior in an experimental interactive task.

Pragmatic theory has made it possible to see the artifacts of some classic methods. For example, Tanz (1980, 1983) documented a variety of pragmatic artifacts in her own and other studies of semantic development. Her principal technique was to ask a child to ask a third person a question; she then examined what the child said, looking for immature language errors and also for what appeared to be mistakes in the child's interpretation of her instructions. One persistent kind of interpretation error that her subjects made caused Tanz to reinterpret some of the results of one of the most famous early works on language development, Chomsky's (1969) *The Acquisition of Syntax in Children from 5 to 10*. In the paperback edition of that work, the cover design shows two comic strip-style speaker "balloons." One balloon says, "Ask him who this is." The other balloon says, "Mickey Mouse." This epitomizes one of Chomsky's generally accepted conclusions: children, even after age 5, may interpret both "ask" and "tell" as meaning "tell."

Tanz replicated this result, first accidentally (Tanz, 1980) and then by deliberate experimental manipulation (Tanz, 1983) of pragmatic conditions. She found that a number of children interpreted "ask" as either "ask" or "tell" according to pragmatic considerations. If they didn't know the answer, they asked the question. If they did know or if they had a stake in a particular answer, they showed a tendency to provide it. This suggests that children who tell when requested to ask may not have a problem with the semantics of "ask," after all. Rather, instead of interpreting instructions to ask someone something as a request to be carried out literally, they may interpret them as a sincere request for information; being cooperative, they simply go ahead and supply the information if they know it.

Other widely accepted conclusions about syntactic and semantic development have been reevaluated in recent years and have been shown to be based on experimental designs that induced pragmatic artifacts (see Foster-Cohen's, 1994, study of binding theory, which concludes that "pragmatic factors must be systematically controlled in any evaluation of syntactic knowledge" [p. 237], and Clark & Grossman's 1998, reexamination of the role of "mutual exclusivity" in early word learning, which is discussed in chap. 17, this volume). Other famous developmental conclusions may also be ripe for pragmatically based reconsideration. For example, Donahue discusses Siegal's (1991) demonstration that the classical administration of the Piagetian number conservation task ("Are there more in this [closely spaced] row or this [widely spaced] row?") is contaminated by pragmatic artifacts that systematically underestimate the age at which number conservation is achieved. One is reminded of Clark's (1992) citation of a sign that he said was posted for years in a London hospital: "No head injury is too trivial to ignore." (Read it again!)[7]

Moral: When it is (or seems to be) obvious what something ought to mean, bottom–up processing of the syntax and semantics is likely to be short-circuited or overruled by pragmatics, in production as well as in comprehension. After all, someone *wrote* that sign!

A LOOK AHEAD

The chapters that follow include paradigms old and new, approaches reconsidered, re-configured, and refined to gain increasing insight into the complexities of language acquisition and use. They range across the age span, across levels of human ability, and across contexts in which language is used and learned. Some of the paradigms described here involve one experimenter and simple stimuli; others involve complex situational prompts; still others cannot be contained in the laboratory or clinic but rely on observation of language in its natural context of use.

Some contributors to this volume follow Berko Gleason in using novel or invented linguistic forms, or they prompt children to create them (Berman, chap. 5; Clark, chap. 4; Gropen, chap. 6; Nelson, chap. 7). Others eschew the question of what speakers might do to investigate what speakers actually do, in the real and messy laboratory called life (Ely, Wolf, McCabe, & Melzi, chap. 12; Ervin-Tripp, chap 13). From the phoneme to the conversation, these authors explore the most fruitful methods for obtaining data and analyzing language use. They range from

---

[7] In case that sentence still seems to make sense to you, suppose it said "No head injury is too trivial to treat." That means "Every head injury is important and should be treated." So "No head injury is too trivial to ignore" should mean "Every head injury is important and should be ignored."

a focus on the implications of narrow transcription (Johnson, chap. 9) to the broadest contexts of conversational interaction (Andersen, chap. 11; Ervin-Tripp, chap. 13). Johnson points out that (just as in a pointillist painting) the whole is dependent on the smallest of parts: Our very concepts of children's grammatical development are inextricably linked to the adequacy of our representation of their speech attempts.

Cross-linguistic testing of research hypotheses is also necessary to the construction of adequate theories of language. From discussion of acquisition patterns in languages other than English, to disordered language use, to second language acquisition, the contributors tackle the sometimes difficult considerations of how to translate (a) questions originally asked about English development and use into (b) equivalent questions about languages of considerably different structure (Andersen, chap. 11; Berman, chap. 5; Clark, chap. 4; Leonard, chap. 16; Menn, chap. 19).

The main axis used to organize the chapters of this book is the degree of control that the researcher attempts to exert over what the person being studied will say. This could be considered, conversely, as the degree to which the language produced is intended to be representative of natural speech; for as control loosens, naturalness increases. The tightest control and the most contrived language is in elicited imitation; the loosest control and the most natural language occur in "fly-on-the-wall" studies of people deeply involved in conversation with one another. The more natural a study is, the more it tells you about what people do say (under the circumstances of the particular interaction); but the less it may tell you about what people can say if they need to. A natural study in July will find no evidence for the knowledge of Christmas carols; a July study that elicits Christmas carols will find that people can indeed sing them, but it will completely lack information as to how, where, and why they are sung.

The naturalness–control continuum has been understood and exploited reasonably systematically since Labov's sociolinguistic work of the late 1960s (Labov, 1972), and presumably all researchers understand that there is no single right method for studying language production. The only issue is whether the results of the method a researcher plans to use give results that are a valid basis for the type of argument he or she wants to make. As noted earlier, even the wug task is not immune to pragmatic bias and the kind of light it sheds on the child's linguistic knowledge. But as researchers we can only wish that despite our own methodological shortcomings, our work will survive the test of time as well as the wug has.

The opening contributions to this volume address relatively structured methods of eliciting language production from children and adults. As we continue to debate the impact that imitation may have on children's lexical development, Masur (chap. 2) considers the methodological implications of how we define our terms: What counts as imitation, and what counts as spontaneity? As stated previously, she weighs the relative value of knowing what children can do versus what they tend to do when unencumbered by the researcher's desires. As a bridge between naturalistic and structured settings, Masur explores the value of using her subjects' mothers to elicit behavior from infants, in natural settings, and is successful in constructing contexts that elicit imitation. By carefully manipulating the mothers' interactions with language-learning infants, she discovers that infants' imitation of novel words in the second year of life is a potent predictor of vocabulary growth.

Gerken (chap. 3) evaluates the application of elicited production (imitation) to the study of children's language development (see also Ratner, chap. 14). In particular, Gerken discusses the pragmatic contexts that facilitate children's success with the given task, and she offers useful and creative tips for the researcher who would like to utilize the paradigm with very young children. These include modifications to reinforcement strategies as well as design, ordering, and presentation of stimuli. Finally, she suggests how the researcher can gauge the representativeness of children's performance by comparing experimental findings with analysis of their spontaneous productions.

Clark (chap. 4) considers the question of how children coin new words, including the almost universal processes of affixation and compounding. Drawing on her extensive work in this area, Clark notes that establishment of a pragmatic context for word innovation is essential for eliciting novel word coinages. Furthermore, as other contributors emphasize, insight into stages and processes of language development is best obtained when the investigator uses converging methods to evaluate a specific hypothesis about language knowledge. To this end, Clark contrasts child and adult behaviors when asked to produce novel forms, interpret them, or judge the well-formedness of options presented by the researcher. Clark ends her chapter with an observation that finds echoes throughout the volume: Regardless of how successful a particular technique has been in furthering research, it is clear that no single paradigm can unequivocally answer important questions about language acquisition and use.

Berman (chap. 5) continues the focus on derivational morphology by exploring children's acquisition of nominal and verbal forms in Hebrew.

She bypasses controversy regarding children's manipulation of nonsense forms by asking her subjects to create novel verbs from known nouns and, vice versa, to go from "known to new," as she says. Her experimental paradigm is guided by careful analysis of the kinds of novel coinages observed in children's spontaneous language, thereby using naturalistic data to shape experimental hypotheses and stimulus construction. Results of her work suggest important differences (a) in how children approach the task of learning and using derivational morphology across languages, and (b) between children's facility in coining nouns and verbs.

Gropen (chap. 6) tackles methods for exploring children's acquisition of verb argument structure. This is a complicated domain of inquiry because children's apparent syntactic errors may merely reflect errors of verb meaning or novel coinages. Thus, naturalistic data may be much less easily interpretable than data obtained under more controlled conditions. Gropen reviews the benefits and limitations associated with research on real verbs, e.g. by doing large corpus analysis using databases such as CHILDES. He then explores how novel verbs might be used to shed light on grammatical and lexical knowledge. For example, he reports his efforts to teach young children novel verbs, such as "to moop" or "to keat," and contrasts what can be learned from such paradigms with longitudinal designs that explore the process by which linguistic knowledge is acquired, as in the classic Carey and Bartlett (1978) chromium study. Gropen then demonstrates how it is possible to combine aspects of both approaches, in work that explores patterns of acquisition for novel forms presented by parents to young children in varying linguistic and extralinguistic contexts.

Other subtle aspects of language learning occupy Nelson's (chap. 7) attention. From the question of how children might learn the plurals for novel words, Nelson moves to the larger question of how children learn new words themselves: His "fiffin" studies examine the question of what children believe a wug to be after it is first introduced to them. His discussion of rare event learning mechanisms emphasizes that some forms of language learning, whether lexical or grammatical, may be based on relatively sparse exposure to exemplars at a time when learning is most opportune for the child. Viewing child language acquisition from perspectives of input and interaction, Nelson discusses methods for not only observing child language development, but facilitating it. He moves from observation of acquisition in the typical child to those with handicapping conditions such as autism, deafness, and SLI. Together with Leonard (chap. 16), Nelson is concerned about how the methods employed in research on language acquisition and use can be applied to intervention strategies. To this end, his focus is not so much on how to obtain language from children as on how to ensure that the child is given maximum opportunities to learn what we as researchers later hope to observe. Such opportunities appear to be numerous, but they often require us, as other contributors (e.g., Masur, chap. 2) also note, to understand the individual child's current state of knowledge and learning style, rather than the characteristics of the child's cohort in general.

Doughty and Long (chap. 8) offer, in their survey of approaches to L2 acquisition, a classic "good news–bad news" scenario. Because L2 learners under study tend to be older than the children on whom many language-elicitation tasks have been developed, experimenters may have the increased flexibility that arises from subject literacy and greater attention span. Such advantages have been widely exploited, making it possible to examine a broader array of research questions and more systematic approaches to data collection and analysis. The older L2 subject has cognitive maturity and life-span experiences that make even narrative analysis much easier than what can be expected in the appraisal of children (cf. Doughty & Long; Ely et al., chap. 12, this volume).

Such advantages, Doughty and Long note, can be counterbalanced by the analytical and response biases of older subjects, who may show much greater disparity between performance on constrained elicitation tasks and spontaneous language sampling than is typically observed in the study of young children. In particular, the older learner has the capacity to avoid use of certain morphosyntactic features of L2. This means that researchers have had to develop elicitation paradigms that demand specific morphosyntactic forms. Without this, it is not possible to evaluate claims about the best ways to characterize the progress of speakers in mastering second and subsequent languages.

Doughty and Long discuss the fact that the rapidity of language acquisition for some L2 learners offers interesting possibilities for longitudinal research. Relatively sophisticated narrative samples can be explored for a wide variety of patterns of morphosyntactic development. In the last part of chapter 8, Doughty and Long note the evolution of L2 research approaches that emphasize the social and interactional properties of the language acquisition process—an evolution that is also evident in the first language chapters, especially those that consider naturalistic settings.

Although Johnson (chap. 9) does not specifically address how children's language data are elicited, her concerns about transcription have ramifications for virtually all treatments of linguistic data—especially those obtained in naturalistic settings. Johnson's focus is not so much on how researchers obtain data, but how it is transcribed and coded for analysis. Orthographic transcriptions necessarily identify children's utterances as consisting of well-formed words, even when they in fact contain ambiguous "maybe-that-was-a-word-and-maybe-it-wasn't" strings. Johnson shows how this categorical judgment, imposed by writing children's early utterances as fully resolved strings of words, makes it appear that development itself is more categorical and less continuous than the phonetic data can support. As she makes clear, the underlying developmental continuity is potentially a source of data of major theoretical importance, but it is masked by the use of orthographic rather than phonetic transcription. Shallow or unreliable transcription of young children's linguistic attempts can misrepresent children's knowledge of linguistic forms and rules, obscure the pathways they take toward mastery of language skills, and impair the validity of researchers' accounts of the language acquisition process. Using acquisition of interrogatives as a case in point, Johnson convincingly argues that our failure to reach consensus on the path that children typically take toward mastery of interrogative syntax is at least partially due to reliance on orthographic transcriptions; these may obscure a relatively continuous process of development from formulaic to productive mastery of question forms.

Taking the study of language acquisition and use out of the laboratory is a theme of several contributions to this volume. Pan, Perlmann, & Snow (chap. 10) focus on the unique opportunities that observation of the everyday dinner conversations of families allows the researcher. Following in traditions begun by Hall, Nagy & Linn (1984) and continued in a longitudinal project directed by Berko Gleason and collaborators, Pan et al. explore the potential for dinner-table talk to shed light on processes of language development that are not easily observable by other methods of data collection. In particular, the contexts of language socialization, across populations differing in socioeconomic status and developmental status of the child, have been fruitfully mined using dinner-table talk. For example, the roots of rare vocabulary usage have been successfully charted through the use of such paradigms; this provides a complementary approach to experimental lexical acquisition study methods.

Andersen (chap. 11) explores children's knowledge of registral variation by using a variety of methods. Her "controlled improvisation" paradigm affords rich contextual support for role playing through the use of puppet conversation partners who interact with children in various familiar settings. Cross-linguistic application of this elicitation technique has shed new light on children's gradual mastery of the phonological, lexical, and speech-act characteristics that distinguish a variety of registers; such development greatly informs our understanding of the paths that children take toward socialization. Andersen's highly productive technique, paired with the attention to transcription detail that is emphasized in Johnson's chapter, has also allowed her to identify discourse markers in several languages. The nature and role of these apparently empty words are still being explored, and Andersen's lightly controlled elicitation paradigm provides an effective method for studying their function.

Narrative use is the focus of chapter 12 by Ely, Wolf, McCabe, and Melzi, it evaluates the advantages and disadvantages of diverse approaches to gathering narrative data for analysis. Like Pan et al., these contributors comment on the underappreciated value of the home environment, particularly dinnertime conversation and other routine activities, as a context for observing the actual use of narrative skills. In moving from such natural settings to semistructured or structured narrative tasks, the researcher encounters trade-offs: Increased task control may be compromised by individual or cultural reactions to the task paradigm.

In chapter 13, Ervin-Tripp explores how to observe and analyze natural peer interaction, a notoriously difficult area of inquiry. After discussing the relevant equipment concerns that arise in trying to "bug" natural conversation (another contributor refers to acting as a "fly on the wall"), she evaluates "fertile sites" for the collection of peer conversations, discusses concerns that arise in data transcription, and offers insights into how such peer interactions inform researchers about the nature of children's linguistic and registral skills, as well as the everyday contexts in which they share language.

The focus of the volume next shifts to methodological concerns in the study of developmental disorders. Ratner (chap. 14) continues Gerken's coverage of one of the most frequently used paradigms in research on typical and atypical language acquisition: elicited imitation (EI). After considering its strengths and weaknesses as an indicator of children's linguistic knowledge, Bernstein Ratner proposes another purpose to which the method can be applied, namely, the study of trade-offs between aspects of linguistic functioning in children with developmental disorders. In her work with stuttering children, EI revealed interesting interactions between fluency and syntactic demand: These patterns are consistent with those that can be extrapolated from analysis of naturalistic samples, but they are more clearly confirmed by using paradigms such as EI that provide a high level of control in manipulating task demand.

Tager-Flusberg (chap. 15) discusses challenges posed by the study of children with autism. A key feature of their disorder is a lack of interest in communicating with others, and this poses severe obstacles to conventional approaches to studying their language knowledge. Tager-Flusberg considers what can be learned from study of the natural language samples produced by children with autism, particularly when the child's caretaker or other familiar person serves as the conversational partner to increase the child's level of participation.

A unique problem in dealing with the language of children with autism is how to identify and analyze their echolalic utterances. Tager-Flusberg and her colleagues have contrasted echolalic and nonecholalic productions, and they have identified systematic patterns of development not unlike those of typically developing children and children with Down syndrome. Although assessment of language skills through standardized test administration is difficult with this population, the creative approaches to language production typified by the wug task have not yet proved feasible in children with autism. Tager-Flusberg closes her chapter with suggestions for the development of methods for the future study of language in this population.

Leonard (chap. 16) notes that the performance of children with SLI can be difficult to appreciate unless the researcher expands the scope of study to include not only age-matched, typically developing children, but also children whose language age more closely matches that of the children with SLI. Although many methods used in the study of SLI in children mirror those discussed elsewhere in the volume, researchers who use treatment efficacy studies are increasingly evaluating the process by which such children learn new skills (see also Nelson, chap. 7). In particular, Leonard focuses on the evaluation of productivity in children with SLI, and he contrasts results of wug like tasks used in this population with findings from tasks that teach nonsense inflections as opposed to nonsense words. Leonard extends what we have learned from such structured tasks to cross-linguistic analysis of patterns observed in the speech of children with SLI, and he weighs the data against competing accounts of the underlying deficit that produces the symptoms of SLI.

Donahue (chap. 17) examines methods for the study of children's pragmatic knowledge. After analyzing how children with learning disabilities (LD) respond to ambiguous messages, she concludes that some patterns of performance reflect their attitudes and beliefs about the causes of communication breakdown, rather than inadequate pragmatic knowledge. Her studies (in which children with LD were compared to typically developing peers in terms of their ability to act as talk show hosts and guests) suggest that the differences between the groups of children included a number of "nonlinguistic" features, including the children's personal views about conversational interactions. In particular, Donahue notes that children with LD come to view their role in conversations somewhat differently from the way that children without LD do. She concludes that their conversational failures reflect accurate social observations, not merely linguistic deficits. Moreover, as her work shows, attacking only the linguistic deficits can misdirect intervention strategies away from approaches that would effectively permit children with LD to mobilize what skills they possess and apply them when appropriate.

The next three chapters address methods for studying language production in adults with acquired language disturbance. Goodglass (chap. 18) notes that the particular questions that arise in the study of aphasia, coupled with the special limitations of patients' test-taking abilities, have prompted the development of a number of methodologies for the investigation of their language performance. Goodglass notes that Berko Gleason turned her attention to the aphasic population almost immediately after the wug study, and that she has contributed extensively to assessment approaches used and expanded on today.

Menn (chap. 19) continues the focus on the study of aphasia by examining methods for the study of macropragmatics and micropragmatics in left- and right-hemisphere-damaged adults. After surveying some prior research on these topics, she turns her attention to two areas in micropragmatic analysis of aphasic behavior: the expression of empathy, and the effect of expectedness of information. Because of the linguistic deficits in aphasia, it is often difficult to know whether pragmatically inadequate communicative attempts reflect the impact of depressed syntactic function or a deeper problem in pragmatic orientation. Using a specifically designed set of picture stimuli, Menn and her colleagues found evidence that empathy can be expressed linguistically by aphasic speakers, albeit in distinct ways that reflect the limiting filter of their language impairment.

Another difficulty in working with aphasic patients, especially nonfluent ones, is that they tend to avoid attempting the elaborated syntactic structures that give them difficulties, such as locatives or passives. One way to try to elicit such language for study is to confront the speaker with stimuli that are unusual enough to prompt comment. Menn's group found that locatives were attempted when these patients were asked to describe unexpected arrangements of objects (e.g., a pillow located at the foot, rather than at the head, of a bed). Of particular interest to the general design of language production studies is her finding that details of stimulus construction, item similarity, and ordering induce a unique discourse setting; the responses appropriate to the transient discourse world of the test may completely mask the question originally posed by the researcher.

Obler and De Santi (chap. 20) voice concerns about the particular test demands that arise when researchers attempt to study the dissolution of language performance that accompanies Alzheimer's disease (AD). In particular, because patients with Alzheimer's disease are distinguished from those with many types of aphasia by specific interactional behaviors during conversation, it is necessary for the researcher who is studying Alzheimer's disease to expand assessment of function to areas beyond those typically targeted by aphasia batteries or tasks. A number of conversational tasks illuminate language function in Alzheimer's disease; one approach that Obler and De Santi explore in some depth is stimulus repetition, returning to a theme broached by Masur and by Ratner. Obler and De Santi also raise the ethical concerns posed by studying adults who, for the most part, are not competent to offer their consent for participation, a situation not otherwise frequently encountered in language studies beyond childhood.

The chapters in this volume offer the reader a wide array of approaches to the study of language production. We trust that they will stimulate readers to explore the richness of diverse methodologies for better understanding of language acquisition and use, continuing a tradition of innovation in language study begun forty years ago.

ACKNOWLEDGMENTS

We are grateful to our contributors, especially Mavis Donahue and Sue Ervin-Tripp, for their comments on this chapter.

REFERENCES

Allman, W. (1991, August 19). The clues in idle chatter. *US News and World Report*, 111, p. 61.
Anisfeld, M., & Tucker, G. R. (1967). English pluralization rules of six-year-old children. *Child Development*, 38, 1201-1217.
Bar-Adon, A. & Leopold, W. (1971). *Child language: A book of readings.* Englewood Cliffs, NJ: Prentice-Hall.

Bellaire, S., Plante, E., & Swisher, L. (1994). Bound morpheme skills in the oral language of school-age, language-impaired children. *Journal of Communication Disorders, 27,* 265–279.

Berko (Gleason), J. (1958). The child's learning of English morphology. *Word, 14,* 150–177.

Berko Gleason, J., and Ratner, N. B. (1998). *Psycholinguistics* (2nd ed.). Mahwah, NJ: Lawrence Erlbaum Associates.

Berman, R., & Slobin, D. (1994). *Relating events in narrative: A crosslinguistic developmental study.* Hillsdale, NJ: Lawrence Erlbaum Associates.

Berry, M. (1969). *Language disorders of children—the bases and diagnoses.* NY: Appleton-Century-Crofts.

Biasca, D. H. (1999). *Language development in Jacobsen (11-q deletion) syndrome: The interaction of language and genetics.* Unpublished doctoral dissertation, University of Colorado, Denver.

Bock, J. K., Lobell, H., & Morey, R. (1992). From conceptual roles to structural relations: Bridging the syntactic cleft. *Psychological Review, 99,* 150–171.

Bock, K., & Levelt, W. (1994). Grammatical encoding. In M. A. Gernsbacher (Ed.), *Handbook of Psycholinguistics.* San Diego: Academic Press. 945–984.

Bogoyavlenskiy, D. (1973). The acquisition of Russian inflections. In C. Ferguson & D. Slobin (Eds.), *Studies of child language development* (pp. 284–292). NY: Holt, Rinehart & Winston.

Brown, R. W. (1973). *A first language.* Cambridge, MA: Harvard University Press.

Brown, R. W. (1957). Linguistic determinism and the part of speech. *Journal of Abnormal & Social Psychology, 55,* 1–5.

Bryant, B., & Anisfeld, M. (1969). Feedback versus no feedback in testing children's knowledge of English pluralization rules. *Journal of Experimental Child Psychology, 8,* 250–255.

Carey, S., & Bartlett, E.. (1978). Acquiring a single new word. *Papers and Reports on Child Language Development, 15,* 17–29.

Channell, R., & Ford, C. (1991). Four grammatic completion measures of language ability. *Language, Speech and Hearing Services in Schools, 22,* 211–218.

Chomsky, C. (1969). *The acquisition of syntax in children from 5 to 10.* Cambridge, MA: MIT Press.

Clark, E. V., & Grossman, J. G. (1998). Pragmatic directions and children's word learning. *Journal of Child Language, 25,* 1–18.

Clark, H. (1992). *Arenas of language use.* Chicago: University of Chicago Press.

Clark, H., & Clark, E. V. (1977). *Psychology and language: An introduction to psycholinguistics.* NY: Harcourt, Brace Jovanvich.

Derwing, B., & Baker, W. (1979). Recent research on the acquisition of English morphology. In P. Fletcher and M. Garman (Eds.), *Language acquisition* (pp. 209–224). Cambridge: Cambridge University Press.

Derwing, B. & Baker, W. (1986). Assessing morphological development. In P. Fletcher & M. Garman (Eds.). *Language Acquisition* 2nd edition, 326–338. NY: Cambridge Univ. Press.

Dever, R. (1972). A comparison of the results of a revised version of Berko's test of morphology with the free speech of mentally retarded children. *Journal of Speech and Hearing Research, 15,* 169–178.

Dever, R., & Gardner, W. (1970). Performance of normal and retarded boys on Berko's Test of Morphology. *Language and Speech, 13,* 162–181.

Duffy, L., & Wishart, J. (1994). The stability and transferability of errorless learning in children with Down syndrome. *Down Syndrome Research and Practice, 2,* 51–58.

Ellis Weismer, S., & Hesketh, L. (1993). The influence of prosodic and gestural cues on novel word acquisition by children with specific language impairment. *Journal of Speech and Hearing Research, 36,* 1013–1026.

Ervin, S. (1964). Imitation and structural change in children's language. In E. Lenneberg (Ed.) *New directions in the study of language* (pp. 163–189). Cambridge, MA: MIT Press.

Ferguson, C. A., & Slobin, D. I. (Eds.) (1973). *Studies of child language development.* New York: Holt.

Foster-Cohen, S. H. (1994). Exploring the boundary between syntax and pragmatics: Relevance and the binding of pronouns. *Journal of Child Language, 21,* 237–255.

Fussell, R., & Krauss, R. (1989). The effects of intended audience on message production and comprehension: Reference in a common ground framework. *Journal of Experimental Social Psychology, 25,* 203–219.

Glucksberg, S., Krauss, R., & Weisberg, R. (1966). Referential communication in nursery school children: Method and some preliminary findings. *Journal of Experimental Child Psychology, 3,* 333–342.

Goad, H., & Rebellati, C. (1994, May–December). Pluralization in Specific Language Impairment: Affixation or compounding? *McGill Working Papers in Linguistics,* 24–40.

Gopnik, M., & Crago, M. (1991). Familial aggregation of a developmental language disorder. *Cognition, 39,* 1–50.

Gould, S. J. (1998). Writing in the margins. Natural History, 107 (9), 16–20.

Gray, V., & Cameron, C. (1980). Longitudinal development of English morphology in French immersion children. *Applied Psycholinguistics, 1,* 171–181

Hall, W., Nagy, W., & Linn, R. (1984). *Spoken words: Effects of situation and social group on word usage and frequency.* Hillsdale, NJ: Lawrence Erlbaum Associates.

Hiriartborde, A., & de La Bouillerie, N. (1973). Sur La generalization de guelgues marques grammaticales dans la languagage d'enfants de 3 ans. Etudes de Linguistique Appliguée, 9, 101–124.

Isbell, B. (1972). Acquisition of Quechua morphology: An application of the Berko Test. In Proceedings of Colloquium Paedolinguisticum. The Hague: Mouton.

Jaeger, J., Lockwood, A., Kemmerer, D., Van Valin, R., Murphy, B., & Khalak, H. (1996). A positron emission tomography study of regular and irregular verb morphology of English. *Language, 72,* 451–497.

Krauss, R., & Glucksberg, S. (1977). *Social and non-social speech. Scientific American, 236* (2), 100–105.

Labov, W. (1972). *Sociolinguistic patterns.* Philadelphia: University of Pennsylvania Press.

Levy, Y. (1987). The wug technique revisited. *Cognitive Development, 2,* 71–87.

Lewis, D., & Windsor, J. (1996). Children's analysis of derivational suffix meanings. *Journal of Speech and Hearing Research, 39,* 209–217.

Lyytinen, P. (1987). Cognitive skills and Finnish Language inflections. *Scandinavian Journal of Psychology, 28,* 302–312.

MacWhinney, B. (1978). The acquisition of morphophonology. *Monographs of the Society for Research in Child Development, 43,* 1–123.

MacWhinney, B. (1995). The CHILDES Project: Tools for analyzing talk (2nd ed.). Hillsdale, NJ: Lawrence Erlbaum Associates.

Mahoney, D. (1994). Using sensitivity to word structure to explain variance in high-school and college reading ability. *Reading and Writing, 6,* 19–44.

Maratsos, M. (1979). How to get from words to sentences. In D. Aronson & R. Rieber (Eds.), *Psycholinguistic research: Implications and applications* (pp. 285–356). Hillsdale, NJ: Lawrence Erlbaum Associates.

McDaniel, D., McKee, C., & Smith Cairns, H. (1998). *Methods for assessing children's syntax.* Cambridge, MA: MIT Press.

Menn, L., & MacWhinney, B. (1984). The repeated morph constraint: Toward an explanation. *Language, 60,* 519–541.

Menn, L. & Obler, L. K. (1990). Agrammatic & Aphasia: A Cross-Language Narrative Sourcebook. Amsterdam: John Benjamins.

Miller, W., & Ervin, S. (1964). The development of grammar in child language. *Monographs of the Society for Research in Child Development, 92,* 9–34.

Perez Pereira, M. (1989). The acquisition of morphemes: Some evidence from Spanish. *Journal of Psycholinguistic Research, 18,* 289–312.

Pinker, S. (1991). Rules of language. *Science, 253,* 530–535.

Pinker, S. (1994). *The language instinct: How the mind creates language.* New York: Morrow.

Prasada, S., & Pinker, S. (1993). Generalisation of regular and irregular morphological patterns. *Language and Cognitive Processes, 8,* 1–56.

Prideaux, G. (1985). *Psycholinguistics: The experimental study of language.* New York: Guilford Press.

Rabe, M., & Matlin, M. (1978). Sex-role stereotypes in speech and language tests. *Language, Speech and Hearing Services in Schools, 9,* 70–76.

Ramer, A., & Rees, N. (1973). Selected aspects of the development of English morphology of black American children of low socioeconomic background. *Journal of Speech and Hearing Research, 16,* 569–577.

Ramsberger, G., & Menn, L. (in press). Co-constructing Lucy: Adding a social perspective to the assessment of communicative success in aphasia. In C. Goodwin (Ed.), *The pragmatic life of brain damaged patients: Situating language impairments within conversation,* in press. New York: Oxford University Press.

Ratner, N. B. (1998). Atypical language development. In J. Berko Gleason (Ed.), *The development of language* (4th ed., pp. 348–397). Boston: Allyn & Bacon.

Roland, D., & Jurafsky, D. (1998). How verb subcategorization frequencies are affected by corpus choice. In *Proceedings of COLING/ACL-98,* 1122–1128.

Rubin, H., Patterson, P., & Kantor, M. (1991). Morphological development and writing ability in children and adults. *Language, Speech and Hearing Services in Schools, 22,* 228–235.

Rumelhart, D., & McClelland, J. (1986). On learning the past tenses of English verbs. In D. Rumelhart & J. McClelland (Eds.), *Parallel distributed processing: Explorations in the microstructure of cognition,* Vol. 2: *Psychological and biological models* (pp. 216–271). Cambridge, MA: Bradford.

Safire, W. (1994, May 8). On language. *New York Times Magazine, 143,* p. 14.

Saporta, S. (Ed.) (1961). *Psycholinguistics: A book of readings.* New York: Holt.

Seidenberg, M., & Hoeffner, J. (1998). Evaluating behavioral and neuroimaging data on past tense processing. *Language, 74,* 104–122.

Sherzer, J. (1982). Play languages: With a note on ritual languages. In L. K. Obler & L. Menn (Eds.), *Exceptional language and linguistics* (pp. 175–99) New York: Academic Press.

Siegal, M. (1991). Knowing children: Experiments in conversation and cognition. Hillsdale, NJ: Lawrence Erlbaum Associates

Slobin, D. (1973). Introduction to inflections: English. In C. Ferguson and D. Slobin (Eds.), *Studies of child language development* (pp. 209–211). NY: Holt, Rinehart & Winston.

Sokolov, J., & Snow, C. (Eds.). (1994). *Handbook of research in language development using CHILDES.* Hillsdale, NJ: Lawrence Erlbaum Associates.

Tanz, C. (1980). *Studies in the acquisition of deictic terms.* Cambridge: Cambridge University Press.

Tanz, C. (1983). Asking children to ask: An experimental investigation of the pragmatics of relayed questions. *Journal of Child Language, 10,* 187–194.

Treiman, R. (1991). Phonological awareness and its roles in learning to read and spell. In E. J. Sawyer & B. J. Fox (Eds.), *Phonological awareness in reading: The evolution of current perspectives* (pp. 159–189) New York: Springer-Verlag.

Wiig, E., Semel, E., & Crouse, M. (1967). The use of English morphology by high-risk and learning disabled children. *Journal of Learning Disabilities, 6,* 457–465.

Wood, J. (1985). Morphology and reading comprehension in young moderately learning disabled pupils. *Research in Education, 34,* 79–88.

Zakharova, A. (1973). Acquisition of forms of grammatical case by preschool children. In C. Ferguson & D. Slobin (eds.), *Studies of child language development* (pp. 281–283). New York: Holt, Rinehart, & Winston.

I
Eliciting Knowledge Of Language

2

Infants' Verbal Imitation and Their Language Development: Controversies, Techniques, and Consequences

Elise Frank Masur
Northern Illinois University

Eliciting infants' verbal imitation in order to investigate its relation to language acquisition is not a new technique (Berko Gleason, 1993), but it has often been a controversial one. As an aspect of language development and, more broadly, of developmental psychology, the study of infants' and children's language-related imitation has frequently become the arena for enacting theoretical conflicts arising from these larger fields. Indeed, several disputes over philosophy and approach among imitation researchers can be regarded as reflections of distinct (but not entirely independent), well-known and enduring controversies within developmental psychology. The three discussed here include conflicts (a) between causal explanations that rely on nature versus nurture, (b) between investigations that focus on universal patterns versus individual differences in development, and (c) between emphases on aspects of behavioral functioning that are intrapersonal versus interpersonal. Although it is certainly the case that many investigators hold intermediate or interactionist positions on these points, regarding them as struggles between countervailing forces allows one to view the contrasting perspectives and issues most clearly.

This chapter describes how the three debates have shaped the purposes and, thereby, the processes of inquiry into infants' imitation and its possible role in language acquisition. In particular, I describe how these questions have affected methodological decisions in my own research on infants' vocal and verbal imitation, as well as the findings that research has yielded.

LANGUAGE IMITATION AND THE NATURE–NURTURE CONTROVERSY

Imitation researchers have often been unwilling warriors in the more general battle between nativists, who hold that language is primarily—if not exclusively—biologically determined, and environmentalists, who maintain that the social context plays a vital role in its acquisition and development. For many nativists, imitation is regarded as a behavioristic mechanism, peripheral or even irrelevant to the process of language acquisition, whereas many environmentalists accord it considerable, sometimes even central, status (see Bohannon, 1993; Snow, 1981). One's stance on the nature–nurture controversy, then, may influence whether the role of imitation in language acquisition is regarded as a legitimate domain of study. It may also govern perceptions of the nature and scope of imitation itself, a term whose meaning has ranged from "simple mimicking in which the child does not comprehend what she is reproducing" (Tomasello, 1992, p. 72) to "a form of encoding that continues the processing of information that is necessary for the representation of linguistic schemas (both semantic and syntactic) in cognitive memory" (Bloom, Hood, & Lightbown, 1974, p. 418).

Disagreement on the role of imitation in language acquisition has been strongest regarding its place in syntactic development (see Bloom et al., 1974; Snow, 1981, for reviews). Views have ranged from denying any position to asserting an important position for imitation. For example, Snow (1981) cited "the child's creative use of imitations for syntactic growth," maintaining that young children's imitation, especially expanded imitations that include additional morphemes beyond those copied, "might . . . provide the learner with linguistic material which is susceptible to segmentation and further analysis" (p. 211). But Ervin-

Tripp (1973) examining imitation more narrowly, had declared that "there is not a shred of evidence supporting a view that progress toward adult norms of grammar arises merely from practice in overt imitation of adult sentences" (p. 397). Researchers with diverse perspectives have been more likely to acknowledge the possibility of a role for imitation in lexical acquisition (see Bloom et al., 1974; Snow, 1981), an attitude that has motivated my own investigations into this question. Yet even in 1986, a grant reviewer disparaged a proposal to investigate the role of imitation in lexical acquisition as well, insisting that "it has not been established that verbal imitation is instrumental in language learning, and on the contrary, there is a tendency in the literature to minimize its contribution to the learning process."

The debate over imitation is undiminished, however, as prominent theorists and researchers again propose a significant place for it in language acquisition. Tomasello's (1992) social-pragmatic view has claimed a central role for "imitative learning" that involves reproducing and finally acquiring a novel "piece of adult language" in "both its appropriate form . . . and function" (p. 72) through participating in meaningful activities together with the adult. Furthermore, Nelson (1996) claimed that imitation is "critical" not only in developing language but also more generally in transmitting culture:

> It goes without saying that acquiring language depends in total on the capacity for reproducing the sounds and signals of others. . . . Of course, language acquisition requires more than "mere" imitation (which is why imitation has been given such short shrift in language research in recent years). But its critical role in human cognition and communication development in the early years should be widely recognized, not only for learning language but also for learning the ways and meanings of the culture, and thus furnishing the mind. (p. 102)

Despite the controversy over the role of imitation in language development, the value of studying it as an aspect of infants' overall psychological development in its own right has been clearly recognized. Indeed, there is a distinguished research tradition from Baldwin (1895) and Piaget (1962) through Meltzoff (1988) tracing developmental changes in infants' imitative performance and capabilities. However, this tradition has generally emphasized action imitation and often overlooked or slighted vocal and verbal imitation (e.g., Abravanel, Levan-Goldschmidt, & Stevenson, 1976; McCall, Parke, & Kavanaugh, 1977; Meltzoff, 1988). It seemed to me crucial to trace infants' vocal and verbal imitative development in relation to their gestural and action imitation, in order to ascertain whether language-related imitation follows the same developmental course. This would be the first step toward the larger goal of examining the relation between verbal imitation and one aspect of language acquisition—lexical development. Although language imitation has been studied both experimentally and spontaneously, infants' action imitation has most often been investigated experimentally. Thus, to explore both vocal and action matching at the same time, it seemed wise to examine them under controlled conditions first, before examining naturally occurring spontaneous imitation. Thus, our longitudinal research has involved an experimental imitation task involving vocal, verbal, and action behaviors presented to a sample of children seen at four ages spanning a period of dramatic linguistic development—from the end of the first to the end of the second year of life.

Methodological Implications

Examining similarities or contrasts between vocal or verbal and action imitation has necessitated developing procedures for coding repetition that are equally appropriate to diverse behaviors. A key issue to be resolved has been the criteria for counting a response as imitative. One dimension influencing such judgments has been the immediacy of the response. Although deferred or delayed imitation was of interest to some as an index of infants' mental representational ability (Meltzoff, 1985; Piaget, 1962), practical considerations have limited most experimental studies to relatively immediate production. However, the definition of *immediate* varies widely. Studies of spontaneous language development may require replication in the next utterance (Ervin-Tripp, 1973), in the next turn (Folger & Chapman, 1978), or within five utterances (Bloom, Hood, & Lightbown, 1974). In contrast, experimental studies presenting both vocal and motor items typically provide a brief interval for a response. That interval may be as short as 2 seconds (Uzgiris, Vasek, & Benson, 1984) but is more likely to be as long as 15 seconds (Abravanel et al., 1976; McCall et al., 1977), the period we have adopted (Masur, 1993; Masur & Ritz, 1984).

Another dimension influencing judgments of imitation has been the degree of similarity between the model and the response. Studies of action imitation have typically required that the reproduction be either an exact copy or a close approximation (Masur, 1988; Uzgiris, 1984), although a systematic response that did not approximate the model has occasionally been coded (McCall et al., 1977). Researchers of spontaneous verbal imitation, in contrast, have often disagreed in their requirements for complete versus only partial overlap between the copy and the entire model, variously accepting or rejecting exact, reduced, or expanded production of prior utterances (see Snow, 1981, for a review). Because the verbal behaviors presented in this investigation were single words rather than syntactic utterances, this definitional argument could be avoided. We counted any exact production or close approximation of the word within the 15-second interval, regardless of whether any other words were also produced.

UNIVERSAL PATTERNS VERSUS INDIVIDUAL DIFFERENCES APPROACHES TO IMITATION

Whereas the nature–nurture controversy has primarily influenced the question of the legitimacy of investigating language imitation, diverging emphases on universal patterns versus individual differences in development have differentially directed the purpose and manner of the inquiry. McCall (1981) argued that there are "two realms of developmental psychology" (p. 1)—two emphases in the field that coexist but are not integrated. Advocates of the first perspective accentuate the universal developmental function underlying a particular trait, the "measured value of a given attribute plotted across age" (p. 2). Followers of the second position, however, concentrate on assessing "the relative consistency of individual differences over age" (p. 3).

The contrast between searching for the developmental function and analyzing diverse patterns of behavioral change is represented as well in approaches to conceptualizing infants' imitation. Piaget's (1962) work stands as the exemplar of the universalistic approach, recording qualitative changes in infants' imitation through his stages of sensorimotor thought during the first two years of life: Infants' imitation progresses from replication that is immediate to delayed; and the characteristics of the behaviors matched develop from simple to complex, familiar to novel, and visible to nonvisible (i.e., actions that infants cannot see themselves perform, such as patting the top of the head).

Following Piaget (1962), many imitation researchers have viewed infants' imitation performance, both motoric and vocal, as an index of their underlying cognitive competence (Kuhn, 1973; McCall, 1979;

Uzgiris & Hunt, 1975). Thus, contrasts in infants' imitative performance, such as between infants who copy only familiar actions and sounds and those who repeat novel behaviors not previously present in their performance repertoires, would be assumed to reflect differences in their attained developmental levels along the universal trajectory, with the latter infants demonstrating a qualitative advance over the former. In keeping with that point of view, Kuhn (1973) declared that imitation is "an *aspect* of overall cognitive functioning, from which it cannot be strictly separated, rather than a unique *process* of behavior acquisition" (p. 163).

Uzgiris (1981), in contrast, has indeed claimed imitation as a process of acquisition, a means of mastering new behavior. She sees imitation as a strategy infants can utilize for representing and encoding new behaviors, linguistic as well as motoric, and incorporating them into an existing repertoire. In this view, individual differences in performance between infants who replicate novel actions or words and those who do not would be considered to represent dissimilarity in adoption of strategies rather than contrasts in competence. However, the strategy of preferentially replicating novel rather than familiar acts should have an advantage for behavioral learning. Whether infants who preferentially match novel, but not familiar, words develop larger vocabularies was one question addressed by our research.

These two divergent views of infants' imitation, as an index of universal development or as a strategy for mastery that some children adopt, are reflected also in separate purposes for examining infants' language reproduction—to measure children's achieved or emerging linguistic capabilities (e.g., Corrigan & di Paul, 1982; Fraser, Bellugi, & Brown, 1973) or to identify individuals who may recruit imitation for acquisition of words or structures (e.g., Bloom et al., 1974; Ramer, 1976; Snow, 1981). These two perspectives also yield discrepant predictions of imitative performance. If imitation is an index, all children should follow a universal pattern and imitate equally, although some may do so earlier than others if their development progresses more rapidly. On the other hand, if it is a strategy, infants should display marked and persistent individual variation in imitativeness. Following these expectations, some cognitive and language developmentalists analyze cross-sectionally for average differences across age groups (e.g., Abravanel et al., 1976; Corrigan & di Paul, 1982; McCall et al., 1977), whereas others often closely track longitudinal similarities and differences in the progress of individual children (e.g., Bloom et al., 1974; Ramer, 1976; Snow, 1981, 1989).

Methodological Implications

These theoretically distinct perspectives had implications for our methodological choices as well. In experimental studies, researchers must decide if their goal is to derive an estimate of the children's underlying competence. As with all attempts to measure competence, eliciting imitation involves a complex interplay between ability and motivation. Researchers with a competence goal strive to assess what infants can actually do, given that they are willing to make the effort. This requires endeavors to motivate infants sufficiently in order to remove, as much as possible, error variance attributable to "mere performance." In contrast, researchers who look for and expect individual variation are more concerned with eliciting imitation performance that is truly representative of infants' usual patterns of behavior. Several aspects of our imitative procedure were designed to take advantage of both theoretical possibilities: Some were developed to engage and motivate the children as much as possible to display their best performance, and others were designed to be more likely to elicit representative behavior.

Although the vast majority of elicited imitation studies, whether they include vocal or verbal items or not, take place in the laboratory with an experimenter as the model (e.g., Abravanel et al., 1976; Killen & Uzgiris, 1981; McCabe & Uzgiris, 1983; McCall et al., 1977; Meltzoff, 1988; Rodgon & Kurdek, 1977), our procedure took place in the children's own homes with their mothers serving as the models. Abravanel et al. (1976) suggested this change in order to enhance the likelihood that children would be willing to repeat less appealing behaviors, such as actions without objects. We adopted that procedure, with special care to instruct the mothers, for an earlier cross-sectional study (Masur & Ritz, 1984) and retained it for the longitudinal investigation (Masur, 1993, 1995). Besides possibly increasing infants' motivation to attend and/or repeat the behaviors, we hoped that their performance under more natural circumstances would reveal their typical interactive patterns and imitative strategies with their mothers in their homes as well.

Moreover, certain aspects of the battery of items presented to the infants were designed to evoke their optimum performance. Before the test items were introduced, two warm-up behaviors, clapping hands and patting knees, that are frequently part of routine imitative games were presented. The intent was to get the children in the mood for playing interactive games with their mothers. The items in the test battery were divided into two halves, and the halves were presented in counterbalanced order across children, with a rest period in between for them to recover from possible fatigue. Within each half, vocal or verbal items were alternated with actions to increase variety and interest. The behaviors in each half were presented in a sequence ordered from easier to more difficult, as on a standardized test, so that infants' performance on early behaviors might foster their continued engagement in the task. Thus, familiar behaviors preceded novel ones, and visible actions preceded nonvisible ones. Both familiar (e.g., wave) and novel (e.g., beckon) actions as well as vocalizations and words were also designed to be conventionally meaningful, because meaningfulness has been shown to be a factor influencing infants' performance (Killen & Uzgiris, 1981; Masur & Ritz, 1984). Furthermore, many of the items involved patterns in threes—three claps, the vocalization *ba-ba-ba*, and the provision for up to three trial presentations—in a manner intended to capitalize on infants' interest in repetition and patterning.

Despite these several techniques intended to maximize infants' performance, there was one procedure we were unwilling to include: We did not tell the children to imitate. The mothers called out the infants' names to attract their attention and then performed the behaviors when the children were watching. The mothers then paused for about 15 seconds to give the children time to respond, if they chose to. Setting expectation implicitly rather than explicitly is common in studies of action imitation (e.g., Abravanel et al., 1976; Killen & Uzgiris, 1981; McCabe & Uzgiris, 1983), but untypical of many elicited verbal imitation studies (e.g., Corrigan & di Paul, 1982; Fraser, Bellugi, & Brown, 1973). However, giving directions might have preferentially advantaged older infants who could understand the verbal instructions. In addition, we felt that infants' willingness to undertake replication of the sounds and actions without explicit instruction would more closely reflect their usual interactive habits. Of course, telling nearly-two-year-olds what to do might have been counterproductive anyway!

INTRAPERSONAL VERSUS INTERPERSONAL FUNCTIONS OF IMITATION

Whether as a sign of infants' developing representational ability or as an individual strategy for mastering novel behaviors, these conceptualizations emphasize the intrapersonal, cognitive aspects of imitation.

Yet imitation is always both a cognitive and a social phenomenon, as Uzgiris (1981, 1984) stressed. As an aspect of interpersonal interaction, infants' imitation "communicat[es] mutuality and shared understanding with another person" (Uzgiris, 1981, p. 1). Infants may employ action or vocal imitation in a social interchange or conversation to acknowledge the partner and respond to his or her contribution, to fill a social or conversational turn, and to maintain the interactional focus or discourse topic (Bloom, Rocissano, & Hood, 1976; Keenan, 1974; Uzgiris, 1984).

In addition to contributing to and expressing an existing social relationship, imitation may facilitate aspects of social development itself. Meltzoff (1990) asserted the following:

> imitative interactions provide infants with a unique vehicle for elaborating the similarity between self and other and for understanding that others, like the self, are sentient beings with thoughts, intentions, and emotions. In other words, imitation may be an important, primitive building block in the nascent development of a "theory of mind" . . . in the child. (p. 141)

Meltzoff's claims echo the earlier arguments of Baldwin (1895) that imitation is a significant process in children's social understanding of self and others: "My sense of myself grows by imitation of you, and my sense of yourself grows in terms of my sense of myself. Both ego and alter are thus essentially social; each is a socius and each is an imitative creation" (Baldwin, 1895, p. 338).

The cognitive and social aspects of imitation are the yin and yang of every imitative reproduction—each present in all instances. However, cognitive and social perspectives may differentially highlight separate components of the imitative act (Masur, 1989). For example, researchers with an intrapersonal viewpoint may concentrate on the quality of the behavior produced, paying special attention to the emergence of infants' cognitive ability to replicate novel behaviors and to recruit imitation as a behavioral acquisition process. In contrast, those with a social or interpersonal focus might emphasize infants' achievement of a behavioral match with a partner, without regard for the familiarity or novelty of the act. Infants' repetition of familiar behaviors may, in fact, be prompted less by cognitive-strategic and more by social-interpersonal purposes, perhaps reflecting their typical involvement in imitative routines and games (Masur, 1988; 1993).

Methodological Implications

Because reproduction of novel and of familiar behaviors may signify different aspects of the imitative act, we thought it important to distinguish between them and study both. Many previous studies of elicited imitation, either action or verbal, failed to consider whether the behaviors presented were novel or familiar to the children (Abravanel et al., 1976; McCall et al., 1977; Rodgon & Kurdek, 1977). Others (e.g., Corrigan & di Paul, 1982) have deliberately presented only familiar words to their subjects. Even investigations of spontaneous verbal imitation have often omitted the distinction between novel and familiar word matching (e.g., Folger & Chapman, 1978; Snow, 1989).

The goal of presenting each child with both novel and familiar behaviors leads to a methodological dilemma: Proper experimental controls would ideally require presenting all children with the same items, the same number of items, and the same numbers of novel and familiar items. However, because different items are familiar or novel to different children, in practice only two of those three conditions are likely to be attainable at any given time. The essential ingredients change with the purposes of the experiment, and we have employed each of the possible combinations at some time. In an earlier cross-sectional study (Masur & Ritz, 1984), all children received the same 21 behaviors that varied in kind and in difficulty. Later we ascertained which behaviors were familiar or novel for each child. Thus, all children received the same behaviors and the same number of items, although unfortunately the numbers of novel and familiar behaviors received by each child could not then be controlled.

Our more recent longitudinal research (Masur, 1993) made use of the two other alternatives. Interviews with mothers about one week before the imitation sessions took place included a checklist of all words, sounds, and actions on the lists of standard and alternate items for the imitation battery. Based on the mothers' reports of the familiarity of each behavior, one or two sounds or actions on the alternate list were substituted for standard ones in all cases when their use would advance the goal of presenting each infant with two familiar and two novel behaviors of each type. Thus, all children received four sounds, four visible actions, and four nonvisible actions; and most received two novel and two familiar behaviors of each kind, although the specific items varied among the children and for any particular child over time.

We were, however, reluctant to employ the same procedure for the verbal imitation items. Because experimental language imitation studies usually present all children with the same words or sentences in order to trace developmental changes in particular structures (e.g., Corrigan & di Paul, 1982; Nelson, 1973; Rodgon & Kurdek, 1977), we wanted to chart infants' reproduction of the same four standard words (*car*, *book*, *chalk*, and *gnome*) longitudinally, while still providing them with at least two novel and two familiar words whenever possible. Thus, we presented all children with these four words and added the occasional one or two from the alternate list only when that advanced the goal of providing two familiar and two novel words to each child. Usually an additional familiar word was added. In effect, all children received the same words and, when at all possible, the same minimum number of novel and familiar words. Slight differences in numbers of words were handled by employing percentages in several analyses.

INFANT'S LANGUAGE-RELATED IMITATION DEVELOPMENT

All the methodological decisions previously discussed were undertaken to explore developmental changes in the vocal, verbal, visible action, and nonvisible action imitation of infants from the end of their first to the end of their second year of life. Of particular interest were issues of similarity, difference, and relationship between language-related and other matching behavior during this period of rapid linguistic development. Furthermore, the research investigated whether imitation of novel behaviors might serve as an effective strategy for acquiring new vocabulary; this was done by examining if children's early imitation of novel, but not necessarily familiar, words would predict their later lexical development. Complete descriptions of the studies and findings are available in reports by Masur (1993, 1995).

As part of a more extensive investigation of mother–infant interaction and children's imitation and language development, 10 girls and 10 boys and their mothers participated in a longitudinal study conducted from 1986 to 1988. The children were visited in their homes twice at each of four ages: 10, 13, 17, and 21 months. These ages were chosen to correspond to normative milestones in children's communicative development: the acquisition of conventional communicative gestures at the end of the first year (Masur, 1983); the emergence of spontaneous symbolic words at the beginning of the second year (Goodwyn & Acredolo, 1993); a rapid acceleration in lexical acquisition for many children in the middle of the second year (Goldfield & Reznick, 1990); and the appearance of rudimentary grammatical utterances toward the end of the second year of life (Nelson, 1973). Seventeen children were observed at all four ages, and three joined the study at 13 months.

The first visit involved videotaping the children interacting with their mothers during three situations: bathtime and two kinds of free play. At the end of these activities, the mothers were interviewed about their children's language development using a Words, Sounds, and Actions Checklist that was adapted from a language interview developed by Bates, Bretherton, and Snyder (1982). This maternal report yielded a measure of the children's productive noun and non-noun lexicons and also included other vocalizations and actions in order to determine the familiarity or novelty of behaviors on the standard and alternate lists from which the imitation items were drawn. All behaviors reported as produced by the children were counted as familiar; all others were considered novel.

The second visit took place about 1 week later and consisted of the experimental imitation task, which was also videotaped. The mothers and infants were asked to sit facing each other on the floor or sofa in the living room or another place from which toys and distracting objects had been removed. As described previously, each mother served as a model after careful instruction and presented to her child the set of novel and familiar words (e.g., car, gnome), sounds (e.g., ba-ba-ba, eeee), visible actions (e.g., wave hand, beckon), and nonvisible actions (e.g., pat head, raise eyebrows) selected from the standard and alternate lists.

The pace of presentation was determined by an experimenter who handed the mother a separate index card explaining each item only when the child appeared calm and attentive. The mother called the child's name and then modeled the behavior when the child looked at her. Item presentation was repeated up to three times. Mothers were instructed not to react to their children's responses, but to smile encouragingly throughout. Vocalizations were presented without objects; but when words were presented, the toy or referent object was placed in front of the child. The child's best performance on each imitation item was coded from the videotape according to preestablished criteria and later compared with ratings completed by the experimenter during the session (see Masur, 1993).

Analyses of developmental change in the overall proportions of behaviors of each kind imitated revealed that infants' performance of vocalizations and both kinds of action increased gradually and similarly, from means of 0.18 to 0.20 at 10 months to means of 0.29 to 0.34 at 21 months. However, replication of words followed a different trajectory: Infants' imitation of words trailed their production of all other behaviors at 10 months ($M = 0.05$) but greatly exceeded all other matching at 21 months ($M = 0.62$; see Masur, 1993).

Analyses of reproduction of familiar versus novel behaviors again revealed distinctions between imitation of words and other behaviors. Although infants matched more familiar than novel vocalizations and actions, there was no significant difference in their overall performance of familiar and novel words. Furthermore, infants' matching of novel words surpassed their imitation of novel vocalizations and nonvisible actions at 17 months and of all novel behaviors at 21 months, although the same findings did not prevail for familiar acts. Infants' replication of novel words, then, even beyond their production of familiar ones, produced the surge in verbal imitation. Thus, although infants' novel word imitation was occasionally correlated with their repetition of other novel items, its developmental course diverged from that of the other behaviors, even from nonverbal vocalizations, during this period of burgeoning linguistic growth (Masur, 1993).

INFANTS' IMITATION AND THEIR LEXICAL DEVELOPMENT

This was the pattern that emerged when the infants' average performance at each age was analyzed. Yet an examination of individuals uncovered a different picture: The accelerating average novel word imitation scores had masked marked differences among the children. Although only 4 children repeated any words at 10 months, by 13 months about half the children, 9 out of 20, reproduced at least one novel word, and almost all of them continued to match novel words at the succeeding assessments. If imitation can indeed serve as a strategy for acquiring new behaviors, including words, then early reproduction of novel words, but not performance of familiar words, should predict later vocabulary development. The group of early novel word imitators allowed us to test this hypothesis.

The concurrent and subsequent noun and non-noun lexicons of the 13-month-olds who did reproduce novel words (the imitators) and those who did not (the nonimitators) were compared (Masur, 1995). Because the infants' noun and non-noun lexicons at 13 months were significantly related to the extent of their vocabularies of both types at 17 months, it was important to remove any current vocabulary size as a possible confounding factor. Consequently, separate repeated measures analyses of covariance for noun and non-noun production were computed, with imitation group (imitators vs. nonimitators) and age (17 and 21 months) as factors and lexical production in the given domain at 13 months as the covariate. The analyses demonstrated that even when initial vocabulary levels were controlled, the early novel word imitators had significantly larger noun and non-noun lexicons than did the nonimitators at both 17 and 21 months (Masur, 1995).

Correlational analyses corroborated and extended these findings. Infants' novel word reproduction at 13 months was unrelated to their concurrent lexicon size. However, infants' frequency of novel word imitation early in the second year was a significant predictor of their noun vocabularies by the middle of the second year and their non-noun vocabularies by the end of it. Subsequent partial correlations confirmed these results: Children who imitated more novel words at 13 months had significantly greater noun lexicons at 17 months and non-noun lexicons at 21 months, even when earlier vocabulary levels were controlled. Moreover, as expected, this pattern of findings held only for infants' imitation of novel words, but not for reproduction of other novel behaviors or for replication of familiar words; infants' familiar word repetition was associated with their current rather than future lexicons (Masur, 1995).

CONCLUSIONS AND FUTURE DIRECTIONS

These results demonstrate the value of investigating infants' verbal imitation, of considering nurture as well as nature in the language acquisition process. In both the studies described, infants' reproduction of novel words exhibited a different pattern from their replication of other familiar or novel behaviors. This distinction suggests a special and specific function for novel verbal imitation during a period of significant language growth. Infants' verbal performance outstripped their repetition of all other kinds of behaviors by the end of the second year. In particular, their reproduction of novel words matched their familiar word performance and surpassed other novel imitation by the middle of the second year. More important, infants who reproduced novel words early in the second year developed larger vocabularies by the middle and end of that year. Children's early imitation of novel words, but not their repetition of familiar words, predicted, and perhaps facilitated, their later lexical development (Masur, 1995).

An infant's ability to match behaviors never before produced not only marks the achievement of a new step along the universal developmental trajectory. It also signals the emergence of a capacity that can be recruited as an individual strategy for adding new acts to one's behavioral repertoire (Masur, 1995; Uzgiris, 1981). Although not all children utilize imitation, novel word matching has the potential to advance vocabulary acquisition by aiding the processes of representing, analyzing, and practicing linguistic structures (Bloom et al., 1974; Snow, 1981). As our findings suggest, it may be the combination of early progress along the universal pathway and early utilization of novel verbal imitation as an individual strategy that is instrumental in rapid vocabulary growth; later development or later strategy adoption may not be as effective. In fact, Nelson (1973) reported that children's spontaneous imitation rates at the end of the second year were nonsignificantly but negatively related to their lexical development.

Certainly, the correlational nature of our research precludes the inference that these children's early adoption of a strategy for novel word imitation did indeed produce their greater lexical advancement. However, although only a future experimental investigation could establish a causal connection, it is noteworthy that in this study the relationship between early novel word reproduction and later vocabulary size held—even when early lexical levels were statistically controlled (Masur, 1995). In addition, children's imitation of other novel behaviors, perhaps indicating developmental achievement without adoption of a specific novel verbal imitative strategy (cf. Snow, 1989), was unrelated to their later lexical development.

Besides functioning as a potential intrapersonal strategy for acquiring new behaviors, imitation is, of course, an interpersonal enterprise (Uzgiris, 1981, 1984). As an aspect of social relations, infants' reproduction of both familiar and novel sounds and words can further interactional and conversational purposes, from acknowledging a relationship to taking a turn or maintaining a topic (Bloom et al., 1976; Keenan, 1974; Uzgiris, 1984). Our experimental procedure, with mothers labeling presented objects, was designed to parallel maternal object-naming practices and evoke infants' usual imitative patterns during natural dyadic interactions. Indeed, we can meaningfully account for the predictive association between these infants' early novel word imitation and their later lexical development only if their imitation in our sessions reflects their typical imitative style (Masur, 1995). Thus, it would be critical to ascertain whether these infants' experimental performance actually mirrors their spontaneous verbal matching. That is the aim of our analyses of the previously videotaped mother-infant bath and play episodes now under way. So far we have charted the developmental characteristics of infants' naturally occurring vocal, verbal, and action imitation (Masur & Rodemaker, in press). Our eventual goal is to uncover the relations between infants' spontaneous and experimental verbal imitation. As with infants' elicited imitation performance, we expect that infants' ability and willingness to imitate novel, but not familiar, words during natural interactions with their mothers will predict their later lexical advancement. Such findings would underscore the value of studying infants' verbal imitation for insights into the processes of language acquisition.

ACKNOWLEDGMENTS

I would like to thank the many people who were involved in aspects of this research program over a number of years, including Shari Larson, Margaret Roschmann, Susanne Thomas, Patrick Wolf, Tena Simpson, and the participating mothers and children.

REFERENCES

Abravanel, E., Levan-Goldschmidt, E., & Stevenson, M. B. (1976). Action imitation: The early phase of infancy. *Child Development, 47,* 1032–1044.

Baldwin, J. (1895). *Social and ethical interpretations in mental development.* New York: Macmillan.

Bates, E., Bretherton, I., & Snyder, L. (1982). *Language comprehension and production interview.* Unpublished manuscript.

Berko Gleason, J. (1993). Studying language development: An overview and a preview. In J. Berko Gleason (Ed.), *The development of language* (3rd ed., pp. 1-37). New York: Macmillan.

Bloom, L., Hood, L., & Lightbown, P. (1974). Imitation in language development: If, when, and why. *Cognitive Psychology, 76,* 380–420.

Bloom, L., Rocissano, L., & Hood, L. (1976). Adult–child discourse: Developmental interaction between information processing and linguistic knowledge. *Cognitive Psychology, 8,* 521–552.

Bohannon, J. N., III. (1993). Theoretical approaches to language acquisition. In J. Berko Gleason (Ed.), *The development of language* (3rd ed., pp. 239–297). New York: Macmillan.

Corrigan, R., & di Paul, L. (1982). Measurement of language production in two-year-olds: A structured laboratory technique. *Applied Psycholinguistics, 3,* 223–242.

Ervin-Tripp, S. M. (1973). Imitation and structural change in children's language. In C. A. Ferguson & D. I. Slobin (Eds.), *Studies of child language development* (pp. 391–406). New York: Holt, Rinehart and Winston.

Folger, J. P., & Chapman, R. S. (1978). A pragmatic analysis of spontaneous imitation. *Journal of Child Language, 5,* 25–38.

Fraser, C., Bellugi, U., & Brown, R. (1973). Control of grammar in imitation, comprehension, and production. In C. A. Ferguson & D. I. Slobin (Eds.), *Studies of child language development* (pp. 465–485). New York: Holt, Rinehart and Winston.

Goldfield, B., & Reznick, J. S. (1990). Early lexical acquisition: Rate, content, and the vocabulary spurt. *Journal of Child Language, 17,* 171–183.

Goodwyn, S. W., & Acredolo, L. P. (1993). Symbolic gesture versus word: Is there a modality advantage for onset of symbol use? *Child Development, 64,* 688–701.

Keenan, E. (1974). Conversational competence in children. *Journal of Child Language, 1,* 163–184.

Killen, M., & Uzgiris, I. C. (1981). Imitation of actions with objects: The role of social meaning. *Journal of Genetic Psychology, 138,* 219–229.

Kuhn, D. (1973). Imitation theory and research from a cognitive perspective. *Human Development, 16,* 157–180.

Masur, E. F. (1983). Gestural development, dual-directional signaling, and the transition to words. *Journal of Psycholinguistic Research, 12,* 93–109.

Masur, E. F. (1988). Infants' imitation of novel and familiar behaviors. In T. R. Zentall & B. G. Galef, Jr. (Eds.), *Social learning: Psychological and biological perspectives* (pp. 301–318). Hillsdale, NJ: Lawrence Erlbaum Associates.

Masur, E. F. (1989). Individual and dyadic patterns of imitation: Cognitive and social aspects. In G. E. Speidel & K. E. Nelson (Eds.), *The many faces of imitation in language learning* (pp. 53–71). New York: Springer-Verlag.

Masur, E. F. (1993). Transitions in representational ability: Infants' verbal, vocal, and action imitation during the second year. *Merrill-Palmer Quarterly, 39,* 437–456.

Masur, E. F. (1995). Infants' early verbal imitation and their later lexical development. *Merrill-Palmer Quarterly, 41,* 286-306.

Masur, E. F., & Ritz, E. G. (1984). Patterns of gestural, vocal, and verbal imitation performance in infancy. *Merrill-Palmer Quarterly, 30,* 369–392.

Masur, E. F., & Rodemaker, J. E. (in press). Mothers' and infants' spontaneous vocal, verbal, and action imitation during the second year. *Merrill-Palmer Quarterly.*

McCabe, M., & Uzgiris, I. C. (1983). Effects of model and action on imitation in infancy. *Merrill-Palmer Quarterly, 29,* 69–82.

McCall, R. B. (1979). Qualitative transitions in behavioral development in the first two years of life. In M. H. Bornstein & W. Kessen (Eds.), *Psychological development from infancy: Image to intention* (pp. 183–224). Hillsdale, NJ: Lawrence Erlbaum-Associates.

McCall, R. B. (1981). Nature–nurture and the two realms of development: A proposed integration with respect to mental development. *Child Development, 52,* 1–12.

McCall, R. B., Parke, R. D., & Kavanaugh, R. D. (1977). Imitation of live and televised models by children on to three years of age. *Monographs of the Society for Research in Child Development, 42* (5, Serial No. 173).

Meltzoff, A. N. (1985). Immediate and deferred imitation in fourteen-and twenty-four-month-old infants. *Child Development, 56,* 62–72.

Meltzoff, A. N. (1988). Infant imitation and memory: Nine-month-olds in immediate and deferred tests. *Child Development, 59,* 217–225.

Meltzoff, A. N. (1990). Foundations for developing a concept of self. In D. Cicchetti & M. Beeghly (Eds.), *The self in transition* (pp.139–164). Chicago: University of Chicago Press.

Nelson, K. (1973). Structure and strategy in learning to talk. *Monographs of the Society for Research in Child Development, 38,* (1–2, Serial No. 149).

Nelson, K. (1996). *Language in cognitive development: Emergence of the mediated mind.* Cambridge: Cambridge University Press.

Piaget, J. (1962). *Play, dreams, and imitation in childhood.* New York: Norton.

Ramer, A. (1976). The function of imitation in child language. *Journal of Speech and Hearing Research, 19,* 700–717.

Rodgon, M. M., & Kurdek, L. A. (1977). Vocal and gestural imitation in 8-, 14-, and 20-month-old children. *Journal of Genetic Psychology, 131,* 115–123.

Snow, C. E. (1981). The uses of imitation. *Journal of Child Language, 8,* 205–212.

Snow, C. E. (1989). Imitativeness: A trait or a skill? In G. E. Speidel & K. E. Nelson (Eds.), *The many faces of imitation in language learning* (pp. 73–90). New York: Springer-Verlag.

Tomasello, M. (1992). The social bases of language acquisition. *Social Development, 1,* 67–87.

Uzgiris, I. C. (1981). Two functions of imitation during infancy. *International Journal of Behavioral Development, 4,* 1–12.

Uzgiris, I. C. (1984). Imitation in infancy: Its interpersonal aspects. In M. Perlmutter (Ed.), *The Minnesota symposium on child psychology* (Vol. 17, pp. 1-32). Hillsdale, NJ: Lawrence Erlbaum Associates.

Uzgiris, I. C., & Hunt, J. McV. (1975). *Assessment in infancy.* Urbana: University of Illinois Press.

Uzgiris, I. C., Vasek, M. E., & Benson, J. B. (1984). *A longitudinal study of matching activity in mother–infant interaction.* Paper presented at the Fourth Biennial International Conference on Infant Studies, New York, NY.

3

Examining Young Children's Morphosyntactic Development Through Elicited Production

LouAnn Gerken
University of Arizona

WHY ELICITED PRODUCTION?

Since the early years of research on language development, the most common source of data used to infer young children's linguistic knowledge has been their spontaneously produced utterances. The popularity of such data stems in part from the relative ease and naturalness of its collection: With many children who have begun to talk, the researcher need only create a comfortable and interesting environment and prepare to deal with an abundance of linguistic information. The recent availability of computerized databases of transcribed spontaneous utterances allows researchers to analyze this information without even interacting with children at all. What could be better?

Although spontaneously produced utterances are a crucial source of information, they are insufficient for at least two reasons. First, there is growing evidence that children's linguistic representations are often more mature than their utterances would suggest. Second, if children's intended utterances are often different from what they actually produce, researchers cannot determine the exact form of the intended utterance from the actual utterance. For example, imagine that a child produces the utterance in (1a) in the context of an adult making a bear puppet kiss a dog puppet. What exactly does the child mean by this utterance? Was the intended utterance more like (1b), (1c), (1d), or (1e)? Even a sensitive observer would be hard pressed to answer these questions.

(1a) Bear kiss dog.
(1b) The bear is kissing the dog.
(1c) The bear kisses the dog.
(1d) The bear kissed the dog.
(1e) You're making the bear kiss the dog.

Clearly, the relation between intended and actual utterances provides potentially important information about the process of becoming a mature language user. One way to access such information is to provide children with "target" utterances for production. Brown (1973) and his colleagues demonstrated several decades ago that children modify target utterances in ways that closely resemble their own spontaneous productions. The advantage of eliciting utterances in this way is that because the target or intended utterance is known, the pattern of modifications that children make can be determined and analyzed.

For example, imagine that in the example described previously the adult had asked the child to say the target in (1c) and the child produced the output in (2a), following. Next imagine that the adult had asked the child to produce the target in (1d). This time, the child produced the output in (2b). Assuming that it continues over several instances, the pattern of adult targets and child outputs yields at least two observations. First, the object determiner is sometimes produced, but the subject determiner never is. Second, the object determiner only appears when the verb inflection is past tense and nonsyllabic. These observations suggest that variable production of a linguistic element (e.g., a determiner) may not be random but instead is governed by potentially important principles. These principles are simply not discernible from studies of children's spontaneous speech alone.

(2a) Bear kisses dog.
(2b) Bear kissed the dog.

Having established that elicited productions provide important and unexpected insights into language development, now let us consider how to most successfully elicit utterances from young children. At least four factors need to be considered: characteristics of children who are good candidates for elicited production, the elicitation procedure, properties of the target utterances, and the relation between elicited and spontaneous utterances. Each of these factors is discussed in the following sections.

CHILD CHARACTERISTICS

When the subject population of interest is normally developing children, 24 to 30 months appears to be the most appropriate age range for the elicited production technique. Eliciting phrase-length utterances from children younger than 24 months is usually unsuccessful. Eliciting such utterances from children older than 30 months often yields exact repetitions of the target, which are not useful if the goal is to examine the relation between target and child utterance. The child's mean length of utterance (MLU) is also a predictor of whether or not the elicited imitation technique will be successful, with MLUs between 1.50 and 3.50 being optimal. Elicited production has also been used successfully with 4- to 6-year-old children with specific language impairment exhibiting MLUs in the same range.

With normally developing children, perhaps the single most significant factor influencing the success of the elicitation task (aside from age) is whether the child's parents normally engage in "can you say" activities at home. Therefore, when recruiting children to participate in research, it is useful to ask the parents about such activities. It is also useful to inform parents before the experimental visit that you will attempt to elicit utterances from their child, because children whose parents have told them what to expect from the visit are generally more cooperative.

ELICITATION PROCEDURES

Very few children repeat utterances on demand without the repetition being incorporated into an interpretable pragmatic context. One frequently used context involves a picture book, either one that is commercially available or one that is created by the experimenter. Most children attempt to repeat object or action labels when the label is associated with a picture in a book. However, eliciting phrasal targets in this way is often difficult. Sometimes it is possible to ease children into phrasal targets by beginning with word targets. For example, the experimenter and child can spend several minutes looking at a book depicting both static objects as well as more complex scenes. The experimenter first names some objects without asking the child to say anything, then attempts to elicit object names, and finally attempts to elicit phrases or sentences describing the more complex scenes.

A slight modification of the book elicitation procedure involves allowing children to put stickers in the book each time they attempt the target utterance. For example, the experimenter might create a book about a hippopotamus that eats a variety of foods, with each target utterance describing a new food eaten. After children attempt to produce each target, they are allowed to place stickers of each food in the hippo's mouth. Employing such a procedure often maintains children's interest longer than simply asking them to repeat what the experimenter says after looking at each picture in a book.

Another elicitation procedure involves using props instead of a book. For example, if the experimenter wants the child to attempt a sentence like (1d), mentioned earlier, she or he might enact the relevant scene with puppets, say the sentence, and ask the child to repeat it. A slight modification of this sequence is sometimes more motivating to the child: The experimenter says the sentence and then asks the child to repeat it, and the experimenter acts out the scene only after the child attempts a repetition.

Yet another modification of the props procedure involves asking the child to serve as an interpreter for the experimenter. In this procedure, the child is presented with tape-recorded sentences that are ostensibly produced by a puppet or other toy. For example, a small speaker can be placed inside a puppet or beside a toy robot. The experimenter says that she or he cannot understand what the puppet/robot says and the child can help by repeating the puppet's/robot's utterances. This story is made more plausible by recording the target utterances in synthetic speech or an unusual voice (see the section following on properties of the target utterances). Child repetitions in this procedure can be followed by the experimenter enacting the sentence with other props, although this addition makes the game too complex for some children to follow.

Although I have never attempted a video elicitation procedure, it seems possible that it might be successful with children who watch *Sesame Street* and similar television programs. The video program might depict and describe interesting scenes, and the video narrator might ask children to repeat the description. Similarly, a computer presentation might be very successful with some children.

In all the procedures described earlier, an often successful method of asking the child to repeat a target utterance involves saying the target at least twice. A typical elicitation script can be seen in (3), following. Note that the target is the last utterance produced by the experimenter before it is the child's turn to speak. Also note that the instructions to repeat are in the form of a statement (e.g., "Say that"). It is possible to use a question (e.g., "Can you say that?"); however, some children respond to this format by simply saying "yes" or "no." (See the next section for other considerations in the elicitation script.)

(3) The bear kisses the dog. Say that. The bear kisses the dog.

One issue to keep in mind when choosing among various elicitation procedures is whether the target utterances contain any words that children are unlikely to know. Perhaps because many parents introduce novel words in book contexts, children appear willing to attempt targets containing novel words when the book elicitation procedure is used. They may also do so with a video procedure. However, they appear reluctant to attempt targets containing novel words in the props procedure. In the latter procedure, asking them to tell a parent or sibling about the scene being shown with props is sometimes successful.

PROPERTIES OF THE TARGET UTTERANCES

The linguistic, physical, and contextual properties of target utterances are critical to the success of the elicited production task. One linguistic property of target utterances that must be controlled is target length measured in syllables. Children with MLUs of 1.50 and 3.50 generally attempt targets of between three and five syllables, usually producing an utterance with one or more syllables omitted. Children at this developmental stage often either refuse to attempt longer targets or produce only the final word or syllable. In order to keep the target within a syllable range that the child will attempt while still creating a plausible elicitation context, an experimenter might produce a longer sentence but ask the child to say only part of it. An example is given in (4).

(4) The bear is kissing the pig. Say that. Kissing the pig.

The physical properties of target utterances often interact with the utterance elicitation procedure used. When target utterances are produced by the experimenter, care must be taken to standardize the presentation as much as possible across targets and across children. Differences in stress placement and other prosodic properties of the target can have substantial impact on children's productions. For example, if the target utterance is a statement, it may not be wise to embed the target in a "can you say" sentence like the one in (5), following, because it is not produced with falling fundamental frequency common to statements. In contrast, the format in (3) and (4), mentioned earlier, yields a target with falling pitch while making it clear to the child that she or he should repeat the utterance. Similarly, the placement of focal stress on either the verb or object of declarative targets has been shown to significantly influence whether and how children produce sentential subjects.

(5) The bear is kissing the pig. Can you say "kissing the pig"?

Aside from the experimenter practicing target utterances many times before beginning to test children, the most obvious way to control the physical properties of targets is to record them. The use of recorded speech, both natural and synthetic, was mentioned as one of the possible elicitation procedures in the previous section. I have had good success using synthetically produced targets (e.g., using DECtalk and other computerized text-to-speech synthesizers). However, children occasionally find synthetic speech frightening or difficult to comprehend. Given the wider availability of sound-editing software, it is becoming increasingly feasible to record natural speech and modify it in ways that might fit different elicitation contexts. One caution regarding the use of recorded natural speech stimuli is that children can become quite confused if the experimenter's voice is the one on the recording.

A final issue to keep in mind when creating sets of target utterances is the sequencing of individual targets with respect to one another. Because sequences of targets can often be treated as a story, children appear to apply to these sequences certain pragmatic principles governing narratives. For example, Levinsky and Gerken (1995) found that when the same character name was the subject of several sentences in sequence, children began to change the name to a pronoun. To prevent children from imposing a narrative interpretation on sequences of targets, the experimenter can take frequent breaks between targets, insert unrelated filler items, or use target sentences that refer to a variety of characters.

Another issue concerning the sequencing of targets is carryover effects from one sentence form to another. For example, imagine a study comparing children's productions of sentences like (6a) and (6b), following. Children asked to produce such sentences often choose one of the two tenses and apply it to all the sentences. One way around such carryover effects is to have different groups of children say the two types of sentences. However, such between-subjects designs have the disadvantage of introducing greater variability into the data. Another method is to present targets of each tense in a block, with the two blocks separated by a long play break or even a few days. In the latter approach, the ordering of blocks should be counterbalanced across children.

(6a) The bear kissed the pig.
(6b) The bear kisses the pig.

RELATION BETWEEN
ELICITED AND SPONTANEOUS
UTTERANCES

As noted in the first section, there is typically a strong relation between the forms children use in their spontaneous speech and the forms they produce in an utterance elicitation task. However, it is prudent to determine if this relation holds each time the task is used. The simplest method for confirming that elicited production data are consistent with spontaneous utterances is to establish the correlation between the average number of syllables or morphemes produced in the elicitation task and MLUs obtained from the same children's spontaneous speech. A significant positive correlation confirms that there is a good match between utterance length in the two measures.

A more rigorous test is to look for the production of specific linguistic elements in elicited and spontaneous utterances. This approach is more difficult, because, as noted in the first section, the intended form of children's spontaneous utterances is difficult to determine. Therefore, trying to determine the frequency with which particular elements are omitted is conceptually difficult. Nevertheless, it is sometimes possible to find a conceptually reasonable comparison. For example, Gerken (1991) found that children omitted subject articles more frequently than object articles in elicited sentence productions. This pattern was confirmed in spontaneous speech by comparing (a) the frequency of articles appearing before nouns in utterances composed of a single noun phrase with (b) the frequency of articles appearing between a verb and a noun.

In summary, elicited production is an excellent complement to spontaneous speech data. Taken together, these measures promise a clearer picture of the child's developing knowledge and mastery of language.

ACKNOWLEDGMENTS

Manuscript preparation was supported by NSF grant #SBR9696072. Thanks to Diane Ohala for helpful comments and suggestions on a previous draft.

REFERENCES

Brown, R. (1973). *A first language*. Cambridge, MA: Harvard University Press.

Gerken, L. A. (1991). The metrical basis for children's subjectless sentences. *Journal of Memory and Language, 30,* 431–451.

Levinsky, S., & Gerken, L. A. (1995). Children's knowledge of pronoun usage in discourse. In E.V. Clark (Ed.), *Proceedings of the twenty-sixth annual child language research forum* (p. 129-196). Palo Alto, CA: Stanford University Press.

4

Coining New Words: Old and New Word Forms for New Meanings

Eve V. Clark
Stanford University

One domain in language that children tackle at an early age is word formation. In this chapter, I review some of the ways this aspect of acquisition has been studied in young children who are acquiring different languages. My focus is on children's creation of new words—whether they use new forms or old ones to express new meanings that contrast with the meanings of words they already know. I consider different sources of data and discuss some of the techniques researchers have used to elicit new word forms. I also discuss how to choose an elicitation technique in order to answer a question about acquisition.

Observations of Spontaneous Speech

One invaluable source of information about what children know, consists of observations of their spontaneous speech, whether in the form of daily diary entries or regular recording sessions that are then transcribed. Numerous researchers have kept detailed, often daily observations of what their children say and how they say it. Among these diarists are several who have looked at various aspects of word formation (e.g., Berman & Sagi, 1981; Bowerman, 1977, 1982; Clark, 1982, 1993; Stern & Stern, 1928). These diary observations have included numerous coinages constructed from either old or new forms in the language. For example, children may use familiar forms to express new meanings, as when they use a noun as a verb to talk about the relevant activity in context (e.g., *scale* for *weigh*, or *broom* for *sweep* in English). Or they may construct new forms for their new meanings by adding suffixes to familiar stems (e.g., *spy* + *er* for *spy*, *drill* + *er* for *drill* among nouns; *hay* + *y* for 'covered in hay,' *salt* + *er* for 'more salty,' *fly* + *able* for 'able to fly' among adjectives). In English, children also construct compound nouns from combinations of stems or stems and suffixes (e.g., *snow* + *car* for 'car covered in snow,' *tea* + *sieve* for 'small sieve' in contrast to a much larger *water-sieve*, *candle* + *cake* for 'birthday cake'). Examples like these of children's spontaneous coinages offer researchers a good idea of what children are likely to know and make use of. But diary data tend to be based on observations of single children, and although they offer exceptionally detailed observations, it may be hard to assess how representative they are for children in general.

An alternative source of observational data is the CHILDES Archive (MacWhinney & Snow, 1985, 1990). This archive contains the transcriptions of many hours of recorded data from a variety of children learning many different languages. The longitudinal records cover anywhere from a year up to four years, with recordings made for about an hour every 2 to 3 weeks. These data also contain a range of coinages (e.g., Becker, 1994); however, identifying a child's innovations in such data may occasionally be difficult because of the virtual absence of contextual notes. At the same time, like diary data, these observations of spontaneous use offer general indications of when children start to use different word-form types—stems, suffixes, and combinations of these—in coining new words. These observations therefore offer important information about what children probably learn first in word formation, what is most productive for them, and which paradigms they identify early in a specific language. Data from children's spontaneous coinages help identify a baseline in terms of what children are likely to know at age 2, or age 4, and so on. But to establish more precisely what they know about how to coin words in their first language, researchers need to be able to elicit coinages from larger numbers of children by persuading them to create new words on demand.

ELICITING COINAGES

The pioneer in eliciting word forms is Jean Berko. In 1958, she reported a series of tests that she used to determine what 5- to 7-year-olds know, for instance, about how to form the plural in English, or how to construct an adjective to express a notion like 'covered in spots.' She emphasized mainly English noun and verb inflection (for nouns: plural -*s* in its three variants: /-s/, /-z/, and /-əz/; and, possessive -*s*, with the same variants; for verbs: durative -*ing*, past tense -*ed* in its three variants: /-t/, /-d/, and /-əd/; and simple present -*s*, again in three variants). In eliciting these inflections, Berko relied on use of nonsense syllables in place of familiar words so she could be sure, when a child added an inflection, that the child was not just reproducing a stem-and-inflection combination already heard from others. Berko also included a few questions about word formation where she attempted to elicit an adjective ending in -*y* (with comparative and superlative forms in -*er* and -*est*) and a compound noun, also using nonsense stems. And she asked children to give definitions of the meanings of a few familiar compounds like *birthday*, *breakfast*, or *blackboard*—a task in which they appeared unable to analyze the compounds into their component parts. In short, while Berko's technique was very successful in eliciting inflectional endings for novel (nonsense) stems from the children, it appeared to be rather less successful in eliciting information about word formation (see also Derwing, 1976). This may have been because children had not yet learned the relevant forms, but observations from vocabulary studies and other sources of spontaneous speech suggest that the difficulty somehow lay in the task itself. One possible reason for this was the use of nonsense stems *(dak, ruk)*, rather than stems with an already familiar meaning, as the basis for the new word form.

When speakers coin a word to express some new meaning, they do so because they are trying to express something that is not expressed by the words they already know. The meaning they have in mind contrasts with existing meanings and so cannot be carried by an existing conventional form. To convey the new meaning, therefore, the speaker must coordinate with the addressee to make sure that that addressee will in fact grasp the meaning intended on that occasion (Clark & Clark, 1979). One aspect of this consists of choosing an appropriate word form (stem or stems with appropriate meaning, affixes likewise, etc.), and then, in context, making sure that the addressee can compute this new meaning. For children, the occasions that seem to require coinages may be more numerous than for adults, because children lack so much of the conventional vocabulary known to adult speakers. In investigating what young children know about coining words, then, the meanings to be expressed seem to offer a key. But if children are simply offered a nonsense-word stem and asked to coin a new word, they have little or no established meaning to go on. So we reasoned that asking children to coin words with familiar, known word stems rather than nonsense words might be more effective in tapping their knowledge of word formation. This indeed proved to be the case. Let me give some examples.

New Words for Agents and Instruments.   In one study of word formation, we looked at what children aged from 3 to 5 years know about coining words for agents and instruments (Clark & Hecht, 1982). To elicit forms for these noun types, we specified the meanings the children were to express, using instructions like "What could you call someone who throws buttons?" (for a new agent noun) or "What could you call something that moves boxes?" (for a new instrument noun). The essential point was that we chose kinds of agents and instruments for which there was no existing term in English, so expression of these meanings required construction of a new form by the child-speakers. None of the children who took part in this task objected to the questions we posed, and all appeared to find it perfectly reasonable to come up with terms to express the meanings that had been specified. Moreover, few children tried to make use of ready-made conventional expressions (ones that captured only part of the meaning specified). The proportions of each response-type (coinage, established term, or other, including "don't know") are shown in Table 4.1.

With increasing age, children coined higher numbers of terms, and their choices of forms were more likely to fit the conventions on how to coin new agent and instrument nouns in English. That is, they shifted toward a steadily greater reliance on the suffix -er added to the relevant verb stem for agents first and then for instruments as well. These data are shown in Table 4.2. English-speaking children also favor -er when they coin compound nouns for agents and instruments (Clark, Hecht, & Mulford, 1986).

Cross-Linguistic Comparisons.   When the same method was used to look at these noun-types in other languages, the general results were very similar: Children 3 to 6 years of age tend to master agentive forms before instrumental ones, even where these rely on the same suffix—as in Icelandic, where innovative uses of the agentive and instrumental suffix -ari appear to be very similar to those for English -er as shown by the summary in Table 4.3 (Mulford, 1983). In fact, the numbers of coinages vs. other responses in the two languages are very close indeed.

In Hebrew, however, there are several different options for agents and for instruments, with little or no sharing of forms across the two noun-types, at least among established conventional options. Yet children (and adults)

TABLE 4.1
Percentage of Innovative Agent and Instrument Nouns

Age	Coinage		Established Term		Other	
	Agent	Instrument	Agent	Instrument	Agent	Instrument
3;0–3;8	76	48	3	28	21	24
3;9–4;5	95	73	2	8	3	19
4;6–5;2	81	73	10	10	9	17
5;3–6;0	93	82	10	3	4	12

Note. Based on Clark & Hecht 1982: 16–17.

TABLE 4.2
Percentage Uses of -er by Age in English

Age	Agent	Instrument
3;0–3;8	55	42
3;9–4;5	90	71
4;6–5;2	76	70
5;3–6;0	91	72

Note. Based on Clark & Hecht 1982: 12.

TABLE 4.3
Percentage Uses of -ari by Age in Icelandic

Age	Agents	Instrument
3;0–3;8	57	43
3;9–4;5	83	49
4;6–5;2	87	80
5;3–6;0	98	78

Note. Based on Mulford 1983: 115.

favored one particular word pattern with the suffix -*an* for both new agent and new instrument nouns (Clark & Berman, 1984; see also Berman, chap. 5, this volume). They also relied on zero-derived and compound noun forms. As in the initial English study, children readily took to the task of coining words for the new meanings they were asked to express, and as before, few children refused to do this task or failed to do it. The percentages of each coinage type in Hebrew for each age group are given in Table 4.4.

Finally, there are similar results for this elicitation of agent and instrument nouns for two Romance languages—French (Seidler, 1988) and Italian (Lo Duca 1990). In these languages, though, children have to take two factors into account: the suffixes for these noun types and the appropriate stem to which a suffix can be added. Even so, the number of coinages, compared to other responses, remains very high, similar in amount to those in the other languages studied. In short, giving children the meanings to be expressed, in the form of extended paraphrases,[1] offers a highly reliable tool for eliciting word forms for new meanings. This finding is not limited only to words for agents and instruments; it holds more generally for words for objects as well.

New Words for Objects.   Children also coin words for objects and in doing so make use of a number of options, depending on the language being learned. In English, for example, young children rely heavily

TABLE 4.4
Percentage Uses of Innovative Noun Forms in Hebrew

Age	-*an Suffix*		*zero-derivation beynoni noun*		*Compound Noun*		*Other Noun Pattern*	
	Agent	*Instrument*	*Agent*	*Instrument*	*Agent*	*Instrument*	*Agent*	*Instrument*
3;1–3;11	15	10	31	18	5	5	4	1
4;2–4;9	62	43	3	5	8	8	3	8
5;0–5;9	77	34	2	1	8	18	3	3
7;3–8;0	65	36	3	10	22	30	8	6
11;0–12;0	63	54	6	8	18	20	4	5

Note. Based on Clark & Berman, 1984: 564–565.

---

[1] As in questions like "What could you call someone who throws buttons?" or "What could you call something that opens doors?" (see further Clark & Berman, 1984; Clark & Hecht, 1982).

on noun–noun compounds (e.g., *candle-cake* for a birthday cake with candles on it, or *lion-box* for the lion-shaped box for Duplo blocks—both at age 2;3), where the first element specifies the modifier and the second the head (i.e., the kind of category being denoted). Innovative compounds of this type first emerge spontaneously as early as 1;8–1;10 and are common in the speech of 2-year-olds (e.g., Clark, Gelman, & Lane, 1985; Clark, 1993). In French, children rely on zero derivation (with bare stems, e.g., *une roule* [for a ball, at 1;10]) and stems with suffixes added (e.g., *une saignure* [for a cut, at 3;4]) for new words for objects (e.g., Aimard, 1975; Grégoire, 1939, 1947). And in Hebrew, children rely both on zero derivation with verbs used as nouns and, to a much lesser extent, on noun–noun compounds (e.g., Berman & Sagi, 1981).

In each language, children appear to be sensitive to the options available for expressing the requisite kind of meaning. They pick out word forms—and suffixes—that are used for designating objects in that language. And, early on, they identify some of the functions of specific word forms. For example, in both English and Hebrew, compound nouns consisting of a modifier and head serve to designate subcategories of the type denoted by the head noun alone. For example, an *oil-spoon* is a kind of spoon (for cod-liver oil), a *spear-page* is a kind of page (with a picture of people carrying spears), and so on (Clark, 1993).[2]

In English, however, such compounds place the head after the modifier, while in Hebrew the head appears first, before the modifier. Yet in both languages, children are at ceiling for comprehension by about 2;6 in their ability to identify the referents of the modifier and head nouns in novel noun–noun compounds (see Clark et al., 1985; Berman & Clark, 1989). This can be established by asking children to identify candidate referents (pictures) for novel compounds, where the picture may contain only information relevant to the head noun, say, or where there may be two head-noun referent pictures but only one that also contains information predicated by the modifier noun. Children's ability to do so well at such an early age in these tasks suggests that being able to talk about subcategories is an important resource, one they learn to exploit early when they lack other terms for the (sub)categories in question. The same children also produce

---

[2] All the compound-types mentioned so far are endocentric compounds where the head-noun designates the kind of category being talked about. English also makes use of exocentric compounds such as *pick-pocket* (someone who picks pockets). In these compounds, there is no direct relation between the rightmost noun and the type of entity being designated. In English, exocentric compound forms are relatively unproductive compared to endocentric compound patterns (see further Jespersen, 1942; Marchand, 1969).

such compounds on demand in English when they are shown pictures of novel subcategories (Clark et al., 1985), but they are rarely able to do so that young in Hebrew (Berman & Clark, 1989).

When children are acquiring languages that rely extensively on compounding, they appear to grasp this process early as an option for coining new words. As a result, children learning Germanic languages, for example, make much more extensive use of compounding than those learning Romance languages (e.g., Elbers, 1988; Smedts, 1979; Stern & Stern, 1928; Clark, 1993).

Words for Actions.   Young children do not only coin words for talking about objects; they also coin words for talking about actions. But they are more likely to do this at an early age when the language in question offers some readily accessible means for doing so. In English, for example, speakers readily form verbs from nouns with zero derivation. And in their spontaneous speech, children acquiring English do the same, and do so from as young as 2;0 to 2;6 (e.g., Bowerman, 1982; Clark, 1982, 1993). Innovative verbs also appear in the spontaneous coinages of children learning other Germanic languages—for instance, German (e.g., Stern & Stern, 1928) and Swedish (e.g., Gustafsson, 1979).

Eliciting novel verbs has proved much harder than eliciting novel nouns. This may be because children rely instead on such general-purpose verbs as *do* in a language like English which, when used in context, very clearly picks out the target action. But when children are faced with a situation in which several related actions are contrasted, they are much more likely to coin new verbs for them than to use *do* again and again (Berman, chap. 5, this volume). That is, immediate contrasts among actions offer a pragmatically more natural occasion for coining contrasting verbs than a series of unrelated but novel actions. So if children have to talk about a set of different locations where someone put things (on a table, on a stool, in a jar, etc.), they are more likely to come up with novel verbs like to *stool* or *to jar*, than if the actions do not contrast within the target domain.

New Words for Undoing Actions.   Contrast is also the motivating factor in a study we did of what children know about the meaning of the prefix *un-* and where it can be used in English (Clark, Carpenter, & Deutsch, 1995). We looked for a situation in which contradiction was expected, almost routine, and found it in the interactions between Oscar the Grouch and other characters on *Sesame Street*. So we used this, a setting and characters familiar to the children we were working with, to elicit the forms we were interested in. The experimenter took the role of one puppet-character, and asked her accomplice (another adult) to carry out various actions, and the child took on the role of Oscar and spoke for the Oscar puppet. In the process, the child contradicted each of the requests that had been made by the experimenter.

This method allowed us to look at the means children favored at different ages. We used it to study the forms they preferred when the initial action was described with a verb-and-particle form in English (e.g., *turn on, plug in*), where in some cases the contradiction of the action was a reversal marked by a different particle (e.g., *turn off*) and in others by a verb prefix (e.g., *unplug*). We also looked at suppletive relations among verb pairs, where one lexical verb was used to talk about the reversal of the action of its pair (e.g., *bend, straighten*) and about verbs for actions that were not reversible (e.g., *hit, burn*), as shown in Table 4.5.

We also compared the patterns observed in English-speaking children up to age 5;0 with those observable in children acquiring German, where particles provide the main resource for reversal and where there is no general prefix with the scope of English *un-*. (*Sesame Street* and the relevant characters were just as familiar to German-speaking as to American English-speaking children.)

This study, then, was successful in finding a pragmatically natural, familiar situation in which to elicit the target forms and constructions. The situation of contradiction (argument) was already known to all the children from *Sesame Street* and probably also from play with their own siblings and friends; the characters from *Sesame Street* and Oscar's propensity for disagreeing with everyone was also known to them. So although we were using a variety of different verbs as the basis for eliciting the target forms we were interested in, children found the task itself a

TABLE 4.5
Reversal Forms in *un-* for Three Types of Verb by Age

Age	un-Prefix	Suppletive	Irreversible
2;8–3;5	54	44	2
3;6–3;11	70	32	3
4;0–4;5	94	74	3
4;6–5;0	80	64	4

Note. Based on Clark, Carpenter, & Deutsch, 1995: 649.

natural one. They participated readily and rarely refused to offer a form when in the role of Oscar, so the number of "don't know" responses and failures to respond was very low.

DEALING WITH UNFAMILIAR FORMS: COMPREHENSION COMES FIRST

Studies of acquisition have consistently found that comprehension precedes production, often with a long lag (e.g., Clark & Hecht, 1982; Clark & Berman, 1984). This décalage, I have argued, plays a critical role in the actual process of acquisition as well as in language use for both adults and children, since the child's representations for comprehension (what has been stored in memory) offer a basis for recognition on the one hand and a template for the child's own eventual production on the other (see Clark, 1982; Clark & Hecht, 1983; Windsor, 1994). That is, the child attends to the adult's speech and stores certain forms for subsequent recognition. The same forms serve as models for the child's own attempts at production. So when children encounter unfamiliar forms, they must first attach some meaning to them (which may be extensively revised over time) and then store meaning and form in memory for recognition on subsequent occasions. This will allow children to distinguish totally new forms from forms heard previously and to make systematic attempts to interpret any form encountered before. Only after this will children try to produce such a form under what they judge to be appropriate circumstances.

One major step in this process involves coming up with a possible meaning. How do children decide on possible meanings? What information do they identify as pertinent in context? In general, I suggest that they attend to what speakers appear to intend on each occasion—what they are looking at, attending to, gesturing toward, and comparing the new object or action to. That is, the locus of joint attention restricts the possibilities as children assign a first possible meaning to an unfamiliar word (e.g., Tomasello, 1995). The range of possibilities is limited by the prior conversational context and the current common ground shared by speaker and addressee (H. Clark 1996). When there is no prior conversational context or common ground, the possible meanings of a new term or expression are less constrained and may show greater variation from one person to another (e.g., Clark & Gerrig, 1984). For children encountering new expressions, the same guideline holds: If there is no prior conversation and little or no common ground inferable in context, new words may be interpreted in a range of different ways.

Even when the experimenter constructs novel compounds with certain semantic relations in mind, there may be nothing to constrain the glosses children offer of their possible meanings. For example, in assessing children's (and adults') ability to give plausible interpretations of novel compounds (of the relations that could hold between the entities denoted by the head and modifier nouns), we elicited a wide range of possible interpretations (Clark & Berman 1987). For the novel Hebrew compound *ben^pilim,* 'son^elephants = (an) elephant-child', for instance the commonest interpretation contained *shel* (as in 'child *of* elephants'), but agentives such as 'a child that raises elephants,' 'a child that trains elephants,' and 'a child that likes elephants' were also very common. Another compound that elicited a range of different interpretations was *gamadey^shabat,* 'elves^sabbath = sabbath-elves': for this, 5-year-olds offered, among other plausible glosses, 'elves who come into the house on the sabbath,' 'elves that light the sabbath candles,' and 'elves that make the blessing over the sabbath candles.' There was, of course, no single interpretation that was counted as correct: From a pragmatic point of view, any plausible relation linking head and modifier was as good as any other in the absence of further information about the speaker's intended meaning. In fact, the number of distinct meanings attributed to each novel compound presented for interpretation ranged from seven to twelve, all of which took the head noun as indicating the kind of category and the modifier as telling more about that category.

In short, with innovative words, as with other unfamiliar forms, children (like adults) assign possible meanings as best they can, and do so in accord with what they know about modifiers and heads as well as what they do or don't have by way of common ground (Clark & Clark, 1979). What such glosses tell us, for innovative word forms, is whether speakers know how to relate stem and affix or combinations of stems when they are asked to provide a possible, plausible meaning. The glosses elicited in studies of innovative agentive and instrumental nouns (Clark & Berman, 1984; Clark & Hecht, 1982; Mulford, 1983), as well as of innovative compound nouns (Clark & Berman, 1987), suggest that this ability emerges early and consistently precedes the ability to produce the relevant forms.

MAKING JUDGMENTS ABOUT
WORD FORMS

Children are also willing to make judgments about what people say and to decide whether something is being done appropriately or not. One common context for this is to ask for judgements about what an incompetent speaker is saying—whether the incompetence stems from the fact that the speaker is a toy, a very young child, or a second-language learner. Children appear quite willing to take on the role of judge under these circumstances and both to make judgements about the appropriateness of the forms used, and to offer alternative formulations in place of defective forms or utterances (e.g., Clark & Carpenter, 1989).

In word formation, this willingness to judge can be used to ask about the appropriateness of a form for a specific meaning. For example, if children are shown a picture of a hat being worn by a little boy outside in the snow and are told that one person calls this a *hat-snow* and another a *snow-hat*, they can readily judge which of the two is the more appropriate term to use (Clark & Barron, 1988). In fact, their judgements of modifier–head order in compound nouns in English, for example, consistently precede their ability to produce compound nouns with appropriate modifier–head order. In general, children seem to master forms in comprehension first, then become able to make selective judgements, and then able to produce appropriate forms for themselves. This ordering seems likely to hold across domains.

Children are also able to choose which suffix is the most appropriate for expressing a particular meaning. For example, they have a preference for more productive forms over less productive ones, as when they opt for *-er* over *-ist* or *-ian* for the expression of agency in English. In fact, when they are trying to reconstruct unfamiliar words from memory, they rely on what they know about the more productive suffix and make use of it even on stems where it had never occurred on the original words being "remembered" (Clark & Cohen 1984). They also choose suffixes that are semantically appropriate over ones that are not (e.g., *-er* over *-ly* for agency). In fact, children's choices of forms typically follow adult judgements of productivity, with more productive forms favored over less productive ones in children's word formation (e.g., Berman, 1987; Chmura-Klekotowa, 1971; Clark & Berman, 1984; Clark & Cohen, 1984). Adults can also distinguish between natural or everyday productivity and normative uses in the formation of new words (Berman, 1987). Older children are presumably able to do this too.

CONCLUSIONS

Meaning plays a critical role in the acquisition of word formation. This is just as true for the child acquiring each word form as for the experimenter trying to study what the child knows at each stage in this acquisition. And attending to the meanings of the forms under study is critical in the elicitation of word forms and of judgements about word forms. Another critical factor is the pragmatic context of word formation and hence the extent to which child-addressees are able to take account of the speaker's intended meaning in context. The speaker, ideally, coins a new word only in circumstances where it is possible, indeed easy, for the interlocutor to compute what the new word means, given the prior conversation and the common ground of speaker and addressee on that occasion. This in turn suggests that the contexts for studying the formation of new words should be pragmatically natural ones where the speaker's motive in coining a word is transparent and so makes sense to the child-addressee.

The coining of new words occurs in adult speech in response to the need for a form to express a particular meaning not expressed by the conventional vocabulary available. The same pragmatic needs govern children's usage, and hence are important as considerations in designing pragmatically natural tasks in which to study derivation, compounding, and other aspects of word formation. The same considerations hold for all study of the process of acquiring a first language. Uses of language should always make sense.

Pragmatically unnatural tasks may lead children to adopt ad hoc strategies for dealing with adult questions (e.g., Siegal, 1997), and that in turn often disguises or obscures what they actually know. Why should they coin a new word if there is no reason to? And if there is no reason for it, why give any response? If the meaning of a new form is not readily construable in context, children may opt not to respond, whether in giving a gloss of the potential meaning or in constructing a new word form (e.g., Berko, 1958; Derwing, 1976). Such nonresponses may suggest, erroneously, that children have not yet acquired the forms in question. The word games and tasks devised for asking questions about language acquisition, then, need to make sense, in context, to the children who are participating in them.

In short, children look for things to make sense in answering questions about language, just as they do in answering questions about anything else. It's up to us as researchers to be as ingenious as possible in devising appropriate ways of eliciting what children know under a range of circumstances as we explore the process of acquisition. This requires prior decisions about the exact question being asked. But a method can only chosen once the question has been clearly identified. Methods on their own cannot show anything. The first imperative is to be clear on what hypothesis is being addressed and on what constitutes data relevant to answering each question raised by that hypothesis. Again, ideally, one should collect data using several different methods to make sure the findings converge. But that too will depend on the question being asked. Knowing what works and what doesn't is helpful, but methods don't identify hypotheses and neither do they pose questions. That is the purview of the researcher alone, and that must take priority. Good methods simply provide useful tools for collecting data adequate to the task of supporting or disconfirming a hypothesis.

REFERENCES

Aimard, P. (1975). *Les jeux de mots de l'enfant*. Villeurbanne: Simép.

Berko, (Gleason), J. (1958). The child's learning of English morphology. *Word, 14*, 150–177.

Becker, J. (1994). "Sneak-shoes," "sworders," and "nose-beards": a case study of lexical innovation. *First Language, 14*, 195–211.

Berman, R. (1987). Productivity in the lexicon: New-word formation in Modern Hebrew. *Folia Linguistica, 21*, 425–461.

Berman, R., & Clark, E. V. (1989). Learning to use compounds for contrast: data from Hebrew. *First Language, 9*, 247–270.

Berman, R., & Sagi, Y. (1981). al darxey tecurat hamilim vexidushan bagil haca'ir [Word-formation processes and lexical innovations of young children]. *Hebrew Computational Linguistics Bulletin, 18*, 36–62.

Bowerman, M. (1977). The acquisition of rules governing "possible lexical items": evidence from spontaneous speech errors. *Papers & Reports on Child Language Development* [Stanford University], *13*, 148–156.

Bowerman, M. (1982). Reorganizational processes in lexical and syntactic development. In E. Wanner & L. R. Gleitman (Eds.), *Language acquisition: the state of the art* (pp. 319–346). Cambridge: Cambridge University Press.

Chmura-Klekotowa, M. (1971). Neologizmy slowotworcze w mowie dzieci [Derivational neologisms in children's speech]. *Prace Filologiczne* [Warsaw] *21*, 99–235.

Clark, E. V. (1982). The young word-maker: a case study of innovation in the child's lexicon. In E. Warnner & L. R. Gleitman (Eds.), *Language acquisition: the state of the art* (pp. 390–425). Cambridge: Cambridge University Press.

Clark, E. V. 1993. *The lexicon in acquisition*. Cambridge: Cambridge University Press.

Clark, E. V., & Barron, B. J. S. (1988). A thrower-button or a button-thrower? Children's judgements of grammatical and ungrammatical compound nouns. *Linguistics, 26*, 3–19.

Clark, E. V., & Berman, R. A. (1984). Structure and use in the acquisition of word-formation. *Language, 60*, 547–590.

Clark, E. V., & Berman, R. A. (1987). Types of linguistic knowledge: interpreting and producing compound nouns. *Journal of Child Language, 14*, 547–567.

Clark, E. V., & Carpenter, K. L, (1989). On children's uses of *from*, *by*, and *with* in oblique noun phrases. *Journal of Child Language, 16*, 349–364.

Clark, E. V., Carpenter, K. L., & Deutsch, W. (1995). Reference states and reversals: undoing actions with verbs. *Journal of Child Language, 22*, 633–662.

Clark, E. V., & Clark, H. H. (1979). When nouns surface as verbs. *Language, 55*, 767–811.

Clark, E. V., & Cohen, S. R. (1984). Productivity and memory for newly-formed words. *Journal of Child Language, 11*, 319–325.

Clark, E. V., Gelman, S. A., & Lane, N. M. (1985). Noun compounds and category structure in young children. *Child Development, 56*, 84–94.

Clark, E. V., & Hecht, B. F. (1982). Learning to coin agent and instrument nouns. *Cognition, 12*, 1–24.

Clark, E. V., & Hecht, B. F. (1983). Comprehension, production, and language acquisition. *Annual Review of Psychology, 34*, 325–349.

Clark, E. V., Hecht, B. F., & Mulford, R. C. (1986). Coining complex compounds in English: Affixes and word order in acquisition. *Linguistics, 26*, 3–19.

Clark, H. H. (1996). *Using language*. Cambridge: Cambridge University Press.

Clark, H. H., & Gerrig, R. J. (1984). Understanding old words with new meanings. *Journal of Verbal Learning & Verbal Behavior, 22*, 591–608.

Derwing, B. L. (1976). Morpheme recognition and the learning of rules for derivational morphology. *Canadian Journal of Linguistics, 21*, 38–66.

Elbers, L. (1988). New names from old words: related aspects of children's metaphors and word compounds. *Journal of Child Language, 15*, 591–617.

Grégoire, A. (1939, 1947). *L'apprentissage du langage* (2 vols). Paris/Liège: Librairie Droz.

Gustafsson, A. (1979). *Treåringars språkliga kreativitet* [The linguistic creativity of three-year-olds] (Paper No. 2). Stockholm University, Child Language Research Institute.

Jespersen, O. (1942). *A Modern English grammar on historical principles; part 6: Morphology*. Copenhagen: Ejnar Munksgaard.

Lo Duca, M. G. (1990). Creatività e regole: studio sull'acquisizione della morfologia derivativa dell'italiano [Creativity and rules: a study of the acquisition of derivational morphology in Italian]. Bologna: Il Mulino.

MacWhinney, B., & Snow, C. (1985). The Child Language Data System. *Journal of Child Language, 12*, 271–295.

MacWhinney, B., & Snow, C. (1990). The Child Language Data System: an update. *Journal of Child Language, 17*, 457–472.

Marchand, H. (1969). English word-formation (2nd rev. ed.). München: C. H. Beck.

Mulford, R., C. (1983). On the acquisition of derivational morphology in Icelandic: learning about *-ari*. *Íslenskt mál og almenn málfræði, 5*, 105–125.

Seidler, S. (1988). *Untersuchung znm Erwerb von Wortbildungsregeln Deverbativa Nomina (Agens und Instrument) im Französischen* [Investigation of the development of word-formation rules for deverbal nouns (agent and instrument) in French]. Unpublished master's thesis, Universität Hamburg.

Siegal, M. (1997). *Knowing children: experiments in conversation and cognition* (2nd ed.). Hove, Sussex: Psychology Press.

Smedts, W. (1979). *Lexicale morphologie: de beheersing van de woordvorming door vlaamse 'brugkassers'* [Lexical morphology: control of word formation by Flemish middle-school children]. Ph. D. dissertation, Catholic University of Louvain, Belgium.

Stern, C., & Stern, W., (1928). *Die Kindersprache: eine psychologische und sprachtheoretische Untersuchung* (4th rev. ed.). Leipzig: Barth.

Tomasello, M. (1995). Joint attention as social cognition. In C. Moore & P. Dunham (Eds.), *Joint attention: its origins and role in development* (pp. 103–130). Hillsdale, NJ: Lawrence Erlbaum Associates.

Windsor, J. (1994). Children's comprehension and production of derivational suffixes. *Journal of Speech & Hearing Research, 37*, 408–417.

5

Children's Innovative Verbs Versus Nouns: Structured Elicitations and Spontaneous Coinages

Ruth A. Berman
Tel Aviv University

This chapter concerns derivational morphology, a domain that was marginal to the Berko wug task (3 or 4 of nearly 30 production items). Yet the research reported here derives directly from this classic study because it, too, makes use of structured elicitation for evaluating children's productive, rule-bound knowledge of morphological alternations. Two questions of principle serve as background to discussion of methodology in language acquisition research: how children construe nouns versus verbs as a universal linguistic contrast, and the impact on this process of language-particular factors in the acquisition of Hebrew as a first language. Findings from a structured elicitation task in which subjects coin new words from familiar lexical items are then compared with studies based on nonsense-words and with children's spontaneous lexical coinages.

NOUNS VERSUS VERBS IN ACQUISITION

The distinction between how children acquire nouns and verbs has been considered from different perspectives: the relative order of noun and verb acquisition at the one-word stage and the proportion of items from different word classes in children's early vocabulary in different languages (e.g., Bloom, Tinker, & Margulis, 1993; Gentner, 1982; Gopnik & Choi, 1995; Tardif, 1996; Tomasello & Farrar, 1986); the distribution of nouns as compared with verbs in early caregiver input (e.g., Goldfield, 1993; Slobin & Kuntay, 1995; Tardif, Shatz, & Naigles, 1997); and the acquisition of word classes as syntactic categories (e.g., Braine, 1987; Maratsos, 1988; Pinker, 1984; Tomasello, Akhtar, Dobson, & Rekau, 1997). The present analysis, in contrast, examines how children distinguish between nouns and verbs morphologically. Focus is thus on the word-internal form and structure of these two classes of words rather than on their syntactic distribution or their communicative function.

All languages appear to make a major lexical-class distinction between categories corresponding to nouns and verbs, although membership in the two classes does not fully overlap across languages (Anderson, 1985; Hopper & Thompson, 1984, 1985; Langacker, 1987).[1] This distinction falls into the category of what Chomsky (1965) termed "substantive" as compared with "formal" universals, akin to Keenan's (1975) idea of "naive universals" shared by all languages. The implication for acquisition, in this as in other areas of linguistic form/function mapping, is that children are from the start predisposed to attend to such distinctions (Berman, 1988, 1993a). What they need to learn is (a) how the relevant categorial distinctions are marked in the language they are acquiring, and (b) what lexical and grammatical consequences this has in their own target language

NOUNS VERSUS VERBS IN HEBREW

Children acquiring Hebrew have both a relatively easy and a rather difficult task in distinguishing between verbs and nouns. Words in the two classes typically take different morphological forms, so children have formal surface cues to help them identify the class membership of the words they hear. From the point of view of comprehension, their task in a Semitic language may thus be simpler than it is for children learning a more analytic language such as English, in which there are often only syntactic cues to distinguish between, say, *to cook ~ a cook; his (shoe)laces ~ he laces*

---

[1] Maratsos (1991), in contrast, suggests that given languages like Tagalog, "the only candidate for a universal form-class category is nouns, and the only universal distinction, that of noun-other" (p. 68).

his shoes, compared with the corresponding Hebrew terms *le-vashel ~ bashlan*[2]*, ha-srox ~ sorex.* But in producing forms in a language with a rich bound morphology such as Hebrew, children cannot rely on simply using a given word as either a verb or a noun. Instead, they have to obey numerous language-specific constraints in order to produce words that are morphologically appropriate to a given word class (verb versus noun) and often also to a particular subgroup in that class (e.g., transitive versus intransitive verb, agent versus place noun).

Most content words in Hebrew—all verbs, and most nouns and adjectives—are made up of consonantal roots and associated affixal patterns. This is illustrated in (1) for verbs and nouns formed from the two roots *g-d-l* standing for something like "grow, increase in size" and *k-t-v* meaning "write, represent linguistic signs graphically." The symbol C stands for any root consonant; affixal consonants and vowels are represented with their phonetic values; verbs are listed in the masculine singular, third person, past tense; stress is word-final, except where marked by an acute accent on the penultimate vowel; and three dashes --- represent accidental gaps in the established lexicon.

(1) Verbs and Nouns based on the consonantal roots g-d-l, k-t-b ~ x-t-v [see note 2]:

	g-d-l	"grow"	k-t-v	"write"
Verbs:				
Pattern 1	*gadal*	"grow" [Intransitive]	*katav*	"write"
Pattern 2	——		*nixtav*	"be written" [Passive]
Pattern 3	*gidel*	"grow, raise" [Trans]	*kitev*	"write captions'"
Pattern 4	*hitgadel*	"aggrandize" [Reflx]	*hitkatev*	"correspond"
[Reciprocal]				
Pattern 5	*higdil*	"enlarge, magnify"	*hixtiv*	"dictate" [Causative]
Agent Nouns:[3]				
	megadel	"grower, farmer"	*kotev*	"author"
	——		*mekutav*	"addressee"
Action Nominals:				
Pattern 1	*gdila*	"growing, growth"	*ktiva*	"writing, script"
Pattern 3	*gidul*	"growth, tumor"	*kituv-it*	"caption(izing)'"
Pattern 4	*hitgadlut*	"aggrandizement"	*hitkatvut*	"corresponding/ence"
Pattern 5	*hagdala*	"enlarging/ment"	*haxtava*	"dictating/ion"

---

[2] The stop *b* and fricative *v* alternate in a relatively predictable way, which children attend to from very early on (and so, too, for the pairs *p / f, k / x*).

[3] These three agent nouns are the same as present-tense (participial) forms and in this sense can be said to be derived by zero derivation, or syntactic conversion from their associated verbs.

Other Noun Patterns:

CóCeC	gódel	"size"	---	
CCaC	---		ktav	"(hand)writing"
CCiC	---		ktiv	"spelling"
CaCCaC	---		katav	"correspondent, reporter"
CaCCaCa	---		katava	"(news) report"
CCuCa	gdula	"greatness"	ktuba	"marriage-contract"
CaCCan	---		katvan	"typist"
CaCCanut	---		katvanut	"typing, stenography"
CaCCut	gadlut	"grandeur"	---	
CCóvet	---		któvet	"address, inscription"
miCCaC	migdal	"tower"	mixtav	"letter, missive"
taCCiC	tagdil	"(photo) enlargement"	taxtiv	"(a) dictate"
maCCeCa	magdela	"enlarger"	maxteva	"writing-desk"
tiCCóCet	---		tixtóvet	"correspondence"

The forms in (1) illustrate several points relevant to the child's task in acquiring Hebrew derivational morphology. First, the system is not fully productive because there are many gaps for any one pairing of a given consonantal root plus affixal pattern. For example, the root g-d-l has no agent noun in the typically agentive pattern CaCCan (hypothetical "grower"), and neither g-d-l nor k-t-v occurs in the most common of all noun patterns: CéCeC (e.g., késer "knot" from the root k-š-r "tie"; téfer "stitch" from the root t-f-r "sew"). Second, the system is not fully regular because its form–meaning relations are often unpredictable. For example, both g-d-l and k-t-v happen to form nouns in the miCCaC pattern that have a product meaning (migdal "tower" and mixtav "letter"), but other nouns in the miCCaC pattern can belong to other semantic classes (e.g., place names such as mitbax "kitchen," misrad "office," and also mispar "number," mišpat "sentence"). Third, verbs must be constructed out of one of the five verb-pattern binyan conjugations (or in two passive conjugations not considered here). Nouns, in contrast, may be constructed outside of the classical root plus pattern processes, for example, by the word-based process of adding suffixes to stems, as in (1): katvan-ut "stenography" from katvan "typist," and gadl-ut "greatness" from the adjective gadol "big, great."

In learning how to form verbs, Hebrew-acquiring children must select one of a small, structurally defined set of patterns, all constructed out of consonantal roots plus associated internal vowel affixes and in some cases CV(C) prefixes. Nouns offer a much wider range of options. They can be: non-root-based, underived forms (e.g., *ax* "brother," *sus* "horse"); in the linear form of an existing word plus suffix (e.g., *ax-yan* "nephew," *sus-on* "little horse"); in the form of blends or compounds (e.g., *axot-rax-maniya* "nursing sister," *sus-meruts* "race-horse"); loan words (e.g., the place noun *pitsaríya,* the agent noun *shef* "chef"); and also in several dozen root plus affixal patterns. As a result, the Hebrew place noun *madaf* "shelf" could yield only a total of five well-formed, nonpassive verb coinages: in the three transitive patterns P1 *modef,* P3 *midef,* or P5 *himdif* meaning "shelve (something)," or in the intransitive P2 *nimdaf* or P4 *hit-madef* in the sense of "be shelved, get shelved, shelve oneself"; but the activity verb *le-vašel* "to cook" might give rise to dozens of possible innovative nouns, including place nouns such as *béšel, mivšal, mivšala, mavšela, bašaliya, bišuliya, bašlaniya, bašaleriya,* as well as, say, agent nouns like *bašal, bašil, béšel, bošlan, mevašlan, mevašler* (cf. established *bašlan* "gourmet cook," *mevašélet* "house-cook").

Two conflicting predictions emerge from the contrast between language-general factors and the Hebrew-particular facts noted here. On the one hand, across languages, children should find it easier to derive nouns than verbs because nouns serve the basic referential function of naming, whereas verbs are more abstract relational elements for which suppletive, general-purpose terms are readily available (e.g., *to bang, to hit* for the act of using a hammer; *to put in, put on* for placing something in a crate or on a shelf). On the other hand, Hebrew-acquiring children might find it easier to coin verbs than nouns because in their language verbs occur only in a small, restricted set of obligatory morphological patterns based on a consonantal root combined with interdigited affixes, whereas nouns can take a far wider range of forms.

FROM KNOWN TO NEW:
ELICITED INNOVATIONS

To test these predictions, I employed a research design first used by Clark and her associates in a range of studies with children speaking different languages (e.g., Clark & Hecht, 1981; see especially Clark, 1993), including Hebrew (e.g., Clark & Berman, 1984, 1987). In production tasks of the kind discussed here, children are given familiar words as source input items, and they are required to use these as a basis for coining innovative target output items. This design has formed the basis for several studies on children's knowledge of derivational morphology in Hebrew (summed up in Berman, 1995), whereas studies based on Clark have served for cross-linguistic Hebrew–English comparison, as shown in (2).

(2) Structured elicitations of Hebrew word formation:[4]

1. *Domain*: **Verb-Transitivity Alternations** [Berman, 1993a, 1993b]
   Ages: 2, 3, 8, adults
   Task: (a) Changing established intransitive verbs to their estab-lished transitive counterparts and vice versa (b) Coining novel intransitive verbs from established transitives and novel transitives from established intransitives
   Example: (a) **Source:** "Here the mother is washing [= *roxétset*] the little boy, and here . . ."
   Target: He's washing (himself) [= *mitraxets*].
   (b) **Source:** "Here the little boy is crawling [= *zoxel*], and here . . ."
   Target: His Daddy is crawling him [= **mazxil,* or **mezaxel*].

2. *Domain*: **Endstate Resultatives = Passive Participles** [Berman, 1994]
   Ages: 2, 3, 4, 5, 7, adults
   Task: Turning known active, transitive verbs to passive participles
   Example: **Source:** "Here's a razor to shave [= *le-galéax*] the man, and here . . ."
   Target: The man is shaven [= *megulax*].

3. *Domain*: **Compound Nouns** [Berman, 1987; Clark & Berman, 1987]
   Ages: 3, 4, 5, 7, 9, adults
   Task: Coining novel compounds from periphrastic phrases and clauses
   Example: **Source:** "What would you call (a) blanket [= *smixa*] you use to cover a doll [= *buba*], a blanket that is for a doll?"
   Target: **smixat + buba* "blanket + doll" = 'a doll-blanket'

4. *Domain*: **Deverbal Noun Formation** [Clark & Berman, 1984]
   Ages: 3, 4, 5, 7, 9, adults
   Task: Coining novel (agent, instrument, and place) nouns from established verbs

---

[4] An asterisk marks novel items not in the established lexicon.

Example: **Source:** "What would you call a person whose job is to jump [= *likpoc*], someone who likes to jump?"
Targets: **kofec,*kafcan, *kapac, *mekapcan*

5. *Domain*:   **Denominal Verb Formation** [Berman, 1989; Berman & Clark, 1993]

Ages: 3, 4, 5, 7, 9, adults

Task: Coining novel verbs from established (place, object, instrument) nouns and (state to causative) adjectives

Example: **Source:** "I'm putting these beads in a box [= *kufsa*], what am I doing to the beads, what do I do with the beads when I put them in the box?"
Targets: **kofes, *mekafes,* or **makfis, *makpis*

Like the original Berko test, this design neutralizes the effect of rote learning of familiar vocabulary items that may be acquired and stored as unanalyzed amalgams, in order to examine children's creative knowledge of rule-based morphological processes. But these studies differ from the classic wug task in which the input items were mainly nonsense words that do not occur in the conventional lexicon. Following Berko, nonsense words have been used as input items for acquisition research in various domains of morpho-syntax. These include passives (Pinker, Lebeaux, & Frost, 1987), causatives (Maratsos, Gudeman, Gerard-Ngo, & DeHart, 1987), verb-argument relations (Braine, Brody, Fisch, & Weisberger, 1990), and the early lexicon (Tomasello & Akhtar, 1995).

However, a range of studies on Hebrew derivational morphology shows that children succeed in coining semantically appropriate and grammatically well-formed novel items earlier, and better, on the basis of familiar input items than when they are required to manipulate nonsense forms. Even 4-year-olds had difficulty in alternating verb patterns to reflect changes in transitivity in a Hebrew version of Braine et al.'s (1990) study (Alroy, 1992), whereas they succeed in tasks based on the methodology used here from age 3 or even younger (Berman, 1995). Difficulty was also shown by children age 4 and older in Sokolov's (1988) comprehension study of causative alternations using nonsense verbs based on established nouns. And in two separate studies that required children to alternate verb-pattern transitivity with both known and novel words, results were significantly higher for familiar than for nonsense items, including at school age (Berman, 1993b; Zadonasky-Ehrlich, 1995). Nonsense words used in such studies lack an established semantics, and thus require prior training in the sound–meaning relation in order to be elicited. In contrast, the methodology used here provides "strong clues as to the intended semantics of the words" (Levy, 1987, p. 73).

Additionally, studies of inflectional morphology using nonsense words (e.g., Hecht, 1985; Levy, 1987) indicate that children do better with real words than with nonsense words as source input items. Karmiloff-Smith (1986) argues that this discrepancy is due to the vulnerability of newly acquired knowledge prior to speakers' eventual automated, procedural performance based on fully consolidated, mature representations. Ravid (1995b) offers a similar explanation in her study of a wide range of inflectional alternations in Hebrew.

In contrast to studies using nonsense items as input, experimental studies like those reported here and by Clark (chapter 4, this volume) typically require children to coin new words from familiar lexical items, for example, nouns from verbs as in (2-4) and verbs from nouns as in (2-5). The task of having subjects devise novel target forms from established source forms that are already in their lexical repertoire ensures both "that children are not relying on rote-learning, since they have to apply their knowledge of form–meaning relations in interpreting and producing novel words . . . and that new words have established semantic associations to motivate their coining of new words" (Berman & Clark, 1992, p. 8). This procedure is particularly suitable in the domain of derivational morphology because it impels children to apply rules to items that do exist in the established lexicon but that happen not to undergo the particular alternation at issue (e.g., from intransitive verb or statal adjective to causative verb, or from verb to noun and noun to verb).

FROM KNOWN TO NEW:
SPONTANEOUS INNOVATIONS

Data from such structured elicitations (see subsequent discussion of the Structured Elicitation Test) were supplemented by innovative noun and verb usages from the naturalistic speech output of Hebrew-speaking children from 18 months through early school age. These coinages form part of a collection of nearly 1,000 unconventional lexical usages recorded from the longitudinal speech samples from six children age 1;6 to 3;6 and from diary data and parental reports for another two dozen children. Such data reflect children's natural propensity for coining new terms to name entities or to refer to situations for which they lack a readily accessible conventional label.

The need to fill gaps in one's personal lexical repertoire is the basis for lexical innovation in general. This is what adult speakers (particularly but not only those with an official concern for language usage, such as journalists, language-policy makers, and translators) do when they encounter a notion for which they do not have a lexicalized label. Children innovate for this reason as well. For example, Varda, age 5;7, coins a novel verb when she says to her mother: _telamni_ li et ha-te "lemon + FEM my tea for me = put lemon in my tea," denominated from the noun _limon_ "a lemon"; and 4-year-old Ronen makes up a new noun when he calls his father a good _taknay_ "fixer" from the P3 verb _le-taken_ "to fix." Children also coin words for referents that do have conventional terms in the current lexicon but that may be either not known or not accessible to them at the time of speaking. The asterisked forms in (3) illustrate such lexically unconventional, but structurally well-formed, Hebrew items—nouns in (3-1 – 3-3) and verbs in (3-4 – 3-6).

(3) Nouns and verbs coined in spontaneous speech output:

1. _ha-*nixut_ azra li kše hayiti ayef.   < _la-núax_ "to rest"
   The _rest(ing)_ helped me when I was tired   cf. established _menuxa_ "rest(ing)"
           [Matan, boy, 3;1]

2. _eyfo ha-*ma'ataf la-matana?_   < _la'atof_ "to wrap"
   Where's the _wrapper_ for the present?   cf. _nyar-atifa_ "wrapping paper"
           [Nir, boy, 3;9]

3. _ani meta mi-*tsemi'ut, ani roca lishtot._   < _tsame_ "thirsty"
   I'm dying of _thirstiness_, I want to drink.   cf. _tsima'on_ "thirst"
           [Shelli, girl, 5;0]

4. _uf, ima, at *maxnik-a_ [P5+ FEM] _oti kaxa!_   cf. _xonek-et_ [P1 + FEM]
   Oh, Mom, you're _making-choke_ me now!   "choke," TRANSITIVE
           [Hagar, girl, 4;0]

5. _ima *mashtiya oti im ha-mits._   < _shota_ [P1 + FEM] "drink,"
   Mom _makes/gives-drink_ me the juice.   INTRANS cf. _mashka_
           [Eshel, boy, 4;4]   "water + TRANSITIVE"

6. _*tesharveli li et ha-xultsa._   < _sharvul_ "(a) sleeve"
   Sleeve my shirt for me.   cf. _tekapli_ "fold, roll-up"
           [Asaf, boy, 3;7]   + FEM, IMPER

These coinages show that Hebrew-speaking children as young as age 3 coin words both to fill genuine lexical gaps and to replace conventional terms in the adult lexicon. They produce both novel nouns and verbs. And they construct these items in keeping with Hebrew-specific constraints on combining consonantal roots with appropriate affixal patterns for new-word formation. Therefore, why not rely exclusively on this rich natura-listic, communicatively motivated data base to examine children's ability to "go from known to new" in innovating novel verbs and nouns? The answer lies in the general usefulness of structured elicitation tasks in acquisition research, particularly in the lexicon. Carefully designed tests ensure representativeness across children, across structural and/or lexical categories, and across test items, where naturalistic data are sporadic, incidental, and nonexhaustive in coverage.

The present study attempts to overcome what Karmiloff-Smith (1979) termed "the experimental dilemma," by considering findings for novel verbs and nouns coined in both structured and open-ended settings. To this end, the naturalistic database was a starting point for deciding which words to select as test items by serving (a) to check which words are typ-ical of young children's speech output, (b) to ascertain what form–mean-ing slots create the lexical gaps that children try to fill spontaneously, and (c) as a basis for comparison with findings for the lexical coinages pro-duced in a structured test situation.

THE STRUCTURED ELICITATION TEST

The two tests illustrated in (2-4) and (2-5) in the previous discussion were given to the same group of 60 children, 12 at each age group: preschoolers age 3 (range 3;0 – 3;10, mean age 3;5), 4 (range 4;0 – 4;11, mean age 4;4), and 5 years (range 5;0 – 6;0, mean age 5;6); and schoolchildren age 7 (mean 7;5) and 9 years (mean 9;6—Grades 2 and 4), compared with 12 adults (mean age 35 years) with males and females balanced in each group.

Procedures

In the denominal task (which involved deriving a novel verb from a familiar place noun) subjects were told, for example, "I'm putting these beads in a box [in Hebrew, the loan-word *karton* "carton," *argaz* "crate," or *kufsa* "box"]; what am I doing to the beads?" A suitable response might be *mekarten, me'argez,* or *kofes / mekafes / makfis,* respectively;[5] to coin a new verb from a familiar instrument noun, children might be told,

"Here's a teddy bear who likes to use all kinds of things to do different jobs, he likes to use different instruments to do a lot of actions, what is he doing with the hammer [= *patish*?]" possible responses are *potesh, mefatesh,* or *maftish,* in three different verb patterns. Source items on the denominal test were in four semantic classes: place and instrument nouns as in these two examples, and also object nouns (e.g., "I'm giving this room a window [= *xalon*], a carpet [= *marvad*]; what am I doing to the room?") and adjectives (e.g., "This soup has no taste and no color; I want to help make it better to eat, I am going to make the soup sharp [= *xarif,*] or green [= *yarok*]; what am I doing to the soup?").

On the deverbal task, subjects were given familiar verbs in the three active, transitive *binyan* patterns, and they were required to derive novel target nouns and adjectives from them in four target semantic classes: place, instrument, and agent nouns; and resultative adjectives. For example, subjects were shown pictures of people in different states and performing different activities in unidentifiable places without any obvious instruments or means, and they were told to elicit place nouns, "What would you call a place that is used for buying, where people buy things [P1 infinitival *li-knot,* impersonal plural *konim*], for cooking, where people cook [P3 *le-vashel, mevashlim*] ?"; to elicit instrument nouns, "What would you call a thing, an instrument that is used for finding, that people find things with [P1 *li-mtso, mots'im*], for cleaning, that people clean with [P3 *le-nakot, menakim*]"?; and for agent nouns, "What would you call a person whose job is to fix, who likes fixing things [P3 *le-taken*], or a person whose job is to boil, a person that works at boiling things [P5 *le-hartiáx, martixim*]?."[6]

All subjects were given both tests. Half were presented with the denominal test (to coin novel verbs) before the deverbal test (to coin novel nouns), and the other half were first given the deverbal task and then the denominal task.[7] Responses were elicited from preschool children through age 6 with the aid of props for the denominal test (beads that

---

[5] The input nouns *karton, argaz* contain more than the canonic three consonants (*k-r-t-n,* ʔ*-r-g-z*), so they are most suited to verbs formed in the P3 *pi'el* activity pattern (chosen by all 12 adults on this test). The noun *kufsa* "can, box," in contrast, includes only three consonants (*k-f-s*), and so can be the basis for a verb in any of the three verb patterns illustrated here—not only P3 *mekafes* but also P1 *kofes* or P5 *makfis.*

[6] Verbs were always presented in the inflectally marked forms of infinitives (with a prefixal *l-*) and impersonals (with a plural *-im* suffix) to avoid using the third person present tense or participial form of verbs as input, because these could serve as agent or instrument nouns (e.g., P3 *menake* "cleaner," P5 *martiax* "boiler").

[7] Preschoolers (age 3, 4, and 5) and in some cases 7-year-olds as well were given each test at a separate session, a day or two apart. Older subjects were given both tests at a single session.

were put in or on different places, a teddy bear wielding different instruments, a felt stick-on dollhouse for adding objects to) and using pictures
for the deverbal test. For each semantic class of input item, subjects were
given two sample coinages. On the denominal test, examples of novel
verbs were given in the three *binyan* verb patterns used for activity verbs;
on the deverbal task, examples of novel nouns were given in a range of
noun patterns applicable to each class of item in the established lexicon.

Results

To maximize comparability between the denominal and deverbal studies,
results are presented for three of the four classes of input items in each
test: verbs derived from instrument, object, and place nouns, and nouns
derived from instrument, agent, and place nouns; Table 5.1 shows the
breakdown of novel items produced by subjects when required to coin
innovative verbs from familiar source nouns. These novel items were
rated as "appropriate" when the form produced was in one of the three
morphological patterns used for encoding activity verbs; "other" coinages
were verbs in an intransitive pattern or with a morphologically indeter-
minate form; "ill-formed" responses either were not in any Hebrew verb
pattern or violated phonological constraints on verb formation. The
inverse of total coinages (not specified in the table) are "non-responses"
of three kinds: no response, "don't know," or repetition of the input item.

Table 5.1 shows that by 4 years of age, children reach near ceiling (87%)
in coining novel verbs in one of the five *binyan* verb patterns available for

TABLE 5.1
Breakdown of Innovative Responses in Coining
Verbs from 30 Familiar Nouns

Age	Appropriate	Other	Total Coinages	Ill Formed (%)
3 years	48	7	55	6
4 years	74	13	87	9
5 years	86	3	89	1
7 years	97	1	98	3
9 years	95	1	96	2
Adults	98	1	99	—

Note. N = 12 per age group.

constructing nonpassive verbs in their language. From 3 years of age, the vast bulk of these innovations were also semantically appropriate: They were formed in one of the three verb patterns for describing activities rather than change-of-state achievements. However, the 3-year-olds were able to perform this task appropriately only around half the time. That is, the youngest group had difficulty in coining novel verbs from familiar source nouns; although when they did so, it was overwhelmingly in accordance with the structural constraints dictated by the grammar of verb formation in their language. The proportion of ill-formed responses out of total innovations was very low, less than 5% overall, even among 3- and 4-year-olds, with a slight peak in amount of error at age 4. These errors typically violated morphophonological constraints within verb-pattern formation. There were very few instances of the non-Hebrew processes of zero derivation or of adding a prefix or suffix to the source noun (e.g., a verb prefix such as present-tense *me-* as in ill-formed **mekise* from *kise* "chair" [Tal 7;0], cf. possible P3 *mekase,* or the infinitival prefix *le-* as in **le'aron* from *aron* "closet" [Michal, 9;3], cf. possible P3 *le'aren;* or a nominal suffix to yield diminutive noun forms, impossible as verbs, e.g., *madaf-it* "shelfie" from *madaf* "shelf," *maxteron* "tiny needle" from *máxat* "needle" [Rotem, 4;4]). Overwhelmingly, when children produced novel verbs based on familiar source nouns, they constructed them in a form consistent with the morphological verb patterns stipulated by their grammar.

A different picture emerges for how the same subjects performed when asked to coin novel nouns from familiar verbs. Table 5.2 shows (a) the percentage of morphologically innovative noun forms given by each age

TABLE 5.2
Breakdown of Innovative Responses in Coining Nouns
from 30 Familiar Verbs

Age	Total Coinages	Ill formed (%)
3 years	83	19
4 years	88	32
5 years	87	18
7 years	89	17
9 years	86	4
Adults	98	2

Note. N = 12 per age group.

group, and (b) the proportion of these that were ill formed (i.e., they violated morpheme-structure rules constraining the form of possible nouns in Hebrew).

The findings in Table 5.2 strongly confirm the prediction that children will coin novel nouns very readily. Even the youngest group, the 3-year-olds, reached ceiling in amount of total coinages (83% compared with only 55% verb coinages from the same children). Yet they often violate structural constraints in doing so, an average 23% of all innovations from age 3 through 7 years. Responses revealed three main deviations from conventional noun-formation, which we defined as ill-formed: (a) forms that violate morphophonological constraints on the syllable structure of possible words in Hebrew (e.g., *ritíax* for a person whose job is to boil things — *le-hartíax* [Tom, 5;11]; *ramdedant* for an instrument used for putting people to sleep — *le-hardim* [Lior, 3;10]); (b) words that use verbal affixes with nounlike stems (e.g., the infinitival prefix *le-* in *le'acbon* for an instrument used for irritating people, from the verb *le-acben* [Omer, 3;10]; *le-hashkeket* for a place for watering from the verb *le-hashkot* [Amit, 3;9]); and (c) words that are structurally well formed as nouns but inappropriate for a given semantic class (e.g., the passive participle form *merutax* "(that has been) boiled" to name a person whose job is to boil things, *le-hartiax* [Tomer, 4;0], or the coinages *bishlut* [Naama, 5;2] and *mevashlan* [Yaniv, 5;5], both possible nouns in Hebrew but suited to naming an abstract state with the *-ut* suffix or an agent with *-an*, respectively, and both misapplied here to name a place where people perform the activity of *le-vashel* "cooking."[8]

The fact that until as late as age 7 nearly one quarter of the novel output nouns produced in response to familiar input verbs were what we characterized as ill formed, and as many as one third of the innovative responses produced at age 4, suggests that children find it hard to coin novel nouns that meet the structural and semantic constraints on form–meaning relations in Hebrew nominal patterning. And it contrasts markedly with the performance of the same children in producing novel verbs, where from age 3 they only occasionally, and from age 5 almost never, violated constraints on semantically and structurally appropriate verb formation in their language.

---

[8] Several responses involved two or all three of these deviations. For example, for a place where people waste things or are busy wasting—*le-bazbez*—the response *lebazbezan* [Naama, 4;1] is an impossible word in Hebrew, because it combines the verbal prefix *le-* with the nominal suffix *-an*, the favored device for innovative agent and occasionally for instrument nouns, but not used to name places.

VERB AND NOUN
INNOVATIONS IN SPONTANEOUS
SPEECH OUTPUT

Items characterized as noun or verb coinages were analyzed from our corpus of unconventional lexical usages recorded from Hebrew-speaking children (see previous section "From Known to New"). This yielded a total of some 500 innovative items, nearly 60% (285 out of 493) verbs and 40% nouns. This appears to contradict the findings for coinages in these two classes in the structured elicitations. On the tests, 3-year-olds coined far fewer verbs than nouns, whereas children across ages 3 to 7 years coined on average the same amount of verbs as nouns (82% versus 86%, respectively). Note, however, that many of the children's spontaneous coinages were form–meaning pairings for which a conventional item is available in the established lexicon of Hebrew (e.g., *mashketa* for conventional *mamtera* "sprinkler," cf. *le-hashkot* "to water"). If we compare the proportion of genuine gap-filling innovations, rather than forms coined as alternatives to items in the established lexicon, the proportion of innovative verbs versus nouns is quite consistent across the two types of data—the structured elicitation test and the spontaneous speech samples, respectively.

Extreme caution is necessary in making such comparisons for methodological reasons. In the structured elicitation tests, care was taken to ensure equal representation of specific morphological and semantic classes of input items so that the forms produced by subjects could unambiguously be related to a given source or input form. The rich but sporadic set of spontaneous innovations that constitute the naturalistic database, in contrast, could not guarantee a representative sampling of form–meaning matchings. No less important, there is no unequivocal way of deciding what the source item was for any given coinage, because in most cases this is not specified in the context in which a child happens to produce a given innovation. Besides, this type of sampling does not allow for reliable developmental claims because unlike the structured elicitations, there was no preselection of children by age group.

Such difficulties are inherent in attempting to seek parallels between spontaneous speech sampling and structured elicitations in new-word formation, as in other domains of acquisition. Yet naturalistic data like these provide a rich supplementary source of information on how young children relate to form–meaning matchings outside the conventional word-stock of their language. And some comparisons between the two types of situations do suggest themselves. For example, one explanation for the relatively larger number of verb coinages in the spontaneous speech sample could be that most (67%) appeared to be related to other verbs rather than derived denominally (from established nouns), as was required by the test.

Examples of spontaneous coinages that were clearly denominal include: the P1 verb *la-tsun* "to put sheep into the fold" from the noun *tson* "sheep" [Itamar, 3;11], P3 *mexalel* "spacing, revolving" for a rocket moving in outer space = *xalal* [Asaf, 5;8], and P5 *mashligim* "sliding in the snow" from the noun *shéleg* "snow" [Nir, 4;1]. Apart from denominated forms like these, three main types of verb coinages occurred in the naturalistic sample: pattern switching, overmarking, and gap filling. (a) In pattern switching, children innovate by using a verb pattern different from the one used for that form–meaning slot in the established lexicon. For example, Ran, age 5;9, says *ha-tmunot* P2 *nexlafot* "the pictures change" of a board with pictures that switch when one turns a button (cf. conventional P4 *mitxalfot)*, from causative P5 *maxlif* "to switch" + TRANSITIVE, root *x-l-f ;* and in the opposite direction, Erez, age 5;6, tells his mother that he needs *le-hitrashem* [P2] = "to sign up for school" (cf. conventional P4 intransitive *le-herashem)*, from P1 transitive *lir-shom,* root *r-š-m.* (b) In overmarking, children explicitly mark verbs from the basic P1 pattern to indicate change-of-state unaccusativity with the P2 or P4 patterns if intransitive, and for causativity using the P3 and P5 pattern if transitive. For example, Keren, age 3;6, says she went swimming in deep water and yet *lo* P2 *nitbáti* "I did not be-drowned" in place of conventional *taváti* "I drowned"; and Ran, age 4;9, says that the sun *mamash* P5 *masrif oti* "really makes-burn-up me" in place of conventional P1 *soref.* (c) In gap filling, around 20% of the verb-based unconventional verbs coined by children fill genuine gaps in the established lexicon. For example, Hila, age 3;4, creates an onomatopoeic verb in P3 in the form *meyamem* for a cat that meows all the time; and Nir, age 4;3, coins a causative P5 verb to describe someone who makes the chair creak, *maxrik* (cf. conventional P1 *xorek*), as does Shelli, age 4;7, when complaining that her mother causes her to dive down, P5 *matslila,* in the bathtub (cf. conventional P1 *tsolel*).

These examples suggest that children find it natural to coin new verbs from familiar verbs by moving across and between the five verb patterns. As noted, they tend less to use familiar nouns as a basis for verb coining, the task required by the test. This accords well with the finding that the task of denominal verb formation appeared quite difficult for the 3-year-olds (only 55% of their responses took the form of verb coinages). Besides, in the naturalistic sample, less than one third of the noun-based verb coinages were recorded from children age 2 to 4, in contrast to well over half the verb-related verb coinages. In general, then, in Hebrew, younger children might tend more naturally to coin verbs from inside the verb system by following the typically Semitic device of verb-pattern alternation or innovation, rather than by deriving them from nouns or adjectives.

In contrast to innovative verbs, the bulk of the noun coinages in the naturalistic sample fill genuine gaps. That is, they name objects or states that lack conventional labels, rather than replacing established lexical items. Spontaneously innovated nouns further contrast with verb innovations because they reveal considerable variety, in both content and form. Semantic innovations included instrument, agent, and place nouns, action nominals, and abstract states, illustrated in (4).

(4) Innovative nouns in spontaneous speech

1. *ani carix *makneax.*
   I need (a) <u>wiper</u>.   [Ran, boy, 4;11]

   < P3 *le-kaneax* "wipe (one's nose)"
   cf. *memxata* "handkerchief"

2. *aba, ani rotse et ha-*maglexa selxa.*
   Dad, I want your <u>shaver</u>. [Uri, boy, 3;6]

   < P4 *le-hitgaleax* "shave (oneself)"
   cf. *mexonat-giluax* "shaving machine = razor = razor"

3. *hi mamash *mats'anit, Miri.*
   She's a real <u>finder</u>, Miri. [Hila, girl, 3;9]

   < P1 *li-mtso* "to find"
   (speaking about her babysitter, who is good at finding things)

4. *aba sheli hu *kavar shel ha-xayot shelanu.*
   My dad is the <u>burier</u> of our dead pets.
   [Shelli, girl, 4;10]

   < P1 *li-kvor* "to bury"
   cf. *kavar* "gravedigger"

5. *ze bet-sefer le-*neginut.*
   It's a school for <u>instrumenting</u>.
   [Sivan, girl, 4;8]

   < P3 *le-nagen* "to play (musical instruments)"
   cf. *negina* "playing instruments, making music"

6. *at cerixa la-tet li kley-*negiva.*
   You have to give me objects of <u>wipery</u>.
   [Ben, boy, 5;1]

   < P3 *le-nagev* "to wipe"
   cf. *niguv* "(act of) wiping"

The most favored noun coinages were objects, particularly instruments, one third of all noun coinages, as in (4-1, 4-2); about 20% were agent-nouns, as in (4-3, 4-4); and next most common were abstract action or state nominals, as in (4-5,4-6). Children coined relatively few place nouns, although on the structured test they coined the same amount of place nouns as instrument and agent nouns.

Analysis of naturalistic coinages thus appears to offer partial support for the trends revealed by the structured elicitations, both in (a) overall proportion of verbs versus nouns that were innovated, and (b) subdivision of these items into semantic classes. In morphological structure, too, spontaneous innovations are on the whole consistent with those elicited by the tests. Verbs were without exception coined in one of the five verb patterns, and nearly all denominal coinages were in the P3 activity pattern, as they were on the test. Nouns, in contrast, were innovated in dozens of different forms, both on the test and in the spontaneous coinages, reflecting the much more open-ended range of possible noun structures in the target language. And in both the test and the spontaneous sample, most took the form of some possible root plus affixal noun-pattern combination (e.g., maCCeC(a) or miCCaCa for instruments and places; CaCaC, CoCCan, or CaCCan for agents; CiCuC, CóCeC, or CCiCa, haCCaCa for abstract action or state nominals): over two thirds (69%) on the test and three quarters (75%) in the spontaneous sample. Far fewer coinages (31% and 25%, respectively) took the form of a stem plus suffix (e.g., -*it* for instruments, -*ay,* -*on* for agents, -*iya* for place nouns, or -*ut* for abstract nominals). Also, both samples yielded very few noun coinages in the present tense or participial *benoni* form, which is available for zero derivation of agent or instrument nouns from the corresponding verb form. Finally, both the test and the spontaneous speech sample contained relatively few items that were morphologically ill formed in the sense that they violated constraints on the form of a possible word in Hebrew. Naturalistic coinages included only an occasional ungrammatical verb and rather more ill-formed nouns: around 2% compared with 5% of verbs produced by 3- to 7-year-olds on the test, and around 9% compared with nearly 20% of the nouns they produced on the test.

Thus, despite the cautionary note that the two databases are not strictly comparable—in terms of representation of structural and semantic categories, communicative situation, and population selection—findings for noun and verb coinages among Hebrew-speaking children do reveal generally consistent patterns across the two contexts of naturalistic speech output and structured elicitation. Additionally, certain patterns that failed to emerge in the deliberately restricted structured elicitations could be detected in the spontaneous speech sample. For example, children appear to find it easier or more natural to coin verbs that relate to existing verbs in the language rather than deriving them from nouns. And a larger proportion of children's innovations, both verbs and nouns, appear to fill temporary gaps, substituting for words in the established lexicon, rather than being "creative" new words that lack conventional labels in the target language.

DISCUSSION

The wug technique was adopted for present purposes as highly appropriate for examining children's knowledge of rule-dependent versus rote-bound linguistic structure. In the area of derivational morphology, however, grammatical rule and lexical convention and accident interact in complex ways. Accordingly, it has proved useful to tap this aspect of linguistic knowledge by enabling children to go "from known to new," by requiring them to derive innovative terms from familiar lexical items. This procedure makes it possible to compare how the same children coin new verbs from old nouns as against how they coin new nouns from old verbs. Results of these structured elicitations also provide important support for findings about how and where children spontaneously coin innovative verbs and nouns when faced with the need to fill a genuine, often temporary gap in the course of their natural speech production.

To conclude, I consider implications of these analyses for children's command of word-formation constraints from the perspectives of language development and language typology, on the one hand, and of methodological principles in the study of language production, on the other.

In terms of developmental trends, the present study confirms earlier findings along two important lines (Berman, 1995). Command of derivational morphology typically follows, and is embedded in, mastery of basic clause structure, including such domains as word order, case marking, and inflectional marking of agreement (in the case of Hebrew—number, gender, and person) and tense/mood distinctions. I suggest that irrespective of their particular target language, children around age 2 to 3 years focus on morphology as it interacts with the grammar of clause structure more than in relation to the structure of the lexicon and vocabulary extension. Thus, structural overregularizations and other creative errors will initially be found mainly in the domain of grammatical inflection, and only subsequently in the area of lexical innovation.

Children appear to start working seriously on derivational morphology from age 3 up, busying themselves with analyzing word forms into their component roots, stems, and affixes in terms of lexical form–meaning mappings, and in relation to categories such as causativity or inchoativity in the verb system, or of agent, instrument, and location in the noun system. Developmentally, age 4 emerges as a period of instability: 4-year-olds indulge in considerable experimentation with word-formation conventions, they reveal the highest degree of across-child and across-item variability, and they tend to also produce the most grammtically ill-formed coinages. These patterns provide evidence for the superficially U-shaped developmental curve that I have argued for in different domains of language acquisition (Berman, 1986, 1987, 1990). In the area under discussion, 2-year-olds by and large do not yet analyze the internal, derivational structure of words; 3-year-olds begin making creative errors; 4-year-olds are the most productive but the least constrained by conventionality in the sense of the form–meaning relations specified in the established lexicon (Clark, 1993); and from age 5, children show an almost adult command of lexical structure and are increasingly bound by lexical convention.

This yields certain predictions about the nature of vocabulary development during and beyond the preschool years. Children early on gain command of the grammatically determined structural constraints on possible word structure in their language; and the stronger the constraints (as in the Hebrew verb system), the earlier will they be mastered. Appropriate form–meaning mappings take longer to develop, so that lexical semantics in this sense follows rather than precedes grammar. When the conventional lexicon starts expanding with school-age developments and the impact of increased literacy, children's creativity takes a dip. Only much later, with the consolidation of metalinguistic skills, do word coinages reveal an upsurge among some although not all speaker-writers, in a conscious attempt to meet genuine lexical gaps in such specialized areas as linguistic humor, advertising, scholarly terminology, and innovative media usage.

These developmental generalizations are constrained by target-language typology and are manifested in ways and at times relative to the particular form–function mappings between the morphological structure of words and the syntactic, semantic, and lexical categories that they encode in different types of languages. The findings of this study reaffirm a view of acquisition that has emerged from cross-linguistic studies in various domains. Work on children's encoding of spatial distinctions comparing languages such as English and Dutch with Korean or Tzeltal (Bowerman, 1996), on children's narrative development in five different languages (Berman & Slobin, 1994), and on compound formation and noun and verb coinages in English compared with Hebrew (Berman & Clark, 1993; Clark & Berman, 1984, 1987) converges to suggest that children from a very young age are attuned to the language–particular way of encoding form-meaning relations in their language. Exactly, when this type of sensitivity finds expression depends on general developmental processes, so that the spatial distinctions noted by Bowerman tend to precede command of derivational marking of linguistic subcategories, and these in turn emerge earlier than rhetorical mastery of form–function relations in extended narrative.

Of all linguistic domains, morphology is the area where cross-linguistic variation is most marked. A reasonable hypothesis might be that universally, in order to coin new words, children initially favor morphologically simple processes such as syntactic conversion (zero derivation) and/or choose the semantically transparent path of adding external affixes to an exisiting word. Work with Clark has shown that comparing acquisition of derivational morphology in English and Hebrew is particularly fruitful, because the two languages are so different in this respect. Thus, as shown by Clark's (1993) naturalistic data, in English even 2-year-olds rely widely on the linear device of affixing to a stem with suffixes such as *-y* for innovating denominal adjectives, and with *-er* for coining agent and instrument nouns from familiar verbs. Moreover, in deriving verbs from nouns, English-speaking children can and do rely on zero derivation. In contrast, Hebrew-speaking children from the start coin all verbs and most nouns like adult speakers of their language, by combining familiar consonantal roots with a given set of affixal patterns. They avoid syntactic conversion, and they use root plus affix formations exclusively for verbs and very widely for nouns. This suggests that a-priori notions of what might be easier or more complex for children must be evaluated in terms of the particular target language to which they are exposed. Each language early on provides children with particular expectations as to the possible, structurally constrained form of words and the preferred, usage-bound form–meaning associations in its current lexicon.

The results of this study suggest that typological factors also play a critical role in how children treat verbs versus nouns in acquisition. As Maratsos (1991) concludes from his cross-linguistically motivated comparison of the acquisition of nouns versus verbs, "we should not expect children's evolution of formal categories to be uniform" (p. 82). On the one hand, Hebrew-speaking children are similar to speakers of any language in that universally they recognize that (a) verbs mark activities, events, and states, and (b) nouns can be coined to name objects, people, places, and abstract situations. And they are like other children in that once they are able to analyze word structure they show an ability for lexical coinage, forming "new words from old" in their language. On the other hand, Hebrew-speaking children, in both structured elicitations and naturalistic speech, restrict the verbs they coin to a small set of root plus affix based patterns, whereas they coin nouns in a wide and heterogeneous range of forms, not all of which conform to the structural constraints on possible word formation in their language. This difference between how they innovate verbs compared with nouns makes them more similar to adult speakers of their own language than to children acquiring a language such as English.

The data reported here point to an area in which further analysis might help to characterize patterns of lexical innovation in adult as well as children's usage, in Hebrew compared with other languages. The sample of spontaneous coinages used here indicates that Hebrew-speaking children derive verbs by relating them to one another, rather than by denominating them from the nouns in their vocabulary. But they prefer to produce nouns from verbs and adjectives to name objects and states that lack established labels. It is not immediately obvious whether in this they are observing preferences for new-word formation in contemporary Hebrew usage in general. The question might be partially resolved by dictionary searches to ascertain the distribution patterns of relatively recent innovations in the current Hebrew lexicon. But such survey data would need to be refined by structured elicitations comparing (a) how children and adult speakers of typologically distinct languages derive new verbs both from other, established verbs and from nouns, with (b) how they coin novel nouns from established terms in each of the two major classes of the lexicon.

As a final note on methodology, in order to avoid both under- or overestimation of children's knowledge and abilities, research should ideally follow the advice I give my graduate students. Start with the richest naturalistic data available as a basis for hypothesis making. Next, design carefully constructed experiments to test your predictions. Afterwards, if possible, go back to check the applicability of your findings in a range of communicative contexts—interactional conversation, elicited narratives, and even, in the case of older children, monologic expository texts. In a domain like the lexicon, where conventionality and representativeness are particularly relevant, it might even be worth checking distributions of form–meaning mappings in established dictionaries and existent corpora of child and adult language usage.

REFERENCES

Alroy, O. (1992). Morphological marking of causativity by Hebrew-speaking children and adults. Unpublished Master's thesis (in Hebrew), Tel Aviv University.

Anderson, S. (1985). Inflectional morphology. In T. Shopen (Ed.), *Language, typology, and syntactic description: Vol. 2 (pp. 150–201).* Cambridge: Cambridge University Press.

Berman, R. A. (1986). A step-by-step model of language learning. In I. Levin, ed. *Stage and structure: Re-opening the debate* (pp. 191–219). Norwood, NJ: Ablex.

Berman, R. A. (1987). A developmental route: Form and use of complex nominals. *Linguistics, 27,* 547–568.

Berman, R. A. (1988). Word class distinctions in developing grammars. In Y. Levy, I. M. Schlesinger, & M.D. S. Braine (Eds.), *Categories and processes in language acquisition* (pp. 45–72). Hillsdale, NJ: Lawrence Erlbaum Associates.

Berman, R. A. (1989, October). *Children's knowledge of verb structure: Insights from Hebrew.* Paper presented at the Boston University Conference on Child Language Development.

Berman, R. A. (1990). Acquiring an (S)VO language: Subjectless sentences in children's Hebrew. *Linguistics, 28,* 1135–1166.

Berman, R. A. (1993a). Developmental perspectives on transitivity: A confluence of cues. In Y. Levy (Ed.) *Other children, other languages: Issues in the theory of language acquisition* (pp. 189–241). Hillsdale, NJ: Lawrence Erlbaum Associates.

Berman, R. A. (1993b). Marking of verb transitivity by Hebrew-speaking children. *Journal of Child Language, 20,* 641–669.

Berman, R. A. (1994). Formal, lexical, and semantic factors in acquisition of Hebrew resultative participles. In S. Gahl, A. Dolbey, & C. Johnson (eds.), *Berkeley Linguistic Society, 20,* 82–92.

Berman, R. A. (1995). Word-formation as evidence. In D. McLaughlin & S. McEwan Eds.), *Proceedings of the 19th Annual Boston University Conference on Language Development: Vol. 1* (pp. 82–95). Somerville, MA: Cascadilla Press.

Berman, R. A., & Clark, E. V. (1992). Lexical productivity in children and adults. *Final Report.* Jerusalem: Binational Science Foundation (BSF).

Berman, R. A., & Clark, E. V. (1993, July). *What children know about coining verbs in English and Hebrew.* Paper presented at the 6th International Congress for Study of Child Language, Trieste.

Berman, R. A., & Slobin, D. I., (1994). *Relating events in narrative: A crosslinguistic developmental study.* Hillsdale, NJ: Lawrence Erlbaum Associates.

Bloom, L., Tinker, E., & Margulis, C. (1993). The words children learn: Evidence against a noun bias in early vocabularies. *Cognitive Development, 8,* 431–450.

Bowerman, M. (1996). Learning how to structure space for language: A crosslinguistic perspective. In P. Bloom, M. Peterson, L. Nadel, & M. Garrett (Eds.), *Language and space.* Cambridge, MA: MIT Press.

Braine, M. D. S. (1987). What is learned in acquiring word classes: A step towards an acquisition theory. In B. MacWhinney (ed.), *Mechanisms of language acquisition* (pp. 65–88). Hillsdale, NJ: Lawrence Erlbaum Associates.

Braine, M. D. S., Brody, R. E., Fisch, M. S., & Weisberger, M. J. (1990). Can children use a verb without exposure to its argument structure? *Journal of Child language, 17,* 313–342.

Chomsky, N. (1965). *Aspects of the theory of syntax.* Cambridge, MA: MIT Press.

Clark, E. V. (1993). *The lexicon in acquisition.* Cambridge: Camridge University Press.

Clark, E. V., & Berman, R. A. (1984). Structure and use in the acquisition of word- formation. *Language, 60,* 542–590.

Clark, E. V., & Berman, R. A. (1987). Types of linguistic knowledge: Interpreting and producing compound nouns. *Journal of Child Language, 14,* 547–568.

Clark, E. V., & Hecht, B. (1981). Learning to coin agent and instrument nouns. *Cognition, 12,* 1–24.

Gentner, D. (1982). Why nouns are learned before verbs: Linguistic relativity versus natural partitioning. In S. Kuczaj (ed.), *Language development: Vol. 2* (pp. 301–334). Hillsdale, NJ: Lawrence Erlbaum Associates.

Goldfield, B. (1993). Noun bais in maternal speech to one-year-olds. *Journal of Child Language, 20,* 85–99.

Gopnik, A., & Choi, S. (1995). Names, relational words, and cognitive development in English and Korean: Nouns are not always learned before verbs. In M. Tomasello & W. E. Merriman (Eds.), *Beyond names for things: Young children's acquisition of verbs* (pp. 63–80). Hillsdale, NJ: Lawrence Erlbaum Associates.

Hecht, B. F. (1985). Situations and language: Children's use of plural allomorphs in familiar and unfamiliar settings. Unpublished doctoral dissertation, Stanford University.

Hopper, P. J., & Thompson, S. A. (1984). The discourse basis for lexical categorization in universal grammar. *Language, 60,* 703–752.

Hopper, P. J., & Thompson, S. A., 1985. The iconicity of the universal categories "noun" and "verb." In J. Haiman (Ed.,) *Iconicity in syntax* (pp. 151–186). Amsterdam: John Benjamins.

Karmiloff-Smith, A. (1979). *A functional approach to child language.* Cambridge: Cambridge University Press.

Karmiloff-Smith, A. (1986). Stage/structure versus phase/process in modelling linguistic and cognitive development. In I. Levin (Ed.), *Stage and structure: Re-opening the debate* (pp. 164–190). Ablex.

Keenan, E. L. (1975). Logical expressive power and syntactic variation in natural language. In E. L. Keenan (ed.), *Formal semantics of natural languages* (pp. 406–421) Cambridge: Cambridge University Press.

Langacker, R. (1987). Nouns and verbs. *Language, 63,* 53–94.

Levy, Y. (1987). The wug technique revisited. *Cognitive Development, 2,* 71–87.

Maratsos, M. (1988). The acquisition of formal word classes. In Y. Levy, I. M. Schlesinger, & M. D. Braine (Eds.), *Categories and processes in language acquisition* (pp. 31–44). Hillsdale, NJ: Lawrence Erlbaum Associates.

Maratsos, M. (1991). How the acquisition of nouns may be different from that of verbs. In N. A., Krasnegor, D. M. Rumbaugh, R. L. Schiefelbusch, & M. Studdert-Kennedy (Eds.), *Biological and behavioral determinants of language development* (pp. 67–89). Hillsdale, NJ: Lawrence Erlbaum Associates.

Maratsos, M., Gudeman, R., Gerard-Ngo, P., & DeHart, G. (1987). A study in novel word learning: the productivity of the causative. In B. MacWhinney (Ed.), *Mechanisms of language acquisition* (pp. 89–114). Hillsdale, NJ: Lawrence Erlbaum Associates.

Pinker, S. (1984). *Language learnability and language development.* Cambridge, MA: Harvard University Press.

Pinker, S., Lebeaux, D. S., & Frost, L. A. (1987). Productivity and constraints in the acquisition of the passive. *Cognition, 26,* 195–267.

Ravid, D. (1995a). The acquisition of morphological junctions in Modern Hebrew: The interface of rule and rote. In H. Pishwa & K. Maroldt (Eds.), *The development of morphological systematicity* (pp. 55–77). Tübingen: Gunter Narr Verlag.

Ravid, D. (1995b). *Language change in child and adult Hebrew: A psycholinguistic perspective.* New York: Oxford University Press.

Slobin, D. I., & Kuntay, A. (1995). Nouns and verbs in Turkish child-directed speech. In D. MacLaughlin & S. McEwen (Eds.), *Proceedings of the 19th Annual Boston University Conference on Language Development: Vol. 1* (pp. 323–334). Somerville, MA: Cascadilla Press.

Sokolov, J. (1988). Cue validity in Hebrew sentence comprehension. *Journal of Child Language, 15,* 129–156.

Tardif, T. (1996). Nouns are not *always* learned before verbs, but why? Evidence from Mandarin speakers' early vocabulary. *Developmental Psychology, 32,* 492–504.

Tardif, T., Shatz, M., & Naigles, L. (1997). Caregiver speech and children's use of nouns versus verbs: A comparison of English, Italian, and Mandarin. *Journal of Child Language, 24,* 535–66.

Tomasello, M., & Akhtar, N. (1995). Two-year-olds use pragmatic cues to differentiate reference to objects and actions. *Cognitive Development,* 201–224.

Tomasello, M., Akhtar, N., Dobson, K., & Rekau, L. (1997). Differential productivity in young children's use of nouns and verbs. *Journal of Child Language, 24,* 373–388.

Tomasello, M., & Farrar, M. J., (1986). Joint attention in early language. *Child Development, 57,* 1454–1463.

Zadonasky-Ehrlich, S. (1995). *"Bootstrapping" morfologi birxishat ha'ivrit kisfat em* [Morphological bootstrapping in acquisition of Hebrew as a first language]. Unpublished master's thesis, Tel Aviv University.

6

Methods for Studying the Production of Argument Structure in Children and Adults

Jess Gropen
McGill University, Montreal, Canada

INTRODUCTION

Argument structure is one of the most challenging topics in the study of language, bringing together the grammar and the lexicon, syntax and semantics. A definition—more comforting than precise—is that *argument structure* refers to knowledge about the expression of arguments (usually noun phrases) in the syntax of a sentence. This chapter discusses how the production of language by children and adults may be studied in order to shed light on argument structure.

The idea that production may be a source of insight into argument structure is based on the simple fact that the speaker bears the burden of syntactically encoding the intended message. Current wisdom holds that each verb in the so-called mental lexicon specifies how its semantic roles map onto grammatical relations, which are then marked in syntax by word order or morphological case, according to the conventions of the language. For example, a speaker interested in communicating the unusual message that a man has bitten a dog must somehow mark the fact that it is the man who does the biting and the dog who is bitten. By looking up the lexical entry for the active verb *bite*, the speaker knows that the semantic roles of "biter" and "bitee" must be encoded as the subject and direct object, respectively. On the other end of the communicative act, the hearer uses the same knowledge to recover the idea that the man bit the dog (vs. the more common idea that the dog bit the man).

A more detailed look at argument structure reveals that it is multifaceted, composed of different types of information (syntactic, semantic, pragmatic), and organized into chunks of different sizes (lexical, grammatical or "constructional," discourse). For this reason, the precise nature of a chosen methodology depends on which aspect of argument structure is being studied. Accordingly, I present a brief overview of different aspects of argument structure. This analysis serves as the basis for my subsequent recommendations about the methodological problems of choosing materials and procedures.

A BRIEF OVERVIEW OF ARGUMENT STRUCTURE: THREE DEPENDENCIES

In this section, I present a short tutorial on how the syntactic expression of a verb's arguments in a sentence depends on the organization of information at three levels of representation: grammatical, lexical, and discourse.

Grammatical Dependencies

Grammatical dependencies involve the fact that the syntax of a sentence depends on the semantic type of event being encoded. It is important to note that the dependency is best stated with respect to two relatively abstract kinds of representations (Pinker, 1989; Grimshaw, 1994; Gropen, 1995; Gropen, Pinker, Hollander, & Goldberg, 1991a; but see Goldberg, 1995): "schematic" semantic representations on the one hand (not rich conceptual descriptions of events), and underlying syntactic representations on the other hand (not surface syntax). For instance, an event in which a woman is melting chocolate may be conceptualized in many intricate ways, including: the thermodynamic details of the process; whether and how an instrument is used for melting the chocolate; the likely purpose for melting the chocolate, involving food-related knowledge about the uses and taste of melted chocolate; associated health-related knowledge about the risks and benefits of eating chocolate; the context of the event, including its time and place; and so on. This information may of course be communicated linguistically, as I have just done. But how much of this information matters when it comes to expressing the basic argument structure of the clause *The chocolate is melting*—in which the entity that melts is the subject of an intransitive form? (Note that I am setting aside myriad variations in surface syntax, such as the use of interrogative forms, etc.) By looking at regularities in how events are encoded in grammar, within and across languages, linguists have discovered that the critical information, for this kind of argument structure, is simply that an entity changes state in some way (e.g., it goes from being solid to being liquid; Levin & Hovav, 1995). In sum, events that express changes of state, such as melting and breaking, tend to be expressed in "unaccusative" intransitive sentences, with a subject Y corresponding to the entity undergoing the change (*The chocolate melted/*The woman melted*; Levin & Hovav, 1995).

Notice that the same event may be semantically construed, and thereby grammatically encoded, in different ways. For example, an event in which a woman melts chocolate may be constructed as a change-of-state event, as just discussed, or as a caused-change-of-state event. Predictably, events that express caused changes of state tend to be expressed in transitive sentences, with a subject X and direct object Y corresponding to the agent and undergoer, respectively (e.g., *The woman melted the chocolate /*The chocolate melted the woman*; Levin, 1985; Levin & Hovav, 1995). If, on the other hand, a different aspect of the event is featured—let's say, corresponding to the fact that the woman is stirring with a spoon—a different semantic construal and argument structure apply: Events that express activities, such as stirring, dancing, and knitting, tend to be expressed in "unergative" intransitive sentences, with a subject X corresponding to the agentive entity performing the activity (*The woman is stirring/*The chocolate is stirring*; Levin & Hovav, 1995).

One interpretation of grammatical dependencies is that they specify the possible ways of encoding a semantic type of event. This way of understanding the dependencies does justice to the universal "linking" tendencies that have been documented (Levin, 1985), yet it also allows for the fact that the actual way of encoding a semantic type of event depends on the particular verb chosen. For example, an event in which an object is made to disappear may be construed as a change of state or as a caused change of state; however, English does not generally allow the verb *disappear* to occur as a transitive (*The ball disappeared; *Tim disappeared the ball*). In this case, one may say that although the grammatical dependencies render it possible to express the causative event in a transitive syntactic form, the vocabulary of English does not instantiate this possibility. Other languages may do so, depending on their set of vocabulary items and cultural norms.

Psycholinguistic support for grammatical dependencies comes from the finding that speakers may produce sentences that violate verb-specific requirements on the expression of arguments. For example, adults occasionally produce causative errors in which a noncausative verb such as *disappear* is used in a syntactically transitive construction to express a causative event (e.g., *Mr. Provenzano had arranged to disappear him*; other examples include *The experience grew me up in a hurry* and *Water will not deteriorate the sockets*; Bowerman, 1982; Pinker, 1989). Although these usages are errors in a strict sense, they nonetheless conform to broad syntax–semantics correspondences of the sort described by linking rules (Pinker, 1989), suggesting that grammatical dependencies act as default biases in event encoding—telling the speaker how to encode semantic relations in the absence of, or in the abeyance of, verb-specific information.

Children—who have less verb-specific information than adults—are even more reliant on grammatical dependencies, in at least three ways. First, children use grammatical dependencies to construct their earliest sentences (Bowerman, 1989; Slobin, 1985; Goldberg, 1998), which typically involve "a restricted set of meanings [having] to do with agency, action, location, possession, and the existence, recurrence, nonexistence, and disappearance of objects" (Bowerman, 1989, p. 137). Second, experimental evidence shows that children can use grammatical dependencies to predict the syntax of unfamiliar verbs (Gropen et al., 1991a), a capacity that presumably plays a role in the acquisition process. Third, verb-syntax errors are more common in children than adults, and in many cases these errors are based on general grammatical dependencies (Pinker, 1989). For example, although adult causative errors are rare events (Pinker, 1989), children's causative errors occur at a rate of about 30% (Gropen, Blaskovich, & DeDe, 1995; Gropen, Blaskovich, DeDe, Potvin, & Guerriero, November 18, 1998).

Lexical Dependencies

Lexical dependencies involve the fact that verbs are "choosy" about how they express their arguments (e.g., the verb *bounce* may be transitive or intransitive, whereas the verb *go* is only intransitive; **John went the ball under the table*), suggesting that there must be some stored representation of verb-specific syntactic information (Pinker, 1989). This stored representation of verb-specific syntactic information is known as verb argument structure (VAS).

Research on lexical semantics has also demonstrated that verbs in English and other languages cluster into classes on the basis of shared semantic and syntactic properties (Levin, 1985, 1993; Levin & Hovav, 1995; Pinker, 1989). For example, all manner-of-motion verbs in English behave in the same way (e.g., *The puck slid/bounced/rolled across the floor; John slid/bounced/rolled the puck across the floor*) and differently from all direction-of-motion verbs (e.g., *The puppy came/went over the hill; Mary *came/*went the puppy over the hill*). One way of thinking about verb classes is that they represent "decisions" by a language about how to lexicalize semantic types of events. That is, instead of deciding that *bounce* can lexicalize causative events of bouncing, *roll* can lexicalize causative events of rolling, and so on for each manner-of-motion verb, English makes the decision once, for all manner-of-motion verbs.

Psycholinguistic research confirms that adults respect both verb-specific syntactic information and verb classes. Although adults generally use conventional verb forms in their speech, they may productively extend new verbs to syntactic frames on the basis of the classes to which the verbs belong. For example, new instrument-of-communication verbs (*fax, e-mail, modem*) are used in the double-object dative construction (*John faxed/e- mailed/modemed her the news*) on analogy with more conventional instrument-of-communication verbs (*John mailed/radioed/wired her the news*) (Gropen, Pinker, Hollander, Goldberg, & Wilson, 1989; Pinker, 1989).

Developmentally, children have less verb-specific and class-specific information than adults do. Research on causative errors (Gropen 1995; Gropen et al., November 18,1998) suggests that these and other verb syntax errors result from the interaction of immature lexical knowledge with default biases in event encoding. As specific verbs are learned, they gradually take precedence over more general dependencies and come to exert more influence on the determination of syntax (Gropen, 1995). Consistent with this view, Bowerman (1982) documented that causative errors occur over a wide developmental range during acquisition of the basic verb lexicon (from roughly 2 to 6 years of age) and that errors for particular verbs decrease gradually in a frequency-dependent fashion.

Discourse Dependencies

Discourse dependencies involve the fact that the surface syntax of a sentence reflects its place in discourse. For instance, there is a strong, universal tendency for the topic of discourse to be expressed early in a sentence (Greenberg, 1966). Thus, a question that focuses on the agent in an event, thereby making it the topic of discourse (e.g., What did John do?), favors a response with the agent as subject (e.g., He rolled the ball across the floor). In contrast, an undergoer-focused question (e.g., What happened to the ball?) encourages a response with the undergoer as subject (e.g., It rolled across the floor). Similar discourse effects are associated with other variations in surface syntax.

The psycholinguistic literature shows that children as well as adults are sensitive to discourse manipulations, which have been successfully used in many experiments as a means of eliciting various syntactic structures. In the case of children, discourse pressure may elicit verb-syntax errors. For example, significantly more causative errors are produced in response to agent-focused questions than in response to undergoer-focused questions (Gropen, Blaskovich, & DeDe, 1995; Gropen et al.). According to Gropen (1995) the full pattern of data, including developmental changes in the tendency to produce errors, may be explained in terms of a response competition between (a) syntax selected on the basis of discourse and grammatical dependencies (i.e., choosing syntax to match the discourse context, as long as it is a possible way of encoding a semantic type of event), and (b) syntax selected on the basis of specific lexical dependencies (i.e., choosing syntax to match the actual VAS requirements of a specific verb, even if it does not match the discourse context).

CHOOSING MATERIALS

One of the main considerations in choosing verbs is whether they are intended to be familiar to subjects, or novel (made-up or rare). As will be seen, the choice of verbs is governed by a number of factors, including whether the focus of study is on grammatical processes of event encoding or the behavior of specific verbs and classes of verbs.

Using Common (Familiar) Verbs to Test Lexical and Grammatical Knowledge

Given that specific verbs are associated with information about how their arguments are expressed, one can document how the acquisition and use of VAS varies as a function of verb frequency, verb class, and other verb properties. For example, in Gropen et al. (1989) we examined the spontaneous speech of five children, age roughly 2 to 5 years, in order to find out what kinds of verbs are used in prepositional dative and double-object dative constructions (e.g., *John gave a gift to Mary* and *John gave Mary a gift*, respectively). Do young children use verbs fairly indiscriminately in these constructions, or do they only use verbs from specific classes? By searching for all dative constructions in this corpus of spontaneous speech, we were able to determine that verbs of giving (e.g., *give, hand, sell*), type of communication (*show, read, tell*), creation (*make, draw, pour*), obtaining (*get, buy, save*), and directed accompanied motion (*bring, take*) were generally used in both constructions. In contrast, verbs of ballistic motion (*throw, toss, kick*) were never used in the double-object form, even though this is permissible in adult English (*John threw/tossed/kicked Mary the ball*), and were only sporadically used in the prepositional form. This finding suggests that children may be slow to extend verbs to compatible constructions. That is, young children may avoid using ballistic motion verbs in the double-object form because the double-object form grammaticizes change-of-possession events, not motion events. On the other hand, the same corpus of data shows that children do not have difficulty with abstract meanings per se (change of possession), with the double-object form, or even with idiosyncratic non-standard verb usages (e.g., idiomatic usages of *give* were produced by four of the children).

In a similar way, familiar verbs can be used in the study of purely grammatical knowledge about encoding events and expressing arguments. For example, when do the prepositional and double-object constructions emerge in children's speech? This question is of special interest because many grammarians have characterized the English double-object dative as "marked" with respect to Universal Grammar (see Stowell, 1981), leading to the prediction that the double-object dative should be difficult for children to acquire (Mazurkewich, 1984; Ritchie, 1985; see Gropen et al., 1989, for discussion). Gropen et al.'s (1989) study of children's spontaneous speech revealed that contrary to this prediction, the double-object dative emerges at roughly the same time as the prepositional dative. In particular: In two children, the double-object form emerged before the prepositional dative; in one child, the prepositional dative emerged before the double-object form; in two children, the two dative forms emerged within one month of each other. The same pattern was found with individual verbs. Of 28 cases in which a child used a verb in both forms, the double-object version came first 16 times, the prepositional version came first 9 times, and both appeared simultaneously 3 times.

One complication in using familiar verbs is that the acquisition and use of VAS cannot always be separated clearly from the acquisition and use of purely grammatical knowledge about encoding events and expressing arguments. For instance, does the earliest use of any verb in a construction (e.g., the use of *give* in the double-object form) indicate the acquisition of that verb's VAS, the acquisition of the construction, or some combination thereof? In many cases this question is impossible to answer, because the earliest use of a verb in a construction may be the first clear expression of that verb's VAS as well as the first clear expression of a syntactic construction. Similar problems arise later in development, in trying to pinpoint the locus of argument structure errors. Fortunately, novel verbs may be used to tease apart lexical and grammatical knowledge about argument structure, as we shall see next.

Using Novel Verbs to Test Lexical and Grammatical Knowledge

In this section I discuss how novel verbs may be used to assess grammatical knowledge independently of lexical knowledge and to assess lexical knowledge in a controlled fashion. The actual task of creating (or finding) novel verbs is given its own treatment in the next section.

Testing Grammatical Knowledge with Novel Verbs: Wug-Type Studies.

By far the most common use of novel verbs— and of novel words in general—is as tools for understanding nonlexical knowledge. Thus, in Berko Gleason's classic paper (1958) on rule use in language, the ability of children to pluralize *wug* systematically to *wugs* shows that there must be some mental rule that allows children to go beyond what they have heard in the input. Indeed, it is the novel nature of these stimuli that allows the researcher to "rule out" the possibility that subjects are simply producing a memorized lexical form.

An example of how novel verbs have been used in the study of grammatical knowledge about argument structure may be found in Gropen et al. (1991a). In this study we tested subjects' sensitivity to the universal linking rule of object affectedness, according to which the argument that is affected in the semantic construal of a situation tends to be encoded as the direct object. Note that this rule states a general, nonlexical correspondence between a semantic type of argument (the thing affected) and an underlying grammatical relation (the direct object). We tested the sensitivity of 3-year-olds, 5-year-olds, 7-year-olds, and adults to this rule by teaching them made-up locative verbs (e.g., *moop, keat*) and varying which argument (the content or the container) was most likely to be construed as affected according to the meaning of the novel verb. After learning each verb, subjects were tested on their willingness to use the novel verb in locative constructions with either the content or the container encoded as the direct object. (Note that I am using *content* and *container* in an extended sense to denote the general relation of bounding.)

In particular, one novel verb in Gropen et al. (1991a)—in the endstate-verb condition—involved moving a cotton ball in a nondescript way to a piece of felt, causing the felt to change color. It was predicted that if subjects were sensitive to the universal linking rule of object affectedness, they would produce container-locative sentences such as *You're mooping the felt (with the cotton ball)*, because the felt was affected according to the meaning of the verb. In contrast, another novel verb—in the manner-verb condition—involved moving the cotton ball to the felt in a zig-zagging manner, but without any resulting change to the felt. Here, it was predicted that subjects would describe the situation by using content-locative sentences, such as *You're keating the cotton ball (onto the felt)*, because in this case the cotton ball was affected according to the verb's meaning. In fact, these predictions were strongly confirmed: In each age group, there was a significant difference in the pattern of locative responses depending on whether the content or container was affected; moreover, in each age group content-locative sentences were in the majority for the manner verb whereas container-locative sentences were in the majority for the endstate verb.

Notice that this result is not really about how subjects learned *moop* or *keat*—it is about their sensitivity to one grammatical rule for encoding events and expressing arguments. In effect, the novel verbs were used as a way of lexicalizing different semantic construals of an event—without having to worry about any memorized VASs clouding the interpretation of the results.

Testing Lexical Knowledge with Novel Verbs: Chromium-Type Studies.   In the wug-style study (after Berko, 1958), as discussed previously, the subjects' knowledge of some nonlexical aspect of language is tested by having them produce language using unfamiliar words. In contrast, in a chromium-style study (after Carey, 1978; Carey & Bartlett, 1978), what is of interest is the process by which the novel item itself is acquired. By tracking the acquisition of a novel word across time, one can study the assumptions about lexical items that children make in the process of acquisition, while controlling for the lexical input itself.

In Carey and Bartlett (1978), fourteen 3- to 4-year-old children were taught the unfamiliar color word *chromium*, which was paired with the color olive. A previous production test had not only verified that the children lacked the color word *olive*, but it also established the particular baseline responses—in most cases, *green*—that children did apply to olive. The new color word was taught in a naturalistic way: For example, in the context of setting a table with trays and cups, where one of the trays was colored olive and the other blue, each child was told individually by a teacher to "bring me the chromium tray, not the blue one, the chromium one." Notice that although the teaching was not explicit, the children were provided with syntactic cues (*chromium* was used as an adjective), lexical-semantic cues (*chromium* was contrasted with the color word *blue*), and conceptual cues (the non-blue tray was an unfamiliar color).

After six weeks, Carey and Bartlett discovered that 8 of the 14 children actually changed their responses from their previous baselines for olive, yet they never chose *chromium* as a response (instead preferring some other color term without stable reference in their lexicons). Furthermore, subsequent teaching and testing revealed that the children fell into two groups: Some children, even after 18 weeks of testing, thought that *chromium* meant green; other children seemed to know that *chromium* signified its own color (e.g., when asked to choose the chromium chip, these children correctly chose the color olive), yet this reference was not stable (e.g., presented with the color olive, children could not produce the label *chromium*). Carey (1978) concludes from this experiment that meanings for new words may be acquired in two parts. First, the word must quickly find its general place in the lexicon on the basis of a "fast mapping" between lexical and conceptual domains. Second, further exposure to the new word over an extended period is needed in order for children to complete the learning process and come to a stable restructuring of the domains involved. Finally, Carey argues that a similar two-stage process applies to words of other syntactic categories, including verbs.

From this study one can also draw several methodological points. First, the most straightforward approach to a chromium-type study is to use a naturalistic yet controlled context for introducing the novel word. In Carey and Bartlett (1978), teachers acting as confederates were able to provide the input in just such a context. Second, Carey and Bartlett show persuasively that the full acquisition of words is an extended process, involving several types of information. Obviously, the study of an extended developmental process cries out for a longitudinal method. Third, because lexical knowledge involves several different types of information, novel verbs must be chosen with a sensitivity to these information types. Thus, Carey and Bartlett's *chromium* was novel in several respects—morphologically, because the word *chromium* was not known by the children at the outset of the study, and conceptually, because no label for the color olive was known by the children at the outset of the study.

Can a *chromium*-type study be applied to the acquisition of verb-argument structure? In principle, certainly. In ongoing research, my colleagues and I are conducting a chromium-type study in order to evaluate Grimshaw's (1994) reconciliation account of how a verb is acquired. The reconciliation account is so named because it offers a motivated compromise between the "syntactic bootstrapping" account of Gleitman and her colleagues (see Gleitman, 1990) and the semantic-based account of Pinker (1984, 1989, 1994). In particular, this account holds that children are able to learn a verb only if the construction in which the verb is heard matches a surface structure generated internally on the basis of the verb's meaning. Furthermore, Grimshaw assumes that children make use of semantic-syntactic linking rules in generating expected constructions on the basis of hypothesized verb meanings. For example, one linking rule maps change-of-state verbs onto unaccusative argument structures, explaining why verbs such as *melt* take the undergoer (acted-on) argument as the subject of the intransitive (allowing sentences such as *The chocolate is melting* but not **The boy is melting*). In contrast, another linking rule maps activity verbs onto unergative argument structures, explaining why verbs such as *eat* take the agent argument as the subject of the intransitive (allowing sentences such as *The boy is eating* but not **The chocolate is eating*).

The reconciliation account makes a strong prediction about when verb learning should fail: Learning should not occur if the construction in which the verb is heard fails to match a surface structure generated internally on the basis of the verb's meaning. This situation would be akin to a child seeing an instance of melting and hearing an unergative-intransitive construction with the verb, such as *The boy is melting*. In order to test this prediction, my colleagues and I are exposing children to novel verbs with meanings that either match or mismatch the constructions in which they occur. For example, one novel verb—drisking—refers to a change-of-state event in which a person adds something to a liquid, causing it to change color (e.g., juice concentrate is added to water, causing it to turn purple). In the match condition, the presentation of the drisking event is accompanied by an unaccusative-intransitive form, such as *The water is drisking*. In the mismatch condition, the accompanying form is an unergative intransitive form, such as *The woman is drisking*.

The presentation of the novel verbs is being conducted through the use of specially written storybooks that feature the novel verbs (among common verbs) in their appropriate extralinguistic and linguistic contexts. Parents are given the storybooks with explicit instructions to read only the text that is actually printed in the book, and to do so on a regular schedule (e.g., once every 2 weeks, for a period of 6 months). This kind of procedure ensures that the input is presented in a naturalistic yet controlled context. Subsequent testing, scheduled at various intervals during the longitudinal period, will reveal whether the novel verbs are being acquired, and if so, how. More generally, we are confident that novel verbs can be used in a *chromium*-type study to investigate basic aspects of how verbs and their argument structures are acquired.

Criteria for Creating Novel Verbs

In this section I discuss several criteria that should be applied in the process of creating novel verbs. In fact, novel verbs may come about in a number of ways, depending on the source of the novel stem and meaning: novel stems and meanings may be created de novo; they may correspond to existing but unfamiliar verb stems with their conventional (unfamiliar) meanings; they may correspond to unfamiliar verb stems with made-up meanings, or made-up verb stems with unfamiliar meanings; or they may correspond to derived stems and meanings. (Note that in this chapter the term *unfamiliar* as applied to novel verbs is short for *existing but unfamiliar*; i.e., low-frequency or archaic.) Each way of creating a novel verb presents its own challenges and may be subject to somewhat different criteria.

The first criterion is that novel verbs must be created or chosen in such a way that they provide a focused test of the hypothesis under consideration. This might be called the criterion of ceteris paribus ("other things being equal"): There may be many reasons why two novel verbs are treated differently by subjects, or why one novel verb is not used as expected; simply put, it is dangerous to assume that "other things are equal." For example, very little can be concluded from the simple failure of a child to dativize a novel verb, because the failure may be attributable to a number of sources (an insensitivity to the relevant linking rules, to the relevant verb-class regularities, to the intended meaning of the novel verb, etc.). The fact of the matter is that lexical knowledge is complex; therefore, a genuinely focused test of a hypothesis demands that a novel verb be created or chosen with sensitivity to many issues. One strategy that often works well in the face of this complexity is to use novel verbs that constitute "minimal pairs"—that is, that differ only in the lexical property under study (e.g., in Experiment 2 of Gropen et al., 1991a, both verbs involved the motion of a cotton ball to a piece of felt; they differed only in whether a particular manner or endstate was also lexicalized).

A second criterion is that a novel verb be semantically well formed or coherent, lest it be rejected or not learned as intended. Coherence is dictated by constraints on the kinds of sub-events that may constitute a verb's meaning, and by constraints on how those sub-events may be related. An egregious demonstration of an incoherent verb meaning, from Pinker (1989, p. 196), is *John zimmed the cat from the roof* to mean "Simultaneously, John yawned and the cat fell off the roof" (also see Carter, 1976). This verb meaning is incoherent because John's yawning has nothing to do with the cat falling off the roof. More generally, Pinker suggests that the different sub-events specified by a verb must always be related to each other in a "quasi-causal" fashion, and Pinker goes on to specify a family of quasi-causal relations based largely on the work of Talmy (1985, 1988).

In this regard, note that one advantage of using existing but unfamiliar meanings is that they are guaranteed to be coherent, for they have been created naturally in the course of acquisition, innovation, or derivation. This guarantee is worth having, because the properties that make for semantic well-formedness are not completely understood. In addition, it is also possible to draw on unfamiliar meanings lexicalized by words in other languages. For example, verbs that incorporate the semantic element of figure (i.e., moving entity; e.g., *spit*) are not well represented in English, but they do represent a major lexicalization pattern in Amerindian languages (Talmy, 1985). In the absence of cross-linguistic data, one might begin to doubt whether or not such lexicalizations were semantically coherent. The existence of these verb meanings in other languages not only guarantees their well-formedness but also offers a rich source of potential materials for creating novel meanings.

A third criterion for creating or choosing novel verbs is that their intended meanings be salient. A lack of salience may make it difficult for learners to grasp the conceptual content of a semantic element, or it may (perhaps as a consequence) lead learners to invoke one semantic element where another is intended. Obviously, technical and scientific vocabulary are difficult for children to grasp, due to children's inexperience with some conceptual domains, yet salience also applies to the vernacular. In particular there is some evidence that, dare I say ceteris paribus, (novel) verb meanings that specify a manner of causation or motion are more easily learned than those specifying a change of state (Gentner, 1978; Gropen et al., 1991a; Gropen, Pinker, Hollander, & Goldberg, 1991b). For instance, in Experiment 1 in Gropen et al. (1991a), we created a novel change-of-state verb in which a packet of marbles was moved to an unsupported piece of cloth (resting on a frame), causing the cloth to sag under the weight of the packet. Although the change in the shape of the cloth was the intended meaning, children tended to focus on the interaction between the agent (i.e., the experimenter/child) and the figure (i.e., the packet of marbles). Indeed, it took a very salient change of state—the color change verb in Experiment 2—to ensure that the intended meaning was the one actually learned.

A fourth criterion for creating or choosing novel verbs is that they be lexically distinct. The issue here is this: How can one ensure that the subject will use the target verb and not a real verb (or that the subject will not covertly "translate" the novel verb into a real one)? In order to prevent this, the novel verb should not be synonymous with any existing, familiar verb, and it should be distinct enough so that subjects will not be tempted to use a more general "superordinate" term. One empirically based approach is to conduct a pilot study on how subjects would label the novel meaning (i.e., present subjects with the novel action, without stem, and elicit verb labels in an action-naming task). If subjects consistently use a single familiar verb, there may be a problem with the lexical distinctness of the novel verb. On the other hand, if there is much variability in subjects' responses, and if they tend to use multiword paraphrases, the novel verb may have its own niche in the lexicon.

Note that the use of existing but unfamiliar verbs is no guarantee of lexical distinctness. Real words are related to each other in many ways, including some approximation of synonymy or semantic similarity and inclusion or troponymy (see Clark, 1987; Gropen, 1995; Miller & Fellbaum, 1991). Paradoxically, perhaps the best strategy to satisfy this criterion is to use novel verbs that are derived from familiar nouns or adjectives, on the grounds that the familiarity of these words will prevent another verb stem from being used. For example, consider the novel verb *to straw*, with the meaning "to move liquid from one location to another by immersing a drinking straw in liquid, creating a vacuum by sealing the top of the straw with a finger, moving the straw, and releasing the liquid in the desired location by removing the finger." What makes the verb *strawing* lexically distinct is that there is no familiar synonym (the closest meaning is that of the unfamiliar verb *pipetting*), and the integral involvement of the straw precludes as less informative the use of more general terms. Furthermore, several factors make it likely that subjects would accept this particular novel verb stem, including the appropriateness of the verb label in this case (verbs are often derived from instrument names; Clark & Clark, 1979), the familiarity of the noun stem *straw*, and the fact that this stem does not have any associated usages as a verb.

Besides the advantage of being lexically distinct, a derived novel verb has the advantage of making it easier for subjects to induce or "fix" the intended meaning of the verb. In addition, such an innovation has a clear connection to known lexical items—it has a place in the system. It is not known whether, or how much, this consideration matters; however, I believe that it helps avoid a situation in which a novel verb is not taken by subjects to be a part of ordinary language.

CHOOSING TESTING PROCEDURES

Regardless of whether familiar or novel verbs are being used, and of whether lexical or grammatical knowledge about argument structure is being assessed, the researcher must decide on one or more appropriate testing procedures for eliciting language from the population under study. In this section, I discuss overt and covert elicitation tasks. The reader is referred to Pan, Perlmann & Snow (Chapter 10, this volume) for discussion of methods for analyzing spontaneous speech.

Overt Elicitation Tasks

At their best, overt elicitation tasks are complementary to analyses of spontaneous speech, allowing the researcher to test focused hypotheses about why a particular language phenomenon occurs, about what knowledge and abilities are within a speaker's capacity, and about the circumstances under which learning is not possible. In addition, they may be used with novel as well as familiar verbs, and they may address lexical and/or grammatical aspects of argument structure. The key to the success of these tasks is that the experimenter intervenes in the "experimental discourse" and attempts to manipulate the nature of what the speaker produces. In overt elicitation tasks, the experimenter is explicit—via instruction, query, or some other form of cueing—about which aspects of language (lexical items, constructions, etc.) are desired in the subjects' responses.

In studying argument structure, the experimenter may exploit all three dependencies discussed earlier in this chapter. First, in order to elicit sentences of a specific underlying kind, the experimenter may manipulate how subjects are likely to construe an event semantically. In these cases, the manipulation involves performing actions that conform to grammatically relevant semantic schemas. An example comes from Gropen et al. (November 18,1998), where we performed either causative or noncausative actions in order to elicit causative or noncausative forms, respectively. In the causative trials, the experimenter used a handpuppet to manipulate a toy (e.g., a lion dropped a boat). In the noncausative trials, a toy participated in an activity without the use of a handpuppet (e.g., the boat fell). As expected, the lack of "handpuppet agency" in the noncausative trials often led the children to use a noncausative form (e.g., an intransitive with the toy as subject).

A second kind of manipulation is to set up discourse contexts that favor one kind of surface syntactic form or another. As discussed previously, one of the simplest ways of doing this involves posing queries in which a constituent (e.g., the undergoer) is focused as the discourse topic (e.g., *What is happening to the boat?*), thereby encouraging subjects to place that constituent at the beginning of their responses (e.g., *The boat is falling*). Manipulations of this sort have been used successfully for many years. More generally, Bock, Loebell, and Morey (1992) argued that these manipulations work because speakers map concepts onto surface grammatical relations on the basis of their conceptual accessibility: Concepts that are more readily activated tend to occur as subjects more often than concepts that are less readily activated, other things being equal. Furthermore, there are many ways of manipulating the accessibility of concepts—ranging from explicit queries and pictured objects to more subtle manipulations of properties such as animacy (Bock, 1982; Bock et al., 1992).

Finally, both the underlying and surface syntax may be influenced by a third kind of manipulation: that relevant to the subject's choice of verb. A fairly common, nondirective approach to eliciting particular verbs is simply for the experimenter to act out the meaning of the verb. This approach may be made more focused by explicitly directing the subject to use a particular verb (e.g., *Can you tell me, using the word fall, what's happening to the boat?*), or—more subtly—by priming the use of a particular verb. An example of the latter approach may be found in Gropen et al.'s (November 18, 1998) study of causative verbs. In that study, each session began with a

priming phase in which the experimenter performed the action corresponding to each target verb (e.g., by dropping the boat) and simultaneously
used the verb in the gerundive form (e.g., *Look! This is called falling*).
Although subjects were not explicitly directed to use particular verbs in the
subsequent testing phase, they nevertheless responded with appropriate target items, showing that the initial priming had been very effective.

I end this section with a cautionary note. Although overt elicitation tasks
have the advantage of using a simple, straightforward set of procedures for
manipulating the attention and conceptual resources of the speaker, they
run the risk of yielding speech that is self-conscious and thereby more
likely to reflect perceived researcher bias, to exhibit carryover effects, or to
degenerate into rote patterns of response. These concerns warrant the following question: Is there any way to achieve some measure of experimental control without running the risk of eliciting self-conscious or reflective
speech? In the following section I discuss one such approach.

Covert Elicitation Tasks

Covert elicitation tasks are those in which the experimenter is not explicit
about which aspects of language are desired in the subjects' responses; they
may employ a form of deception in leading subjects to believe that their
language per se is ancillary to the task. These tasks offer an intermediate
degree of control, being more efficient and less natural than spontaneous
speech but less efficient and more natural than overt elicitation tasks.

A superb example of a covert elicitation task is that of Bock's syntactic priming paradigm (Bock, 1986). In this paradigm, adult subjects are
presented with a long sequence of sentences and pictures, and they are
instructed to make a recognition judgment for recurrences of individual
items (sentences or pictures, depending on the type of trial). Furthermore,
on the pretext of improving memory performance, subjects are instructed
to repeat each sentence aloud or describe each picture (in a single sentence) before making the memory judgment. In a number of studies
(Bock, 1986; Bock & Loebell, 1990; Bock et al., 1992) involving a wide
range of construction types, Bock and her colleagues found evidence for
syntactic priming: The surface syntactic form of a repeated sentence
affects how subjects describe unrelated pictures in subsequent trials.

The power of this technique is not only that subjects produce speech in
an unselfconscious way but also that experimenters can exert some control
over how subjects produce their speech. Syntactic priming is a case in
point: It works, according to Bock, because a given surface syntactic rep-

resentation is being repeatedly accessed and primed. However, by extending the paradigm it should also be possible to exert control over other
aspects of the language-production process. Indeed, Bock and her colleagues have already used this paradigm to test for the priming of event
types (Bock & Loebell, 1990) and underlying syntactic structures (Bock et
al., 1992). Although her results have been negative (i.e., not showing the
priming of these structures), I believe that the paradigm—if suitably modified—can be made relevant to testing for these structures. In addition, it
would be of great interest to adapt the paradigm for use in children and to
address questions that concern the usage of particular verbs. By pursuing
all these modifications, my colleagues and I are attempting to learn more
about the production of argument structure in both children and adults.

ACKNOWLEDGMENTS

Preparation of this chapter was supported by NSERC grant 0GP0121309.

REFERENCES

Berko (Gleason), J. (1958). The child's learning of English morphology. *Word, 14*, 150–177.
Bock, K. (1982). Towards a cognitive psychology of syntax: Information processing contributions to
    sentence formulation. *Psychological Review, 89 (1)*, 1–47.
Bock, K. (1986). Syntactic persistence in language production. *Cognitive Psychology, 18*, 355–387.
Bock, K., & Loebell, H. (1990). Framing sentences. *Cognition, 35*, 1–39.
Bock, K., Loebell, H., & Morey, R. (1992). From conceptual roles to structural relations: Bridging
    the syntactic cleft. *Psychological Review, 99*, 150–171.
Bowerman, M. (1982). Evaluating competing linguistic models with language acquisition data:
    Implications of developmental errors with causative verbs. *Quaderni di Semantica, 3* (Serial No.
    1), 5–66.
Bowerman, M. (1989). Learning a semantic system: What role do cognitive predispositions play? In
    M. Rice and R. Schiefelbusch (Eds.), *The teachability of language* (pp. 133–169). Baltimore:
    Paul H. Brookes.
Carey, S. (1978). The child as word learner. In M. Halle, J. Bresnan, & G. A. Miller (Eds.), *Linguistic
    theory and psychological reality* (pp. 264–293). Cambridge, MA: MIT Press.
Carey, S., & Bartlett, E. (1978). Acquiring a single new word. *Papers and Reports on Child
    Language Development* [Department of Linguistics, Stanford University], *15*, 17–29.
Carter, R. J. (1976). Some constraints on possible words. *Semantikos, 1*, 27–66.
Clark, E. V. (1987). The principle of contrast: A constraint on language acquisition. In B.
    MacWhinney (Ed.), *Mechanisms of language acquisition* (pp. 1–33). Hillsdale, NJ: Lawrence
    Erlbaum Associates.
Clark, E. V., & Clark, H. H. (1979). When nouns surface as verbs. *Language, 55*, 767–811.
Gentner, D. (1978). On relational meaning: The acquisition of verb meaning. *Child Development, 49*,
    988–998.

Gleitman, L. R. (1990). The structural sources of verb meanings. *Language Acquisition, 1*, 3–55.

Goldberg, A. (1995). *Constructions: A construction grammar approach to argument structure*. Chicago: University of Chicago Press.

Greenberg, J. H. (1966). Some universals of grammar with particular reference to the order of meaningful elements. In J. H. Greenberg (Ed.), *Universals of language* (2nd ed., pp. 73–113). Cambridge, MA: MIT Press.

Grimshaw, J. (1994). Lexical reconciliation. *Lingua, 92*, 411–430.

Gropen, J. (1995). A neural net model of argument structure. In *McGill papers in cognitive science* (Tech. Rep. No. 2395). Montreal: McGill University.

Gropen, J., Blaskovich, J., & DeDe, G. (1995, November). *"Come it closer": Causative errors in child speech*. Paper presented at the Twentieth Annual Boston University Conference on Language Development.

Gropen, J., Blaskovich, J., DeDe, G., Potvin, K., & Guerriero, S. (November 18, 1998). *Causative errors in child speech: A processing account*. Manuscript in preparation, Department of Psychology, McGill University.

Gropen, J., Pinker, S., Hollander, M., & Goldberg, R. (1991a). Affectedness and direct objects: The role of lexical semantics in the acquisition of verb argument structure. *Cognition, 41*, 153–195.

Gropen, J., Pinker, S., Hollander, M., & Goldberg, R. (1991b). Syntax and semantics in the acquisition of locative verbs. *Journal of Child Language, 18*, 115–151.

Gropen, J., Pinker, S., Hollander, M., Goldberg, R., & Wilson, R. (1989). The learnability and acquisition of the dative alternation in English. *Language, 65*, 203–257.

Levin, B. (1985). Lexical semantics in review: An introduction. In B. Levin (Ed.), *Lexical semantics in review* (Lexicon Project Working Papers No. 1, pp. 1–62). Cambridge, MA: MIT Center for Cognitive Science.

Levin, B. (1993). *English verb classes and alternations*. Chicago: University of Chicago Press.

Levin, B., & Hovav, M. R. (1995). *Unaccusativity*. Cambridge, MA: MIT Press.

Mazurkewich, I. (1984). The acquisition of the dative alternation by second language learners and linguistic theory. *Language Learning, 34*, 91–109.

Miller, G., & Fellbaum, C. (1991). Semantic networks of English. *Cognition, 41*, 197–229.

Pinker, S. (1984). *Language learnability and language development*. Cambridge, MA: Harvard University Press.

Pinker, S. (1989). *Learnability and cognition*. Cambridge, MA: MIT Press.

Pinker, S. (1994). How could a child use verb syntax to learn verb semantics? *Lingua, 92*, 377–410.

Ritchie, W. C. (1985). Word-formation, learned vocabulary, and linguistic maturation. In Jacek Fisiak (Ed.), *Historical semantics and historical word-formation* (pp. 463–482). New York: Mouton.

Slobin, D. (1985). Cross-linguistic evidence for the language-making capacity. In D. Slobin (Ed.), *A cross-linguistic study of language acquisition, Vol. 2* (pp. 1157–1249). Hillsdale, NJ: Lawrence Erlbaum Associates.

Stowell, T. (1981). Origins of phrase structure. Unpublished doctoral dissertation, Massachusetts Institute of Technology.

Talmy, L. (1985). Lexicalization patterns: Semantic structure in lexical forms. In T. Shopen (Ed.), *Language typology and syntactic description: V of 3*. (pp. 57–149). NY: Cambridge University Press.

Talmy, L. (1988). Force dynamics in language and cognition. *Cognitive Science, 12*, 49–100.

7

Methods for Stimulating and Measuring Lexical and Syntactic Advances: Why Fiffins and Lobsters Can Tag Along With Other Recast Friends

Keith E. Nelson
Penn State University

My grandmother was a great quilter and cook. Until recently, I did not realize she was also my first mentor in understanding language development. If you haven't tasted her whenever-you-crave-it creamed corn with oysters, or her holiday candy called "divinity," or her bread, or feasted your eyes on one of her quilts that transform a thousand small pieces of ties and scarves and who-knows-what into a many-hymned chorus to the harmony of this world, then you have missed out on some wonderful and complex events. If Grandma Nelson had been an academic she could have given an entirely new connotation to "Divinity Studies," for she was very wise and very articulate on the complex patterns in which humidity, temperature, bags of sugar, nuts, and other ingredients interacted to make some mixes optimal for divinity candy. May similar grannies nest in your extended family dwellings!

This chapter is dedicated to Daisy Hayman Nelson for all the reasons just mentioned and also for some wonderful conversations we conducted side-by-side, accompanied by the rhythms of our two chaotically rocking

rocking chairs. (At this point the editors are counting words and wondering will I wind this around back to the topic of children's language and methods and theories connected to the same. Yes, definitely.) I argue for a metaphor of "quilting" language complexity piece-by-piece to make the remarkable, dynamic, super-quick language systems that children usually achieve, although with interesting differences in sophistication and complexity, by around 6 to 8 years in all cultures. Moreover, I argue that language learning conditions, the complex child-and-partner interactional conditions, when properly described, are also complex quiltlike mixes in which truly favorable conditions may produce breakneck speed in language advances, but in which truly lousy conditions can create plateaus in learning and serious language delay.

In order to discover what learning conditions contribute in a causal way to progress in lexical, syntactic, or text development, a range of methods is important. This chapter describes several interrelated programs of research that share key methodological characteristics: on lexical-conceptual development, on syntactic development, and on literacy development. Each tries to include "ecologically valid" experimental methods that examine in systematic fashion some of the same learning processes and relevant learning conditions that apply when the child is progressing (or not progressing) in learning communication skills in varied naturalistic contexts. Further, each looks for convergence in findings and interpretation between experimental and naturalistic studies. In addition, each program of research tries to take individual differences fully into account. Finally, there are interesting theoretical and intervention/educational implications in relation to patterns of results from each research domain. By examining many aspects of the "quilt" of language, one is also led to some conclusions about the nature of a child's mind that supports "stitching along" productively under certain conditions but becomes slowed, stalled, or tangled under other conditions that at first looked promising.

FANCIFUL FIFFIN TOYS

Here I examine procedures, data, and conclusions from a series of experimental studies on young children's learning of new concepts and names for these concepts. The original wug research incorporated two basic techniques that are adapted in the research reported here: (a) a concept example new to a child is given a fanciful, made-up, new name, such as *wug*, and (b) if the child shows generalization of that name to a new situation (e.g., pictures of two wugs), the pattern of that generalization is used to infer underlying lexical and/or syntactic structures. Examples of interesting generalization patterns include the naming of wugs based on the regular plural ending *-s* in English and the naming of multiple fiffins based on the lexicalized concept *fiffin*.

In two experiments, John Bonvillian and I explored how younger children from 18 to 27 months of age fared in acquiring new concepts when both learning and generalization trials were spread over several months. We were interested in learning rates, individual differences, degree of varied responsiveness to different exemplar sets, integration of information from sessions separated by 2 weeks, and theoretical interpretations of all of these. At the outset of these experiments, there was some doubt about whether anyone could demonstrate in children so young under controlled and narrowly circumscribed learning conditions the initial acquisition and systematic generalization of a set of basic object concepts and their English names. By screening children's homes and interviewing parents, we were able to choose unknown English lexical items such as *lobster* and *snorkel* for both studies. In the second study we also compared children's acquisition with fanciful lexical items such as *fiffin* and *lubnik*. In all this work we sought ecological validity. Except for the built-in designs for evidence patterns (which the children were unlikely to recognize as unusual), in other respects adults in the lab did what mothers and fathers do at home. Experimenters and mothers in the lab talked and played with the children, and the mothers mixed in labeling of concept exemplars the children initially did not know how to either categorize or lexicalize. We wanted to establish how children learned to express and comprehend the names for the concepts.

The first study (Nelson & Bonvillian, 1973) was a short longitudinal experiment with 10 children, initially 18 months of age. Our overall method was to let mothers teach but to rigorously control how often the children saw toys and heard the toys' names. For each of 16 concepts, the children first heard the concept names in an initial session where 3 exemplars of each concept were named by the children's mothers. The same labeled exemplars were encountered and again named by the mothers every 2 weeks in new sessions, which continued until the children were almost 24 months of age. Similarly, for each of the 16 concepts there were further exemplars that never were labeled by the mothers. No previous study with preschool children had controlled frequency and patterning of lexical labels, or how many exemplars these labels were applied to, or the number of unlabeled generalization examples available. Each child had the chance to learn these 16 concepts: *barrel, bobber, caboose, canteen, compass, eyebolt, handcuffs, hedgehog, nozzle, oiler, pulley, sifter, silo, sinker, snorkel,* and *whetstone.*

The 18-month-olds did learn, fortunately! This put us in the position to examine and reflect on the remarkable individual differences, despite the close equation of both exemplar sets and lexical labeling patterns across all 10 children. Overgeneralization by adult criteria of one name to another concept (e.g., labeling a *barrel* as a *silo*) was infrequent, as only 12% of the concepts showed any overgeneralization. Individual differences were clearest in terms of the numbers of concepts acquired and named, with some children learning five times as many concepts as the least efficient learners. The very wide range of learning for these young children, even though input was equated closely for the basic object concepts examined, is surprising if one expects that nouns labeling such concepts are the easiest items in early semantic acquisition. However, from naturalistic samples of children's first 50 words acquired, multiple reports establish that social-emotional-expressive words are early acquisitions for many children as well (Bloom, Tinker, & Margulis, 1993; K. Nelson, 1973; K. E. Nelson, 1982; Nelson, Baker, Denniger, Bonvillian, & Kaplan, 1985). For some children the social-emotional-expressive preference even goes so far that all the first 50 words are of this sort. These children raise our awareness of the multiple ways in which emotion and social connection and motivation and personal style are dynamically woven into communicative progress, even at the first-word and first-phrase level. These are processes that I revisit in many ways later in this chapter when syntax and literacy development are addressed.

Fiffins first appeared in a study of 25 children between 22 and 27 months of age. Again, our overall method was to let mothers teach but to rigorously control how often the children saw toys and heard the toys' names. Here the generalization exemplars for 18 different concepts were presented only at widely spaced intervals, forcing the retrieval and application of concept names such as *fiffin, bandock, sifter,* and *lobster* across at least 2-week intervals. The remaining concepts were *compass, oiler, beaver, bobber, pulley, barrel, hedgehog, renscap, teggle, wangsop, dacton, lubdub, sidoy,* and *tellnik.* The total set thus included 9 made-up names and 9 English nouns. The names were distinct in terms of their pronunciations, so that coding of which word a child produced would be clear even if the child produced only part of the name. The design incorporated 10 sessions total, with 7 sessions for learning about adult-named exemplars; but sessions 3, 6, and 9 were restricted to adult-unnamed exemplars that tested generalization of whatever concept and lexical acquisition had been achieved by the child in the prior learning sessions. The generalization examples were also presented once more at the end of session 10. A final methodological point is that across sessions 4 to 10 each concept was tested for comprehension: The child showed correct comprehension by choosing an exemplar (e.g., a *fiffin*) from an arrangement of toys that included 6 incorrect and one correct exemplar.

These procedures ensured that each child received across the full study the same patterns of toys and names for the toys. Methodologically this experimental approach contrasts strongly with another frequently used method for studying early vocabularies: parental reports of word use unaccompanied by reports or observations of when and how relevant object exemplars and namings of these exemplars have been presented (cf. Leopold, 1939; Nelson, 1973). The experiments reported here provide a good basis for observing individual differences in learning precisely because they build in experimental controls on the evidence that children had available to them.

This experiment also varied learning-set size. When two to four exemplars were named by adults per concept, by the end of the study the children had themselves named at least one exemplar appropriately for 83% of the concepts and they averaged 57% naming of all learning-set exemplars. This level of learning for 22 to 27-month-olds suggests a clear improvement in learning rate as compared with similar learning sets employed in 10 sessions by Schwartz (in Leonard & Schwarz 1978) with 14 to 18-month-olds; these younger children named 36% of adult-named exemplars. The Fanciful Fiffin study also provided data on how often the children extended their acquired names to the generalization exemplars that adults had never named. These were named frequently by the children, but at a rate just about half (28% of exemplars) the naming shown for the remaining learning-set exemplars. For these learning sets, note that two factors were at work: Adults named these toys, and the toys were presented in a total of 7 sessions rather than just the 4 sessions for the generalization toys.

When the named learning set is minimal, only one exemplar is available as the basis for the child's learning. This held for six of the concepts. Nevertheless, learning from the minimal or "rare" evidence available took place. Naming of at least one exemplar held for 58% of concepts. Children on average named 19% of all learning-set and generalization exemplars. Clearly, these learning rates are lower than for concepts with two to four adult-named exemplars and three generalization examples. Thus, learning of new lexical items can be based on just one learning-set exemplar, but the 22 to 27-month-olds learned more concepts and learned then more quickly when multiple exemplars were provided in the adult-named learning set (cf. Mervis & Pani, 1980).

Remarkable individual differences lie behind the average data so far presented. In the Fanciful Fiffin study we closely equated which learning sets were provided, the schedule across 10 sessions of presentations of the learning sets and generalization sets, a complete lack of corrective feedback for any errors in naming or comprehension made by the children, and additional procedures for testing comprehension of the lexical items. Despite these equated learning conditions, children differed on a broad range of learning measures. Highlights of these differences are listed here:

• Children learned different numbers of concepts. Comprehension and/or production was shown by one child for just 33% of the concepts, but for 8 of the 25 children 100% of the concepts showed comprehension and/or production. On average, comprehension and/or production was 81% (14.6) of the 18 concepts.

• Even when the same numbers of concepts were learned by subsets of children, the children differed in which concepts met acquisition criteria.

• Even when the same concept and criterion of learning was considered, children differed in the rates at which they met the criteria.

• Comprehension and production of concept names showed varied relationships. Sixteen children led strongly in production, seven led in comprehension, and only two were highly similar in their comprehension and production performance.

• Children varied from (a) no overextensions of concept names to exemplars for other concepts, to (b) overextension of many names (average, 21%).

• *What do you say to a hedgehog-beaver?* These children were tested on extra toys that combined some features of two concepts, what we called "hybrids." At 25 to 27 months of age, with considerable concept learning already under their belts, children were shown 24 such hybrids. One child named these at quite a high rate, 53%. Most were in the range of 8% to 47%. It was fun to see that some names were invented or adapted, including *lobster-fiffin, dacton-pulley,* and *beaver-hedgehog.* These findings complement those of Clark (1981, also chap. 4, this volume) and Nelson (1982).

Summary of Methods and Findings

In these lexical acquisition studies, input was controlled for 18- to 27-month-olds. The children were rewarded by the chance to explore and learn about new toys and names in an atmosphere of low pressure and no correction. The mothers were rewarded by observing their children's language growth. The investigators were rewarded by insights into the impacts of children's individual differences and the experimentally manipulated learning sets. All were rewarded by a picnic with plenty of ice cream and take-home snapshots at the end of the study.

Input definitely mattered. Learning a new concept and its name was more probable and more rapid when larger input sets were provided. Yet "rare event learning" was also observed in the extreme, when a single exemplar named by an adult served as a sufficient basis for many children learning one or more of the six concepts of this sort. There is no contradiction here, because children may be capable of lexical acquisition from learning sets of one or two items encountered only every 2 weeks and still be benefited in their learning rates by larger learning sets and/or more frequent encounters with exemplars.

Children's characteristics also mattered. Variations in learning patterns and rates were very large even though learning conditions had been nearly equalized by the experimental procedures. In addition, children who more extensively generalized their existing (pre-study) words to the new concepts were better at learning the experimental words. Their active naming of the toys, sometimes with clear overgeneralization errors and sometimes with descriptive but not concept-specific words, contributed to their encoding of the toy exemplars and their mastery by the end of the study of appropriate new words and concepts. Total vocabulary size pre-study, as assessed by a detailed interview with the mother, ranged from 18 to 300 words. Our interviews occurred after the children had been learning words for many months—and with no longitudinal methods for examining how much these vocabulary sizes were influenced by the patterns of objects, events, and names the children had experienced. Children with higher pre-study vocabularies learned more of the experimental concept names and also extended their previously known names more often to the experimental concepts.

We can paraphrase the central results in terms of lexical "quilts" of many words that become appropriately understood and interrelated across time. In the Fanciful Fiffin studies the children built up distinctive, individualized language quilts, even when we provided a common set of patches (exemplars, labels) and suggested stitches (our naming patterns). Those children who were more active stitchers—more often overgeneralizing the words they knew from outside the study—were also quickest at sorting out which new words should be mapped to which toy exemplars.

TAG ALONGS: SNEAKING UPTAKE OF TAGS, PASSIVES, ETC. INTO CONVERSATIONAL INTERACTION WITH CHILDREN

In the 1960s, and to this day in some quarters, the peculiar notion has been tossed around (e.g., Chomsky, 1968, 1986; Fodor, 1983, 1985; Lightfoot, 1989; Pinker, 1994) that in language learning children face severely "impoverished input. " This notion in turn is argued as forcing theorizing about language acquisition to the default position that the child brings to language very powerful, linguistic-specific, innate mechanisms. What is so peculiar about the concept of impoverished input is that there has long been evidence that compared to other domains, the typical child in all cultures encounters at ages 1 to 6 years extremely rich and frequent input—albeit from varied mixtures of parents, other adults, and other children in varied cultures. Moreover, since the 1960s there has been a steady accumulation of increasingly differentiated information about the nature of language input and its variations (e.g., Bohannon, Padgett, Nelson, & Mark, 1996; Nelson, 1980, 1991a; Ratner, 1996; Snow, Perlmann, & Nathan, 1987). This section explores some of the methods, theories, findings, and conclusions from work by my colleagues and me that have contributed to an increased understanding of how input varies and how selected aspects of input contribute directly to syntactic progress by children.

Four lines of thinking complemented each other as we began a program of research concerning how input is processed and incorporated into syntactic systems by children. I review the initial thinking and then some of the actual research and its essential methods. Finally, I discuss revisions in theoretical frameworks.

The first line of thought concerned how strong or weak the child's general memory, abstraction, retrieval, and sequential analysis and motor planning capacities may be at 12, 24, 36, 48, and 72-and-over months of age. To the extent that these capacities are on the weak side, input may need to be very "user friendly," with many frequent processing facilitators, in order to allow language learning to progress. However, from the Fanciful Fiffin and other demonstrations of learning or "fast mapping" (Carey, 1978; Mervis & Pani, 1980) based on only one or two exemplars widely spaced in time or even presented on one occasion only, it became plausible to estimate that even by 18 to 24 months of age children have in place extremely powerful general learning mechanisms, and that across 24 months these mechanisms become even more powerful, rapid, and efficient. Because these mechanisms work even with very "thin" or rare input, we labeled them rare event learning mechanisms. As in the Fanciful Fiffin research, children sometimes encounter very salient and highly processable single exemplars and from a single occasion successfully abstract new concepts and new linguistic structures.

A second line of reasoning was from cognitive psychology as applied to both adults and children. Processing efficiency could be expected to vary strongly by context. For preschool children trying to learn syntax in the face of greater limitations on processing than obtain for older children and adults, it seemed likely that no learning would occur in many discourse contexts but that other discourse contexts would support fairly efficient learning. These latter, more favorable contexts would likely be ones that minimize working memory demands, focus memory and abstraction on syntax, and allow relatively long processing "windows" for comparing child–adult syntactic structures.

The third line of thinking on syntax was that we should try to learn something from naturalistic socialization agents about clues to effective strategies for facilitating children's syntactic progress. Because there are so many discourse moves that mothers might use that could potentially facilitate the child's progress, there was a "needle in the haystack" feeling about whether powerful facilitating strategies could be found in analyses of mother–child discourse and longitudinal progress by the child. But along with a handful of other investigators, we began to look through the haystacks of naturalistic data available to us.

As a fourth line of reassuring, from the outset it was clear that experimental language intervention contrasts would be required to test out any specific strategies—any "needles" from the naturalistic stacks of data— to determine whether these strategies could indeed be causal agents for specific syntactic advances by children. Ecologically valid experimental tests were intended that would mimic what occurs in naturalistic discourse patterns associated with children's rapid syntactic advances. Our goal was to bring to children's acquisition of new syntactic structures an experimental rigor of the sort that had proved so productive, from the initial wug experiments onward, in revealing children's existing syntactic structures and in understanding lexical acquisition.

Recasts in the Beginning

We took our initial clues from some of the first chapters of detailed work on child–adult discourse. From the mothers of Adam, Eve, and Sarah, we borrowed and adapted a technique first described as "expansions" (Brown, Cazden, & Bellugi-Klima, 1969). When the child says *The dog running*, an adult expansion could be *The dog is running*. We grouped these filling-in, expanding kinds of replies with many other adult replies that also overlap in meaning with a child's utterance but recast, rearrange, or redisplay such meaning. Recasts became our term for any such reply regardless of whether the preceding "platform utterance" from the child was fully grammatical and regardless of whether the recast reply expanded, reduced, or rearranged the elements present in the child's utterance. To take just two examples, if the child said *The bird was singing,* then two different recasts could be *Yes, it sang* or *That bird was singing brightly, wasn't it?*

Our first experiment on recasts went out on a limb. In the absence of prior evidence of a causal contribution of recasts to children's syntactic advance, we speculated that recasts could play that role. Why? Precisely because they appeared to fit the characteristics described previously in our analytic search for certain discourse events that could optimize the child's on-line processing of new syntactic information during ongoing conversation. The child has just uttered a platform utterance based on his or her current syntactic system and with a particular meaning in mind. When the recast occurs, the overlap in meaning should help maintain the child's attention but at the same time (because the meaning is "old") allow a preponderance of processing capacity to address the relationship between the new syntactic components of the recast and the child's own expressed syntax.

The research design compared progress at the preschool level by a group of children given recasts to that of two control groups. Results clearly indicated that over a few months, recasts provided experimentally do accelerate language progress (Nelson, Carskaddon, & Bonvillian, 1973). This outcome was important because it served as a springboard for considerable programmatic research. However, as in most research on the early stages of a topic, it raised more questions than it answered. Note that *recasts* were here defined in only the most general sense—the recasts could include any aspect of syntax, they were not individualized in any planned way to each child's language profile, and they could be of any length and complexity. Despite this, they worked! But it seemed evident that still more powerful interventions and more refined theory would benefit by the development of more differentiated subsets of recasts. New methodological procedures would be needed for these purposes. Rather than one big "recast needle," we set out in search of smaller, more specialized discourse needles that could help children stitch new pieces of syntax into their language repertoires.

Stitching Tags Into Children's Syntactic Systems

The reasoning behind adult recasting influenced a series of studies on the acquisition of highly specific syntactic structures. Here I use tag questions, as one structure among many investigated, to give the highlights of this work. *The bear ate a lot of candy, didn't she?* and *The boy didn't like the music, did he?* both illustrate tag questions. The tags at the end are highly complex because they must be coordinated precisely with the verb and subject noun and negation/affirmation of the preceding clauses. In each study described, we determined that tag questions were absent in pre-intervention language samples for the children selected for intervention. Other absent structures served as control comparisons. Then we used narrowly focused "growth-recasting" on tags (or focused on other syntactic targets absent before the recasting) to see if this procedure would allow children to acquire ("stitch in") tags, in 5 to 20 hours of recasting spaced across 2 to 3 months. The new language, growth recasts, was adopted for these highly differentiated recast interventions that targeted only those structures in the growth zone beyond the child's current syntactic level.

Preschool children with no disabilities "stitched" intervention targets—tags, other complex questions, or new verbs such as future tense verbs—into their language with high efficiency in the growth-recasting study of Nelson (1977). In fact, each of twelve 29-month-olds acquired new targeted forms after receiving 5 hours (spaced across 2 months) of growth-recasting intervention on syntactic structures well beyond their pre-intervention levels. Control syntactic structures were acquired at a far lower rate. This demonstration of how effective a short-term, well-specified treatment for syntax could be was exciting. It helped fuel many new steps in theorizing and intervention. Within the context of wuglike experimentation that goes beyond naturalistic data, it was also appropriate that it even earned a fanci-ful, hypothetical prize. Brown (personal communication, 1979) wrote that it deserved a "benign intervention award." We were, it was clear, helping children who already were doing just fine in language acquisition. Replications followed for language-normal children in three new studies concerning tags, passives, verbs, and noun phrases (Baker & Nelson, 1984; Nelson, 1989, 1991a). Again, the preschool children showed that they were cognitively and linguistically prepared to learn complex new syntactic structures from short-term interventions (5 to 20 hours, across about 2 months) if these interventions presented target structures as growth recasts to the children's own utterances.

The results described so far at first glance appear to conflict with some earlier work on expansions or recasts. But a close look at methods employed shows that earlier work by Cazden (1965) and Feldman (1971) would not be expected to have similar results (see Nelson, 1987; Nelson & Nelson, 1978). In Cazden's study there was not a clear-cut advantage for a group of children receiving expansions as compared with groups receiving imitative replies or no treatment. However, pre-intervention language lev-els were so different for the three groups that no definitive conclusions could be drawn (even after attempted statistical "adjusting" for initial lev-els). Another factor working against strong impact of expansions or recasts is that in both the Cazden and Feldman studies the adult interveners spoke English dialects different from those the children routinely encountered. Finally, in neither of these studies was there employment of a procedure that on theoretical grounds we have argued would be highly facilitative of abstraction and acquisition by the children—growth recasts tailored to individual children that maintain semantic overlap with the child's preced-ing utterance and that build in syntactic structures found to be lacking in pre-intervention analyses. In order to study the impact of growth recasts, several key methodological steps are required: (a) detailed analysis of spe-cific syntactic structures present and absent in pre-intervention data, (b) on a child-by-child basis, the creation of a treatment plan that gives the child recasting on absent structures, (c) "control" comparisons of other absent structures that do not receive recasting, and (d) specific analyses of the child's use or lack of use of the treated and untreated syntactic structures in everyday conversations after the recasting treatment has been completed.

In three more studies, we again applied growth recasts that we stitched into our conversations with children. But now we worked with children who needed help in syntax, children with delayed syntax but no cognitive or perceptual or emotional disabilities: children with specific language impairment (SLI). Tags and other structures absent at pre-intervention baselines were used in recast interventions tailored to each child's syntactic profile. In all three studies the SLI children acquired the targeted, recasted structures significantly more quickly than they did matched structures serving as controls (Camarata & Nelson, 1992; Camarata, Nelson, & Camarata, 1994; Nelson, Camarata, Welsh, Butkovsky, & Camarata, 1996). Another study demonstrating positive effects of recasting on syntax growth was conducted in sign language with deaf children (Prinz & Masin, 1985).

"Tag-along" experiments were proving useful theory and in building new treatment for language delay. Consider the cases where children acquired tag question structures. Here we recognized four levels of "tagging" in operation— (a) *isn't it, are they*, and so forth tagged along at the end of the adult recasts, (b) the growth recasts were also semantic tag-alongs or extensions, (c) the children somehow "tagged" the new structures (for both storage and retrieval) in their long-term representations during initial learning and subsequent generalizations, and (d) processing by the children during the recasting intervention successfully "stitched" or "tagged" the new structures into the children's syntactic systems.

Summary of Recasting Studies Within a Rare Event Learning Perspective

Something about the recasting procedure was facilitating children's progress in syntax. After all, at statistically significant levels the nine studies just described converged in showing the positive impact of experimentally controlled recasting by adults in triggering progress in syntax (cf. also Fey, Cleave, & Long, 1997; Fey, Cleave, Long, & Hughes, 1993). And the growth recasting studies pinpointed that tags, passives, relatives, gerunds, infinitives, and other structures lacked by an individual child can be introduced into the child's syntactic repertoire by growth recasting focused exclusively on what the child lacks. So far, the theoretical emphasis has been on the way in which child-utterance/adult-recast sequences in discourse enhance processing of the syntactic contrast between adult and child utterances. Attention, working memory, syntactic pattern abstraction, and long-term storage and retrieval all may be enhanced in the simple discourse event, child-utterance followed by adult-recast-with-challenge. In addition, there is a lack of request/demand in the recast for the child to respond immediately, and this lack of discourse pressure may allow extended processing time after the recast. All these processes working together may enhance acquisition across multiple recast occasions of the target structures incorporated into the recasts (Bohannon & Stanowicz, 1989; Nelson, 1980, 1989).

The child by no means needs to learn something from each recasting occasion. Instead, rare event learning capacities permit the child to ignore many recasts and still acquire new tags and other structures. Learning may occur if the child focuses on even a handful of the easy-to-process syntactic challenges that growth recasting makes available in each treatment session. A comparison to another phenomenon that is subject to dynamic, tricky mixes is appropriate. Tornadoes are predictable to an extent. They are far more likely to develop under a complex mix of conditions that are also associated with certain kinds of thunderstorms. But predicting at what moment and in what location the tornado will occur is not possible; tornadoes appear in only a small handful of the potentially sufficient, facilitating opportunities.

AND NOW FOR SOMETHING COMPLETELY DIFFERENT (OR IS IT?): FANCIFUL COMPUTER FUN AS A ROUTE TO LITERACY FOR DEAF AND AUTISTIC CHILDREN

Research strands that begin in different regions sometimes have a tendency to develop and eventually blend or weave together. That certainly is the case for the recasting work on syntax, discussed previously and the program of research now to be reviewed on multimedia approaches for literacy instruction. A number of related methods fit under the definition of recasting, and spelling them out may be helpful to further refinements in both methods and theories.

Our entry into deaf education research began with a recognition of the appallingly low levels of literacy achieved by most deaf children at 12 to 18 years of age. We saw parallels between (a) the frequent (but not consistent) observations of SLI children showing language delay, but with more than half the children demonstrating average to above-average nonverbal cognitive scores (Fey & Catts, 1998; Fey, et al., 1997; Hansson, Hellquist, Leonard, Nettelbladt, & Salameh, 1998; Leonard, 1998; Tallal, Stark, & Curtiss, 1976), and (b) the frequent observation of language delay with average to above-average nonverbal cognitive scores for deaf children (Bonvillian & Folven 1993; Moores, 1978, 1985; Nelson, Prinz, Prinz, & Dalke, 1991). As with the majority of SLI children in our own research, there was the paradox for a great many deaf children of having good-to-excellent cognitive skills as measured by nonlanguage tasks, accompanied by severe language delay and frequent long-term negative consequences in the form of poor academic skills and restricted career opportunities in adulthood (Aram, Ekelman, & Nation, 1984; Aram & Nation, 1980; Bonvillian, Nelson, & Charrow, 1976; de Villiers, de Villiers, & Hoban, 1994; Moores, 1978, 1985; Records, Tomblin, & Freese, 1992; Schlesinger & Meadow, 1976; Strothard, Snowling, Bishop, Chipchase, & Kaplan, 1998). For most deaf children this involved not only low literacy but low sign language and spoken language skills as compared with those of age-mates. Once we extended multimedia approaches to autistic children, a similar combination of low spoken language skills and low literacy had to be faced, along with difficult-to-estimate nonverbal cognitive abilities, in our instructional design.

The strongest overlap in theoretical frameworks between recasting syntax for SLI children and trying to create new learning conditions for deaf and autistic children held at the cognitive-processing level. For all these children who were far behind their age-mates in communication skills, we sought to present new structural challenges that would be easily processed. The challenges were patterned into interactions with an eye on focusing the child's processing capacities squarely on the challenges and their contrasts with what the child already had mastered in language. Even for the children with considerable delay, such as 4 or 5 years, it seemed possible that intact rare event learning mechanisms might be seen if learning conditions were made highly favorable. But how to do this?

We decided to seek a "double facilitation." That is, a mix of methods was chosen for deaf children and autistic children with the dual goals of raising literacy and enhancing first-language skills. Improvements in the latter were needed by the children anyway, and we figured that raising the first language skills would also make it easier to move to more advanced levels of literacy. Teachers were trained to do recasting with the children, in sign language for deaf children and in spoken language for autistic children. The recasting was interspersed between short episodes in which the child actively manipulated text sentences on a multimedia screen so that the text triggered two additional channels of information—graphic animations parallel in meaning to the text sentence, and first language sentences (sign or speech) parallel to both the text and animations. *The alligator chases the girl,* for example, would appear in rapid succession as text, graphics, and first language. Then the teacher and child would converse a bit, with recasting by the teacher. Then a new multimedia sequence would be initiated by the child.

One of the key advantages of multimedia programs is that they are fairly easily adapted for new languages to support highly similar implementation in new locations. So it was not long before a series of studies with American deaf students as well as Belgian deaf students and Swedish autistic and deaf children had been completed. My focus here is on the key results and on some rethinking we did at the theoretical and procedural levels.

In each country, deaf and autistic children readily explored both fanciful, nonrealistic sentences and highly realistic sentences. Tests built into the software and tests on paper-and-pencil measures showed that the children had learned to understand fanciful and realistic sentences equally well. Significant literacy gains were shown in the U. S. studies (e.g., Nelson, Prinz, Prinz, & Dalke, 1991), in Sweden (Heimann, Nelson, Gillberg, & Kärnevik, 1993; Heimann, Nelson, Tjus, & Gillberg, 1995; Nelson, Heimann, & Tjus, 1997), and in Belgium (Nelson, Loncke, & Camarata, 1993; Prinz, Nelson, Loncke, Geysels, & Willems, 1993). Moreover, in some studies first language gains beyond control/comparison gains were examined on the expectation that the recasting side conversations would support such gains. In each such study, accelerated first language progress was in fact observed. American Sign Language gains were reported in Nelson et al. (1991), and Swedish spoken language gains were reported for Swedish autistic children (Heimann et al., 1993; Heimann et al., 1995).

Now I consider in more detail the procedural steps behind the communication gains just summarized. We wanted the children to have fun and give the materials close attention. Thus, the multimedia computer setups we used put the child actively in charge of making lively, enjoyable, animated sequences appear on the screen. Fanciful foxes singing human songs and fanciful dinosaurs feeding carrots to penguins are examples. In all cases, the child rapidly selected (by touching a special pad or clicking a mouse for on-screen locations) pieces of text to activate a complete sentence. For example, by choosing in sequence *the alligator* and *chases* and *the girl*, the child could assemble a complete sentence on-screen. Then the animation for that sentence would run. And then, depending on the child, sign language or spoken language would be presented. Next the teacher and child would converse about what had just happened and any associations to the events, with recasting by the teacher. Our initial framing of these procedural steps was almost exclusively cognitive and linguistic. Within about 20 to 25 seconds the first three steps involving text/animation/first language would be completed and very soon after that the related comment(child)/recast(teacher) steps would also occur. Working memory would thus have multiple opportunities to abstract connections between the to-be-learned text and the other forms of representation "cascaded" before the child. The final step of first language recasting would be the support for abstraction of new first language structures by the child.

Our framing of these events has evolved in two significant ways. First, we gradually recognized the similarity between recasting in child–adult conversation and some varieties of paraphrase or restatement in the software environment. Consider the sentence *The panda put the pizza on the gorilla's table*. After text is chosen to express that sentence on the screen, new presentations of essentially the same meaning but in new communication channels fit the definition of recasts as old-meanings/new-structural-variations. So, text/animation, text/voice, text/sign, animation/sign, and animation/voice may be described as different kinds of recasts. When there are gaps in developmental level between any of these paired elements (as when sign mastery is above text mastery, or animation understanding is above text understanding), working memory may have good opportunities to abstract some new structural understandings. So, within the multimedia-plus-teacher interventions, there are a set of learning opportunities that are similar in their reliance on variations of recasting as potential facilitators (Nelson, 1998; Nelson & Camarata, 1997; Nelson, Heimann, & Tjus, 1997; Nelson & Welsh, 1998).

The second broad change in our conceptualization of learning in the multimedia settings applies to learning in the other research domains we have considered—in lexical acquisition and syntactic progress during language therapy. Accordingly, the next section covers all these domains of learning.

RECASTING THE THEORETICAL FRAME ON LEARNING

In our recent writing, the learning of text and first language structures are both considered within a variant of dynamic system theorizing. My colleagues and I argue that abstractions in working memory and encoding of these into long-term memory—processes at the cognitive heart of learning—are greatly dependent on a converging set of conditions we call a "tricky mix" (Nelson, 1998; Nelson & Camerata, 1997; Nelson & Welsh, 1998; Nelson, Heimann, & Tjus, 1997). Beyond favorable cognitive and linguistic conditions, the probability of learning increases rapidly as a broader mix of favorable learning conditions comes into play. Patterns of text/graphics/sign/speech that make language challenges processable are certainly important, but equally important are the convergence of favorable variables of motivation, emotional regulation, expectancy, confidence, and self-esteem. When many converging, favorable conditions "dynamically collaborate," the learning may be exceptionally rapid and powerful, the pinnacle of progress from a few rare events or episodes. An analogy is that dynamic interaction of many factors similarly can create exceptionally good outcomes in baking bread, playing in a jazz ensemble, or experiencing weather conditions on a beautiful spring day. However, methodological innovations are necessary to help examine not only well-defined "narrow" progress in spoken language, sign language, or literacy but also anything like a "tricky mix" account of learning conditions underlying the children's progress.

REFLECTIONS ON DIVERSE RESEARCH DOMAINS

Many domains have been discussed. Literacy progress, sign language progress, progress in spoken English or Swedish, learning of new names and their mapping to object concepts—all have been examined. At this point reflections across these domains are employed to suggest some of the contributions and also some of the complications—in methods and in theories—for research on children's communicative skills.

Providing Increasingly Differentiated Forms of Effective Intervention

If children were not sensitive to input variations, there would be little point to implementing programs of research to improve interventions for children's language delay. But the preceeding review indicates a very strong sensitivity of syntactic progress rates to learning conditions. For recent research on children with SLI, two very important differentiations have emerged, each based on new methods providing systematic experimental contrasts lacking in earlier research. First, interventions focused on baseline-absent syntactic structures show clear impact on children's syntactic growth, whereas treatment of partly mastered structures does not appear to produce impact—the latter structures reach mastery just as quickly if they are not treated (Nelson, Camarata, Welsh, Butkovsky, & Camarata, 1996). Second, all direct comparisons of commonly used imitative treatments to recent innovations on conversational recasting treatment indicate that the recasting treatments are more effective. Combining these outcomes would lead to differentiated treatments of SLI that incorporate syntactic structures not yet used by an individual child, with conversational recasting "carrying" the target structures (relative clauses, gerunds, etc.) for the child's potential analysis and learning.

More Differentiated Accounts of Individual Differences

Progress in understanding children's development requires meaningful differentiations of their characteristics, despite the convenience of broad terms to summarize development. In theoretical discussions, in method choices, and in intervention decisions, it is crucial to be aware that saying "the child" learns from "the input" is meaningless without further specification of what is known about the child's current level of language and cognition and about prior and current input and interaction conditions. Similarly, phrases such as "the SLI child" or "the language-normal child at Stage IV" or "the SLI child at Stage IV" should be used cautiously as introductions to more differentiated descriptions of the children's learning contexts and their particular social-emotional, linguistic, and cognitive characteristics.

In the experimental work reviewed in this chapter, there were large individual differences in learning rates and patterns despite the experimental structuring of relatively high similarities between the patterns of cognitive/linguistic challenges presented to the children. Thus, patterns of learning fiffins or relative clauses or new text sentences by language-normal children turned out to be surprisingly varied within each area of language learning despite our controls on the numbers and timing of similar exemplars to each child. Likewise, learning rates were quite varied for children who were behind their age-mates in syntactic or literacy domains, even when given the "same" sets of challenges. There were also interesting longitudinal patterns from the Fanciful Fiffin research.

Learning rates at 22 to 27 months were better predictors than general cognitive test scores or overall language scores, when the predicted outcomes were rates of learning new concepts by the same children after they reached 4½ years of age (Nelson & Bonvillian, 1978; cf. Hart & Risley, 1995).

What are the implications of these large individual differences? One is that we need better differentiations in our theories of how individual children, with and without disabilities, learn new communicative structures at various developmental stages. Another implication is that generally effective interventions could be made even more effective if they were tailored, through comparative treatment research, to highly relevant characteristics of individuals. Methods of researchers or instructional methods of schools that bypass such individual tailoring in favor of some single, "standard" intervention for children within a certain classification—SLI, developmental delay, autistic, deaf, and so forth—carry multiple risks. These include oversimplification of learning processes, low motivation on the part of children, and ineffectiveness of intervention for a lot of children.

Tailoring of methods could proceed in many directions. As just one example, there are speculations that working memory characteristics of SLI children affect which pieces of syntactic input will result in "uptake" or "abstraction" of new syntax (Gathercole & Baddeley, 1993; Nelson, 1980, 1989, 1991a). By jointly studying pre-intervention working memory characteristics of the children and their sensitivity to variations on how conversational recasting is conducted, researchers might identify new treatment methods that provide one highly effective treatment to SLI children with the lowest levels of working memory capacity and a contrasting but equally highly effective treatment to SLI children with the highest levels of working memory. The same basic "frame" for jointly studying pre-intervention characteristics of children and their relative sensitivities to a range of treatment variations could be applied to a great many potentially relevant child characteristics. These might include long-term memory retrieval, self-esteem and confidence, social style, cognitive style, emotional regulation, and speed of abstraction of patterns under prior controlled conditions. At the same time, the studies reviewed to this point also make clear that accounting for individual differences in learning rates can be approached from a broader, more transactional framework in which the "same" planned treatment for each child is examined in terms of the varied, emerging experiences of both child and teacher/tutor during the treatment. These are discussed in the following section.

Refining Theoretical Frameworks

Quilting, as Grandma Nelson experienced it, was not a solo activity. A quilting group of six to eight women dynamically conspired to create first the preliminary conditions for a quilt. The needed conditions included piles of patches, a stretched cloth foundation on a wooden frame, needles and countless spools of thread, and the emotional-social "frame" for undertaking stitch after stitch. Then the real quilting began. The precise quilt structure evolved amid apparent chaos, a wild rumpus of talk, high emotion, laughter, and sewing.

Similarly, the learning of lexicon, syntax, and text takes place within dynamically interacting conditions that at times converge in effective patterns to produce communicative advances. There is a rich mix of social-emotional, self-esteem, motivational, strategic, and expectancy conditions that accompany and interact with the key words, sentences, and dialogue that at first were the only measures we examined in research on communicative development. In contrast, we modestly expanded our coding methods when we moved to transactional (cf. Sameroff & Chandler, 1975) and dynamic systems (cf. Fox, 1994; Thelen & Smith, 1994) theoretical framework. All significant learning depends on tricky mixes of learning conditions, with rapid learning occurring only when the tricky and partly chaotic mix of conditions converges strongly (Csikszentmihalyi & Csikszentmihalyi, 1988; Nelson, 1987, 1991a&b, 1998; Nelson & Camarata, 1997; Nelson, Heimann, & Tjus, 1997; Nelson, Welsh, Camarata, Heimann, & Tjus, 1996; Nelson, Perkins, & Lepper, 1997; Nelson & Welsh, 1998). This theoretical approach has the heuristic role of inviting empirical exploration of how the broader range of social, emotional, motivational, and cognitive/linguistic factors interact to create the strong individual differences so evident in each of the communicative domains.

It is still early, but three studies have helped to account for children's rates of language progress and serve to illustrate new methodological steps stimulated by the theory. In each of the studies, videotapes of the first two sessions of intervention were analyzed to determine the child's "enjoyable engagement" or "social-emotional-cognitive" engagement with the teacher/therapist and the teaching materials. These engagement measures included positive affect expressed in the voice or on the face. They also included touching or looking at the toys or computer graphics directly relevant to the sentences provided by the adult or the computer software. Summary scores for enjoyment/engagement were then created for the children and used as predictors (in statistical regression) of how much learning occurred by the end of intervention. In line with tricky-mix theorizing, children's higher enjoyment/engagement scores early in intervention were predictive of larger learning gains across 3 months of intervention. These developmental gains were shown in syntax for language-impaired children in Haley, Camarata, and Nelson (1994), in syntax for language-normal children in Nelson and Welsh (1998), and in reading levels for autistic children (Heimann et al., 1995; Tjus et al., 1998).

Expressed in rare event terms, we infer that the rare events of "stitching" something new about language structures into long-term memory were most likely under dynamic mixes of growth recasts (carrying challenges in language) combined with relatively positive affect, high social engagement with the adult interaction agent, and close attention to both the language structures presented and their nonverbal context. In related work, there is some evidence that children with SLI receive less appropriate prosody, eye gaze, and language complexity from their mothers than are received by language-normal age-mates (Leonard, 1998; Pierart & Harmegnies, 1993). Similarly, from other investigations of language impaired children (Leonard, 1998; McTear & Conti-Ramsden, 1992), autistic children (Bonvillian & Nelson, 1978; Bonvillian, Nelson, & Rhyne, 1981; Koegel & Koegel, 1995) and deaf children (Lederberg, 1993; Maxwell, 1983; Meadow, Greenberg, Erting, & Carmichael, 1981; Prinz & Prinz, 1981; Prinz & Strong, 1998), there are many clues that social and affective conditions can dynamically mix with language modality and discourse structure to produce wide variations, from very low to very high rates of language development. The most productive moments in speech, sign, and text progress are indeed a lot like Grandma Nelson's most productive moments in quilting or divinity making.

It is crucial to learn in further research more about how variables interact, couple, and synergize to affect children's communicative advances. This is quite complex, of course. Multiple experimental methods and naturalistic methods will be essential, with a search for convergent results across samples of children, languages and cultures, and methods applied.

One danger, however, is that sometimes broad, global variables will be researched that appear promising precisely because they combine different kinds of cognitive/linguistic, interactional, and emotional-social variables. One good example is the variable Hart and Risley (1995) labeled Feedback Tone by the parents of children at 1–3 years of age. High scores on this variable were predictors of child language level—not only at age 3 but also at age 9. Relatively high ("affirmative, positive valence") scores reflected, in part, two factors that we showed could work together dynamically both for literacy progress and first language progress—frequent conversational recasts and relatively positive affective tone in the child–adult interactions. Obviously, there is some convergence between the research reviewed in our previous discussion and Hart and Risley's report. But from the latter report it is impossible to disentangle how often the recasts and positive affect were occurring, in part because affect is not directly coded but instead is inferred from confirmations, praise, and approval. An additional complication is that Feedback Tone failed to differentiate varieties of recasts from each other and from similar non-recast discourse replies, and it also included a variable shown in other research not to be associated positively with language growth—adult exact repetition. Refined future work will need to directly code more differentiated affect and social variables along with differentiated coding of adult–child discourse variables, and in relation to children's language growth it will need to more systematically examine the contributions of such differentiated variables as compared with any more global combination variables.

Challenging Prior Assumptions About Children

One potential of research in any field is to "reduce ignorance" (Ray, 1993). This can happen fairly quickly in some domains when new methods lead to the collection of evidence that strongly challenges previous assumptions. In the methods, data, and ideas examined in this chapter, two examples illustrate especially well this kind of progress.

Assumption A

SLI children have learning and processing deficits that prevent their learning language at a normative rate from conversational treatments.

Essential Methods.   Direct, input-controlled and input-matched experimental comparisons of conversational recast treatment of SLI children and language-normal children at the same language stages.

Challenging Evidence.   The SLI children learn real-language, new syntactic structures equally well (Nelson, Camarata, Welsh, Butkovsky, & Camarata, 1996). It thus appears that many SLI children can "quilt" syntax together from conversational opportunities—if these opportunities combine syntactic challenge and processing facilitators

Assumption B

New concepts and their lexical labels must be built up by first encountering a series (examplars 1, 2, 3, 4, etc.), and then abstracting their common features, prototypical structure, or other conceptual structure.

Essential Methods.   Experimental control of input to ensure that the learner encounters only a single exemplar and its name as the potential basis for learning.

Challenging Evidence.   From extremely thin evidence, decidedly rare events, language-normal children from at least 18 months have learned to learn and can actively extrapolate from a single named toy, video event, or picture. From such singular background, concepts such as *wangsop* and *teggle* and *fiffin* have been formed and generalized appropriately to new toys. Children with SLI who are still at Brown Stages II to IV demonstrate similar conceptual skills and rapid mapping of new words to concepts (Dollaghan, 1987; Rice, Buhr, & Nemeth, 1990; Rice, Oetting, Marquis, Bode, & Pae, 1994).

CONCLUSIONS

From the last 30 years of research and writing concerning children's development of spoken languages, sign languages, and literacy, researchers have acquired important insights into these phenomena. This chapter has covered some of the progress made in understanding the environments of children; the input sets and interactions carrying this input; and children's abstraction, acquisition, and uptake of new communicative structures. It has illustrated also how innovations in methods are essential to observed progress.

A number of related prior claims and assumptions have been strongly challenged. It once seemed reasonable to assume that variations in the input and interactions children experience have little or no impact on how they learn or how quickly they learn. It also was assumed by many authors that nearly all children in all cultures achieve essentially full mastery of a first language and that this developmental work is complete by about 6 years of age. These assumptions tended to work against the choice of research procedures that provide close examination of children's variations in language mastery and of input and interactions (and other factors) that might be influences on such variations. Nevertheless, enough investigations have now been completed to support a far different set of claims:

1.   Children vary dramatically in their rates of progress in all domains of language and in their eventual levels of mastery of language as measured at age 6, 10, 18, or later adulthood (Bates, Bretherton, & Snyder, 1988; Bloom, 1991; Fenson, Dale, Reznick, Bates, & Thal, 1994; Fey & Catts, 1998; Nelson, Denniger, Bonvillian, Kaplan, Baker, 1984). A great deal of further empirical and theoretical work is needed to help explain why these differences occur. New methods that incorporate individual tailoring of interventions and experimental contrasts between interventions will be helpful in this work.

2.   Under rigorous experimental variation in input conditions, children show strong sensitivities to the input and interaction conditions provided to them. Both learning rates and learning patterns are changed when the input and interaction conditions vary. These conclusions hold for language-impaired, autistic, deaf, developmentally delayed, and language-normal children alike (Fey, Cleave, Long, & Hughes, 1993; Greenberg, Calderon, & Kusche, 1984; Kaiser, 1993; Kaiser, Yoder, & Keetz, 1992; Nelson, Heimann, & Tjus, 1997). They apply equally to syntactic development, reading and writing development, and lexical development.

3.   Naturalistic input and interaction conditions show rich associations to children's communicative progress (Barnes, Gutfreund, Satterly, & Wells, 1983; Bohannon et al., 1996; Conti-Ramsden, Hutcheson, & Grove, 1995; Cross, 1977, 1978; Farrar, 1992 ; Furrow, Nelson, & Benedict, 1979; Grimm, 1987; Hart & Risley, 1995; Hoff-Ginsburg, 1986; Scherer & Olswang, 1984; Schodorf & Edwards, 1983; Snow, Perlmann, & Nathan, 1987; Yoder, 1989). When "input processing facilitators," shown to be causal positive influences on learning rates in experimental intervention, are examined for naturalistic data sets, convergent conclusions emerge; more facilitators in input are associated with more rapid communicative development. In the naturalistic data sets so far examined, it is common to find that for children at the same language stage (e.g., Brown Stage II) some children receive recasts and other language-learning facilitators 20 times as frequently as other children do (Conti-Ramsden, 1990; Cross, Nienhuys, & Kirkman, 1985; Hart &

Risley, 1995; Hoff-Ginsberg, 1986; Nelson, 1989; Nelson, Welsh, Camarata, Butkovsky, & Camarata, 1995). Moreover, there are very large overall quantitative differences in input—some children receive at least 10 times as many overall utterances and overall words in input during years 1 to 6 as do other children. For some children with Specific Language Impairment it is likely that relatively parental few recasts, relative to non delayed children, is a contributing factor (Conti-Ramsden, 1990; Nelson et al., 1995). By combining information from a few papers that provide information on rates of interaction of children and their conversational partners (Hart & Risley, 1995; Nelson et al., 1984; Wells, 1985), one can make a reasonable estimate that between age 1 and age 6 an average environment for a child includes around 40 million words and 8 million utterances. Many children receive twice that quantity. Within that haystack of input is the likelihood that there are more "needles" with sharp, focused impacts on how children make language progress. What is needed is further, more differentiated research that examines naturalistic/experimental convergences concerning interactional patterns that serve as facilitators of children's progress in their syntax, pragmatics, discourse, and narrative skills.

4.   Developmental science often progresses when similar phenomena are studied with different methods, different children, and different research teams. Recast replies that present new structural patterns while overlapping in basic meaning with the prior communication are a case in point. Different experimental variations and naturalistic data analyses by many research teams converge to suggest that recasts facilitate communicative progress by children. Still further convergence appears through cross-cultural comparisons. When differentiated discourse analyses have been conducted, recasting has shown up as a common strategy by parents talking in Arabic, Swedish, German, and English (among other languages) with children at Brown Stages I to IV (e.g. Conti-Ramsden, 1990; Cross, 1977, 1978; Cross et al., 1985; Grimm, 1987; Nelson, Heimann, Abuelhaija, & Wroblewski, 1989).

5.   The mind is a balancing act. At any moment of potential learning there is a complex and dynamic mix of processes in the mind. Emotion, expectancy, self-esteem, motivation, and strategies are all part of mind, along with representations of spoken and/or sign language and/or text and selected current and past nonlinguistic events. The arguments and data of this chapter suggest that researchers gain insight into how children's minds work by analyzing convergences between the cognitive/linguistic and social-emotional-motivational textures of child–adult interactions.

The "quilt" of communicative advance is built from dynamic convergences among all these processes. Tricky mixes of learning conditions modulate learning rates in the lexicon, syntax, and literacy. By implication, narrative and discourse and phonological processes are similarly affected by tricky combinations of learning conditions.

6. Communicative advances equally depend on the preparation of the human mind even at 18 months of age and even in many children with considerable disabilities. Any child who has the cognitive level of a normative 18-month-old or older child is prepared to learn very efficiently, and further efficiency will come with further general cognitive development (Bowerman, 1985; Elman et al., 1996; Kail, 1991; Nelson & Nelson, 1978; Siegler, 1991; Slobin, 1973, 1985). The child's mind can learn from infrequent, rare, even singular events, if the events include structural challenge accompanied by a rich and dynamically converging set of conditions. Successful learning of significant communicative structures thus reflects a readiness to respond in dynamic fashion to potential learning situations. It also reflects a mind that, even before 2 years of age, incorporates remarkable pattern abstraction, encoding, and retrieval mechanisms with sufficient flexibility to accommodate complex speech, sign, and text modalities and the many complex subdomains of each. (Elman et al., 1996; Maratsos & Chalkley, 1980; Nelson, 1981, 1987, 1991a, 1991b). Future research may identify a language-specific biological structuring of the child's mind that also supports language acquisition. In any case, children's high readiness for learning complex structures is vividly illustrated in the responses by 3-year-olds to growth recasting of challenging passives—thorough mastery is achieved after only brief intervention that parallels what other children (without intervention) achieve much later, at 8 to 11 years of age (Baker & Nelson, 1984; Nelson, 1987, 1989, 1991a). Thus, the children are ready both cognitively and linguistically to handle the relatively high challenges of passives when recasting dialogue carries passive exemplars. Again, though, research establishes that the remarkable readiness of the child's mind for learning is accompanied by a uniquely human vulnerability—no learning or very slow learning will occur unless the child encounters challenges accompanied by specific processing facilitators and by relatively positive levels of affect, motivation, self-esteem, and expectancy (Lepper, Woolverton, Mumme, & Gurtner, 1993; Nelson, Perkins, & Lepper, 1997; Nelson et al., 1998). For any current episode of learning, all the latter factors are highly dependent on previous cycles of supportive social interaction with other human beings. Quilting-in of new communicative

skills today thus directly reflects the dynamic mix of current conditions and indirectly reflects dynamic mixtures, favorable and unfavorable, across the child's previous social experience.

ACKNOWLEDGMENTS

Background research and reflection underpinning the ideas and data presented in this chapter were provided by grants to the author from the National Science Foundation (BNS-8013767), National Institutes of Health (MH 19826h, HD 06254, R01-NS26437, 2R01DC00508, and 1P50 DC0382-01), U. S. Department of Education (G008302959, G008430079, and G0008300361), and Hasbro Children's Foundation.

REFERENCES

Aram, D., Ekelman, B., & Nation, J. (1984). Preschoolers with language disorder: Ten years later. *Journal of Speech and Hearing Research, 27*, 232–244.

Aram, D., & Nation, J. (1980). Preschool language disorders and subsequent language and academic difficulties. *Journal of Communication Disorders, 13*, 159–170.

Baker, L., & Cantwell, D. P. (1982). Language acquisition, cognitive development, and emotional disorder in childhood. In K. E. Nelson (Ed.), *Children's languge: Vol. 3* (pp. 286–321). Hillsdale, NJ: Lawrence Erlbaum Associates.

Baker, N. D., & Nelson, K. E. (1984). Recasting and related conversational techniques for triggering syntactic advances by young children. *First Language, 5*, 3–22.

Barnes, S., Gutfreund, M., Satterly, D., & Wells, G. (1983). Characteristics of adult speech which predict children's language development. *Journal of Child Language, 10*, 65–84.

Bates, E., Bretherton, I., & Snyder, L. (1988). *From first words to grammar: Individual differences and dissociable mechanisms*. New York: Cambridge University Press.

Bloom, L. (1991). *Language development from two to three*. New York: Cambridge University Press.

Bloom, L., Tinker, E., & Margulis, C. (1993). The words children learn: Evidence against a noun bias in early vocabularies. *Cognitive Development, 8*, 431–450.

Bohannon, J. N., Padgett, R. J., Nelson, K. E., & Mark, M. (1996). Useful evidence on negative evidence. *Developmental Psychology, 33*, 551–555.

Bohannon, N., & Stanowicz, L. (1989). Bidirectional effects of imitation and repetition in conversation: A synthesis within a cognitive model. In G. E. Speidel & K. E. Nelson (Eds.), *The many faces of imitation in language learning* (pp. 121–150). New York: Springer-Verlag.

Bonvillian, J. D., & Folven, R. (1993). Sign language acquisition: Developmental aspects. In M. Marschark & D. Clark (Eds.), *Psychological perspectives on deafness* (pp. 229–268). Hillsdale, NJ: Lawrence Erlbaum Associates.

Bonvillian, J. D., & Nelson, K. E. (1978). Development of sign languages in autistic children and other language-handicapped individuals. In P. Siple (Ed.), *Understanding language through sign language research* (pp. 121–150). New York: Academic Press.

Bonvillian, J. D., Nelson, K. E., & Charrow, V. R. (1976). Language and language-related skills. *Sign Language Studies, 12*, 211–250.

Bonvillian, J. D., Nelson, K. E., & Rhyne, J. M. (1981). Sign languages and autism. *Journal of Autism and Developmental Disorders, 11,* 125–137.

Bowerman, M. (1985). Beyond communicative adequacy: From piecemeal knowledge to an integrated system in the child's acquisition of language. In K. E. Nelson (Ed.), *Children's language: Vol. 5* (pp. 369–398). Hillsdale, NJ: Lawrence Erlbaum Associates.

Brown, R., Cazden, C., & Bellugi-Klima, U. (1969). The child's grammar from I to III. In J. P. Hill (Ed.), *Minnesota symposia on child psychology* (pp. 28–73). Minneapolis: University of Minnesota Press.

Camarata, S., & Nelson, K. E. (1992). Treatment efficiency as a function of target selection in the remediation of child language disorders. *Clinical Linguistics and Phonetics, 6,* 167–178.

Camarata, S., Nelson, K. E., & Camarata, M. (1994). A comparison of conversation based to imitation based procedures for training grammatical structures in specifically language impaired children. *Journal of Speech and Hearing Research, 37,* 1414–1423.

Carey, S. (1978). The child as word learner. In M. Halle, J. Bresnan, & G. A. Mutter (Eds.), *Linguistic theory and psychological reality.* Cambridge, MA: MIT Press.

Case, R.. (1985). *Intellectual development, birth to adulthood.* San Diego, CA: Academic Press.

Chomsky, N. (1968). *Languge and mind.* New York: Harcourt, Brace, Jovanovich.

Chomsky, N. (1986). *Knowledge of language: Its nature, origin, and use.* New York: Praeger.

Clark, E. V. (1981). Lexical innovations: How children learn to create new words. In W. Deutsch (Ed.), *The child's construction of language* (pp. 299–328). London: Academic Press.

Conti-Ramsden, G. (1990). Maternal recasts and other contingent replies to language-impaired children. *Journal of Speech and Hearing Disorders, 55,* 262–274.

Conti-Ramsden, G. , Hutcheson, G., & Grove, J. (1995). Contingency and breakdown: Children with SLI and their conversations with mothers and fathers. *Journal of Speech and Hearing Research, 38,* 1290–1302.

Cross, T. (1977). Mothers' speech adjustments: The contribution of selected child listener variables. In N. Waterson & C. Snow (Eds.), *The development of communication* (pp. 151–188). New York: John Wiley & Sons.

Cross, T. (1978). Mother's speech and its association with rate of syntactic acquisition in young children. In N. Waterson and C. Snow (Eds.), *The development of communication* (pp. 199–216). New York: John Wiley & Sons.

Cross, T., Nienhuys, T. G., & Kirkman, M. (1985). Parent-child interaction with receptively disabled children: Some determinants of maternal speech style. In K. E. Nelson (Ed.), *Children's language: Vol. 5* (pp. 247–296). Hillsdale, NJ: Lawrence Erlbaum Associates.

Csikszentmihalyi, M., & Csikszentmihalyi, I. (1988). *Optimal experience.* New York: HarperCollins.

de Villiers, J., de Villiers, P., & Hoban, E. (1994). The central problem of functional categories in the English syntax of oral deaf children. In H. Tager-Flusberg (Ed.), *Constraints on language acquisition: Studies of atypical children* (pp. 9–47). Hillsdale, NJ: Lawrence Erlbaum Associates.

Dollaghan, C. (1987). Fast mapping of normal and language-impaired children. *Journal of Speech and Hearing Disorders, 52,* 218–222.

Elman, J. L., Bates, E. A., Johnson, M. H., Karmiloff-Smith, A., Parisi, D., & Plunkett, K. (1996). *Rethinking innateness: A connectionist perspective on development.* Cambridge, MA: MIT Press.

Feldman, C. (1971). *The effects of various types of adult responses in the syntactic acquisition of two- to three-year-olds.* Unpublished manuscript, Department of Psychology, University of Chicago.

Farrar, M. J. (1992). Negative evidence and grammatical morpheme acquisition. *Developmental Psychology, 28,* 90–98.

Fenson, L., Dale, P. A., Reznick, J. S., Bates, E., & Thal, D. (1994). Variability in early communicative development. *Monographs of the Society for Research in Child Development, 58,* (5, Serial No. 242).

Fey, M. E., & Catts, H. (1998, June). *Can the language basis of reading disability be reduced to problems in phonological awareness? Evidence from a longitudinal investigation.* Paper presented at the Symposium on Research in Child Language Disorders, Madison, WI.

Fey, M. E., Cleave, P., & Long, S. (1997). Two models of grammar facilitation in children with language impairments: Phase 2. *Journal of Speech and Hearing Research, 40,* 5–19.

Fey, M. E., Cleave, P., Long, S., & Hughes, D. (1993). Two approaches to the facilitation of grammar in children with language impairment: An experimental evaluation. *Journal of Speech and Hearing Research, 36,* 141–157.

Fodor, J. A. (1983). *The modularity of mind: An essay on faculty psychology.* Cambridge, MA: MIT Press.

Fodor, J. A. (1985). Multiple book review of *The modularity of mind. Behavioral and Brain Sciences, 8,* 1–42.

Fox, N. A. (1994). Dynamic cerebral processes underlying emotion regulation. In N. A. Fox (Ed.), *The development of emotion regulation: Biological and behavioral considerations* (pp. 152–186). *Monographs of the Society for Research in Child Development, 59,* (Serial No. 240).

Furrow, D., Nelson, K., & Benedict, H. (1979). Mothers' speech to children and syntactic development: Some simple relationships. *Journal of Child Language, 6,* 423–442.

Gathercole, S. E., & Baddeley, A. (1993). *Working memory and language.* Hillsdale, NJ: Lawrence Erlbaum Associates.

Greenberg, M. T., Calderon, R, & Kusche, C. (1984). Early intervention using simultaneous communication with deaf infants: The effect on communicative development. *Child Development, 55,* 607–616.

Grimm, H. (1987). Developmental dysphasia: New theoretical perspectives and empirical results. *German Journal of Psychology, 11,* 8–22.

Haley, K., Camarata, S., & Nelson, K. E. (1994). Positive and negative social valence in children with specific language impairment during imitation based and conversation based language intervention. *Journal of Speech and Hearing Research, 37,* 141–148.

Hansson, K., Hellquist, B., Leonard, L., Nettelbladt, U., & Salameh, E. (1998, June). *Results from screening of phonology, grammar, and language comprehension: A report from an ongoing crosslinguistic project.* Paper presented at the Workshop of the European Child Language Disorders Group, Barcelona.

Hart, B., & Risley, T. R. (1995). *Meaningful differences in the everyday experience of young American children.* Baltimore: Brookes.

Heimann, M., Nelson, K. E., Gillberg, C., & Kärnevik, M. (1993). Facilitating language skills through interactive micro-computer instruction: Observations on seven children with autism. *Scandinavian Journal of Logopedics and Phoniatrics, 18,* 3–8.

Heimann, M., Nelson, K. E., Tjus, T., & Gillberg, C. (1995). Increasing reading and communication skills in children with autism through an interactive multimedia computer program. *Journal of Autism and Developmental Disorders, 25,* 459–480.

Hoff-Ginsberg, E. (1986). Function and structure in maternal speech: Their relation to the child's development of syntax. *Developmental Psychology, 22,* 155–163.

Kail, R. (1991). Developmental change in speed of processing during childhood and adolescence. *Psychological Bulletin, 109,* 490–501.

Kaiser, A. (1993). Parent-implemented language intervention: An environmental system perspective. In A. Kaiser & D. Gray (Eds.), *Enhancing children's communication* (pp. 63–84). Baltimore: Brookes.

Kaiser, A., Yoder, P. J., & Keetz, A. (1992). Evaluating milieu teaching. In S. F. Warren & J. Reichle (Eds.), *Causes and effects in communication and language intervention* (pp. 9–47). Baltimore: Brookes.

Koegel, R., & Koegel, L. (1995). *Teaching children with autism.* Baltimore: Brookes.

Lederberg, A. (1993). The impact of deafness on mother–child and peer relationships. In M. Marschark & D. Clark (Eds.), *Psychological perspectives on deafness* (pp. 93–121). Hillsdale, NJ: Lawrence Erlbaum Associates.

Leonard, L. B. (1998). *Children with specific language impairment.* Cambridge, MA: MIT Press.

Leonard, L. B., & Schwartz, R. G. (1985). Early linguistic development of children with specific language impairment. In K. E. Nelson (Ed.), *Children's language, vol. 5* (pp. 291–318). Hillsdale, NJ: Erlbaum.

Leopold, W. F. (1939). *Speech development of a bilingual child: A linguist's record. Vocabulary growth in the first two years.* Evanston, IL.: Northwestern University Press.

Lepper, M., Woolverton, M., Mumme, D. L., & Gurtner, J. L. (1993). Motivational techniques of expert human tutors: Lessons for the design of computer-based tutors. In S. P. Lajoie & S. J. Derry (Eds.), *Computers as cognitive tool* (pp. 75–105). Hillsdale, NJ: Lawrence Erlbaum Associates.

Lightfoot, D. (1989). The child's trigger experience: Degree-0 learnability. *Behavioral and Brain Sciences, 12,* 321–375.

Maratsos, M. P., & Chalkley, M. (1980). The internal language of children's syntax: The ontogenesis and representation of syntactic categorires. In K. E. Nelson (Ed.), *Children's language: Vol. 2* (pp. 127–214). Hillsdale, NJ: Lawrence Erlbaum Associates.

Maxwell, M. (1983). Language acquisition in a deaf child of deaf parents: Speech, sign variations, and print variations. In K. E. Nelson (Ed.), *Children's language: Vol. 4* (pp. 283–314). Hillsdale, NJ: Lawrence Erlbaum Associates.

McTear, M., & Conti-Ramsden, G. (1992). *Pragmatic disability in children.* Chichester, England: Ellis Horwood.

Meadow, K., Greenberg, M. T., Erting, C., & Carmichael, H. (1981). Interaction of deaf mothers and deaf preschool children: Comparisons of three groups of deaf and hearing dyads. *American Annals of the Deaf, 126,* 454–468.

Mervis, C. B., & Pani, J. R. (1980). Acquisition of basic object categories. *Cognitive Psychology, 12,* 496–522.

Moores, D. F. (1978). *Educating the deaf.* Boston: Houghton Mifflin.

Moores, D. F. (1985). Early intervention programs for hearing impaired children: A longitudinal assessment. In K. E. Nelson (Ed.), *Children's language: Vol. 5* (pp. 159–196). Hillsdale, NJ: Lawrence Erlbaum Associates.

Nelson, K. (1973). Structure and strategy in learning to talk. *Monographs of the Society for Research in Child Development, 38* (149), 1–2.

Nelson, K. E. (1977). Facilitating children's syntax acquisition. *Developmental Psychology, 13,* 101–107.

Nelson, K. E. (1980). Theories of the child's acquisition of syntax: A look at rare events and at necessary, catalytic, and irrelevant components of mother–child conversation. *Annals of the New York Academy of Sciences, 345,* 45–67.

Nelson, K. E. (1981). Toward a rare-event cognitive comparison theory of syntax acquisition. In P. S. Dale & D. Ingram (Eds.), *Child language: An international perspective* (pp. 229–240). Baltimore: University Park Press.

Nelson, K. E. (1982). Experimental gambits in the service of language acquisition theory. In S. A. Kuczaj (Ed.), *Language development, syntax and semantics* (pp. 159–199). Hillsdale, NJ: Lawrence Erlbaum Associates.

Nelson, K. E. (1987). Some observations from the perspective of the rare event cognitive comparison theory of language acquisition. In K. E. Nelson (Ed.), *Children's language: Vol. 6* (pp. 289–331). Hillsdale, NJ: Lawrence Erlbaum Associates.

Nelson, K. E. (1989). Strategies for first language teaching. In M. Rice & R. Schiefelbusch (Eds.), *The teachability of language* (pp. 263–310). Baltimore: Brookes.

Nelson, K. E. (1991a). On differentiated language learning models and differentiated interventions. In N. Krasnegor, D. Rumbaugh, & R. Schiefelbusch (Eds.), *Language acquisition: Biological and behavioral determinants* (pp. 399–428). Hillsdale, NJ.: Lawrence Erlbaum Associates.

Nelson, K. E. (1991b). Varied domains of development: A tale of LAD, MAD, SAD, DAD, and RARE and surprising events in our RELMS. In F. S. Kessel, M. H. Bornstein, & A. J. Sameroff (Eds.), *Contemporary constructions of the child: Essays in honor of William Kessen* (pp. 123–142). Hillsdale, NJ: Lawrence Erlbaum Associates.

Nelson, K. E. (1998). Toward a differentiated account of facilitators of literacy development and ASL in deaf children. *Topics in Language Disorders, 18,* 73–88.

Nelson, K. E., Baker, N. A., Denninger, M., Bonvillian, J., & Kaplan, B. (1985). Cookie versus do-it-again: Imitative-referential and personal-social-syntactic-inititating language styles in young children. *Linguistics, 23,* 433–454.

Nelson, K. E., & Bonvillian, J. D. (1973). Concepts and words in the two-year-old: Acquisition of concept names under controlled conditions. *Cognition, 2,* 435–450.

Nelson, K. E., & Bonvillian, J. D. (1978). Early language development: Conceptual growth and related processes between 2 and 4 1/2 years of age. In K. E. Nelson (Ed.), *Children's language: Vol. 1* (pp. 467–556). New York: Gardner Press.

Nelson, K. E., & Camarata, S. M. (1997). Improving learning conditions for English literacy and English speech acquisition by severely to profoundly deaf children. *Volta Review, 98,* 17–41.

Nelson, K. E., Camarata, S. M., Welsh, J., Butkovsky, L., & Camarata, M. (1996). Effects of imitative and conversational recasting treatment on the acquisition of grammar in children with Specific Language Impairment and younger language-normal children. *Journal of Speech and Hearing Research, 39,* 850–859.

Nelson, K. E., Carskaddon, G., & Bonvillian, J. D. (1973). Syntax acquisition: Impact of experimental variation in adult verbal interaction with the child. *Child Development, 44,* 497–504.

Nelson, K. E., Denninger, M. M., Bonvillian, J. D., Kaplan, B. J., & Baker, N. D. (1984). Maternal adjustments and non-adjustments as related to children's linguistic advances and to language acquisition theories. In A. D. Pellegrini & T. D. Yawkey (Eds.), *The development of oral and written language: Readings in developmental and applied linguistics* (pp. 31–56). New York: Ablex.

Nelson, K. E., Heimann, M., Abuelhaija, L., & Wroblewski, R. (1989). Implications for language acquisition models of children's and parents' variations in imitation. In G. E. Speidel & K. E. Nelson (Eds.), *The many faces of imitation in language learning.* New York: Springer-Verlag.

Nelson, K. E., Heimann, M., & Tjus, T. (1997). Theoretical and applied insights from multimedia facilitation of communication skills in children with autism, deaf children, and children with motor or learning disabilities. In L. B. Adamson & M. A. Romski (Eds.), *Research on communication and language disorders: Contributions to theories of language development* (pp. 296–325). Baltimore: Brookes.

Nelson, K. E., Loncke, F., & Camarata, S. (1993). Implications of research on deaf and hearing children's language learning. In M. Marschark & D. Clark (Eds.), *Psychological perspectives on deafness* (pp. 123–151). Hillsdale, NJ: Lawrence Erlbaum Associates.

Nelson, K. E., & Nelson, K. (1978). Cognitive pendulums and their linguistic realization. In K. E. Nelson (Ed.), *Children's language: Vol. 1* (pp. 223–286). Hillsdale, NJ: Lawrence Erlbaum Associates.

Nelson, K. E., Perkins, D., & Lepper, M. (1997). *Accelerating learning: Why significant learning is rare and what to do about it.* Unpublished manuscript, Pennsylvania State University, University Park.

Nelson, K. E., Prinz, P. M., Prinz, E. A., & Dalke, D. (1991). Processes for text and language acquisition in the context of microcomputer-videodisc instruction for deaf and multihandicapped deaf children. In D. S. Martin (ed.), *Advances in cognition, education, and deafness* (pp. 162–169). Washington, DC: Gaullaudet University Press.

Nelson, K. E., & Welsh, J. A. (1998). Progress in multiple language domains by deaf children and hearing children: Discussions with a Rare Event Transactional Model. In R. Paul (Ed.), *The Speech/Language Connection* (pp. 179–225). Baltimore: Brookes.

Nelson, K. E., Welsh, J. A., Camarata, S., Heimann, & Tjus, T. (1996). A rare event transactional model of language delay. Paper presented to the International Association for the Study of Child Language, Istanbul, Turkey.

Nelson, K. E., Welsh, J. A., Camarata, S., Heimann, M. & Tjus, T. (1999). A rare event transactional dynamic model of tricky mix conditions contributing to language acquisition and varied communicative delays. In K. E. Nelson, A. Koc, & C. Johnson (Eds.), *Children's language, Vol. 11,* to appear. Mahwah, NJ: Lawrence Erlbaum Associates.

Nelson, K. E., Welsh, J. A., Camarata, S. M., Butkovsky, L., & Camarata, M. (1995). Available input and available language learning mechanisms for specifically language-delayed and language-normal children. *First Language, 15,* 1–17.

Pierart, B., & Harmegnies, B. (1993). Dysphasie simple de l'enfant et langage de la mère. *L'Année Psychologique, 93,* 227–268.

Pinker, S. (1994). *The language instinct.* Cambridge, MA: MIT Press.

Prinz, P. M., & Masin, L. (1985). Lending a helping hand: Linguistic input and sign language acquisition. *Applied Psycholinguistics, 6,* 357–370.

Prinz, P. M., Nelson, K. E., Loncke, F., Geysels, G., & Willems, C. (1993). A multimodality and multimedia approach to language, discourse, and literacy development. In B. A. G. Elsendoorn & F. Coninx (Eds.), *Interactive learning technology for the deaf* (pp. 55–70). Berlin: Springer-Verlag.

Prinz, P. M., & Prinz, E. A. (1981). Acquisition of ASL and spoken English by a hearing child of a deaf mother and a hearing father: Phase II, early combinatorial patterns. *Sign Language Studies, 30,* 78–88.

Prinz, P. M., & Strong, M. (1998). ASL proficiency and English literacy within a bilingual deaf education model of instruction. *Topics in Language Disorders, 18,* 47–60.

Ratner, N B. (1996). From "Signal to Syntax:" But what is the nature of the signal? In J. Morgan & K. Demuth (Eds.), *From signal to syntax* (pp. 1–17). Mahwah, NJ: Lawrence Erlbaum Associates.

Ray, W. J. (1993). *Methods: Toward a science of behavior and experience.* Pacific Grove, CA: Brooks/Cole.

Records, N., Tomblin, J., & Freese, P. (1992). The quality of life of young adults with histories of specific language impairment. *American Journal of Speech-Language Pathology, 1,* 44–53.

Rice, M., Buhr, J., & Nemeth, M. (1990). Fast mapping word learning abilities of language delayed preschoolers. *Journal of Speech and Hearing Disorders, 55,* 33–42.

Rice, M. L., Oetting, J. B., Marquis, J., Bode, J., & Pae, J. S. (1994). Frequency of input effects on word comprehension of children with specific language impairment. *Journal of Speech and Hearing Research, 37,* 106–122.

Sameroff, A. J., & Chandler, M. (1975). Reproductive risk and the continuum of caretaker casualty. In F. Horowitz & M. Hetherington (Eds.), *Review of child development research: Vol. 4* (pp. 187–243). Chicago: University of Chicago Press.

Sameroff, A., & Fiese, B. (1989). Transactional regulation and early intervention. In S. J. Meisels & J. Shonkoff (Eds.), *Early intervention: A handbook of theory, practice, and analysis.* New York: Cambridge University Press.

Scherer, N. J., & Olswang, L. B. (1984). Role of mothers' expansions in stimulating children's language production. *Journal of Speech and Hearing Disorders, 27,* 387–396.

Schlesinger, H. S., & Meadow, K. (1976). *Studies of family interaction, language acquisition, and deafness.* San Francisco: University of California Press.

Schodorf, J., & Edwards, H. (1983). Comparative analysis of parent-child interactions with language-disordered and linguistically normal children. *Journal of Communication Disorders, 16,* 71–83.

Siegler, R. S. (1991). *Children's thinking.* Englewood Cliffs, NJ: Prentice-Hall.

Slobin, D. (1973). Cognitive prerequisites for the development of grammar. In C. Ferguson & D. I. Slobin (Eds.), *Studies of child language development* (pp. 175–208). New York: Holt, Rinehart, & Winston.

Slobin, D. I. (1985). Crosslinguistic evidence for the language-making capacity. In D. I. Slobin (Ed.), *The crosslinguistic study of language acquisition* (pp. 1157–1256). Hillsdale, NJ: Lawrence Erlbaum Associatesiates.

Snow, C. E., Perlmann, R., & Nathan, D. (1987). Why routines are different: Toward a multiple-factors model of the relation between input and language acquisition. In K. E. Nelson (Ed.), *Children's language: Vol. 6* (pp. 65–98). Hillsdale, NJ: Lawrence Erlbaum Associates.

Stothard, S. E., Snowling, M. J., Bishop, D. V. M., Chipchase, B. B., & Kaplan, C. A. (1998). Language-impaired preschoolers: A follow-up into adolescence. *Journal of Speech and Hearing Research, 40,* 407–418.

Tallal, P., Stark, R., & Curtiss, S. (1976). The relation between speech perception impairment and speech production impairment in children with developmental dysphasia. *Brain and Language, 3,* 305–317.

Thelen, E., & Smith, L. B. (1994). *A dynamic systems approach to the development of cognition and action.* Cambridge, MA: MIT Press.

Wells, G. (1985). Preschool literacy-related activities and success in school. In D. R. Olson, N. Torrance, & A. Hildyard (Eds.), *Literacy, language, and learning: The nature and consequences of reading and writing* (pp. 229–255). Cambridge: Cambridge University Press.

Yoder, P. (1989). Maternal question use predicts later language development in specific language disordered children. *Journal of Speech and Hearing Disorders, 54,* 347–355.

8

Eliciting Second Language Speech Data

Catherine Doughty
Georgetown University

Michael H. Long
University of Hawaii

Second Language (L2) researchers employ many of the same procedures as their first language (L1) counterparts for eliciting speech data. However, common characteristics of L2 subjects, who tend to be older children or adults, can extend the range of methodological options in some cases and cause problems in others. After considering learner variables of these kinds, we focus on three L2 research domains in which promising procedures are being refined for describing L2 speech production and/or for understanding production-related aspects of L2 acquisition: developmental linguistic profiling, descriptive linguistic profiling, and documenting the role of language production in acquisition.

Although researchers in first and second language acquisition employ many of the same procedures for eliciting speech samples, and the same criteria when developing and assessing the reliability, validity and appropriateness of new instruments and measures (see, e.g., Chaudron, Crookes, & Long, 1988; Gallimore & Tharp, 1981), methodological modifications can be required if, as is frequently the case, the L2 subjects are older children or adults. Depending on the precise ages and values of the other variables involved, the procedures used and/or the variants thereof may need to reflect such matters as older learners' typically greater cognitive maturity, attention span, short-term memory, metalinguistic awareness, and test-wiseness, as well as possible cultural differences, the presence of one or more additional languages in the mix, and the broader range of linguistic features and abilities targeted in many L2 studies. Some of these and other variables can generally facilitate data collection and analysis, whereas others make them more problematic. Table 8.1 indicates the variety of speech elicitation procedures used in second language acquisition (SLA) research, listed roughly in descending order both from most to least constraining on subjects' production, and (potentially, at least) from most to least linguistically focused. References in the table are first to methodological surveys, where available, and then to a representative study (often only one of many reported in the L2 literature) utilizing each procedure.

METHODOLOGICAL IMPLICATIONS OF SOME COMMON L2 LEARNER CHARACTERISTICS

Some common characteristics of older L2 subjects offer investigators increased methodological flexibility. L1 and/or L2 literacy, for example, provide L2 researchers with options, such as reading aloud, that are sometimes unavailable to their L1 counterparts. Reading aloud word lists, dialogues, or short passages that have been seeded with target sounds, often as one of a battery of tasks, has been an especially useful procedure with both older children and adults in certain kinds of developmental and variationist L2 phonology studies (see, e.g., Dickerson, 1975; Major, 1987; Sato, 1984, 1985), as well as in studies of the effects of age of onset and putative sensitive periods on ultimate attainment in L2 phonology (e.g., Bongaerts, van Summeren, Planken, & Schils, 1997; Thompson, 1991). Also capitalizing on subject literacy, almost all studies of interlanguage pragmatics that use discourse completion as an elicitation device have presented subjects with written sociolinguistic vignettes (see Kasper & Dahl, 1991, pp. 221–226) and then had subjects write down what they thought they would say in those situations when requesting, complaining, refusing, and so forth.

More generally, working with subjects who are literate offers investigators additional scope in both the content of elicitation tasks and the delivery of instructions for their performance; the same task type may some-

TABLE 8.1
L2 Speech Elicitation Procedures

Procedure	Survey Reference	Sample Study
Reading aloud	Tarone (1979)	Dickerson (1975)
Utterance completion	Henning (1983)	Fathman (1975)
Elicited imitation	Bley-Vroman & Chaudron (1994)	Naiman (1974)
Elicited translation		Swain, Dumas, & Naiman (1974)
Word association		Soderman (1993)
Picture + oral prompt		Dulay & Burt (1974)
Discourse completion	Kasper & Dahl (1991)	Banerjee & Carrell (1988)
Dictogloss		Swain (1998)
Picture description		Hyltenstam (1984)
Story retelling		Hyltenstam (1988)
Video retelling		Klein & Purdue (1992)
Communication task (a) structure-focused (b) meaning-focused	Yule (1997) Pienemann (1998) Pica et al. (1993)	Lightbown (1983) Pica, Young, & Doughty (1987)
Role play	Kasper & Dahl (1991)	Walters (1979)
Interview schedule	*Studies in Second Language Acquisition,* 1988, 10(2)	Larsen-Freeman (1983)
Structured interview	*Studies in Second Language Acquisition,* 1988, 10(2)	Doughty et al. (1997)
SOPI	Shohamy (1994)	Norris (1996)
OPI	Young (1995)	Ross (1995)
Unstructured interview	Wolfson (1976)	Johnston (1985)
Spontaneous speech	Wolfson (1986)	Sato (1990)

times be usable with younger children, but less efficiently so or with greater difficulty. The Simulated Oral Proficiency Interview (SOPI), for example, is a standardized, pre-recorded oral interview procedure (supposedly) measuring L2 proficiency, available in various foreign languages, which testees can undergo without leaving their educational or work setting before submitting the audiotape of their performance for assessment by trained raters. Similarly, where withdrawing the researcher from the immediate scene has been felt likely to relax subjects and enhance the spontaneity of L2 conversational data, it has been possible to leave literate adults alone in a room for 30 minutes or more, tape recorder running, with booklets containing written instructions and materials for a series of complex tasks, as in Long (1983): conducting informal conversation, experiencing vicarious narrative, giving instructions for two meaning-focused communication tasks, doing the first task (Spot the Difference), doing the second task (Odd Man Out), and discussing the supposed purpose of the research. By way of contrast, in a study of negative feedback in child SLA (Oliver, 1995), when the researcher left the room while pairs of younger children (age 8 to 13) worked on a meaning-focused communication task, knowing that they were being video-recorded, a few children were captured on film promptly cheating—holding up cut-outs above the screen so that their partners could see them, instead of having to identify them from verbal descriptions, and sometimes glancing furtively into the video camera as they did so (Oliver, p.c.). (This is not to suggest that all children cheat whereas all adults are paragons of virtue, of course.)

Increased age and cognitive maturity can free both subjects and researchers from here-and-now constraints, making viable such tasks as describing movie plot-lines or recounting frightening experiences. The effect on L2 speech accuracy, fluency, and syntactic complexity of narrating the same story in the here-and-now or there-and-then (operationalized as presence and absence of visual support in the form of a cartoon strip story and/or an oral prompt to establish time reference) has itself become the focus of some studies (e.g., Robinson, 1995; Robinson, Ting, & Irwin, 1995). General findings are that an orientation to displaced time and space results in trends toward lesser fluency but greater accuracy and complexity of output. Other things being equal, age and cognitive maturity also bring improvements in a subject's general understanding of what is sought by a researcher or required by a speech elicitation task or task-type. Thus, a particular task (e.g., recording instructions for an unseen listener on how to assemble a Lego house) and/or task condition (e.g., performing the Lego instructions task after first spending 10 minutes planning what to say and how to say it, including making written notes, but notes to which subjects are told they will not have access when making the recording [one of the tasks and task conditions used by Crookes, 1989]) could only be meaningful to an older child or adult, quite apart from whether or not the younger child was literate.

A whole range of task-types may not be usable with some younger children at all, yet these have been employed successfully with L2 subjects of greater cognitive maturity and metalinguistic awareness. These include word association (Soderman, 1993; Spadaro, 1998), discourse completion (Banerjee & Carrell, 1988), story retelling (Larsen-Freeman, 1983), video retelling (Fernandez, Gass, Mackey, Plough, & Polio, 1998), various kinds of oral proficiency tests (Shohamy, 1994), and interviews (Johnston, 1985). Some variants of the first three procedures require either L1 or L2 literacy of subjects, however, which is not always present in adult L2 learners either. Surprisingly, word association appears only to have been used in written form in L2 work to date, and discourse completion only in written form in all but one case (Rintell & Mitchell, 1989). The advantages offered by some forms of metalinguistic awareness not only for producing but also for evaluating L2 speech were evident in a cleverly designed study of the ontogeny of the ability to recognize a spoken or written foreign accent (Scovel, 1981). The youngest children the researcher could get to understand an accent-rating task were age 5. Older NS children, adult NSs, adult NNSs, and adult aphasics, conversely, had no problem with the task. In fact, Scovel was able to show that the ability to distinguish NSs and NNSs on the basis of 28-second read-aloud taped speech samples (but not considerably longer written samples from the same subjects, where avoidance and monitoring were possible) matured from 73% accuracy at age 5 to near perfection (97% accuracy) by age 10. The adult NNSs improved with increasing ESL proficiency, but only to 77%, which was comparable to the 5-year-old child NSs' performance and poorer than the aphasic group's mean of 85%.

Greater cognitive maturity and life experience also increase (a) the intellectual challenge a task or task-type can involve, and (b) the knowledge of the world researchers may assume when designing a study. For example, Charlie Chaplin's *Modern Times* has been used successfully as the stimulus for written narratives in a Swedish study of maturational constraints on SLA (Hyltenstam, 1988), and other L2 researchers (Doughty, Byrnes, Connor-Linton, Spielmann, & Tyler, 1997; Fernandez et al., 1998; Klein & Perdue, 1992) have used excerpts from Rowan Atkinson's Mr. Bean series or the Chaplin film as stimuli for oral video-retelling tasks with young adults (see Example 2 in subsequent discussion), despite the life experience required to follow the stories and especially to appreciate the humor and pathos depicted.

Most adults' superior memory and attention span allow researchers greater leeway, too. This can be seen at the macro level in the use of the retelling tasks referred to previously, which are often quite lengthy and complex; in the use of whole batteries of tasks and tests in a single session (e.g., Ortega & Long, 1997); and in the use of interviews lasting an hour or more in some studies (e.g., Johnston, 1985). At the micro level, improved short-term memory and attention span permits (and, given the reconstructive nature of valid elicited imitation tasks, requires) the use of longer utterances as items for older children and adults, which in turn allows researchers to test L2 subjects' control of more complex grammatical constructions relatively easily and efficiently. This is especially valuable with optional constructions such as conditionals, passives, wh-questions, and relative clauses (see, e.g., Munnich, Flynn, & Martohardjono, 1994; Perkins, Brutten, & Angelis, 1986), which may occur very infrequently, if at all, in hours of spontaneous speech. Relative clauses, for example, otherwise require painstaking use of a combination of carefully designed pictures and oral prompts (Doughty, 1991; Hyltenstam, 1984) or of even more artificial "language-like" tasks, such as sentence combining (Gass, 1982).

These are just some of the ways in which literacy, cognitive maturity, metalinguistic awareness, life experience, memory, and attention span can facilitate data collection in L2 studies. Not all common L2 subject characteristics make life easier for researchers, however. Cultural differences often determine whether a procedure, such as the interview, can be used at all, or the degree of success likely. These differences often co-occur with variation in subjects' educational experiences. The latter may not have been with formal education, for example, and certainly may not have included encounters with such procedures as word association, discourse completion, communication tasks, role play, or oral proficiency tests. This can result in such devices being unusable or at least requiring (a) training in the procedures themselves before data can be collected with them, and/or (b) adjustments in the way they are employed (e.g., in the degree of formality of their administration).

Some usually advantageous L2 subject characteristics can be a mixed blessing. Thus, metalinguistic awareness facilitates use of word association, discourse completion, and other task types, but it also burdens researchers with ascertaining whether samples of L2 speech reflect what Labov (1969, and elsewhere) called the basic vernacular style as opposed to other, more "monitored" speech styles (for discussion, see Tarone, 1979, 1988). The effects of attention to speech arising from this ("small m") monitoring may lead, among other things, to intra-subject variation across tasks A and B at times 1 and 2 being confused or confounded with development or regression. The problem can be compounded in L2 research by a more restricted sort of ("large m") Monitoring (Krashen, 1977a, and elsewhere), that is, the use of conscious knowledge of low-level grammatical L2 rules to "edit" performance initiated on the basis of subconscious, implicit L2 knowledge.

Sociolinguists have long questioned the idea that speakers have just one vernacular speech style in Labov's sense, or indeed that formality of style is a function of attention to speech (see, e.g., the critique in Wolfson, 1976, pp. 203–206). Similarly, few SLA researchers accept Krashen's simple bimodal (+/- Monitor) dichotomy as adequate to account for variation in L2 production (for counterevidence, see, e.g., Tarone, 1983), much less Krashen's overall Monitor theory of SLA, of which Monitoring soon became a rather minor part. Many would probably still agree with Krashen, however, that certain kinds of tasks (e.g., discrete-point grammar tests or role plays) performed under certain conditions (e.g., unspeeded and after planning) lead at least some L2 speakers to modify their performance in ways that could be highly undesirable in studies addressing certain research questions.

An example of Monitoring in Krashen's sense is that of learners who know, and can access and apply, grammar rules for simple alternations such as English *a/an* or third person *-s*. They may apply this knowledge while preparing for a role play or a telephone call, or while responding to a simple utterance-completion item or taking part in an oral proficiency interview, and thereby improve their performance, producing, say, *an egg* or *he works* instead of *a egg* or *he work*, which they might say in a hurried (and so, not Monitorable) conversation in which they were attending to message content, not form. Another example would be learners who, aware of a lexical gap or grammatical lacuna in their L2, and being both metalinguistically aware and test-wise, proceed to circumlocute or even alter the message itself to avoid the linguistic problems—resulting in occasions when the absence of items in the data really may reflect ignorance. Such metalinguistic intrusions on normal interlanguage performance (in that instance, in the form of improved accuracy on "easy" plural and third person *-s*) were argued by Krashen (1977b) to account for the "disturbed" morpheme accuracy orders on some tasks reported for adult learners by Larsen-Freeman (1975), thereby disposing of apparent counterevidence to the claim for invariant L2 orders. The use of metalinguistic knowledge that is possible on some elicitation tasks, but not on others, could equally easily affect results in studies of such issues as L2 developmental sequences, the role of synchronic variation in interlanguage change over time, stabilization and (putative) fossilization, and the assessment of learner proficiency. Moreover, although several task-types in Table 8.1, including reading aloud, elicited translation, discourse completion, story retelling, and most interviews, are obviously susceptible to these kinds of "noise" (i.e., two kinds of monitoring and/or avoidance), several others, including picture description, video retelling, and role play, could also be affected if performed under certain conditions, such as after planning or practice of various kinds (Crookes, 1989, 1991; Ortega, 1997). In general, controlling for both task and task condition is even more important for synchronic or diachronic, intra- or inter-learner comparisons than is the case in any other kind of research.

Metalinguistic awareness can be problematic in other ways. Greater awareness of self and of complex status differences involving age, gender, power, and solidarity may, in turn, result in systematic variation in L2 production (e.g., in politeness), and this can show up differentially in elicited and "natural" speech (Wolfson, 1986). Wolfson strongly recommended that researchers begin with qualitative methods, especially nonintrusive observation of spontaneous speech, only then resorting to elicited data and quantification, and often recycling back and forth between qualitative and quantitative data and analyses. The problem in L2 research, however, is that cultural differences between researcher and subjects can make collection of spontaneous speech even trickier than in L1 acquisition research. Cultural differences may influence such matters as what someone considers appropriate speech behavior in an interview, for instance, what is considered a relevant response, or whether the interview is a familiar speech event at all (Wolfson, 1976). Even in cases where interviewer and interviewee are from the same cultural background, and one in which the interview is a recognized speech event, Wolfson showed that the data obtained differ from "natural speech" in important ways. The topics of narratives (often what interviewers wish to elicit from NNSs in L2 studies, e.g., when focusing on tense-aspect-modality systems) are usefully introduced by speakers themselves in natural speech, not by a questioner, as is typically the case in the question-answer format of interviews ("Have you ever had a frightening experience?"). The aspects of stories that interviewees emphasize as a result, and the language they use to do so (e.g., the conversational historical present—frequent in natural speech, rare in interviews) also differ. As Wolfson (1976) put it, in interview narratives "[T]he action is reported and summarized but not performed" (p. 194). Efforts to convert interviews into "spontaneous conversations," she noted, also often failed and were in any case unnatural (violations of the rules for interviews), and the use of group sessions was little more effective.

Natural speech, Wolfson argued, is really no more or less than appropriate speech—appropriate for the situation in which it occurs, varying systematically according to speaker, listener, setting, topic, and other factors, and for speech event. Interviews, at best, are sources of data on appropriate speech for interviews, an alien speech event for NNSs from many cultural backgrounds; it is unjustified, therefore, to assume that results there will reflect the same speakers' speech anywhere else. The only guaranteed way of obtaining the elusive "natural" data sought by so many researchers, Wolfson suggested, is through simple, nonintrusive observation using multiple samples on the same speakers in as many and as varied settings as possible (the researcher's own friends and acquaintances often provide the most likely candidates for frequent observation in that number and variety of settings). Unfortunately, very few L2 studies have been comprehensive enough, lasted long enough, or involved such relationships of friendship. One that did meet those criteria, however, as well as Wolfson's requirements for speech sampling, was Sato's longitudinal study of two Vietnamese brothers acquiring English naturalistically in Philadelphia. Accepted as a family friend by both the boys and their American foster parents for over a decade, Sato focused on several aspects of the children's phonology (Sato, 1984, 1985), the role of conversation in grammatical development (e.g., in the grammaticization of past time reference; Sato, 1986), and precursors to complex syntax (Sato, 1988). Sato also examined intra- and inter-subject synchronic variation and development over time. She used three elicitation procedures to do so throughout the study: reading a text aloud, elicited imitation of words and phrases, and spontaneous speech. The last involved extensive recordings of the boys in conversations with a range of interlocutors in the home, over meals, doing homework, during car journeys, on day trips, at soccer games, on vacation, and elsewhere (for results from the first year, see Sato, 1990).

L2 PRODUCTION:
DATA AND THEORY

Perhaps the most salient difference between normal child language acquisition and adult SLA is the level of ultimate attainment. Native-like spoken production is an elusive goal for almost all (and some researchers say all) adult L2 learners. Particularly in classroom SLA, oral fluency is

the most difficult aspect of the L2 to achieve. Given the gulf that typically exists between adult spoken L2 production and the more receptive
L2 abilities, moreover, the all-too-frequently used measures of comprehension, recognition, intuition, and/or metalinguistic awareness must be
seen only to reveal a portion of overall L2 ability, and the findings of
receptive measures of L2 ability cannot be assumed to reflect productive
ability. For these and other reasons, SLA researchers are becoming
increasingly interested in studying L2 production in greater depth and in
its own right.

Whereas many of the procedures listed in Table 8.1 can be incorporated into a variety of study designs for a range of purposes (see the survey references, and the sample study listed for each procedure in the
table), this section focuses on three examples that illustrate research on
L2 language production in light of recent attention to describing L2 use
comprehensively, and with a view to understanding processes of SLA that
might be dependent on L2 production. The first two examples are taken
from an approach to characterizing language ability, either developmentally or descriptively, known as linguistic profiling. The developmental
approach is theory-driven, based on a theory of SLA that is reflected in a
known developmental sequence, and the predictions of which can be
tested using profiling tasks and procedures. In contrast, as will be seen in
subsequent discussion, the descriptive profiling approach is data-driven,
always starting from the L2 production data, used to formulate a functional theory of SLA in the European Science Foundation (ESF) project
and to describe the L2 use of a particular group of interest, advanced L2
learners, in Georgetown University's Foreign Language Initiatives in
Research and Teaching (FLIRT) project. The third example documents
the development of tasks and procedures used in a line of research, some
(but not all) exponents of which postulate an integral role for L2 production in the SLA process itself, generally known as the Interactionist
Model of SLA. In such studies it is assumed that L2 production is essential, or at least facilitative, for SLA, so both the empirical tasks and the
L2 assessment measures (sometimes one and the same) primarily investigate language production data using a range of discourse analytic procedures. All the examples of linguistic profiling for the study of L2 language production, as well as of interactional discourse analyses that aim
to reveal SLA processes, are discussed very briefly in terms of the relevant SLA theoretical construct(s) assumed and the criteria applied to
assess L2 learners' ability. However, the primary aim of this section is to
exemplify the types of tasks used to collect the L2 production data.

Example 1: Developmental Linguistic Profiling

The developmental approach to linguistic profiling is the one taken in Pienemann's (1998) processability theory, an explanation of SLA that expands extensively on his earlier collaborative work on the Multidimensional Model (Meisel, Clahsen, & Pienemann, 1981), which, among other things, posited a hierarchically arranged set of processing constraints on L2 performance. The aim of processability theory is to answer the question: What causes development of [L2] competence to follow a describable route? This is what Pienemann calls the development problem (1998, p. 16). The construct that is assumed in this theory is that language processing mechanisms constrain SLA. Accordingly, production data are seen to be ideal in the sense that specifiable and predictable features in the language sample embody the effects of the processing constraints. The underlying developmental sequence for SLA in processability theory is morphosyntactic and is based on cross-sectional and longitudinal studies of the acquisition of German, English, Swedish, and Japanese as second languages. In both the Processing Constraints and the Processability versions of Pienemann's theory, the fundamental notion of L2 development is implicational, which can best be represented as continuous stages of development. Put very simply, each successive stage of development requires the processing ability of all the previous stages, such that L2 ability at any one stage implies the existence of L2 ability at all earlier stages. Tables 8.2 and 8.3 provide schematic characterizations of the stages in each version of the theory.

Although the theoretical explanation for the developmental sequence has evolved considerably from one version of the theory to the next, it is important to note that both attempt to explain the same set of observations (i.e., the morphosyntactic features that appear at each stage of development). Table 8.4 exemplifies the L2 developmental sequence with English morphosyntax.

With this background, three important methodological considerations that have arisen during the construction of the processability theory of SLA may now be discussed: the emergence criterion, the structure-targeting problem, and the feasibility of the approach for language ability assessment. It has long been known that accuracy (typically expressed as correct suppliance in obligatory linguistic contexts) is not the best measure of L2 production ability. SLA is complex, parallel, and nonlinear. More often than not, it does not reach the criterion of complete accuracy (in the sense of matching the native-like norm—what is sometimes called mastery) in any reasonably short period, if at

TABLE 8.2
Constraints and Developmental Stages in the
Multidimensional Model

Stage of Development		Rule in Evidence in L2 Data	Processing Constraints
Stage 1	pre-x	single words	chunking
Stage 2	x	canonical order	+ canonical order strategy + subordinate clause strategy
Stage 3	x + 1	adverb preposing	+ canonical order strategy + subordinate clause strategy + initialization - finalization strategy
Stage 4	x + 2	verb separation	- canonical order strategy + subordinate clause strategy + initialization - finalization strategy
Stage 5	x + 3	inversion	- canonical order strategy + subordinate clause strategy - initialization-finalization strategy
Stage 6	x + 4	verb final	- canonical order strategy - subordinate clause strategy - initialization - finalization strategy

Note. For a detailed discussion, see Pienemann 1998: 45–47.

TABLE 8.3
Constraints and Developmental Stages in
Processability Theory

Stage of Development	Processing Resources
Stage 1	• No sequence of constituents
Stage 2	• No exchange of information (canonical order or morphological flags for semantic roles) • Use of local information
Stage 3	• Use of salience principle in word order • Phrasal morphemes
Stage 4	• Exchange of information: internal to salient constituent
Stage 5	• Exchange of information: between internal constituents
Stage 6	• Distinction between main and subordinate clauses

TABLE 8.4
Stages for English L2 Morphosyntax

Stage of Development	L2 English Rules in Data	Examples
Stage 1	Single words, formulas	Yes. How are you? My name is . . .
Stage 2	SVO word order	I like apple
	SVO?	He have brother?
	Third Singular-s	He works here
Stage 3	Neg + V	She don't like
	Do fronting	Do you like Mexico?
	Topicalization	John I know
	Adverb Preposing	Yesterday I see her
Stage 4	Yes/No inversion	Have he went?
	Pseudo inversion	Where is your house?
Stage 5	Aux-2nd / Do-2nd	Where have you study?
	3 singular -s	He does not study English
Stage 6	Cancel inversion	He asked why she left

Note. See also Johnston 1985; Pienemann, Johnston & Bradley 1988.

all. Given this situation, such simplistic measures as accuracy are bound to fail to capture the necessary detail. In the case of developmental linguistic profiling, the important detail of SLA to be captured in the analysis of the data is the very first instance of a stage-criterial feature whose appearance is hypothesized to herald the onset of that level of processability. In other words, as soon as any one feature that defines a stage of L2 development appears in the language production data of an L2 learner, the learner is said to be at that particular stage. Operationally, two things must be guarded against in this type of analysis: language production chunks and human error. Accordingly, the emergence criterion incorporates a requirement for productivity (as defined by use of the feature in two different types of contexts; e.g., for morphology, on two different stems, and for syntax, involving different verb types) and for the appearance of a minimum of five productive instances of the feature. An early criticism of the emergence criterion was that it could not account for oversuppliance of a feature that, by other measures such as targetlike use (Pica, 1983) that mathematically "penalized" learners for overuse (in inappropriate contexts) could be taken into consideration. In response to this, processability theory now includes a distributional analysis component, which, although an improvement, is nonetheless descriptive in that it provides information supplemental to the emergence information rather than integral to it.

Given that emergence is ascertained on the basis of the productive appearance of specified and predictable L2 morphosyntactic features, it is essential that procedures be used that target those features. Particularly for some features in some languages, this aspect of the data collection has been difficult due to the fact that in open-ended, meaning-focused tasks the learners can circumlocute and thereby avoid contexts that require the stage-criterial structures. For example, in some early work on the application of the Processing Constraint model to the assessment of English as a Second Language (ESL), it was observed in interview-based language production samples that learners almost never ask questions, use negation, or need to refer to third persons (thereby avoiding third person singular -s) (Pienemann, Johnston, & Brindley, 1988). The absence of contexts for these features was limiting, as they represent windows into the more advanced developmental stages. To remedy this situation, structure-focused tasks were designed and studied by Pienemann's team at the University of Sydney Language Acquisition Research Center (Mackey, 1994; Pienemann, 1998; Pienemann & Doughty, 1991). Five communication tasks and one informal interview were used (see Table 8.5). Two

TABLE 8.5
Stucture-Focused Tasks for L2 Production Data Collection

Task	Structure	Participants	Procedure
Habitual Actions	3 Sing -s	Subject + Researcher	This task involved a set of photographs depicting "a day in the life of someone such as a librarian or a police officer." Subjects were asked questions such as "What does a librarian do every day?"
Story Completion	Wh-questions	Subject + Researcher	Subjects were shown a set of pictures, which were in order, and then were given instructions to find the story behind the pictures. They were encouraged to ask for information to enable them to guess the story. One example of this task made use of pictures of a man who had been given poison and who needed to buy the antidote.

Continues

TABLE 8.5
Continued

Task	Structure	Participants	Procedure
Informal Interview	General	Subject + Researcher	Subjects were interviewed informally and with sensitivity by the researcher. The situation was designed to be as close as possible to a friendly chat. The researcher asked questions of each subject, and the subjects were encouraged to ask questions of the researcher as well.
Picture Sequencing	Negation Questions	Subject + Subject	Subjects were each given part of a sequence of pictures. Together the parts made up one story. The pictures were lettered so that they could be identified for discussion. In order to sequence the pictures to find the story, questions had to be formed and responses given that were sometimes negative. An example of this task was a story involving a man being assaulted by three different people on his way home from work.
Picture Differences	Negation Questions	Subject + Subject	Subjects were given one picture each of the "spot the difference" variety. They were told that there were X number of differences. They had to ask questions and make positive and negative responses in order to find the differences.
Meet Partner	Questions	Subject + Subject	Subjects in dyads asked each other questions to find out information and then were given the opportunity to introduce each other to the researcher.

(adapted from Pienemann & Doughty, 1991)

tasks and the informal interview involved a single subject interacting with one researcher. The remaining three tasks paired two subjects who interacted with each other; the researcher was present but generally did not participate in the dyadic subject tasks apart from in a brief, supportive way.

In general, with respect to features that had been shown in previous research to be infrequent in unstructured data collection, the Habitual Actions task was successful in eliciting contexts for third person singular -*s*; the Story Completion was excellent in overcoming the barrier to L2 learners asking questions, and the Meet Partner and Picture Differences tasks were relatively successful in obtaining contexts for questions. Although it was designed to elicit questions as well, the Picture Sequencing task did not do so, and none of the six tasks was effective in eliciting negation, a feature that remains problematic (Pienemann & Doughty, 1991). Nonetheless, taken together, this set of structure-focused tasks is effective in eliciting L2 production data that contain sufficient numbers of contexts for the morphosyntactic features that form the L2 developmental sequence.

One final aspect of developmental linguistic profiling is the question of its feasability, or practicality, given the level of complexity of the approach that is mandated by the level of sophistication of processability theory. Very briefly, the procedures have been automated in a computer program called Rapid Profile (Pienemann & Thornton, 1992). While two learners carry out the structure-focused tasks described in Table 8.5, two researchers construct the linguistic profile: One is the task facilitator, and the other observes the interaction and enters information into a computer interface in which the stage-criterial morphosyntactic features appear and can be checked (by a mouse click) as soon as the observer hears the feature being used in a targetlike context. In this way the need for tedious transcription is eliminated, and the Rapid Profile program automatically calculates the stage of the learner, utilizing the emergence criterion described earlier.

Example 2: Descriptive Linguistic Profiling

The advantages of the developmental approach to linguistic profiling are evident in the preceding description: The entire approach is based on substantive cross-linguistic research that has resulted in the establishment of L2 developmental sequences that are constrained by processability; the data collection and measurement procedures have been carefully constructed and empirically tested; and the resulting language assessment is grounded in a well-developed theory of SLA. There is one disadvantage, however: The linguistic profiles are limited to L2 morphosyntax. For other research purposes, such a narrow view of L2 language ability may not be sufficient. Descriptive linguistic profiling takes a more unwieldy, but nevertheless a more comprehensive, approach to the study of L2 language production. The purpose of descriptive linguistic profiling is generally to characterize the overall language ability of L2 learners either by using a data-driven basis for formulating a functional theory of SLA or simply by describing a particular group of learners' L2 use (e.g., in order to characterize advanced learner proficiency). In contrast to the morphosyntactic orientation of developmental linguistic profiling, descriptive profiles are extensive and the analyses are carried out from a naturalistic discourse perspective. Two large-scale, cross-linguistic studies, in turn, exemplify the theory construction and advanced learner characterization uses of descriptive profiling. Both projects utilized a video-retelling procedure to obtain the L2 production data, and the second project illustrates a number of adjustments made to the tasks to take into account the differences in level and experience of the L2 subjects.

In the first project, the ESF project, immigrant workers from six L1 backgrounds (Punjabi, Italian, Turkish, Arabic, Spanish, and Finnish) were studied learning L2s in five countries (UK, Germany, Holland, France and Sweden). The L2 speech data were collected by having the subjects retell the second half of a video montage constructed from a Chaplin movie, *Modern Times*, to a NS interlocutor who had watched the first half of the video with the subjects. This format provides the subject–interlocutor interactants with the same background information and with motivation for the retelling, because the interlocutor has not seen the second half of the video, but is interested to find out what happened. Furthermore, the less linguistically able member of the conversational pair is the one who holds the majority of the information. Data were collected longitudinally, once every 10 months for a total of three cycles of data collection. Because the video retelling helps to solve the problem of the researcher interpreting the beginning learners' intentionality by constraining the range of possible meanings, the L2 production data were analyzed in terms of the emerging systematicity and functional patterns in the learners' utterances. Through analyses such as these, the ESF researchers tried to show how formal L2 features develop in the service of communicative function. Klein and Perdue (1992) discussed some findings of interest that may be summarized here. First, learners were reported to move through three stages: a preverbal utterance stage, a nonfinite verb organization stage, and a finite verb organization stage. Utterance organization was operationalized in terms of the argument orderings expressing semantic relations that the learners were trying to communicate. With regard to the information structure of the utterances, the beginning learners tended to mention the controller of the action first and the focus of the utterance last. Klein and Perdue (1992, p. 303) attempted to demonstrate that development within the noun phrase was related to its function in introducing and maintaining referents. Working from the data upwards, the ESF project used speech elicited by the video retelling as the basis for a functional explanation of SLA.

The FLIRT project at Georgetown University (Doughty, et al., 1997) also utilized the descriptive linguistic profiling approach, but in this case the purpose was to characterize the L2 ability of English-speaking university students, advanced learners of seven L2s, and the English L2 of pre-university learners from a range of L1s. Advanced learners were defined as students in their last year of university who had reached a specific upper-level course. Beyond describing this capacity of the advanced L2 learner, such data are used to identify learning problems that subsequently become the focus of pedagogical intervention studies. The researchers in this project selected linguistic profiling after becoming dissatisfied with the largely discredited oral proficiency interview (OPI) approach (see the special issue of *Studies in Second Language Acquisition, 10* (3), 1988, for a discussion of the limitations of this method of assessment of L2 production). Most problematic in oral proficiency interviews is that data elicited typically are limited to brief learner responses to interviewers' questions. The video-retelling task successfully facilitates the collection of long stretches of advanced learner production. In addition to the retelling, an open-ended question ("What is your view of the social message of the video?") was asked in order to vary the discourse structure; and because the learners in this project were literate adults, both written and oral data were collected.

In the preparatory study, it was found that a number of adjustments had to be made to the ESF methodology to improve the quality of the data. First, it became apparent that it would be necessary to prepare the NNSs (college-age, American students) for the possibility of a social message in advance of viewing the *Modern Times* video. Second, the retelling data in the pilot study resulted in long stretches of speech but not much variation in type of language attempted. Thus, for the main study, the video-retelling portion of the task was limited to 20 minutes, and four directed-conversation topics (based on the video) were developed. The retellings in the main study were learner-to-NS tasks, and the directed conversations took place in learner–learner dyads primarily, with a NS ready to assist. For both studies, extensive training was given to the NSs so that they would not dominate the interaction, as they might otherwise have been expected to do without such training, given their superior language ability.

As in the ESF project, NNSs and NSs viewed the first half of the *Modern Times* montage together. Then the native speakers left the room, and the NNSs viewed the rest of the montage (see Table 8.7 for details). At the completion of the film half the NNSs remained in the viewing

TABLE 8.6
FLIRT Oral Data Collection Tasks and Procedures

Task & Participants	Prompts	Directions/Procedure
Part 1: Video Retelling (oral): Subject - NS Interlocutor	It is your task to be as natural a conversation partner as you can be while at the same time making sure that the subjects provide ample language in the tasks they are given. Exchange a few pleasantries to introduce yourself and make the student feel at ease. A prompt could be something like: I left the room at the scene when Chaplin was in jail. I am of course curious how things went on. Can you tell me what happened after that and how the story ended?	Be encouraging and supportive as you listen carefully to what the subjects have to say. Use various minimal encouraging cues (e.g., uuh-uh; yeah, gestures) to signal that you are following along and have understood. Follow the leads provided by the respondents to encourage them to continue speaking. Skillfully weave subsequent questions into the previous parts of the conversation (e.g., "you just mentioned that you find American humor difficult to understand; could you be a little more specific?"). Do not correct, interrupt, or give the impression of an interrogation or a test. Try not to make lengthy comments of your own. Request clarification only when it is impossible to understand what the student is trying to say.
Part 2: Guided Video Discussion 2 Subjects - 1 NS Interlocutor	Topic 1: Chaplin is considered to be the best comedian of his time. Obviously people then found him funny. I'm not sure I can quite see it that way. Based on this performance, would you consider him to be a great comedian? Why? Why not? Is this the kind of humor you are familiar with? Where are the similarities, where the differences?	In the second part, use the questions listed under each one of the tasks as suggested subtopics that you will carefully weave into the conversation. Do not list them rapid-fire all at once. For topic 2, try to follow the script as well as possible in the conversation. This will result in more comparable data with the writing task. On the other hand, if this does not present itself naturally, it is not necessary to use all prompts in each of the tasks. Simply try to make the conversation as rich and engaging as possible.

Continues

TABLE 8.6
Continued

Task & Participants	Prompts	Directions/Procedure
	Topic 2 (this is also the topic for the writing task): We talked earlier how the movie ends with the young couple happily walking off into the sunset, the cliché of a Happy Ending in American movies. Is there anything particularly "American" about the brand of happiness the movie characters seem to aspire to? Does this kind of happiness also have appeal in **** culture? Is there something like a "right to happiness" in American culture that contributes to the power of the cliché of a "happy ending" in American movies? How does that relate to the economic and political tensions of the time when the movie was made? What constitutes happiness today? How is it depicted in contemporary movies?	Make sure that both students participate roughly equally in the conversation. If necessary, pose a question directly to one or the other. In general, do not help out with specific vocabulary. Let the students circumlocute as well as possible. You might in your feedback use a precise word that could then be picked up by the students.
	Topic 3: The whole notion of heroes, of course, changes over time. In the past heroism was often linked quite closely to combat and war, to physical accomplishments, but also to striving for impeccable ethical standards. What kinds of heroes does this movie show? What makes them people that set an example? What is problematic about that?	
	Topic 4: Chaplin is obviously the hero of the story, a hero of the little people. What makes him a hero in this story? What does that tell us about the needs or the aspirations of people at the time? Who are our heroes today, how do we depict them in movies, what does that say about major societal developments and concerns?	

****Interlocutor inserts the name of the subject's culture.

room to write in their L2 in response to the two prompts shown in Table 8.7, and the other half paired up with NS interlocutors to retell the second half of the video in one-on-one format (Table 8.6). After the retelling, NNSs were put in pairs to discuss up to four topics with each other, as time permitted, one of which was equivalent to the second writing prompt. One NS facilitated the NNS–NNS conversation whenever necessary and ensured that the writing prompt topic was discussed orally. Subjects who wrote first then switched locations with subjects who conversed first, and the entire process was repeated.

A portion of the FLIRT project L2 oral data analysis is under way at the time of the writing of this chapter (Byrnes, Connor-Linton, Jourdenais, & Sanz, 1998). The Spanish contribution compares spoken and written narrations at the two levels of instruction and focuses on frequency, contexts, and avoidance of use of non-Subject Verb Object (SVO) structures. The German study examines differences in clause structure and discourse functions across monologic and dialogic oral tasks in the advanced learner group. The third project investigates the use of case marking in relation to word order by advanced and intermediate learners of Korean in terms of functional needs. The last investigation, using Japanese data, investigates differential use of evaluation devices at the two levels of proficiency in order to profile learners' development as narrators. From the comparisons of the pilot and main studies, it is clear that the task modifications were successful in eliciting language production data that push L2 learners to the limits of their syntactic abilities, discourse (e.g., topic introduction and maintenance), and abstract discussion (e.g., opinion establishment and defense), thereby providing an informative profile of their advanced language ability.

TABLE 8.7
FLIRT Oral Data Collection Tasks and Procedures

Part 3: Video Retelling (written): Subject - NS Interlocutor (displaced)	Writing Prompt #1: In writing, tell someone who has not seen the second half of the movie how the action continues and how the movie ends. Begin with the scene when Chaplin gets out of jail.
Part 4: Guided Video Discussion (written): Subject - NS Interlocutor (displaced)	Writing Prompt #2: Write a review of the movie you just saw for a (German, French, Italian, etc.)-language newspaper. As someone familiar with American culture, you should particularly focus on the use and significance of the well-known American cliché for movie endings, the Happy Ending. As you explain this to your German, French, Italian, etc. readers, consider the following issues . . .

Example 3: The Role of Production in SLA

Some more circumscribed L2 language production elicitation procedures have been developed in a line of research involving interactionist models of SLA in which it is claimed that language is learned conversationally, not synthetically, structure by structure. We refer to these devices as meaning-focused communication tasks. In this line of research, the design of tasks and procedures is integral to the aim of capturing such language learning processes as the negotiation of meaning and grammaticization during the production of comprehensible output. In interactionist approaches, in addition to the acquisitional value of comprehending the L2 input (Krashen, 1982, 1985), it is further claimed that producing language so as to be understood by interlocutors—for instance, during modification of the interactional structure of talk (Long, 1996; Pica, 1992) and/or by attempting comprehensible output (Swain, 1985, 1995)—is critical to SLA. More specifically, it is hypothesized that through attempting to communicate, negotiating meaning to repair a communication breakdown, and noticing and/or having attention drawn to differences in L2 learner and targetlike production, learners' L2 production is "stretched" or "pushed" such that restructuring of the developing interlanguage (IL) occurs (Pica, 1992; Swain, 1995).

This line of descriptive and experimental interactionist SLA research has contributed in a number of ways to an understanding of the role of task variables in the study of L2 production. A number of task features are important if the aim is to foster the kind of interaction in which output is likely to be pushed far enough beyond the learners' usual current level of performance, such that the acquisitional processes of negotiating meaning and noticing formal differences can arise in sufficient numbers as to be documentable and to be studied in terms of effects on SLA. Early studies sought simply to observe the frequency of interactional devices that interlocutors must deploy in order to reach mutual understanding in the context of a potential or an actual communication breakdown. For example, by comparing an opinion-exchange task ("Who on the list of seemingly equally needy patients should be selected for transplantation of a heart that has just become available?") with a jigsaw task (a puzzle-like, garden-planting task in which each participant knows a unique part of the garden plot), Doughty and Pica (1986) showed that the distribution of and requirement for information exchange are essential. When there is no information exchange requirement, one member of the group (whether in an entire class, a small group, or a dyad) tends to dominate the interaction. On the other hand, if the information is distributed equally among participants and the task cannot be completed without each piece of information, then considerable negotiation of meaning occurs. Another task feature some claim to be important is that there should be a convergent rather than a divergent goal (Pica, Kanagy, & Falodun, 1993). If the participants know that all the information individually held must be contributed to the completion of the task, then interaction and, where necessary, negotiation of meaning ensue. Although the value of information distribution and having a convergent goal held in all participation patterns, pairs and small groups benefited more from this task arrangement than did whole classrooms of learners (Doughty & Pica, 1986).

A procedure that is often built into meaning-focused communication tasks as utilized in interactionist SLA research is the manipulation of input to learners, followed by differing conditions under which the manipulated input is to be processed. The general question of interest is whether input that is either simplified or elaborated in advance is more useful during comprehension than is unmodified input that is spontaneously modified during the accomplishment of the communication task. In general, this work has shown that learner–interlocutor interactional modification of input results in greater comprehension during communication tasks, as measured by task outcomes—for example, picking up an object and placing it in the right location (Gass & Varonis, 1994; Loschky, 1994; Pica, Young, & Doughty, 1987). The current and most difficult phase of this research involves establishing a direct link between interactional modifications that result in L2 comprehension and the production of comprehensible L2 output and interlanguage restructuring. A generalized design based on several studies is presented in Table 8.8. The tasks used involve direction giving and direction following under different conditions of input and interactional modification. The overall idea is to present learners with native-speaker baseline input in comparison with input that has been modified in some way by the researcher.

Pica et al. (1987) modified the task-direction input on the basis of common principles of elaboration, such as decomposition, clause simplification, and repetition of key lexical items. Gass and Varonis (1994) offered the methodological improvement of conducting a preparatory study in which a NS performed the tasks with a NNS and the task directions were transcribed as naturally modified by the pair. Comprehension is measured by task success, and such measurement has become increasingly sophisticated, involving video documentation of item selection and placement

TABLE 8.8
Input and Interaction Conditions in Meaning-Focused
Communication Tasks

Step 1:	Task directions are given under varying input conditions (+/- manipulated input): e.g., native input vs. researcher simplified input vs. NS—>NNS pre-modified input.
Step 2:	Tasks are carried out under differing interactional conditions: +/- opportunity for interaction.
Step 3:	Comprehension is measured in terms of success on task, and interactionally modified output is analyzed in the transcripts.
Step 4:	A subsequent task is carried out in which opportunities for use of the previously interactionally modified and comprehended features are examined to determine whether they have been acquired.

(Pica et al., 1987) and the development of a scoring procedure that ties success on task to interactional modifications that are documented in the transcripts. In other words, good guesses on the tasks are ruled out as being interesting to the analyses, as they were not the result of learners and their interlocutors working their way out of communication breakdowns (Doughty, 1996). Finally, studies have incorporated sets of tasks that are designed to provide learners with opportunities to use the same kind of language that was interactionally modified in previous tasks. Subjects are required, for example, to assemble an airplane from cut-out pictures and then immediately, or one week later, assemble a train (Doughty, 1996). Both airplane and train have passengers, servers, engineers/pilots, and the like who are engaged in eating, sleeping, watching movies, and so forth. Two problems remain with these kinds of tasks. First, it has proven very difficult to provide multiple contexts for use of specific linguistic structures in tasks that are relatively naturalistic. Second, the kind of language that is involved in direction-following and assembly tasks tends to be highly referential; it remains to be seen how this approach can be used to study the development of abstract and displaced language. In fact, it remains to be seen whether the kinds of tasks that can promote communication breakdowns do indeed capture SLA processes.

Finally, Swain and her colleagues at the Ontario Institute for Studies in Education have developed a methodology for studying the role of producing comprehensible output in the development of accuracy by very advanced learners. This approach utilizes the dictogloss, the analysis of language-related episodes, and tailored SLA measures (Swain, 1995, 1998). The dictogloss is a short passage that is constructed by researchers to include a previously identified and recalcitrant L2 learning problem (e.g.,

L2 French preverbal object clitics, which L1 English learners interpret as subjects, thereby creating agreement problems). The learners' task is to write down verbatim as much as possible of a passage, which is read to them at a rate so rapid as make this impossible. Learners then work in pairs to reconstruct the exact wording of the passage, verbalizing difficulties and trying out solutions. Swain calls this meta-talking, and she codes these stretches of speech as language-related episodes. Finally, the transcripts are analyzed and tailor-made language assessment measures are developed. This step is necessary because, although the dictogloss is designed to prompt learners to attempt language production that is known to be problematic, other production problems sometimes arise, and learners meta-talk about those. Swain claims that this kind of meta-talk and attempting to produce complex language engages learners in what she calls syntactic processing, a step she claims is necessary for the development of L2 accuracy.

CONCLUSION

The goal of this brief discussion of L2 speech elicitation procedures has not been to provide an exhaustive methodological survey but rather to illustrate some of the diverse options currently employed by SLA researchers, highlighting factors arising from their use with subjects who are typically older than the younger children who figure more prominently (although not exclusively) in L1 work and who come from varying cultural backgrounds. In addition, from the several hundred subdomains that make up modern SLA, sketches were offered of work in just three in order to show how research questions and/or theoretical motivation continue to spur the refinement of existing procedures and to lead to the creation of new ones. These are both developments that will surely continue apace for many years in what is such a vital yet still emergent discipline.

REFERENCES

Banerjee, J., & Carrell, P. L. (1988). Tuck in your shirt, you squid: Suggestions in ESL. *Language Learning, 38*, 313–347.

Bley-Vroman, R., & Chaudron, C. (1994). Elicited imitation as a measure of second-language competence. In E. E. Tarone, S. M. Gass, & A. D. Cohen (Eds.), *Research methodology in second-language acquisition* (pp. 245–261). Hillsdale, NJ: Lawrence Erlbaum Associates.

Bongaerts, T., van Summeren, C., Planken, B., & Schils, E. (1997). Age and ultimate attainment in the pronunciation of a foreign language. *Studies in Second Language Acquisition, 19* (4), 447–465.

Byrnes, H., Connor-Linton, J., Jourdenais, R., & Sanz, C. (1998, March). *Profiling the advanced language learner*. Symposium presented at the annual meeting of the American Association for Applied Linguistics, Seattle.

Chaudron, C., Crookes, G., & Long, M. H. (1988). *Reliability and validity in second language classroom research* (Tech. Rep. No. 8). Honolulu: University of Hawaii. Center for Second Language Research, Social Science Research Institute.

Cohen, A. D., & Olshtain, E. (1994). Researching the production of second-language speech acts. In E. E. Tarone, S. M. Gass, & A. D. Cohen (Eds.), *Research methodology in second-language acquisition* (pp.143–156). Hillsdale, NJ: Lawrence Erlbaum Associates.

Crookes, G. (1989). Planning and interlanguage variation. *Studies in Second Language Acquisition, 11*, 367–383.

Crookes, G. 1991. Second language speech production research: A methodologically oriented review. *Studies in Second language Acquisition, 13* (1), 113–132.

Dickerson, L. (1975). The learner's interlanguage as a system of variable rules. *TESOL Quarterly, 9*, 401–407.

Doughty, C. (1991). Second language instruction does make a difference: Evidence from an empirical study of SL relativization. *Studies in Second Language Acquisition, 13* (4), 431–469.

Doughty, C. (1996). *SLA through conversational discourse*. Paper presented at the Annual Conference of the American Association of Applied Linguistics, Chicago.

Doughty, C., Byrnes, H., Connor-Linton, J., Spielmann, G., & Tyler, A. (1997). *Profiling the Georgetown University advanced foreign language learner* (Teaching-Research Nexus Grant). Washington, DC: Georgetown University.

Doughty, C., & Pica, T. (1986). Information-gap tasks: Do they facilitate SLA? *TESOL Quarterly, 20* (2), 305–325.

Dulay, H., & Burt, M. (1974). Natural sequences in child second language acquisition. *Language Learning, 24* (1), 37–53.

Fathman, A. (1975). Language background, age and the order of acquisition of English structures. In M. Burt & H. Dulay (Eds.), *On TESOL '75* (pp. 33–43). Washington, DC: Teachers of English as a Second Language.

Fernandez, M., Gass, S. M., Mackey, A., Plough, I., & Polio, C. (1998, March). *Task repetition and attention to form/meaning: Effects on linguistic output?* Paper presented at the Pacific Second Language Research Forum, Tokyo.

Flege, J. (1980). Phonetic approximation in second language acquisition. *Language Learning, 30*, 117–134.

Gallimore, R., & Tharp, R. G. (1981). The interpretation of elicited sentence imitation in a standardized context. *Language Learning, 31* (2), 269–392.

Gass, S. M. (1982). From theory to practice. In M. Hines & W. Rutherford (Eds.), *On TESOL '81* (pp. 129–139). Washington, DC: Teachers of English as a Second Language.

Gass, S., & Varonis, E. (1994). Input, interaction and second language production. *Studies in Second Language Acquisition, 16* (3), 283–302.

Hartford, B. S., & Bardovi-Harlig, K. (1992). Experimental and observational data in the study of interlanguage pragmatics. In L. F. Bouton & Y. Kachru (Eds.), *Pragmatics and language learning* (Monograph No. 3, pp. 33–52). University of Illinois at Urbana-Champaign, Urbana: Division of English as an International Language.

Henning, G. (1983). Oral proficiency testing: Comparative validities of interview, imitation, and completion methods. *Language Learning, 33*, 315–332.

Hyltenstam, K. (1984). The use of typological markedness conditions as predictors in second language acquisition; the case of pronominal copies in relative clauses. In R.W.Andersen (Ed.), *Second language acquisition: A cross-linguistic perspective* (pp. 39–58). Rowley, MA: Newbury House.

Hyltenstam, K. (1988). Non-native features of near-native speakers. On the ultimate attainment of childhood L2 learners. In R. J. Harris (Ed.), *Cognitive processing in bilinguals* (pp. 351–368). Amsterdam: Elsevier Science Publishers.

Johnston, M. (1985). *Syntactic and morphological progressions in learner English* (Research Report). Canberra: Commonwealth of Australia, Department of Immigration and Ethnic Affairs.

Kasper, G., & Dahl, M. (1991). Research methods in interlanguage pragmatics. *Studies in Second Language Acquisition, 13,* 215–247.

Klein, W., & Perdue, C. (1992). *Utterance structure. Developing grammars again.* Amsterdam/Philadelphia: John Benjamins.

Krashen, S. (1977a). The Monitor Model for adult second language performance. In M. Burt & H. Dulay (Eds.), *Viewpoints on English as a second language* (pp. 152–161). New York: Regents.

Krashen, S. (1977b). Some issues relating to the Monitor Model. In H. D. Brown, C. Yorio, & R. Crymes (Eds.), *On TESOL '77* (pp. (144–158). Washington DC: Teachers of English to Speakers of Other Languages.

Krashen, S. (1982). *Principles and practice in second language acquisition.* Oxford: Pergamon.

Krashen, S. (1985). *The input hypothesis: Issues and impliciatons.* London: Longman.

Labov, W. (1969). The study of language in its social context. *Studium Generale, 23,* 30–87.

Larsen-Freeman, D. (1975). The acquisition of grammatical morphemes by adult ESL students. *TESOL Quarterly, 9,* 409–430.

Larsen-Freeman, D. (1983). Assessing global second language proficiency. In H. W. Seliger & M. H. Long (Eds.), *Classroom-oriented research in second language acquisition* (pp. 287–304). Rowley, MA: Newbury House.

Lightbown, P. M. (1983). Exploring relationships between developmental and instructional sequences in L2 acquisition. In H. W. Seliger & M. H. Long (Eds.), *Classroom-oriented research in second language acquisition* (pp. 217–243). Rowley, MA: Newbury House.

Long, M. H. (1983). Native speaker/non-native speaker conversation and the negotiation of comprehensible input. *Applied Linguistics, 4,* (2), 126–141.

Long, M. H. (1996). The role of the linguistic environment in second language acquisition. In W. Ritchie & T. Bhatia (Eds.), *Handbook of research on second language acquisition* (pp. 413–468). New York: Academic Press.

Loschky, L. (1994). Comprehensible input and second language acquisition. *Studies in Second Language Acquisition, 16* (3), 303–323.

Mackey, A. (1994). Targeting morpho-syntax in children's ESL: An empirical study of the use of interactive goal-based tasks. *Penn Working Papers in Educational Linguistics, 10* (1), 67–89.

Major, R. (1987). Phonological similarity, markedness, and rate of L2 acquisition. *Studies in Second Language Acquisition, 9,* 63–82.

Meisel, J., Clahsen, H., & Pienemann, M. (1981). On determining developmental stages in natural second language acquisition. *Studies in Second Language Acquisition, 3* (2), 109–135.

Munnich, E., Flynn, S., and Martohardjono, M. (1994). Elicited imitation and grammaticality judgment tasks: What they measure and how they relate to each other. In E. E. Tarone, S. M. Gass, & A. D. Cohen (Eds.), *Research methodology in second language acquisition* (pp. 227–243). Hillsdale, NJ: Lawrence Erlbaum Associates.

Naiman, N. (1974). The use of elicited imitation in second language acquisition research. *Working Papers on Bilingualism, 2,* 1–37.

Norris, J. (1996). *A validation study of the ACTFL Guidelines and the German Speaking Test.* Unpublished master's thesis, University of Hawaii, Honolulu.

Oliver, R. (1995). Negative feedback in child NS-NNS conversation. *Studies in Second Language Acquisition, 17* (4), 459–482.

Ortega, L. (1999). Planning and focus on form in L2 oral performance. *Studies in Second Language Acquisition, 21,* 109–48.

Ortega, L., & Long, M. H. (1997). The effects of models and recasts on the acquisition of object topicalization and adverb placement in L2 Spanish. *Spanish Applied Linguistics, 1* (1), 65–86.

Perkins, K., Brutten, S. R., & Angelis, P. J. (1986). Derivational complexity and item difficulty in a sentence repetition task. *Language Learning, 36,* 125–141.

Pica, T. (1983). Adult acquisition of English as a second language under different conditions of exposure. *Language Learning, 33* (4), 465–497.

Pica, T. (1992). The textual outcomes of native speaker–non-native speaker negotiation: What do they reveal about second language learning? In C. Kramsch & S. McConnell-Ginet (Eds.), *Text and Context* (pp. 198–237). Cambridge, MA: D. C. Heath.

Pica, T., Kanagy, R., & Falodun, J. (1993). Choosing and using communication tasks for second language instruction. In G. Crookes & S. M. Gass (Eds.), *Tasks and language learning. Integrating theory and practice* (pp. 9–34). Clevedon, Avon: Multilingual Matters.

Pica, T., Young, R., & Doughty, C. (1987). The impact of interaction on comprehension. *TESOL Quarterly, 21*, 737–758.

Pienemann, M. (1998). *Language processing and second language development: Processability theory.* Philadelphia: John Benjamin's.

Pienemann, M., & Doughty, C. (1991, March). *Task analysis for rapid profiling.* Paper presented at the Second Language Research Forum. Los Angeles.

Pienemann, M., Johnston, M., & Brindley, G. (1988). Constructing an acquisition-based procedure for second language assessment. *Studies in Second Language Acquisition, 10*, 121–143.

Pienemann, M. & Thornton, I. (1992). Rapid Profile. (Computer program). Sydney, Australia: University of Sydney, Language Analysis Centre.

Rintell, E. & Mitchell, C. J. (1989). Studying requests and apologies: An inquiry into method. In S. Blum-Kulka, J. House, & G. Kasper (Eds.), *Cross-cultural pragmatics: Requests and apologies* (pp. 248–272). Norwood, NJ: Ablex.

Robinson, P. (1995). Task complexity and second language narrative discourse. *Language Learning, 45* (1), 99–140.

Robinson, P., Ting, S., & Irwin, J. (1995). Investigating second language task complexity. *RELC Journal, 25*, 62–79.

Ross, S. (1995). *Aspects of communicative accommodation in oral proficiency interview discourse.* Unpublished doctoral dissertation, University of Hawaii, Honolulu.

Sato, C. J. (1984). Phonological processes in second language acquisition: Another look at interlanguage syllable structure. *Language Learning, 34* (4), 43–57. Also in G. Ioup & S. Weinberger (Eds.), *Interlanguage phonology* (pp. 248–260). Cambridge, MA: Newbury House.

Sato, C. J. (1985). Task variation in interlanguage phonology. In S. M. Gass & C. Madden (Eds.), *Input in second language acquisition* (pp. 181–196). Rowley, MA: Newbury House.

Sato, C. J. (1986). Conversation and interlanguage development: Rethinking the connection. In R. R. Day (Ed.), *Talking to learn: Conversation in second language acquisition* (pp. 23–45). Rowley, MA: Newbury House.

Sato, C. J. (1988). Origins of complex syntax in interlanguage development. *Studies in Second Language Acquisition, 10* (3), 371–395.

Sato, C. J. (1990). *The syntax of conversation in interlanguage development.* Tubingen: Gunter Narr.

Scovel, T. (1981). The recognition of foreign accents in English and its implications for psycholinguistic theories of language acquisition. In J-G. Savard & L. Laforge (Eds.), *Proceedings of the 5th Congress of AILA* (pp. 389–401). Québec: University of Laval Press.

Shohamy, E. (1994). The validity of direct versus semi-direct oral tests. *Language Testing, 11*, 99–123.

Soderman, T. (1993). Word associtaions of foreign language learners and native speakers. In H. Ringbom (Ed.), *Near-native proficiency in English* (English Dept. Publications No. 2, (pp. 94–182) Abo, Finland, Abo Akademi.

Spadaro, K. (1998). *Maturational constraints on lexical acquisition in a second language.* Unpublished doctoral dissertation, University of Western Australia, Perth.

Swain, M. (1985). Communicative competence: Some roles of comprehensible input and comprehensible output in its development. In S. Gass & C. Madden (Eds.), *Input in second language acquisition* (pp. 235–253). Rowley, MA: Newbury House.

Swain, M. (1995). Three functions of output in second language learning. In G. Cook & B. Seidlhoffer (Eds.), *Principle and practice in applied linguistics* (pp. 125–144). Oxford: Oxford University Press.

Swain, M. (1998). Focus on form through conscious reflection. In C. Doughty & J. Williams (Eds.), *Focus on form in classroom second language acquisition* (pp. 64–82). Cambridge: Cambridge University Press.

Swain, M., Dumas, G., & Naiman, N. (1974). Alternatives to spontaneous speech: Elicited translation and imitation as indicators of second language competence. *Working Papers on Bilingualism, 3*, 68–79.

Tarone, E. (1979). Interlanguage as chameleon. *Language Learning, 29*, (1), 181–191.

Tarone, E. (1983). On the variability of interlanguage systems. *Applied Linguistics, 4*, (2), 142–164.

Tarone, E. (1988). *Variation in interlanguage*. London: Edward Arnold.

Thompson, I. (1991). Foreign accents revisted: The English pronunciation of Russian immigrants. *Language Learning, 41*, (2), 177–204.

Walters, J. (1979). Strategies for requesting in Spanish and English: Structural similarities and pragmatic differences. *Language Learning, 29*, (2), 277–293.

Wolfson, N. (1976). Speech events and natural speech: Some implications for sociolinguistic methodology. *Language in Society, 5*, 182–209.

Wolfson, N. (1986). Research methodology and the question of validity. *TESOL Quarterly, 20* (4), 689–699.

Young, R. (1995). Conversation styles in language proficiency interviews. *Language Learning, 54*, (1), 3–42.

Yule, G. (1997). *Referential communication tasks*. Mahwah, NJ: Lawrence Erlbaum Associates.

II
GATHERING PRODUCTION DATA
IN NATURALISTIC SETTINGS

9

What You See Is What You Get: The Importance of Transcription for Interpreting Children's Morphosyntactic Development

Carolyn E. Johnson
University of British Columbia
Vancouver, British Columbia

Transcription is a time-consuming and often tedious task, but it is a non-trivial one with far-reaching consequences. Transcriptions provide the data that are analyzed by researchers interested in language production. However, they are not comprehensive or direct records of what speakers actually say and mean. It is generally acknowledged that setting up a particular recording situation, most often with the observer present, influences what the participants say and how they say it and, consequently, what can be concluded from the data. Choosing a means of recording speech and interactions—for example, audio or video recorder, stationary or remote microphone—further constrains what can become part of the permanent record. Transcription puts the data one step further from what speakers say and do because transcribers must select which aspects of the speech signal and interactional context to record in print. Should the transcriber make a written record of every phonetic detail, pause, gesture, change in direction of gaze, and situational feature to approach a complete and accurate representation? The answer is clearly "no," for reasons of—among others—readability, affordability, and perhaps even sanity. Ideally, each transcription should be tailored to the purpose of the investigation for which it constitutes the data. In any case, there is no such thing as a neutral transcription. As Ochs (1979) put it in her aptly named chapter, Transcription as Theory, "transcription is a selective process reflecting theoretical goals and definitions" (p. 44).

The format of transcripts has received considerable attention in recent years because of increases in (a) data sharing through databases such as CHILDES (MacWhinney, 1991; Sokolov & Snow, 1994), and (b) discourse and conversational analysis research. This new discussion of a process that until recently has largely been taken for granted is guided by general principles such as accessibility, readability, and standardization (see, e.g., Edwards, 1992, 1993; Edwards & Lampert, 1993; MacWhinney & Snow, 1985, 1992). This chapter foregrounds another aspect of transcription that is important to the interpretation of exisiting research as well as relevant to future research and data sharing; it focuses on one specific type of transcription—that of the speech of children under age 3;6 or so. I propose that attention to phonetic data is crucial to making judgments from production data about young children's acquisition of morphosyntactic categories and constraints or rules.

With very few exceptions, analyses of children's language production at levels other than phonological are based on transcriptions made with standard orthographic symbols, often with child pronunciations represented by spellings such as *dat* for *that* and *wanna* for *want to*. Generally speaking—and for obvious reasons—the younger the children, the more likely it is that transcripts of their speech will include phonetic symbols or other indicators of nonadultlike pronunciations. Early word production and researchers' decisions about what should even count as a word are clearly tied up with 1-year-olds' ability to pronounce; this is emphasized in work by, for example, Ferguson and Farwell (1975), Halliday (1975), Menn (1976), Peters (1977, 1983), Scollon (1976), and Vihman and McCune (1994). However, a mere handful of studies deals with phonetic detail in the speech of children starting to combine words and use grammatical morphemes. For example, Bowerman (1973) refers to "copious phonetic notes" (p. 19) supplementing the orthographic transcription in her study of Finnish children's early word combinations. Bernhardt and Johnson (1995), Bloom (1970, 1973), Dore, Franklin, Miller, and Ramer (1976), and Peters and Menn (1993) are among a small number of researchers whose discussion of such phenomena as transitional forms, false starts, and filler syllables depends on observation of phonetic phenomena.

In reports of the next stages of morphosyntactic development, phonetic transcription and even explicit mention of the transcription process are rarer still. It is worth noting that of Adam, Eve, and Sarah (the transcripts of whose speech provide us with many of our generalizations about children's language) only some of Sarah's speech was transcribed phonetically. This does not mean that the transcripts are not detailed and careful; they are. Brown (1973) noted that the transcribers "took great pains over grammatically significant and phonetically minimal features like inflections, prepositions, articles, and contracted auxiliaries. It is a tribute to their immense care, I know, that the data described in Stage II are so remarkably orderly" (p. 52). And early users of this database were careful to interpret such features conservatively, as illustrated by Bellugi (1965), Brown (1968), and Klima and Bellugi's (1966) description of the children's early formulaic *wh*-questions and Brown's (1973) discussion of Adam's segmentation of *it's, that-a, have-a,* and other forms (pp. 390–398).

But individual researchers' care in interpreting orthographic transcripts does not eliminate the dangers of failing to take phonetic data into account. Once a child form is written on a transcript in standard orthography, it tends to be taken at face value. This is especially true in the case of shared data, if the current analyst has never heard the original tapes. In describing the morphemic level at which Adam and Eve's speech was transcribed, Brown (1973) reported that "if a meaningful element was sounded well enough to be recognized, it was recorded in normal English spelling with no effort being made to render the particularities of the child's pronunciation" (p. 52). How well is "well enough to be recognized"? How will researchers accessing these data through CHILDES (MacWhinney & Snow, 1985) interpret these morphemic renderings? Peters and Menn (1993) reported a case of a CHILDES orthographic transcription showing *it* in object position for one child at age 2;6. Listening to the tape, Menn's student Bettina Perregaard observed that the child's actual pronunciations of this form varied among [ɪt], [ə], and zero. Peters and Menn concluded that "the transcribers were forced to choose between underrepresenting or overspecifying Patricia's knowledge, and chose the latter. This underscores the inherent inadequacy of orthographic transcriptions for understanding transitional phenomena in morphological development" (p. 753, fn.). In accord with Peters and Menn, I maintain that failure to attend to and transcribe phonetic details can (a) lead to over- or underrepresenting children's knowledge of linguistic forms and rules, and (b) obscure the process of acquisition.

In this chapter, I demonstrate these consequences by examining the early stages of interrogative acquisition. In this discussion, *knowledge* should be interpreted to mean "knowledge for spontaneous production," recognizing that complete assessment of a child's knowledge in a linguistic domain can only be done with a triangulation of results from comprehension experiments and data from spontaneous production, imitation, elicitation, and perhaps metalinguistic tasks (depending on the child's age) in addition to spontaneous production in a variety of circumstances.

THE ACQUISITION OF QUESTION WORDS AND INTERROGATIVE SYNTAX

Children's questions have been the subject of investigation for linguists, psychologists, and educators from the time of the earliest diary studies. Studies of question words (also called "*wh*-words" because of their form in English), for the most part, have been motivated by interest in order and determinants of acquisition (e.g., Bloom, Merkin, & Wooten, 1982; Smith, 1933; Tyack & Ingram, 1977). Studies of interrogative syntax, starting with analyses of the Harvard children (Brown, 1973; see, e.g., Bellugi, 1965; Brown, 1968; Klima & Bellugi, 1966), were done first to show that children's language was systematic and rule governed rather than imitative (Bellugi, 1971, p. 95), then to verify particular claims of syntactic theory (e.g., Hurford, 1975; Mayer, Erreich, & Valian, 1978), and most recently to "suggest modifications in linguistic theory, or to help in deciding among competing accounts in adult grammar based on intuitions" (de Villiers, 1995, p. 2). The continuing interest in interrogative acquisition warrants attention to the nature of the production data that informs analyses, generalizations, and arguments. Some of the most recent research depends on data reported in earlier studies (e.g., Radford, 1994) or archived in CHILDES (e.g., Stromswold, 1990, 1995), and new production data will surely be collected and transcribed. In the discussion of interrogatives, I focus on the acquisition of question words and auxiliary inversion because (a) they belong to the early stages when children's pronunciation is likely to be immature, and (b) they have been studied extensively.

Question Words

Some of the most congruent reports of language acquisition concern the acquisition of question words. The consistency holds, with only minor deviations, across longitudinal and cross-sectional studies, comprehension and production modes, normal and deviant language populations, a number of different languages, and first- and second-language learning. The developmental sequence that emerges is (roughly) (a) *what* and *where,* (b) *who, why, how,* and *whose,* and (c) *which* and *when* (or corresponding words in other languages; see, e.g., Bloom et al., 1982; Cairns & Hsu, 1978; Chapman, 1973; Ervin-Tripp, 1970; Ingram, 1972; Johnson, 1980, 1981; Lightbown, 1979; Smith, 1933; Tyack & Ingram, 1977; Wode, 1976). In production studies the sequence is determined by either first occurrence or frequency of each word and is explained in terms of lexical semantics, input frequency, and/or cognitive development. Although these factors are surely important, I suggest that at least some of the universality of these results can be attributed to how researchers interpret what children mean relevant to specific situations, rather than what the children actually say. In this way, they overrepresent children's knowledge of individual question words and their semantics and obscure the history of their development. These consequences impact on how researchers understand the development of interrogative syntax and the relation between words and conceptual development.

Studies of a number of different languages provide scattered evidence that children's earliest interrogatives are assigned to question-word categories even when no question word is phonetically present in the utterance. The question type appears to be categorized on the basis of (a) a question frame, such as English [sæt] *go* interpreted as "Where's that go?" or [sæt] *called* interpreted as "What's that called?" or (b) extralinguistic context, such as [sæt] categorized as either *what's that?* or *who's that?* depending on whether the perceived referent is animate or not. Embla, a Swedish child, asked a number of such questions between 1;11 and 2;1 (at Brown Stages I and II, based on mean length of utterance, or MLU) as shown in (1):

(1) *är det?*   "(What) is it/that?"
     heter det?   "(What) is it/that called?"
     gjörde barnet?   "(What) did the child do?"
     sa Ragnhild nu, mama?   "(What) did R. say now, mama?"
     andra ögat?   "(Where) the other eye?"
                                Lange and Larsson, 1973, p. 84

None of the 13 questions interpreted as *vad heter* + NP? "What is called + NP?" during this period contain the *vad.* About half of them began with the phonetic element [a], [ə], or [ɔ], which might attest to Embla's awareness of the missing word.

Stern and Stern (1928/1965) reported similar examples in German for their daughter, Hilde, between 1;6 and 1;8 (pp. 30, 191):

(2) Hilde   Adult target
     das hier?   *(Was ist) das hier?*
     "that here'"   "(What is) that here?"
     is 'n das?   *(Was) ist denn das?*
     "is (the)n that"   "(What) is then that?"
     das?   *(Was ist) das?*
     "that"   "(What is) that?"
     is 'n da?   *(Wer) ist denn da?*
     "is (the)n there"   "(Who) is then there?"

Wode (1976) noted other German examples in his daughter's speech when she was about 2;9 (*wem* "to whom," *wo* "where," and *wie* "how" did not appear where interpreted), as well as an example from Bulgarian (Gheorgov, 1908) in which the child omitted an interpreted *kadé* "where."

French examples are provided by Guillaume (1973), who reported a child at 1;10.7 omitting *où* in the imitations in (3), when there was "no possible doubt about the meaning of the question" (p. 241):

(3) *il est?*   "(Where) is he?"
     il est l'autre de maman?   "(Where) is it, mama's other one?"
     il est maman chérie?   "(Where) is it, dear mama?"

Similar results from an imitation task in English are provided by Brown and Fraser (1963); for example, "Where does *Daddy go*?" imitated as *daddy go*? and "Where does it go?" imitated as *go*?

Studies of spontaneous English production cite name-eliciting questions without *what*; for example, Ervin-Tripp's (1977) Sally, age 1;10, used *this*?, and Menn's (1976) Jacob used [esa] at 1;4.28, with [zɪ] (possibly from *what's this*) added a month later. Bellugi (1965) reported Adam's alternation of *where boy go*? with the equivalent *boy go*? during the first stage of interrogative development, observing that "It is not even clear that there is always a structural distinction between *wh* and *yes/no* questions at this stage" (p. 115). Radford (1995, p. 489) provided further examples, shown in (4):

(4) bow-wow go?   (Where did the) bow-wow go? (Louise 15)
     mummy doing?   (What is) mummy doing? (Daniel 21)

car going?	(Where is the) car going? (Jem 21)
doing there?	(What is he) doing there? (John 22)
mouse doing?	(What is the) mouse doing? (Paula 23)

Such examples show that researchers are confident about saying what type of *wh*-word should be present. They raise the question of what child productions were included in counts that contribute to conclusions about *wh*-word development—and it is likely that at least some were, because the studies sampled children as young as 1;6 (when *wh*-interrogatives are formulaic) and it is often easy to infer what children mean. Counting *wh*-questions without *wh*-words may not ultimately affect order of acquisition of question types (e.g., [sæt] may evolve into *what is that?* before *why* is learned), but it does overrepresent what children know about the *wh*-words themselves—phonologically, semantically, and as a class that participates in syntactic constructions. It also raises the related question of how researchers count apparent *wh*-words that are not pronounced accurately, especially in situations in which the meaning seems straightforward.

Some years ago I charted the development of interrogatives for eight monolingual English-speaking children, ages 1;6 to 3;0 and representing Brown's (1973) developmental Stages I–V (Johnson, 1980, 1981, 1983, 1999). Congruent with claims by Bellugi (1965), Brown (1968, 1973), Klima and Bellugi (1966), and others, these children's earliest *wh*-interrogatives were rigidly formulaic, many of them containing either no phonetic trace of a *wh*-word or else one that was phonetically incomplete and/or ambiguous. These formulas could regularly be predicted to occur within certain interaction routines. For example, all but the two youngest children typically produced a series of [sæt] (or an equivalent) utterances while taking plastic animals out of a purse (cf. Ninio & Bruner, 1978, on book reading).

Given such formulaic beginnings, how do children's interrogatives evolve into real *wh*-questions? What does it mean for a child to "know" a *wh*-word? There is considerable evidence that *wh*-formulas are learned in specific interaction contexts and used for specific pragmatic purposes (see Johnson, 1981, 1999, for discussion). A child who has learned a routine of this type must separate the *wh*-word from its linguistic and interactive environments. This involves identifying and segmenting the phonological substance of the *wh*-word, assigning it a meaning ultimately detached from a particular context of use, and figuring out how it participates in syntactic rules. My data (Johnson, 1980, 1981, 1999) show that, in common with other kinds of word learning, this does not happen all at once; over the gradual course of development children provide evidence of partial knowledge in the form of inaccurate pronunciation, incomplete and erroneous segmentation, and semantically and syntactically inappropriate use.

The children providing the data for this discussion were a boy and a girl at each 6-month age interval from 1;6 to 3;0. They were audio- and video-recorded playing in a livingroom setting in a television studio. The recording situation—low ambient noise, first rate equipment and tape, and placement of microphone and video camera—is critical for data of this sort. (Such studies must, of course, be balanced with studies of children in more natural environments; this is an old issue.) Each child was recorded over a period of approximately 2½ months. All child and adult utterances were transcribed orthographically, and the 2,407 child utterances coded as interrogatives were transcribed phonetically with IPA symbols (International Phonetic Association, 1979) and diacritics developed specifically for transcribing the speech of young children (Bush et al., 1973). Two coders independently identified *wh*-interrogatives[1] and categorized them according to *wh*-type with greater than 90% agreement. The categorization, intended to be comparable to that of earlier studies, was independent of the phonetic quality of the *wh*-word, which was coded separately. In cases where neither phonetic nor contextual information clarified which *wh*-word was intended, the utterance was coded as ambiguous. Coding yielded 984 *wh*-interrogatives, which are the data for this discussion.

Taking the *wh*-types at face value and using order and frequency of occurrence as criteria, the order of acquisition was consistent with earlier reports. *What* and *where* were clearly the earliest and most frequent, together accounting for 90% of all *wh*-interrogatives recorded. *When* (not used by any child) and *which* were the latest, with *who, why,* and *how* falling somewhere between. However, the order reveals little about the interrogatives in this sample.

About one third of the children's codable (unambiguous) *wh*-words were counted as phonetically accurate, on the criteria of correct syllable

---

[1]I refer to "*wh*-interrogatives" because I am discussing a syntactic mood, without reference to the communicative functions it can serve. These include, for example, politeness formulas (e.g., "How are you?"), invitations, requests for action, permission or attention, rhetorical questions, and moves to be included (e.g., "What are you doing?"). This distinction is highly relevant to generalizations about children's early language. See Johnson (1981) for discussion.

structure, essentially correct consonants, and reasonable vowel quality. Examples include [wʊtsæt], [wʌdɪzɪt], and [phonetic symbols]. (Note that this coding does not go the next step to claim that the child has segmented *what + 's + that*, for example.) The proportion of accurate and complete *wh*-words increased with the children's linguistic growth, especially in Stage V. There was a corresponding decrease in the proportion of partially incomplete pronunciations, which included at least the correct initial consonant or the [t] in *what*, such as [wʌsæt], [hʌtsæt], [wɛsɪsgo], and [wɛdnɑɾɚwɑn]. *Wh*-words were coded "phonetically ambiguous" when an inaccurate pronunciation overlapped another *wh*-word, such as [hʊzə] for *where's a* and [wəs] for *where's*; no change could be tracked on this dimension. Until Stage V, about 20% of the interrogatives had no phonetic trace of a *wh*-word, although the children contributed unevenly to this figure. For example, 3-year-old Anthony, who developed from Stage III to Stage V over the course of the study, omitted *wh*-words in almost one third of his *wh*-interrogatives (and pronounced *wh*-words accurately in only half the remaining interrogatives), contrasting with his age-mate, Lindsay, who omitted *wh*-words in only 6% of hers. All but one of the missing *wh*-words should have been *what* or *where*.

Phonetic variability in the youngest children's utterances contributed to the inaccuracy of forms possibly meant to be *wh*-words, as shown in (5). In this example, Chloe, 2;3.8, Stage I, was holding a peg from a pegboard in her hand and looking all around while speaking.

(5)   Chloe: mommy [ʌʔ / əˈʒɪ / aˈɹæ / həm / ˈæli / li bal]
      Mother: Hm?
      Chloe: mom [ˈleː / / ˈgæs]
      Mother: Wanna put that somewhere?
      Chloe: yeah.

Chloe seemed to be tying to communicate something to do with location of the peg board, possibly trying to ask her 2-year-old version of "Where does this go?" or "Where's the thing this goes in?" She tried repeatedly to repair her message in order to be understood (cf. Scollon, 1976), but her mother clearly had to rely on the nonverbal context to formulate a response.

For several of the children, [h] varied freely with [w] word-initially, and vowels showed a high degree of variation. This led to phonetic overlap of target *where* with *what*; *what* and *where* with *how* and *who*; and *how* with *who*. The overlap was more complete when *what* and *where* lacked final consonants, as they often did in formulaic *what's that*? and *where's this go*? In such cases it is difficult to come to any conclusions about what these children knew about the size and shape of specific *wh*-words, or whether they distinguished interrogative type by the *wh*-words themselves. This is illustrated by Jane at 2;6.28, Stage III, who asked the interrogatives in (6) within one half-hour period:

(6)   [wəsæ?wʌnɪsaʊfɛnɪʃ]   whats that one is all finish?
       [wəsikgoɪ]   wheres he/it going?
       [wʌsɪskat]   whats this called?
       [wʌsɪsgɔ]   wheres this go?
       [ʌsɪs]   whats this?
       [ʌsdɪkgo]   wheres this go?

Notice that I have paired *what* and *where* interrogatives to demonstrate that the contrast is often at the end of the frame, not in *wh*-word position, where there is complete overlap. (In the glosses the apostrophes are omitted in an attempt to avoid overinterpretation of the child's analysis of the phrases, but even the spaces between words represent an interpretation of what Jane knows.) In such formulaic questions, children may be signaling their intended meaning by the whole phrase, or by phrase-final contrasts, rather than by inclusion of a specific *wh*-word. If this is the case, what do they know about the words themselves, and how can we use production data to find out?

The strongest evidence of acquisition of specific *wh*-words comes from their appearance as contingent single-word queries, as shown by example (7) from Anthony at 3;3.4, Stage V:

(7)   Mother: We saw a big long train with three engines.
     Anthony: Where?
     Mother: Yesterday.
     Anthony: Where? Downtown?

This example is particularly convincing because Anthony responded to his mother's temporal answer with a repetition of his original question and a suggested answer that makes his pursuit of locative information very clear. The three oldest children in this study produced such queries with *what* and *where*, starting at Stage IV, and the two oldest additionally used *why*. It is interesting to note that Stage IV—for those who make reference to Brown's (1973) stages—is the developmental level that linguists connect with the acquisition of interrogative syntax (e.g., Davis, 1987; O'Grady, 1997).[2]

In the developmental time between their exclusive reliance on rigid *wh*-formulas and the competence exemplified by (7), the children provided several types of evidence that they were beginning to segment the formulas into useful constituents: (a) self-repairs, (b) paradigmatic substitutions, and (c) segmentation errors. Observing each of these types requires a phonetic record of their occurrence.

Repairs (Clark & Andersen, 1979; Sacks, Schegloff, & Jefferson, 1974) occurred in interrogatives with false starts, with the second attempt more accurately pronounced than the first, as shown in (8):

(8)   Darcy (Stage III)
　　[wɪzə/wɛɹzənʌðɚbinbæg]　　wheres another beanbag?　(2;6.18)
　　[wʌs/wʌtsɔvəðɛɚ]　　　　　whats over there?　　　　(2;7.1)

The children sometimes repaired *wh*-interrogatives that their mothers did not answer, as shown in (9), an example from Graham at 2;4.20, Stage III:

(9)　Graham:　　　　[aɪz] another [fi]?
　　　(no answer)
　　　Graham:　　　　[waɪz] another tree?
　　　(no answer)
　　　Graham:　　　　[wɛɹz] another tree?
　　　Mother:　　　　There's one.

Examples 5 and 9 call to mind Scollon's (1976) observation that the child is willing to repeat and modify until the adult signals understanding.

---

[2]There has been some confusion in the auxiliary and interrogative-acquisition literature about whether Stage III or Stage IV is the developmental level at which auxiliaries proliferate and subject–auxiliary inversion begins to be learned. This may be due to Brown's use of Levels I to V in his 1968 article on questions, which are equivalent to Stages I to V of his 1973 book. In this article he did not distinguish between his levels and Bellugi's interrogative stages, based on her periods A to F (1965, 1967), which were defined over equal time segments as opposed to MLU values. The matter is further confused because, in her 1965 paper, Bellugi reported that she had combined the periods two at a time, which should yield interrogative stage 1 as periods A + B, stage 2 as periods C + D, and stage 3 as periods E and F. The lack of agreement among different summaries of the same data, plus other investigators' failure to specify whether they are using Brown's or Bellugi's stages, make this a point worth noting.

Before internal paradigmatic substitutions appeared, the children used formulas as combining forms, for example, early [wʌsæt] followed by productions such as [wʌsæt] *thing?*, [wʌsæt] *over there?* and [wʌsæt-dæwʌn], which did not provide evidence of internal analysis. Substitutions within formulaic interrogatives can provide supportive evidence that analysis is taking place. The five most linguistically advanced children produced alternations such as [wʌtɪzæt] and [wʌtɪzɪt] and *what you make, Mommy?* with *what we make, Mommy?,* as well as filling open slots in frames such as [wɛrzə_____]. Paradigmatic substitutions must be considered in conjunction with other evidence of analysis, however; sometimes what appears to be analysis is actually just another formula added to the child's inventory. An example comes from Graham, at 2;4.20, Stage III, who asked [wɛɹaɹdeɪ] while searching for a single cup.

Segmentation errors show that analysis is under way but not complete. Instances in this study appeared in Stage III, as shown by the examples in (10):

(10) Graham   (2;4.20)   [wʌsætdæwʌn]

whats-that that one?

Jane   (2;6.28)   [wʌsætwʌnɪzaʊfɛnɪʃ]

whats-that-one is all finish?

Darcy   (2;6.18)   [wʌtsɪtʃʊgɚ]

whats-it sugar? (= "want some sugar")

The last example from Darcy illustrates an interesting type of error, what Bolinger (1977) called "collocation mixing," which adults do when they say, for example, "The rain petered off" instead of either "petered out" or "tapered off." This instance was part of a series of utterances during a pretend tea party, during which Darcy repeatedly offered his mother salt to put in her tea (*want some salt?* was a routine part of all his tea parties; it was a collocation for him). When his mother insisted on sugar instead of salt, Darcy was forced to break up his collocation; it is likely that in so doing he mixed in one of his other collocations, *whatsit,* which attests to its storage as a ready-made phrase.

Collocations are also relevant to the stage of language development at which children have analyzed *wh*-words and are using them productively. In her first three sessions, when Jane's (2;6.28–2;8.2) MLU and upper bound put her in Brown Stage III, all her *wh*-interrogatives were formulaic. Her first *where* questions were variants on [wʌsɪsgo]. By the second session her frames started to open up, and she asked questions of the type [wɛɹz] NP?

and [wɛɹz] NP *go?*, including an accurately pronounced [wɛɹdɛmgɔ]. In session 4 (2;8.16, Stage IV) she asked *where?* as a single word 10 times but only one query that might have been a *where* formula; and in 15 of her 19 *where* interrogatives, she correctly pronounced [wɛɹ], providing strong evidence of knowledge of the word *where*. In session 6 (2;8.30) all her potential *where* interrogatives were again formulaic, and only two of them were not ambiguous. This is illustrated with the sequence of interrogatives in (11), asked while Jane was trying to fit plastic shapes into a Tupperware ball. Jane's mother interspersed comments during this interchange, mostly of the type, "Well, you just turn that ball a little bit and you might find it."

(11) [wʌtsdɪswʌŋgɔmɑm]
[wʌsdɪswʌn/gɔmɑm]
[wʌsdɪswʌn]
[wʌtsɪswʌgɔmɑm]
[wʌsɪswʌn/gɔ]

The *where* interrogatives here overlap the semantic territory of "How do I do this?" because Jane asked some of them when she had already found the correct hole but could not get the piece in, but the pronunciation of the *wh*-forms is characteristic of her pronunciation of *what* in earlier sessions. How can we explain this apparent regression? The play context strongly predicted Jane's use of her formulaic *wheres-this-go?* This is a characteristic of formulaic utterances; structure and context make a package, whether the formula is the adult's "Hi, how are you?" or the child's "Trick or treat" (Berko Gleason & Weintraub, 1976) or "What's that?" Although she was capable of generating a novel *where* interrogative at this developmental stage, Jane pulled this one from her repertoire ready made.

Bolinger (1976) suggested that children and adults learn in both collocation and word-size units; as collocations are analyzed, "stored units are to be found in three overlapping levels, corresponding to morphemes, words and collocations. For any given collocation I would maintain that all three may coexist" (p. 9). (For further discussion of language production based on collocation-size units as well as creative constructions, see Clark, 1974; Ferguson, 1976; Fillmore, 1979; Hayes-Roth, 1977; Johnson, 1981; Peters, 1983; Van Lancker, 1973; Vihman, 1980; Wong Fillmore, 1979.) This interpretation raises problems for students of child language. Not all child utterances provide data of equal value for describing the child's grammar. Should we try to decide which utterances in a transcript are formulaic and eliminate them from analysis? If so, how?

The task becomes possible to consider if we take both phonetic and situational facts into account, along with some knowledge of the child's current grammatical level of competence. Brown (1973, pp. 390–398) and Peters (1983, pp. 7–12) suggested criteria to guide linguists' decision making, including, for example, whether the child's utterance (a) is a particular "chunk" that occurs frequently and without alteration, (b) coheres phonologically, (c) is situationally dependent, and (d) sometimes seems inappropriate in particular contexts. An example of the last criterion is Graham's (2;4.20, Stage III) use of [wʌsæt] in (12), where it appears that he did not know how to ask *what color*, so he used a means he did know for obtaining the desired information (an example of using an old form for a new function; Slobin, 1973):

(12) Mother: What color's that one?
     Graham: that's a green one
     Mother: Don't think so.
     Graham: [wʌsæt]
     Mother: Looks red to me.

To summarize, studies that use production data to determine acquisition of *wh*-words are likely to overrepresent children's knowledge unless they involve careful analysis of phonetic (and contextual) data. Children's early *wh*-interrogatives are unanalyzed formulas used predictably in definable interaction contexts. Attending to phonetic data, we can see that a considerable number of these formulas do not show any phonetic evidence of a *wh*-word, whereas others include only incomplete or inaccurate pronunciations that may obscure distinctions among *wh*-words. From these routines, children's developmental course is gradual, with evidence of partial analysis and knowledge in the form of substitutions within the formulas, repairs, and segmentation errors. Even when children demonstrate knowledge of *wh*-words, they sometimes use old formulas in contexts to which they are bound, or to extend question-asking into unfamiliar semantic territory, which raises questions about which child utterances should be included in morphosyntactic analyses. Each of these points is important because we not only make claims about the relationships between children's *wh*-words and their ability to conceptualize locative, temporal, and causal relations and so on, but we also make assumptions about a class of *wh*-words that—at least according to some linguistic theories—move to the front of sentences, represent empty categories and leave traces in the clauses where they originated (in English and many other languages), and are associated with auxiliary inversion. Phonetic data can help pinpoint the time at which linguists and psychologists are justified in making such generalizations about *wh*-words.

Subject–Auxiliary Inversion

Subject–auxiliary inversion (SAI, also called "auxiliary inversion," "inversion," and "I-to-C movement") is a mechanism many languages use to differentiate interrogative from declarative sentences. In English, the auxiliary occurs after the subject in declarative sentences, for example, "She had pointed at the wugs," but before the subject (and after the *wh*-word) in matrix questions, for example, "What did she point at?" Children learning English are reported to learn inversion at Brown Stage III (e.g., Brown, 1968; Radford, 1994) or Stage IV (e.g., Davis, 1987; O'Grady, 1997; see note 2), but there is considerable controversy over just how this acquisition proceeds. To learn this rule of English, children must be able to identify words (and sometimes abbreviations of words) that count as auxiliaries and understand that they belong to a class of elements that behave in the same way under certain syntactic conditions, such as in the formation of interrogative and negative declarative sentences.

This acquisition problem became especially interesting to linguists when Bellugi (1965) observed that during her question development stage 3, Adam, Eve, and Sarah inverted auxiliaries in *yes/no* interrogatives but not in *wh*-interrogatives, as illustrated by Adam's *Do you take it out?* and *What I can put them in?* Since that time, researchers have investigated whether children generally do, in fact, go through a stage during which they do not invert auxiliaries, and whether they differentially invert *yes/no* and *wh*-interrogatives, as Bellugi found. Stromswold (1990, p. 137) summarized the results from nine such studies and reported that (a) seven of the nine did not find a "failure-to-invert" stage; (b) two found no difference in rate of inversion for *yes/no* and *wh*-interrogatives, two found inversion in *yes/no* but not *wh*-interrogatives, and two found inversion to be more common in *wh*- than *yes/no* interrogatives; and (c) *wh*-word affected the rate of inversion, with *what* and *where* questions showing the most inversion and *why* and *when* the least.

How can we explain the apparently contradictory results? Stromswold (1990, 1995) herself analyzed the CHILDES transcripts of 14 children for whom there is longitudinal data (MacWhinney & Snow, 1985) (and which included Adam, Eve, and Sarah) and found a very high inversion rate (93%) and no stage during which there was a differential inversion rate for *yes/no* and *wh*-interrogatives overall, although individual children followed each of the patterns described in (b), preceding paragraph. She suggested that children vary for extralinguistic reasons such as input differences, ability to monitor what they say, and willingness to make linguistic generalizations (Stromswold, 1990, pp. 192–196). But methodological decisions are also behind some of the disparity. For example, Bellugi's analysis of the stage 3 interrogatives included child productions with and without auxiliaries (also see Brown, 1968; Klima & Bellugi, 1966), so many of her "uninverted" *wh*-interrogatives in fact had no auxiliary to invert. Stromswold, on the other hand—looking at the same (as well as other) transcripts—analyzed only sentences that included auxiliaries, so she and Bellugi came to different conclusions about the same children.

However, the main methodological point I would like to raise here is again one concerning transcription. At least some of the studies Stromswold summarized included interrogatives with what appeared to be contracted auxiliaries (given orthographic transcripts). For example, Ingram and Tyack's (1979) was one of the studies that found a similar inversion rate for auxiliaries in *yes/no* and *wh*-interrogatives, except during period A (matched to Bellugi's period A by age, with reference to Adam), when inversion was more frequent in *wh*-interrogatives. Recall that this is a period for which Bellugi and others claimed that *wh*-interrogatives were formulaic and the children did not produce auxiliaries. Ingram and Tyack themselves suggested the possibility that the apparently contracted auxiliaries were not always productive and thus did not demonstrate auxiliary movement. In fact, given evidence such as that presented in my section on *wh*-words, even forms written down as uncontracted auxiliaries might not have been productive. The data collectors in Ingram and Tyack's study were the children's mothers, who were instructed to "write down every question the child asked for a continuous period until 225 questions were collected" (p. 336). These mothers (among whom I numbered) recorded their children's questions orthographically, making clues to their interpretation as formulas or novel constructions inaccessible to the researchers. Also, like Stromswold, Ingram and Tyack included only interrogatives judged to contain auxiliaries— analyzed or not—in their calculation of inversion rate. It is not surprising that their results conflicted with Bellugi's and showed no stage 3-type differential inversion.

Linguists studying children's interrogative syntax in recent years have tried to eliminate the problems associated with interpreting unanalyzed forms by excluding formulaic interrogatives from their analyses and discussion (e.g, Davis, 1987; O'Grady, 1997; Radford, 1994, 1995; Stromswold, 1990, 1995). It is not always clear, however, whether researchers do this on an utterance-by-utterance basis or whether they include all interrogative utterances once a child has gone beyond the developmental level at which all *wh*-interrogatives are formulas. Nor is there agreement on what should be considered a routine. For example, Radford (1994) explicit excluded "potential routines such as *what dat?*" from his analysis of Stage 1 interrogatives, but he included utterances such as *what cowboy doing?, what doing?, where milk go?,* and *where horse go?* (p. 212). On the basis of these data, he argued that children's interrogatives at even this stage are formed by *wh*-movement—but recall the problems with even saying there are *wh*-words at Stage I. Although he went on to discuss Stage II and III interrogatives, he did not mention routines again. Stromswold (1990, p. 47; 1995, p. 21) did not include utterances that were "obvious routines" such as *what's that?* in her analysis; on the other hand, she criticized Radford's 1990 analysis of early interrogatives because "he was quite liberal in what he considered to be a formulaic question. For example, he ignored questions such as *what squirrel doing?* or *where doggie go?* because he considered them to be routines" (1995, p. 17). Stromswold noted that context of utterance can be used to minimize, but not eliminate, the likelihood of including a routine in the data set (1995, p. 21), and she further minimized this likelihood in her 1990 work by excluding "contracted auxiliaries" from her analyses.

As noted earlier, not all researchers exclude contracted auxiliaries, and these are especially open to overinterpretation by the simple fact of being recorded orthographically. An example of how this sort of interpretation is hard to budge once it becomes established is an article by Weinberg (1990) in which she cited Davis (1987) and Ingram and Tyack's (1979) research as evidence that "some children begin to invert in *wh*-questions at the same time that they invert in yes/no questions" (p. 167). Agreeing that the auxiliaries at this stage might be unanalyzed (the most likely possibility, given what is known about this stage), she argued that children might "allow unanalyzed material to surface in [initial] position" (p. 169) and "that there could be a stage before [verb-ending] concord is mastered where the *auxiliary and verbal forms are mastered as unanalyzed units* [italics added], allowing the auxiliary to appear exclusively in initial position" (p. 170). It is hard to understand what such a claim could mean, given that the "auxiliaries" in these unanalyzed interrogatives are the instances of, for example, [s] in forms such as [sæt] and [wʌsɪfeŋgo], which, by definition, are not separable from the preceeding or following phonetic material.

But [s] (or 's) is not the only "auxiliary" that presents segmentation problems. Peters and Menn (1993, p. 751) reported one child's use of nasal filler syllables in preverbal position, which developed gradually into *can, did, do, are,* and *shall,* as well as unsegmented forms such as *did-you, do-you, can-you, let's,* and *shall-we.* Peters (1995) explained that the child's did-you, pronounced [dɪdʒə] or [dɪdʒu], was an unanalyzed "single unit that marked action just completed by himself," for example, saying (at age 2;0) *did-you hear car,* meaning "I heard a car" (p. 470). She went on to note that "Seth had similar problems disentangling *what* from *are, do, did,* and *a* . . . which all tend to be elided into something like /wətə/" (p. 470).

As in the case of *wh*-words, interpretation of children's ability to invert auxiliaries in interrogatives is dependent on the quality of the transcriptions that are the data, as well as analytic decisions made by the researcher. Phonetic information is crucial for making decisions about children's grammars, particularly when the analysis involves units that occur first in unanalyzed routines. The researcher is much more likely to pause and carefully consider the composition of [wʌsɪfeŋgo] than *where's this thing go?*—that is, there is less danger of overrepresenting the child's syntactic expertize when provided with phonetic information.

Taken together, studies of *wh*-word development and subject–auxiliary inversion illustrate opposing interpretations of interrogative development arising from different uses of transcriptions of production data. Studies based on orthographic transcriptions present a sharp discontinuity between formulaic and syntactically constructed interrogatives, with the formulas either dismissed as irrelevant forms or an uninteresting stage prior to the development of interrogative syntax (e.g., O'Grady, 1997; Stromswold, 1990, 1995) or overinterpreted as evidence of immature syntactic constructions (e.g., Radford, 1994; Weinberg, 1990). On the other hand, studies that seriously take into account the phonetic detail of children's interrogatives (e.g., Johnson, 1981) suggest a continuity of development, with formulas gradually yielding their internal structure as phonologically defined chunks that can then be assigned semantic and syntactic values.

CONCLUDING COMMENTS

The discussion of the importance of phonetic transcription in the study of children's early morphosyntactic development has focused on two aspects of interrogatives: *wh*-words and subject–auxiliary inversion. The same points could have been made from other domains of language development. One domain that has been treated in this way is grammatical morphology, which is particularly interesting given the interrelationships between morphology and phonology. It is worth noting that pioneering studies by Berko Gleason (1958) and Brown (1973) included discussion of allomorphs, often not considered in more recent studies of morphological development.

A few studies reported "empty forms" (Bloom, 1973; Leonard, 1975), "phonetically consistent forms" (Dore et al., 1976), or "filler syllables" (Peters, 1977) as children make the transition to two-word utterances and utterances with grammatical inflections. However, most of these studies did not follow the development of these forms from their first appearance to their endpoint as fully fledged morphemes. An exception is a careful and comprehensive analysis of two children's early morphemic development by Peters and Menn (1993), who explained that they had

> so few cases to work from because the overwhelming majority of transcriptions, for children who are beyond the one-word stage, focus on syntax and provide no phonological information. (The present work should demonstrate that the theoretical payoff for phonetic transcription extends well beyond the study of the acquisition of phonology.) (p. 746)

Their fine-grained analysis focused on the process of acquisition and allowed them to track phonologically underspecified syllables and other phonological units in a variety of morpheme positions as they gradually developed into adultlike morphemes, thereby avoiding overrepresentation of the children's knowledge at any given point in time and revealing different paths of development for the two children. This study intersects with the interrogative-acquisition studies in that one child produced nasal fillers and unsegmented forms in auxiliary position, as mentioned earlier. Menn and Peters's data led them to conclude that each child, while following a different path, gained access to morphology by "making use of 'phonological toeholds' in which growing ability to reproduce relatively meaningless sounds provides exposure to the distributional information necessary for sorting out the combinatory rules" (p. 746). Their micro-analysis also motivated their argument that both children and adults can have partial knowledge of the form and meaning of morphemes.

Also based on a phonetic and distributional analysis of filler syllables, Bernhardt and Johnson (1995) appealed to speech production models in an attempt to explain the difference between what a child with a severe phonological impairment knew about language and what he actually said in any given utterance. This child, like Seth in Peters and Menn's study, used filler syllables when he was just learning a new form. As his phonology, morphology, and syntax developed, the filler syllables changed function. Detailed analysis of the syllables and their privileges of occurrence suggested that sentence encoding restrictions at—variously—phonological, lexical, syntactic, and discourse levels limited phonetic encoding of particular classes of words, including third person pronominal subjects, deictic terms, *wh*-words, and connectives (p. 275). This analysis led Bernhardt and Johnson to recommend further development of sentence production models that can account for children's productions, with a view to developing better motivated intervention for children with language disorders.

The cases of interrogative and morphological development discussed in this chapter demonstrate the importance of phonetic transcription—as a record of what children actually say—to (a) avoiding overrepresentation of what children know, (b) providing insight into how development proceeds, and (c) explaining how children get to what they say from what they know. If we thus acknowledge the utility of phonetic transcription, where do we go from here? Phonetic transcription of every child corpus, regardless of what the research is about, is unlikely to happen and perhaps not even desirable on grounds such as expense, accessiblity, and readability of data.

The answer may lie in each researcher's careful consideration of the forms likely to be relevant to addressing particular research hypotheses. Given the guidance of a good-quality orthographic transcript and access to the sound (and perhaps video) recording it represents, the researcher can identify and transcribe just those child utterances or portions of utterances that bear on the research question. If the researcher is using a database and analysis system such as CHILDES (MacWhinney & Snow, 1985), the phonetic transcription can go on a separate coding line (keeping the main line readable) and the resulting transcript can be contributed back to the database. This approach to research using archived data will become more feasible as digitized auditory records linked to transcripts become more available (MacWhinney & Snow, 1992). MacWhinney and Snow support Peters et al. (1990) in arguing that "the inclusion of a complete CHAT '%pho' line does much to guarantee real data accountability, particularly at the youngest ages" (p. 469). In the meantime, students of early child language who are collecting new production data would do well to buy the best recording equipment they can afford and hone their phonetic transcription skills.

REFERENCES

Bellugi, U. (1965). The development of interrogative structures in children's speech. In K. Riegel (Ed.), *The development of language functions* (Report No. 8, pp. 103–137). Ann Arbor; Michigan Language Development Program.

Bellugi, U. (1967). *The acquisition of negation*. Unpublished doctoral dissertation, Harvard University.

Bellugi, U. (1971). Simplification in children's language. In R. Huxley & E. Ingram (Eds.), *Language acquisition: Models and methods* (pp. 95–119). New York: Academic Press.

Berko (Gleason), J. (1958). The child's learning of English morphology. *Word, 14,* 150–177. Reprinted in A. Bar-Adon & W. Leopold, *Child language: A book of readings* (pp. 153–167). Englewood Cliffs, NJ: Prentice-Hall.

Berko Gleason, J., & Weintraub, S. (1976). The acquisition of routines in child language. *Language in Society, 5,* 129–136.

Bernhardt, B., & Johnson, C. E. (1995). Sentence production models: Explaining children's filler syllables. In C. E. Johnson & J. H. V. Gilbert (Eds.), *Children's language: Vol. 9* (pp. 253–281). Mahwah, NJ: Lawrence Erlbaum Associates

Bloom, L. (1970). Language development: Form and function in emerging grammars (Research Monograph No. 59). Cambridge, MA: MIT Press.

Bloom, L. (1973). *One word at a time: The use of single-word utterances before syntax.* The Hague: Mouton.

Bloom, L, Merkin, S., & Wooten, J. (1982). *Wh*-questions: Linguistic factors that contribute to the sequence of acquisition. *Child Development*, 53, 1084–1092.

Bolinger, D. (1976). Meaning and memory. *Forum Linguisticum, 1,* 1–14.

Bolinger, D. (1977). Idioms have relations. Forum *Linguisticum, 2,* 157–169.

Bowerman, M. (1973). *Early syntactic development: A cross-linguistic study with special reference to Finnish.* Cambridge: Cambridge University Press.

Brown, R. (1968). The development of Wh questions in child speech. *Journal of Verbal Learning and Verbal Behavior, 7,* 279–290.

Brown, R. (1973). *A first language: The early stages.* Cambridge, MA: Harvard University Press.

Brown, R., & Fraser, C. (1963). The acquisition of syntax. In C. Cofer & B. Musgrave (Eds.), *Verbal behavior and learning* (pp. 110–122). New York: McGraw-Hill.

Bush, C., Edward, M. L., Luckau, J. M., Stoel, C., Macken, M., & Petersen, J. (1973). *On specifying a system for transcribing consonants in child language: A working paper with examples from American English and Mexican Spanish.* Stanford, CA: Stanford University, Child Language Project.

Cairns, H., & Hsu, J. (1978). Who, why, when and how: A development study. *Journal of Child Language, 5,* 477–488.

Chapman, R. (1973). *The development of question comprehension in preschool children.* Paper presented in the annual convention of the American Speech and Hearing Associations, Detroit.

Clark, E. V., & Andersen, E. S. (1979). Spontaneous repairs: Awareness in the process of acquiring language. *Papers and Reports on Child Language Development, 16,* 1–12.

Clark, R. (1974). Performing without competence. *Journal of Child Language, 1,* 1–10.

Davis, H. (1987). *The acquisition of the English auxiliary system and its relation to linguistic theory.* Unpublished doctoral dissertation, University of British Columbia, Vancouver.

de Villiers, J. (Ed.). (1995). Introduction to the Special Issue on the Acquisition of *wh-* questions [Special issue]. *Language Acquisition, 4,* 1–4.

Dore, J., Franklin, M., Miller, R., & Ramer, A. (1976). Transitional phenomena in early language acquisition. *Journal of Child Language, 3,* 12–19.

Edwards, J. A. (1992). Computer methods in child language research: Four principles for the use of archived data. *Journal of Child Language, 19,* 435–458.

Edwards, J. A. (1993). Perfecting research techniques in an imperfect world: Response to MacWhinney & Snow. *Journal of Child Language, 20,* 209–216.

Edwards, J. A., & Lampert, M. D. (Eds.). (1993). *Talking data: Transcription and coding in discourse research.* Hillsdale, NJ: Lawrence Erlbaum Associates.

Ervin-Tripp, S. (1970). Discourse agreement: How children answer questions. In J. Hayes (Ed.), *Cognition and the development of language* (pp. 79–107). New York: Wiley.

Ervin-Tripp, S. (1977). From conversation to syntax. *Papers and Reports in Child Language Acquisition, 13,* K1–21.

Ferguson, C. A. (1976). The structure and use of politeness formulas. *Language in Society, 5,* 137–152.

Ferguson, C. A., & Farwell, C. (1975). Words and sounds in early language acquisition. *Language, 51,* 419–439.

Fillmore, C. J. (1979). On fluency. In C. Filmore, D. Kempler, & W. Wang (Eds.), *Individual differences in language ability and language behavior* (pp. 85–101). New York: Academic Press.

Gheorgov, I. (1908). *Ein Beitrag zur grammatischen Entwicklung der Kindersprache* [A treatise on the grammatical development of child language]. Leipzig: Engelmann.

Guillaume, P. (1973). The development of formal elements in the child's speech (E. V. Clark, Trans.). In C. A. Ferguson & D. I. Slobin (Eds.), *Studies of child language development* (pp. 240–251). New York: Holt, Rinehart and Winston. (Pages 216–229 from original work, Le développement des élements formels dans le language de l'enfant, 1927. *Journal de Psychologie, 24,* 203–229.)

Halliday, M. A. K. (1975). *Learning how to mean: Explorations in the development of language.* London: Edward Arnold.

Hayes-Roth, B. (1977). Evolution of cognitive structures and processes. *Psychological Review, 84,* 260–278.

Hurford, J. (1975). A child and the English question formation rule. *Journal of Child Language, 2,* 299–301.

Ingram, D. (1972). The acquisition of the English verbal auxiliary and copula in normal and linguistically deviant children. *Papers and Reports on Child Language Development, 4,* 79–91.

Ingram, D., & Tyack, D. (1979). Inversion of subject NP and AUX in children's questions. *Journal of Psycholinguistic Research, 8,* 333–341.

International Phonetic Association (1979). *The principles of the International Phonetic Association* (Handbook of the IPA). London: London University College.

Johnson, C. E. (1980, October). The ontogenesis of question words in children's language. Paper presented at the Fifth Annual Boston University Conference on Language Development, Boston.

Johnson, C. E. (1981). Children's questions and the discovery of interrogative syntax. Unpublished doctoral dissertation, Stanford University, Stanford, CA.

Johnson, C. E. (1983). The development of children's interrogatives: From formulas to rules. *Papers and Reports in Child Language Development, 22,* 108–115.

Johnson, C. E. (1999). *What does it mean to "know" a wh-word?* Manuscript in preparation.

Klima, E., & Bellugi, U. (1966). Syntactic regularities in the speech of children. In J. Lyons & R. Wales (Eds.), *Psycholinguistics papers* (pp. 183–208). Edinburgh: University Press. (Reprinted in *Child language: A book of readings*, pp. 412–424, by A. Bar-Adon & W. Leopold, Eds., 1971, Englewood Cliffs, NJ: Prentice Hall)

Lange, K., & Larsson, S. (1973). *Syntactical development of a Swedish girl Embla between 20 & 40 months of age: Part I, Age 20–25 months* (Project Child Language Syntax Report No. 1). Stockholm: Stockholms Universitet, Institutionen für Nordiska Språk.

Leonard, L. (1975). On differentiating syntactic and semantic features in emerging grammars: Evidence from empty form usage. *Journal of Psycholinguistic Research, 4*, 357–364.

Lightbown, P. (1979). Question form and meaning in the speech of young children learning French. *Working Papers on Bilingualism, 18*, 103–130.

MacWhinney, B. (1991). *The CHILDES project: Tools for analyzing talk.* Hillsdale, NJ: Lawrence Erlbaum Associates.

MacWhinney, B., & Snow, C. (1985). The child language data exchange system. *Journal of Child Language, 12*, 271–296.

MacWhinney, B., & Snow, C. (1992). The wheat and the chaff: Or four confusions regarding CHILDES. *Journal of Child Language, 19*, 459–471.

Mayer, J., Erreich, A., & Valian, V. (1978). Transformation, basic operations and language acquisition. *Cognition, 6*, 1–13.

Menn, L. (1976). *Pattern, control, and contrast in beginning speech: A case study in the development of word form and word function.* Unpublished doctoral dissertation, University of Illinois at Urbana-Champaign (University Microfilms International No. 76–24, 139)

Ninio, A., & Bruner, J. (1978). The achievement and antecedents of labeling. *Journal of Child Language, 5*, 1–15.

Ochs, E. (1979). Transcription as theory. In E. Ochs & B. Schieffelin (Eds.), *Developmental pragmatics* (pp. 43–75). New York: Academic Press.

O'Grady, W. (1997). *Syntactic development.* Chicago: University of Chicago Press.

Peters, A. M. (1977). Language learning strategies: Does the whole equal the sum of the parts? *Language, 53*, 560–573.

Peters, A. M. (1983). The units of language acquisition. *Cambridge Monographs and Texts in Applied Psycholinguistics*, S. Rosenberg (Ed.), Cambridge: Cambridge University Press.

Peters, A. M. (1995). Strategies in the acquisition of syntax. In P. Fletcher & B. MacWhinney (Eds.), *The handbook of child language* (pp. 462–482). Oxford: Blackwell.

Peters, A., Fahn, R., Glover, G., Harley, H., Sawyer, M., & Shimura, A. (1990). *Keeping close to the data: A two-tier computer-coding schema for the analysis of morphological development.* Unpublished manuscript, University of Hawaii, Honolulu.

Peters, A. M., & Menn, L. (1993). False starts and filler syllables: Ways to learn grammatical morphemes. *Language, 69*, 742–777.

Radford, A. (1990). *Syntactic theory and the acquisition of English syntax: The nature of early child grammars of English.* Oxford: Blackwell.

Radford, A. (1994). The syntax of questions in child English. *Journal of Child Language, 21*, 211–236.

Radford, A. (1995). Phrase structure and functional categories. In P. Fletcher & B. MacWhinney (Eds.), *The handbook of child language* (pp. 483–507). Oxford: Blackwell.

Sacks, H., Schegloff, E., & Jefferson, G. (1974). A simplest systematics for the organization of turn-taking in conversation. *Language, 50*, 696–735.

Scollon, R. (1976). *Conversations with a one-year-old: A case study of the developmental foundation of syntax.* Honolulu: University Press of Hawaii.

Slobin, D. (1973). Cognitive prerequisites for the development of grammar. In C. Ferguson & D. Slobin (Eds.), *Studies of child language development* (pp. 175–208). New York: Holt, Rinehart, & Winston.

Smith, M. (1933). The influence of age, sex, and situation on the frequency, form, and function of questions asked by preschool children. *Child Development, 4*, 201–213. (Reprinted in *Readings in language development*, pp. 278–291, ed. by L. Bloom, 1978, New York: John Wiley and Sons.)

Sokolov, J., & Snow, C. (1994). *Handbook of research in language development using CHILDES.* Hillsdale, NJ: Lawrence Erlbaum Associates.

Stern, C. & Stern, W. (1965). *Die Kindersprache, eine Psychologische und Sprachtheoretische Untersuchung* [Child language, a psychological and linguistic investigation]. Darmstadt, Germany: Wissenschaftliche Buchgesellschaft. (Unchanged reproduction of the 4th ed., Leipzig, 1928)

Stromswold, K. (1990). *Learnability and the acquisition of auxiliaries.* Unpublished doctoral dissertation, Massachusetts Institute of Technology, Cambridge. (Distributed by MIT Working Papers in Linguistics, MIT, Cambridge, MA)

Stromswold, K. (1995). The acquisition of subject and object *wh*-questions. The acquisition of *wh*-questions [special issue], J. de Villiers (Ed.), *Language Acquisition, 4,* 5–48.

Tyack, D., & Ingram, D. (1977). Children's production and comprehension of questions. *Journal of Child Language, 4,* 211–224.

Van Lancker, D. (1973). Language lateralization and grammars. In J. Kimball (Ed.), *Syntax and semantics: Vol. 2* (pp. 197–204). New York: Academic Press.

Vihman, M. M. (1980). Formulas in first and second language acquisition. *Papers and Reports in Child Language Development, 18,* 75–92.

Vihman, M. M., & McCune, L. (1994). When is a word a word? *Journal of Child Language, 21,* 517–542.

Weinberg, A. (1990). Markedness versus maturation: The case of subject-auxiliary inversion. *Language Acquisition, 1,* 165–194.

Wode, H. (1976). Some stages in the acquisition of questions by monolingual children. In W. von Raffler-Engel (Ed.), *Child Language—1975* (pp. 261–310). [Equivalent to *Word, 27,* International Linguistic Association]

Wong Fillmore, L. (1979). Individual differences in second language acquisition. In C. Fillmore, D. Kempler, & W. Wang (Eds.), *Individual differences in language ability and language behavior* (pp. 203–228). New York: Academic Press.

10

Food for Thought: Dinner Table as a Context for Observing Parent–Child Discourse

Barbara Alexander Pan
Harvard Graduate School of Education

Rivka Y. Perlmann
Boston Institute for Psychotherapy

Catherine E. Snow
Harvard Graduate School of Education

Most studies of children's spontaneous speech and of parent–child interaction have collected data in dyadic contexts, those in which activities designed to elicit dyadic talk (book reading, toy play) were prescribed or encouraged and then observed. These activities are constrained in a number of ways: They may not be common occurrences in some homes, where parent–child relations do not revolve around play; and they are by nature biased toward child interests—the books and the toys typically chosen are designed for children and are limited to child-appropriate topics and entities. Although some work has been done on adult–child interaction in more ecologically valid care-taking situations such as bathing, dressing, and diapering (e.g., Aukrust, 1995, 1996; Masur, 1987, 1989), this too has tended to be dyadic in participation structure. Although dyadic talk is relatively easy to observe, transcribe, and code, it has obvious limitations—both as a source of information about children's language environments, which are often multiparty, and as a context for observing certain kinds of interactive phenomena that may only emerge in larger groups.

One context for observing parent–child interaction that has gone beyond the constraints of the child-focused, dyadic setting has been mealtime conversations. These have been included in language corpora since the project by Hall and collaborators (e.g., Hall, Nagy, & Linn, 1984) and the project by Berko Gleason and her colleagues (Studies in the Acquisition of Communicative Competence), both begun in the mid-1970s. In Berko Gleason's project, children were observed systematically in dyadic contexts with mother and father and then at a family mealtime with both parents. Subsequently researchers such as Beals (1993), Becker (1990), Blum-Kulka (1993, 1994, 1997), Ochs and colleagues (Ochs, Taylor, Rudolph, & Smith, 1992), and others have used mealtimes as contexts for observation with the justification that these are naturally occurring events, that they reflect familial processes, and that they tap into cultural norms about contexts for and types of interaction.

In this chapter we examine the value of dinner-table conversations as a context for observing child language and parent–child interaction, in order to address the following question: Is the dinner-table context one that generates information about children's language interactions not available in other contexts?

In order to answer this question, we consider the uses that have been made of the large corpora of mealtime conversations, starting with that produced under Berko Gleason's direction. We also provide an overview in table form of available corpora of mealtime conversations (see Table 10.1) and try to include reference to all published research on mealtime talk in our bibliography. In reviewing past research about mealtime conversations, our goal is to discuss the advantages of multiparty, naturally occurring conversations as a basis for drawing conclusions about language development and language interaction. To present a balanced picture, though, we start with (a) a discussion of some of the challenges associated with collecting and analyzing mealtime data, and (b) some methodological guidelines.

TABLE 10.1
Major Corpora of Mealtime Data

Corpus	N of Families	Characteristics of Sample	Observation Conditions	Age of Target Children	Major Focus
Aukrust	44	22 Norwegian, 22 American	videotaped, no observer	2;9–4;0	cultural norms
Becker	5	middle class, observed longitudinally	audiotaped, no observer	mean 3;5 at start of study	language socialization
Berko-Gleason*	24	middle class, English-speaking	audiotaped, no observer	2–5 years	language socialization
Blum-Kulka	34	Native Israeli, American immigrants in Israel, American Jewish	audio- and videotaped, observer present	6;1–17;2	socialization, cultural differences, code-switching
Davidson	12	middle class, English-speaking	audiotaped, no observer	4;11–5;9	language input to precocious readers
Hall*	39	middle and working class, black & white, English-speaking	audiotaped, observer present	4;6–5;0	language input
Hooshyar*	31	middle class, families with children with Down Syndrome, English-speaking	videotaped, observer present	3;2–11;2	language input, language socialization
Kasuya	5	middle class, Japanese-English bilingual	audiotaped, observer present	2;10–4;10	code-switching, Japanese acquisition
Ochs	12	middle to working class, English-speaking	videotaped, no observer	5 years	narrative co-construction
Pan	10	middle class, Chinese-speaking, living in the U.S.	audiotaped, no observer	4;0–6;0	code-switching, language maintenance
Snow	81	working class, English-speaking, observed longitudinally	audiotaped, no observer	3 to 13 years at start of study	predictors of literacy development

* Available through CHILDES (MacWhinney, 1991)

THE CHALLENGE OF
COLLECTING AND ANALYZING
DINNER-TABLE TALK

Overview

Although we are convinced of the many advantages of dinner-table conversations for certain research purposes, we must point out that collecting and analyzing mealtime talk poses inherent challenges. Some are technical ones associated with recording quality and difficulty of transcription, which require thoughtful decisions about recording equipment, about the advantages of videotaping versus using audio alone, and about the role of an observer. Other challenges have to do with ecological validity—ensuring that the mealtime taped is as natural as possible, deciding how to proceed if families do not typically eat together, creating a culturally appropriate role for any observer, deciding on appropriate instructions for the family, and so on. Yet another set of challenges relates to the possibly illusory comparability of mealtimes across social classes and cultures. In fact, differences in the rules governing mealtimes abound. In some cultures they constitute opportunities for children to talk with adults as equal conversational partners, whereas in others a hierarchical structure imposes relative silence on youth. In some cultures mealtimes are quite formal, and in others they offer a time to relax. In some cultures the mealtime is limited to the nuclear family, in others to friends and larger family groups, and in yet others it is a time for open-handed inclusion of anyone in the vicinity. All these challenges must be kept in mind when deciding on whether to collect and how to use mealtime data.

Technical challenges

Multiparty interaction is more difficult to transcribe and analyze than is dyadic interaction. The time invested in transcribing 20 minutes of a mealtime conversation can be several times greater than the time involved in transcribing a dyadic interaction of similar length. Problems the transcriber faces include discriminating among speakers (especially if there is more than one child); the greater likelihood of overlapping speech and conflicting topics/agendas; the frequent impossibility of determining who the addressee(s) are; the likelihood of noise from dishes and silverware, burps and slurps; and the possibility that milk was spilled into the tape recorder.

Observing a mealtime requires making a decision about whether the observer should be present or not. The presence of an observer involves both pros and cons. Observing a mealtime without participating in it typically creates an extremely awkward situation, but by participating the observer can influence the mealtime talk to a considerable degree (see Blum-Kulka, 1997, for discussion); s/he generally takes on the role of guest, and transforms the dinner into a more formal event than normal. Cultural norms about the degree to which a visitor at dinner is a typical or an exceptional event may make cross-group comparisons difficult; for example, in the Blum-Kulka (1997) study the observer was always invited to eat with the Israeli families, but often was not invited by families observed in the United States. Transcribing is easier if an observer has been present, in particular one who can remember the event well or make field notes surreptitiously. The presence of an observer can provide assurance that the taping was uncensored—which might, however, lead people to be more selective of their topics and more careful of their speech. Participants sometimes forget after a while that the tape recorder is there, but it is more difficult to forget that an observer is present.

When data are to be collected without an observer present, the choice of recording equipment and guidelines to the families for placement of the microphone become particularly crucial. Difficulties in audibility can result if the microphone is placed close to a noisy infant, for example, or if a radio or television is left on during the meal. The tape recorder needs to be in relatively close proximity to the most important speakers—but it should also be in a position that is relatively protected from the banging of dishes and from disruption as people move to and from the table.

Similarly, a decision is needed about video- versus audiotaping. Some researchers choose to videotape (Ochs et al. 1992, had fieldworkers set up a videocamera and then leave, and on other occasions she had families audiotape themselves), which makes identification of speakers easier but has many of the same drawbacks as the presence of an observer.

Ecological Validity

Allowing families to tape an unobserved mealtime, such as was done in the Home-School Study (Snow, 1991), might provide more naturalistic data and give families more control in the submission of a "good" mealtime. However, this procedure has the disadvantage of providing considerable freedom, which some families take advantage of to avoid ever taping a meal. For any given year of the study, 18% to 37% of the families in the Home-School Study failed to produce a mealtime tape.

The mealtime context may be less ecologically valid for some families than for others; in some families, meals at which the whole family sits down to eat together, without television or radio on, is the exception rather than the rule. For those families, there may be other contexts in which extensive adult–child or multiparty interaction is more common (e.g., car rides, walks to the bus stop, talk while engaged in household tasks such as cleaning or food preparation). For other families, however, multiparty interaction around the dinner table may be more ecologically valid than a context such as "free play," which assumes that adults regularly engage in play with their children.

Mealtime conversations are particularly interesting as contexts for observing whole-family interactions. The nature of mealtime conversations can be quite different, though, when the family constellation is itself dyadic or when other familial circumstances such as parental work schedules make whole-family meals impractical. In the Home-School Study, for example, single mothers with only one or two young children reported not typically eating an organized dinner. Tapes submitted from families like this included meals that consisted of the children eating Cheerios in front of the television and, in a couple of families, interaction during meal preparation rather than during the meal itself. Thus, focusing on families in which the parents and children normally eat together might constitute a limitation to a very biased sample. Alternately, including mealtimes that vary over the full range of participant structures generates difficulties in comparability.

Care and thoughtfulness about the instructions to families can ensure optimal data quality. It is generally best to let families know why their mealtimes are of interest and to emphasize that the variety of ways in which families organize talk at mealtimes is part of the research focus, unless doing so threatens the research goals. In the Home-School Study, where the focus of most of the data collection was the young child in the family, that child was often given a privileged position during recorded mealtimes—encouraged to speak up and included explicitly in the conversations. This possibly unnatural treatment might have been avoided had more explicit instructions been given that the mealtimes were meant to provide a source of information about the whole family. Blum-Kulka (1997) instructed her subjects that the mealtimes were being taped as part of a study comparing Israeli and Jewish-American families, without mentioning that language used, politeness, or narrative discourse would be of special interest; but the interviews conducted outside the mealtime focused on matters of cultural identification, language proficiency, and academic aspirations for the children—inclusion of these topics might well have influenced how parents talked during the meal.

These various challenges make clear that using mealtime data does not automatically solve problems of obtaining optimal family interaction data. No data are perfect. Mealtime data are, however, a rich and often highly informative source of certain kinds of information, and generally they are an invaluable supplement to other, more structured and focused types of data.

USING MEALTIMES IN RESEARCH ON ACQUISITION

Research in English-Speaking Families

In 1975 when Jean Berko Gleason wrote a proposal to the National Science Foundation to fund the collection of child language data, she had two primary interests: the differences between mothers and fathers in their styles of interaction with their children, and the use of the language of socialization—parental attempts to display and elicit politeness routines and other socially appropriate language forms. Thus, she designed a study in which mothers and fathers would interact dyadically with their children reading a picture book, playing with a take-apart car toy, and engaging in make-believe play. In addition to these dyadic settings, though, she asked the families to tape a dinner-table conversation in which both parents and child were present. These conversations were recorded without an observer present.

The dinner-table conversations collected by Berko Gleason constituted the data analyzed in Berko Gleason, Perlmann, and Greif's (1984) paper, "What's the Magic Word?" The authors analyzed parental strategies for enforcing the production of politeness forms by their children (e.g., *what do you say? what's the magic word?*). Simple frequency counts of politeness routines used by participants during the meal yielded rich material about the types of politeness routines, their pervasiveness, their form and function, and their social as well as linguistic purposes. The unequal linguistic and social status of children and parents could be seen in these everyday interchanges. The parents' didactic and directive style in dealing with their children, and their one-sided strategies used to elicit the politeness routines from their children, emerged clearly in numerous examples such as the following:

Child:	More juice, more juice, more juice, more juice, more juice.
Father:	I didn't hear, uh, the magic word, Katie.
Child:	*Please.*

The existence of a routine such as *May I please be excused?* accentu-
ates the status difference between parents and children because this is a
form that is basically reserved for children; an adult who intends leaving
the table may say *excuse me*, but only a child must ask for permission and
wait for it to be granted:

Mother:	All right, what do you ask daddy, what do you ask?
Daughter:	Please.
Mother:	Please what?
Daughter:	(mumbles unintelligibly)
Mother:	May I be excused, right?

This example is interesting because the parent provides in one episode
a series of increasingly explicit demands for the routine, beginning with
elicitation (*what do you ask?*), continuing with a prompt of a more specific nature (*please what?*), and ending with a model (*may I be excused?*).
The following exchange between 4-year-old girl and her mother also
exemplifies the parent's increasingly exacting demand of the child to produce the desired form:

Child:	Mommy, I want more milk.
Mother:	Is that the way you ask?
Child:	Please.
Mother:	Please what?
Child:	Please gimme milky.
Mother:	No.
Child:	Please gimme milk.
Mother:	No.
Child:	Please . . .
Mother:	Please, may I have more milk?
Child:	Please, may I have more milk?

Berko Gleason and her colleagues argued that the teaching of politeness routines served not only a socialization function but a linguistic one
as well. The examples cited showed how adults were not just teaching
their children how to be polite when they insisted that the children change
the form of their utterance to a more polite variant. They were also exposing them to their first lessons in stylistic variation.
    Perlmann (1984) analyzed the Berko Gleason corpus from the per-
spective of the content of dinner-table conversations. Perlmann developed a coding scheme that captured individual differences in speaking

style among the homogeneous sample of middle-class families available in the Berko Gleason corpus. She showed that these families were fairly uniform in some features of their speaking style and highly variable in others. She looked at dimensions such as the amount of speech, the degree to which it revolved around the child, the presence of abstract discourse, and the degree of focus on discipline and control. Perlmann found that the amount of talk over dinner was not a good yardstick for measuring individual differences among this group of families. This dimension of loquaciousness may display more variability when examined across different ethnic or socioeconomic groups. However, families displayed wide individual differences in the degree to which they talked about abstract matters with their children. Some parents never talked to their child in a style that conveyed general concepts and principles about how the world works (e.g., illustrating parallels between gravy spoons collecting meat juices and the ways that rivers and lakes work). Furthermore, families whose conversations contained this kind of "world knowledge" tended to have fewer exchanges focused on discipline and control. Perlmann's descriptions illuminated subtle variations in parental styles and their linguistic expression. Ultimately, variations in parental style may contribute to the emergence of individual differences in children. The analysis carried out by Perlmann presaged the use of dinner-table conversation to answer questions about the cognitive content of familial conversations, a theme later taken up by Ochs and her colleagues and in Snow's study (Ochs et al., 1992; Snow, 1991).

Inspired by Berko Gleason's work with normally developing children, Hooshyar collected similar data on a large group of children with Down syndrome, looking as well in the same study at families with normally developing children and those with children with specific language impairment (Hooshyar, 1985, 1987). Hooshyar subsequently made the corpus of conversations in families with a child with Down syndrome available through the Child Language Data Exchange System (CHILDES) archives (MacWhinney, 1991; MacWhinney & Snow, 1985, 1990). Comparisons between children in the Berko Gleason and in the Hooshyar corpora revealed use of fewer inner state words, especially those referring to affect or cognition, in maternal speech to children with Down syndrome (Tingley, Berko Gleason, & Hooshyar, 1994). Another comparison of these two groups, including as well data from the Hall and the Home-School Study corpus (see subsequent discussion), was carried out by Snow, Perlmann, Berko Gleason, and Hooshyar (1990). They looked at the use of politeness forms in the speech of fathers and mothers in three groups: middle-class parents with normally developing children, working-class parents with normally developing children, and parents whose children had Down syndrome. They found that the speech addressed to children with Down syndrome was more conventionally polite, but they did not find the expected social class differences or differences between mothers and fathers in politeness in the dinner-table context.

Another sizable corpus of dinner-table conversations comes from the work of Hall, who recorded 39 Black and White, middle and working class families with 4-year-old children in a variety of naturally occurring settings. Hall's analyses of these data focus primarily on frequency of vocabulary used by children and adults at home, at school, and in transit (Hall, Nagy, & Linn, 1984), and for the most part they do not consider the dinner-table context apart from other home contexts. However, because specific contexts such as the dinner table are faithfully indicated in the transcripts (also now part of the CHILDES archives), the Hall corpus is a valuable source of dinner-table data for other studies focusing on language socialization and parent–child interaction more generally, such as that by Snow, Gleason, and colleagues (Snow et al., 1990).

The Home-School Study of Language and Literacy Development, (HSSLLD), a longitudinal study that began with 81 working-class families (Snow, 1991), attempted to collect dinner-table conversations yearly from all the participating families. Like Berko Gleason's and Hall's, this study documented parent–child interaction in a variety of contexts, but most of these were somewhat scripted, dyadic, mother–child interactive contexts. Only the dinner-table conversations were naturally occurring and taped without an observer present. Because the researchers were interested in exposure to extended discourse as a predictor of later language and literacy outcomes, analyses of the Home-School Study dinner-table conversations focused on issues such as the frequency of occurrence of narrative and of explanatory talk. Beals (1991, 1993) categorized the explanatory talk available in 31 dinner-table conversations collected during the first few years of the study, providing a picture of naturally occurring extended discourse that was much enriched beyond that available from the more common analyses of narrative. Beals and De Temple (1993) analyzed the incidence of both narrative and explanation in the same mealtimes as a predictor of later child outcomes and found that the amount of explanatory talk that a 3-year-old is exposed to at mealtimes is associated with vocabulary and discourse abilities at age 5. Beals and Snow (1994) described the ways in which narrative and explanatory talk relate to one another within mealtimes—with explanations often being buttressed by narratives and vice versa. They found that families that tended to produce a high proportion of narrative talk were also likely to produce more explanatory talk than the average.

An additional aspect of mealtime talk analyzed within the context of the Home-School Study was the use of rare or sophisticated vocabulary during mealtimes. Rare words were defined as those that fall outside the 3,000 most common words of English (and their inflected forms). Beals and Tabors (1995) described the frequency of rare words produced by Home-School Study participants during the dyadic and the mealtime contexts. They found mealtimes a particularly rich source of rare vocabulary; they also found that mealtime rare vocabulary use was a better predictor of later child outcomes (particularly in the domain of receptive vocabulary) than was rare vocabulary use in other contexts. Rare words used by low income families in the sessions analyzed by Beals and Tabors included *oxygen, seahorse, shrimp, bureaucrat, budget, government*, and *carbohydrates*. Weizman (1995; Weizman & Snow, 1998) extended this analysis, using Home-School Study mealtimes as well as dyadic interactions collected when the children were 5 years old. Weizman's work replicated and extended that of Beals and Tabors; rare vocabulary at mealtimes was the best predictor of child vocabulary and, in fact, the significant relationships found extended for 2 years, predicting 2nd-grade vocabulary. Not just the incidence of rare vocabulary, but also the degree to which the vocabulary is conversationally embedded in a rich semantic context, emerged in Weizman's analysis as a significant predictor. Thus, for example, the following conversation, in which considerable information about the meaning of the word was available from the language in which it was embedded, exemplified the kind of talk heard by children with the largest vocabularies:

> **Child:** Mom, can I have a sausage?
> **Mother:** Yes you may, help yourself.
> **Mother:** Oh you ate that up with *gusto*, honey!
> **Mother:** Please be careful, okay?

In contrast, the following interaction gives minimal help in understanding what the rare word *cholesterol* might mean:

> **Mother:** No, you've had enough.
> **Mother:** You're not supposed to eat a lot of chicken skin like that.
> **Mother:** It's not good for you.
> **Mother:** There's *cholesterol* in it.
> **Mother:** Can you say "cholesterol"?
> **Mother:** Let me see you say it.

A study related to the Home-School Study was undertaken by Davidson (1993), looking at similar dyadic and whole family interactive situations for two groups of 5-year-old children from highly literate, middle class families. Half the children Davidson studied were early, untutored readers, whereas the other half were matched on social variables but did not read until after having been provided with formal reading instruction. Davidson's dinner-table conversations were longer than most collected by the Home-School Study and were full of rich cognitive and linguistic information. The families Davidson studied—both those with early readers and those whose children did not read spontaneously— engaged in a very high proportion of extended discourse and of talk that Perlmann (1984) would have characterized as related to "world knowledge" (Davidson & Snow, 1995, 1996). For example, the following interaction was initiated by a child question:

Child:	Do you know what sharks' chunks weigh?
Mother:	Sharks' what?
Child:	When they eat it.
Mother:	Sharks' what?
Child:	Chunks, when they eat it.
Mother:	When they eat what?
Child:	You know how much . . . when the . . . their chunks weigh when the shark eats the chunk?
Mother:	No, how much does a chunk weigh?
Child:	Fifteen pounds.
Mother:	A chunk of . . .
Father:	You mean that a shark can take a bite out of another fish fifteen . . . a fifteen pound bite out of another fish?
Mother:	Really?
Child:	Uh-huh.

An analysis of the differences in rare vocabulary use between families of 5-year-olds in the Home-School Study and in Davidson's study also reveals striking differences (Davidson & Snow, 1999).

A somewhat distinct approach to the analysis of dinner-table conversations was taken by Ochs et al. (1992), who collected data from 12 families across a range of social classes. All the families included children age 4 to 6. Operating from a more anthropological perspective, Ochs and her colleagues also focused on narrative and explanatory talk but emphasized the value of dinner-table conversations as a context for socializing children's capacities to take perspective, engage in critical thinking, and develop other intellectual skills relevant to school success. Ochs et al. present a picture of dinner-table conversation as a context for solving everyday problems by co-constructing interpretations of events through narration and renarration.

Research in Bilingual Families

Mealtime conversations become particularly rich sources of information in families that are bilingual or bicultural. Portraits of interaction within bilingual families are often based on the presumption of dyadic interaction—that the child speaks one language with the mother and the other with the father. But what happens in families like these when mom, dad, and children sit down together for a meal? This question was addressed by Kasuya (1997) in a study of families living in the United States in which one parent speaks Japanese and one English as a native language. Kasuya found that English predominated at the dinner table, even in families where the American parent spoke Japanese and the Japanese-speaking parent was successful in maintaining Japanese in dyadic interactions.

Kasuya's findings are less surprising, in some sense, than Pan's (1988, 1995) findings from a study of 10 middle class Chinese families in which the parents had immigrated to the United States as adults and, although competent speakers of English, were trying to maintain Mandarin as the home language. Target children were all first-born, had been spoken to primarily in Mandarin by caregivers since birth, and were 4 to 6 years old at the time of observation. Parent–child dyads were tape-recorded reading a wordless book, and parents were asked to audiotape a family dinner at which both parents and the target child were present. The focus of the study was on patterns of code switching—who bids to move the conversation from Mandarin to English or vice versa, and how compliant other family members are with the shift. One of the unexpected findings was that children participated much more extensively in family discourse at the dinner table than they did in dyadic interaction around book reading with either parent. Because children were more likely to shift from Mandarin to English, and adults were more likely to comply with child shifts than children were to comply with those of adults, the end result was that the dinner table became a context in which children had considerable influence on family language choice. This was the case even though there were two adults present, both of whom professed a commitment to maintaining Mandarin as the home language and each of whom was, in principle, available to model, recast, or otherwise support the child in producing appropriate Mandarin initiations and responses. The dinner-table context was crucial in revealing the degree to which family interaction was shifting toward English in those families in which the use of English by the child was tolerated by the parents.

Mealtimes as a Context for Studying Cultural Differences

Another study of code switching was carried out by Blum-Kulka (1997) as part of her analysis of interaction in American families who had immigrated to Israel. Because proficiency in English is highly valued in Israel, and because the Hebrew proficiency of the parents was often more limited than their English proficiency, these families regularly used a considerable amount of English during dinner-table conversations, often despite a preference on the part of the children for Hebrew. Blum-Kulka's study encompassed as well analysis of dinner-table conversations in native Israeli families and in Jewish families living in the United States. She used dinner-table talk as a context for analyzing cultural norms for parent–child relationships, for narrativization of experience and participants' rights and opportunities to participate in narratives, and for socialization talk.

One striking finding from Blum-Kulka's analysis was that her three groups of families were all quite similar in their levels of conventional and unconventional politeness. This finding contrasts with those from other kinds of comparisons of Israeli with American interactions, in which Israelis are usually described as being more direct and less conventionally polite (e.g., Blum-Kulka, House, & Kasper, 1989). It seems that mealtimes, in addition to revealing culturally specific norms for interaction, can disclose underlying similarities across quite different groups. This finding also recalls that from Snow et. al.'s (1990) study that fathers and mothers did not differ in politeness at the dinner table, although men and women do differ in politeness in other interactive contexts.

One other use of dinner-table conversations to illuminate questions about cultural differences is reported in Aukrust and Snow (1998). Families in Norway were matched on family constellation and social level to families in the United States, and an analysis was carried out based on Beals' (1993) and Beals and Snow's (1994) descriptions of narrative and explanatory talk in U.S. mealtimes. Aukrust and Snow found that narratives predominated in the Norwegian conversations, whereas explanations predominated in the U.S. conversations. Furthermore, the narratives that U.S. families produced tended to be about "big events" such as trips or family outings, whereas the Norwegian narratives focused on much more minor incidents such as events in the child's day-care classroom. Consistent with this difference in focus, the Norwegian explanations that did occur tended to deal with matters of social importance— explanations for minor deviations from the expected in the interpersonal realm, for example—whereas the American explanations were more likely to deal with matters of physical causality. Aukrust and Snow interpreted these findings as relating to broader cultural themes of individualism and autonomy in the United States and of egalitarianism and local belongingness in Norway.

THE DISTINCTIVE VALUE OF MEALTIME CONVERSATIONS

We have reviewed a variety of interesting findings and conclusions drawn from analyses of mealtime conversations. In this section we consider why mealtimes may yield different kinds of data and uniquely valuable data when compared to dyadic book reading or freeplay contexts.

• Much talk at the dinner table goes beyond the here-and-now topics related to eating, requesting, and serving food, in contrast to freeplay or book-reading situations in which the vast majority of talk between adults and young children is related to the ongoing activity or joint focus of attention. Thus, the dinner table is a context that may generate more talk about the nonpresent, more narratives, and types of negotiating talk that go beyond negotiating the immediate activity (Ochs et al., 1992; Perlmann, 1984).

• Because multiple agendas are played out at the dinner table— including serving, requesting, and consuming food, as well as socialization of children, exchange of information necessary for planning family affairs, and living up to the societal norm of having a pleasant conversation—children as well as adults must shift from one to another frame of talk. Making transitions across these different tasks and keeping several of them active simultaneously (e.g., interrupting an anecdote to pass the noodles) forces family members to use specific language forms and to deal with certain cognitive challenges that are less likely to occur in dyadic interaction.

• Because mealtimes tend to be multiparty contexts, and contexts in which adults and children are physically constrained to share space for some period, they also tend to be situations in which socialization is given high priority (Ochs et al., 1992; Snow et al., 1990), thereby providing a valuable window onto the transmission of cultural norms from parents to children.

• Similarly, mealtime conversations require taking into account simultaneously the multiple perspectives of the various participants and thus demand from children more work to make their narratives comprehensible and to understand their interlocutors' narratives than may be the case in dyadic interactions, where it is easier for the adult to adapt to the child's level and to the degree of their shared background knowledge.

• Natural interactions between children and their fathers are most likely to be observed, in traditional households at least, at the dinner table. Thus, dinner-table conversations become a unique source of information about paternal input to young children. This is of particular importance in light of the widespread findings that fathers are more likely than mothers to engage in talk that is less adapted to the child's level and thus more challenging (Berko Gleason, 1975; Mannle & Tomasello, 1987).

• Mealtime can also be a context in which there is considerable verbal interaction between adults and children (unless the culture is one in which talk by children at the table is discouraged). Dinner-table context sometimes yields more talk by young children than does a task such as book reading in which the child may be more content to let adults take the lead, as found in Pan's analysis of Chinese families (1988, 1995).

• Mealtimes can be considered to be a "sheltered workshop" in which children develop their extended discourse skills, with considerable help from adults in constructing their narratives for wider comprehensibility (as exemplified in the data from the HSSLLD and from Blum-Kulka's narratives). Talk is often about topics on which speaker and some but not all listeners have shared knowledge, so those who share knowledge can help provide support for the teller (Blum-Kulka & Snow, 1992).

• Some evidence suggests that dinner-table talk may be a more potent predictor of children's later language development than characteristics of talk in other settings. For example, the use of rare vocabulary items during dinner-table conversations was found to relate more strongly to child vocabulary outcomes than the use of rare vocabulary in book-reading or toy-play settings—perhaps because the multiparty conversations at the dinner table provided a richer basis for learning about the meaning of those rare words (Beals & Tabors, 1995; Weizman, 1995).

PROCESSING MEALTIME DATA

Mealtime transcripts are deeply rich and reanalyzable. When Berko Gleason included mealtime recording in her study in the mid-1970s, there was no single hypothesis she was interested in testing. Rather, she proceeded on the assumption that interesting data would emerge; and subsequent analyses of those transcripts fully justified that assumption. Although some subsequent studies have collected mealtime data with more targeted goals, the resulting data, albeit messy, always lend themselves to analyses that go beyond the original plans.

As researchers have become more aware of the potential of mealtime data, they have become more planful about analysis prior to data collection. Thus, we now know that mealtimes are ideal contexts for looking at language socialization and teaching of politeness, for seeing language choice in bilingual families, for observing narratives and explanations, and for documenting child exposure to relatively rare vocabulary items. In fact, mealtimes more than many other sorts of interactions belie the traditional notion that parents engage in no explicit language teaching.

Precisely because mealtime conversations are suitable for so many different sorts of analyses, it is difficult to provide a-priori guidelines about coding. Coding decisions should in any case reflect research questions, not data sources. However, it is clear from Table 10.1 that mealtime data lend themselves particularly well to certain kinds of coding, such as identifying extended discourse forms, distinguishing between cognitively challenging and practical talk, and coding minimally informative versus highly supportive contexts for novel lexical items.

CONCLUSION

Over the past few decades, child language research has evolved in ways that have made the dinner-table context a particularly rich source of data. The field has moved from an emphasis on dyadic to multiparty interaction, and from diary studies of single subjects to studies of larger samples of children and families. What researchers in the field have retained of the early diary methodology is a recognition of the importance of collecting naturalistic data about children's spontaneous language production. At the same time, there has been (a) burgeoning interest in children's acquisition of pragmatic as well as morphosyntactic and lexical knowledge, and (b) a corresponding shift in the unit of analysis from linguistic unit to speech event (Blum-Kulka, 1997). This widening of the lens has allowed researchers to investigate the development of extended discourse, including narratives and explanations, as well as children's utterance-level skills. Finally, the connections between child language research and anthropology have been highlighted as researchers more explicitly examine the parallel processes of language acquisition and socialization. For some communities, at least, the dinner table seems to be a prime site for the verbal transmission of cultural norms.

Berko Gleason could hardly have known that the corpus of dinner-table talk she collected in the mid-1970s would eventually be joined by corpora from the variety of samples and cultures represented in the literature today. Nor could she have foreseen how well the mealtime context would suit so many of the trends in child language research over the past two decades. The decision to contribute her transcripts to the CHILDES archives, though, and the support and advice she offered to students and colleagues alike in undertaking mealtime data collection, was intentional, ensuring that dinner-table talk from children and their families will continue to provide food for thought for child language researchers for years to come.

REFERENCES

Aukrust, V. G. (1995). *Fortellinger fra stellerommet. To-åringer i barnehage: en studie av språk-bruk—innhold og struktur* [Narratives from the nursery room. Two-year-olds in nursery school: a study of language use—content and structure] (Report No. 4/95). Oslo: University of Oslo, Institute for Educational Research.

Aukrust, V. G. (1996). Learning to talk and keep silent about everyday routines: A study of verbal interaction between young children and their caregivers. *Scandinavian Journal of Educational Research, 40,* 311–324.

Aukrust, V. G., & Snow, C. E. (1998). Narratives and explanations during mealtime conversations in Norway and the U.S. *Language in Society, 27,* 221–246.

Beals, D. E. (1991). *"I know who makes ice cream": Explanations in mealtime conversations of low-income families of preschoolers.* Unpublished doctoral dissertation, Harvard Graduate School of Education, Cambridge, MA.

Beals, D. E. (1993). Explanations in low-income families' mealtime conversations. *Applied Psycholinguistics, 14,* 489–513.

Beals, D. E., & De Temple, J. M. (1993, March). The where and when of whys and whats: Explanatory talk across settings. *Paper presented at the biennial meeting of the Society for Research in Child Development,* New Orleans.

Beals, D. E., & Snow, C. E. (1994). "Thunder is when the angels are upstairs bowling": Narratives and explanations at the dinner table. *Journal of Narrative and Life History, 4,* 331–352.

Beals, D. E., & Tabors, P. O. (1995). Arboretum, bureaucratic and carbohydrates: Preschoolers' exposure to rare vocabulary at home. *First Language, 15,* 57–76.

Becker, J. (1990). Processes in the acquisition of pragmatic competence. In G. Conti-Ramsden & C. E. Snow (Eds.), *Children's language: Vol.7* (pp. 7–24). Hillsdale, NJ: Lawrence Erlbaum Associates.

Berko Gleason, J. (1975). Fathers and other strangers: Men's speech to young children. *In Georgetown University Roundtable on Language and Linguistics* (pp. 289–297). Washington, DC: Georgetown University Press.

Berko Gleason, J., Perlmann, R., & Greif, E. (1984). What's the magic word: Learning language through politeness routines. *Discourse Processes, 7,* 493–502.

Blum-Kulka, S. (1993). "You got to know how to tell a story": Telling, tales, and tellers in American and Israeli narrative events at dinner. *Language in Society, 22,* 361–402.

Blum-Kulka, S. (1994). The dynamics of family dinner-talk: Cultural contexts for children's passages to adult discourse. *Research on Language and Social Interaction, 27,* 1–51.

Blum-Kulka, S. (1997). *Dinner talk: Cultural patterns of sociability and socialization in family discourse.* Mahwah, NJ: Lawrence Erlbaum Associates.

Blum-Kulka, S., House, J., & Kasper, G. (Eds.) (1989). *Cross-cultural pragmatics: Requests and apologies. Advances in discourse processes, Vol. 31.* Norwood, NJ: Ablex.

Blum-Kulka, S., & Snow, C. E. (1992). Developing autonomy for tellers, tales, and telling in family narrative-events. *Journal of Narrative and Life History, 2,* 187–217.

Davidson, R. (1993). *Oral preparation for literacy: Mothers' and fathers' conversations with precocious readers.* Unpublished doctoral dissertation, Harvard Graduate School of Education, Cambridge, MA.

Davidson, R., & Snow, C. E. (1995). The linguistic environment of early readers. *Journal of Research in Childhood Education, 10,* 5–21.

Davidson, R., & Snow, C. E. (1996). Five-year-olds' interactions with fathers versus mothers. *First Language, 16,* 223–242.

Davidson, R., & Snow, C. E. (1999). *Social class differences in rare vocabulary.* Manuscript in preparation, Harvard Graduate School of Education.

Hall, W. S., Nagy, W. E., & Linn, R. (1984). *Spoken words: Effects of situation and social group on oral word usage and frequency.* Hillsdale, NJ: Lawrence Erlbaum Associates.

Hooshyar, N. (1985). Language interaction between mothers and their nonhandicapped children, mothers and their Down syndrome children, and mothers and their language-impaired children. *International Journal of Rehabilitation Research, 4,* 475–477.

Hooshyar, N. (1987). The relationship between maternal language parameters and the child's language constancy and developmental condition. *International Journal of Rehabilitation Research, 10,* 321–324.

Kasuya, H. (1997). *Sociolinguistic aspects of language choice in English/Japanese bilingual children.* Unpublished doctoral dissertation, Harvard Graduate School of Education, Cambridge, MA.

MacWhinney, B. (1991). The CHILDES project: Computational tools for analyzing talk. Hillsdale, NJ: Lawrence Erlbaum Associates.

MacWhinney, B., & Snow, C. E. (1985). The Child Language Data Exchange System. *Journal of Child Language, 12,* 271–295.

MacWhinney, B., & Snow, C. E. (1990). The Child Language Data Exchange System: An update. *Journal of Child Language, 17,* 457–472.

Mannle, S., & Tomasello, M. (1987). Fathers, siblings, and the bridge hypothesis. In K. E. Nelson & A. van Kleek (Eds.), *Children's language, Vol. 6* (pp. 23–42). Hillsdale, NJ: Lawrence Erlbaum Associates.

Masur, E. F. (1987). Imitative interchanges in a social context: Mother-infant matching behavior at the beginning of the second year. *Merrill-Palmer Quarterly, 33,* 453–472.

Masur, E. F. (1989). Individual and dyadic patterns of imitation: Cognitive and social aspects. In G. E. Speidel & K. E. Nelson (Eds.), *The many faces of imitation in language learning* (pp. 53–71). New York: Springer-Verlag.

Ochs, E., Taylor, C., Rudolph, D., & Smith, R. (1992). Storytelling as a theory-building activity. *Discourse Processes, 15,* 37–72.

Pan, B. A. (1988). *Patterns of language choice in bilingual parent-child discourse.* Unpublished doctoral dissertation, Boston University.

Pan, B. A. (1995). Code negotiation in bilingual families: "My body starts speaking English." *Journal of Multilingual and Multicultural Development, 16,* 315–327.

Perlmann, R. (1984). *Variations in socialization styles: Family talk at the dinner table.* Unpublished doctoral dissertation, Boston University.

Snow, C. E. (1991). The theoretical basis for relationships between language and literacy in development. *Journal of Research in Childhood Education, 6,* 5–10.

Snow, C. E., Perlmann, R., Berko Gleason, J., & Hooshyar, N. (1990). Developmental perspectives on politeness: Sources of children's knowledge. *Journal of Pragmatics, 14,* 289–305.

Tingley, E. C., Berko Gleason, J., & Hooshyar, N. (1994). Mothers' lexicon of internal state words in speech to children with Down syndrome and nonhandicapped children at mealtime. *Journal of Communication Disorders, 27* (2), 135–155.

Weizman, Z. O. (1995). *Sophistication in maternal vocabulary input at home: Does it affect low-income children's vocabulary, literacy, and language success in school?* Unpublished doctoral dissertation, Harvard Graduate School of Education, Cambridge, MA.

Weizman, Z. O., & Snow, C. E. (1998). *Lexical input as related to children's vocabulary acquisition: Effects of sophisticated exposure and support for meaning.* Manuscript submitted for publication.

11

Exploring Register Knowledge: The Value of "Controlled Improvisation"

Elaine Andersen
University of Southern California

As a graduate student at Stanford University in 1974, I had recently published a paper (Andersen & Johnson, 1973) showing how an 8-year-old appropriately modified her speech to reflect both the age of the addressee and the nature of the task (e.g., telling a story vs. explaining a game vs. free play), and I was about to embark on a doctoral thesis examining in more detail young children's knowledge of the form and functions of Babytalk, or caregiver's speech. Then I met a scholar from Boston who was visiting for the year at the Center for Advanced Studies in the Behavioral Sciences. I soon learned that the scholar, Jean Berko Gleason, was at least one step ahead of us in this line of inquiry; she had already published the results of a naturalistic study that examined stylistic variation in the speech of toddlers, preschoolers, and first or second graders in five families (1973) and was planning a series of more controlled studies that would investigate different aspects of children's communicative competence, focusing especially on their acquisition of social/communicative routines (see, e.g., Berko Gleason & Perlmann, 1982; Berko Gleason, Perlmann, & Greif, 1984; Berko Gleason & Weintraub, 1976; Greif & Berko Gleason, 1980).

Becoming aware of this work, as well as the much cited Society for Research in Child Development monograph by Shatz and Gelman (1973), convinced me, in my naiveté, that this subject had been exhausted and I had better look elsewhere for a thesis topic. Fortunately, in large part through my growing friendship with Jean and her encouraging support that year (and ever since), I decided that it made more sense to expand the topic rather than abandon it. After all, Babytalk is not the only "register," or style of speech, that children must learn as they acquire communicative competence in their language. Indeed, during the early years of language socialization they are exposed to a wide range of registers in the speech of others, long before they have the opportunity to use these forms themselves. The question then is: Do children have passive knowledge of registers that an investigator would never have the opportunity to observe in naturalistic settings? Now began many years of research looking at the acquisition of register knowledge across a variety of language communities in the United States, Europe, and Latin America. This research required the development of an elicitation technique that had been little used in the study of language acquisition (see, however, Bates, 1976; Bates & Silvern, 1977). Explanation of the usefulness and nature of this technique forms the core of this chapter.

In what follows, I first briefly describe the general domain of inquiry (i.e., register knowledge and its acquisition) and argue for the need for and benefits of the experimental methodology that I have referred to as controlled improvisation. I then summarize and illustrate very generally some of the major findings of a series of cross-linguistic studies that have used slight variations of this technique. Finally, I focus on the investigation of discourse markers to more explicitly illustrate the application of this technique in exploring children's knowledge of the ways in which subtle linguistic forms can reflect or create social meaning.

REGISTER VARIATION

Language varies to reflect such nonlinguistic factors as the formality of the situation and the age, gender, or social class of speakers. Those varieties that reflect characteristics of the users are called dialects; those that reflect characteristics of the situation in which language is being used are often referred to as registers. The term *register* was first used and defined by Reid (1956) and later developed in the work of Ellis and Ure (1969), Ferguson (1977), and Andersen (1990), among others. More recent discussion of a variety of different registers is contained in Biber and Finegan (1994). In general, all these studies point out that register variation is sensitive to a wide range of social factors, including the context and topic of talk, as well as different aspects of the relationship between interlocutors (e.g., how well they know one another and the power relationship between them).

In any society, everyone controls a variety of registers; a given individual can be both a mother and a chemist, or a surfer, a student, and a doctor, and that individual speaks differently depending on the role he or she is playing at the time and the situation or setting of the discourse. Linguistically, registers can vary lexically (e.g., choice of *stomach*, *abdomen*, or *tummy*), phonologically (e.g., choice of *swimming* or *swimmin'*) and morphosyntactically (e.g., choice of an active or passive sentence: *He mixed the chemicals* or *The chemicals were then mixed*). Much has been written, for example, about the specialized vocabulary, intonation patterns, and morphosyntax of professional registers such as classroom language and medical talk (e.g., Atkinson & Biber, 1994; Cazden, 1988; Sinclair & Coulthard, 1975) and of simplified registers such as Babytalk and Foreignertalk (Andersen, 1990; Ferguson, 1975, 1977; Snow, 1972; Snow & Ferguson, 1977).

The Acquisition of Register Knowledge

The aspect of communicative competence covered by the notion of register knowledge has also been discussed by various researchers under the labels of "usage patterns," "style variation," or "codes." Although she does not use the term *register*, it is exactly this aspect of communicative competence that Berko Gleason (1973) was concerned with when she pointed out that:

> Somewhere along the road to language acquisition children must gain control over not only a vast vocabulary and a complicated grammar, but a variety of styles of speaking to different people under differing circumstances. . . .
>
> Paradoxically, until recent times, those of us who have studied child language have restricted ourselves to samples of the child's language to us, the interviewer, or to the child's mother or teacher, and we have assumed that that was it: child language. . . . In order to investigate code switching in children's language, it is necessary to observe the same child in a number of different speech situations. (p. 159)

The acquisition of register knowledge, then, is the process by which children learn to use language that is appropriate for the situation. This involves the coordination of several types of knowledge at once. First, children must have the linguistic tools necessary to exhibit the kinds of register variation characteristic of their society—for example, they must have available different names for the same referent *(potty* vs. *toilet)* and different grammatical forms to express the same speech act (the imperative request *Close the door* vs. the interrogative request *Would you please close the door?* vs. the declarative hint *It's noisy in the hall,* which can also serve as a request for the addressee to close the door). Second, they must be aware of those aspects of discourse participants and setting that demand register shifts in their society—for example, does one simplify one's speech for both children and foreigners, as in many western societies (Ferguson, 1975), or does one register shift for only one of these groups as in Western Samoa (Ochs, 1988; Shore, 1982)? Third, children must know the exact nature of the relationship between linguistic and social variation—that is, which particular linguistic forms cluster together to form the register that is appropriate for a particular social situation. For example, it is not enough to know that in middle-class American society it is appropriate to simplify one's speech for very young children and for adult foreigners because they are both considered "incompetent" in some way; one must also realize that exaggerated intonation is appropriate to use when speaking to the child, whereas flat intonation is more characteristic of speech addressed to a foreigner.

CONTROLLED IMPROVISATION

Naturalistic studies like the early Berko Gleason work (1973) on children's "code switching" in the family setting may well be the most ecologically valid way to test children's sociolinguistic skills; such studies demonstrate how children use language in familiar situations with familiar people. However, naturalistic studies are limited in a number of ways: Most important, they eliminate the possibility of assessing knowledge that children may have acquired but never display because of the limited roles they actually get to play in everyday (vs. pretend) life. For example, most American children have experienced numerous doctor's appointments by the time they are 4 or 5 years old, but it will be many years before any of them get to medical school and play the role of doctor for real.

Therefore, in my own work (e.g., Andersen, 1984, 1990; Andersen, Brizuela, Dupuy, & Gonnerman, 1995) I have used a method that I have labeled "controlled improvisation" to explore the range of linguistic devices (morphosyntactic, lexical, pragmatic, and phonological) for marking distinct registers that young children have available at different stages of acquisition. My main concerns in developing this task were to find a procedure that would meet four criteria: (a) It should be a task that children would find familiar and comfortable, (b) it should allow for comparison along the same nonlinguistic (social) dimensions across children, (c) it should neither constrain the children's creativity nor limit the range of sociolinguistic markers to any preconceived set (because children's categories do not always coincide with those of adults), and (d) it should facilitate children's ability to demonstrate their full range of knowledge.

After piloting a number of other techniques that were unsuccessful either in terms of keeping the children's limited attention focused on the task or in producing transcribable recordings (i.e., in which there were not several children speaking at once), I chose to use a number of role-specific puppets for whom the children had to "do the voices" in contexts set up by the experimenter. This procedure satisfies the first criterion by taking advantage of the fact that when preschoolers are involved in pretend play they often spontaneously adopt consistent speech patterns in accordance with the social categories involved (e.g., mothers, babies, doctors, etc.). The use of puppets and predetermined contexts also has the advantage of helping to control the situation (e.g., a child with puppets representing a doctor and a nurse is unlikely to suddenly switch to playing "robot" or "space warriors" with them), thereby allowing for comparisons across children and satisfying the second criterion. At the same time this technique allows the child a great deal of freedom to be imaginative and creative within the given limits, satisfying the third criterion. But most important, the technique allows children to demonstrate, through role play, knowledge of appropriateness rules governing language use for roles that are otherwise not available to them. Thus, each of the four goals for eliciting reliable results are met by the use of controlled improvisation.

The Application of "Controlled Improvisation"

This technique has now been used in at least six projects that have explored children's developing communicative competence in a variety of speech communities, including the following: middle-class monolingual

English-speaking American children (Andersen, 1990); middle-class monolingual French children (Andersen, 1996; Andersen et al., 1995); working-class bilingual Chicano children (Brizuela, Andersen, & Stallings, 1998); middle-class monolingual Spanish-speaking Argentinean children (Brizuela, Dupuy, & Andersen 1998; Brizuela, Gil, & Andersen, 1997); and middle-class bilingual Basque-Spanish children (Amorrortu, 1997). In the earliest project on English, the participants were 18 pre-school and first-grade children age 4 to 7 years; in the other projects the children ranged in age from 4 to 13, with the older children's speech used as the model that the younger children were acquiring. More specifically, 36 children age 4 to 13 participated in the French study, 20 children age 6 to 10 in the Chicano study, 36 children age 6 to 11 in the Argentinean study, and 8 children age 8 to 10 in the Basque study. For each study, the population constituted equal numbers of boys and girls.

In each of these studies the children participated in two or three sessions with different pretend settings, including a family setting, a medical setting, and a classroom setting. In the sessions the children had the opportunity to role-play a variety of characters including mother, father, spouse, doctor, nurse, teacher, and foreigner, as well as the more natural (for them) roles of son or daughter, patient and student. To ensure that speech samples were comparable across subjects, the experimenter suggested a distinct context in each session and used a single, distinct set of puppets for each. The puppets were hand-puppets in the form of "mittens" about 10 inches long, with very large mouths and arms hanging at the sides. Four fingers were used to move the upper part of the puppet's mouth, and the thumb operated the lower part. The hard-puppets were designed this way, with the mouth the only part that the children could manipulate easily, to encourage "talking" and discourage communication by gesture or other actions.

In the original American study, I first tried involving two children in each session, with one child playing one or two roles while the other child played the other(s). This technique turned out to be problematic because the use of puppets appeared to encourage the children to become aggressive: They would try to bite the other child's puppet with their puppet(s) or pull its hair. Although it may have been that they were reflecting the kind of violence portrayed in skits such as Punch & Judy, it is also clear that pretend play allows one to relax inhibitions against taboo behaviors. Therefore I instead tested children individually. Each child was asked to play two roles at a time, so as to elicit contrasting speech "styles"; the experimenter took the third role in each setting, with the purpose of keeping the session going if the role playing otherwise stalled. Occasionally, additional puppets were introduced into each setting by the children; this was tolerated for continuity of discourse in each session and often contributed additional distinctions among speech styles. From time to time, if a child appeared to forget what role he or she was playing, the experimenter would slip out of the "frame" and ask: "Is that the daddy/mommy/baby speaking?" At an appropriate juncture in a session, children would exchange one of their puppets for the experimenter's puppet; in this way, every child got the opportunity to do the voices for all three roles. Although I had intended to test children as young as age 2 or 3, pilot work soon made it clear that the task is too cognitively complex for children this young. (See Andersen, 1990, p.175, for further discussion of what 3-year-olds could and could not do.)

In the second project, in France, we found that the children preferred and produced much more fluent discourse when interacting with other children rather than with the experimenter. Because, unlike their American peers, they did not exhibit unusually aggressive behavior in this context, the method was modified for them so that two children at a time role-played together, each playing one or two roles and exchanging roles so that each child played every role. The experimenter was present only to set up the play and encourage its development. Other slight modifications of controlled improvisation that have been used in different language communities are described in greater detail in the papers cited in the previous discussion.

The Settings

In the following discussion, I describe the general scenario suggested by the experimenter for the three different contexts (family, doctor, and classroom) in the original study.

The Family Situation.   The three basic puppets in the family situation were (a) a mother, identifiable as a female adult by a dress, long hair in a bun, and earrings; (b) a father, identifiable as a male adult by a tie and a mustache; and (c) a young child, identifiable as such by flannel pajamas and ribboned pigtails. (Other puppets occasionally added to this session at the child's insistence included a grandmother; other young children (as siblings or friends); and occasionally a teacher, a doctor, and a nurse.) The experimenter introduced the setting for the family session in the following way:

Now today, let's play family; we have a daddy, a mommy, and a young child who's just learning how to talk. Why don't we pretend that it's the child's bedtime and the daddy/mommy is going to tuck her in and tell her a story. Then they can talk about what they're going to do tomorrow— maybe the child is going to be 3 years old tomorrow and they'll have a birthday party. Now why don't you play the daddy/mommy and the child, and I'll be the other parent. So you'll make that one talk like a daddy/mommy, right? And the other one talk like a young child, okay?

The Doctor Situation.   In the "doctor's office," the experimenter again offered three puppets: (a) one with a mustache and white hair on a balding head, wearing a white uniform; (b) another with blond hair in a bun, wearing a white uniform and a hat with a red cross on it; and (c) a third puppet recognizable as a patient by a bandaged forehead and one arm in a splint. Although the children were not told which puppets were to represent the doctor and the nurse, all of them in the American study assumed that the "male" was the doctor, the "female" the nurse. This turns out to be something of a problem for analysis because it confounds two social variables (gender and professional status), making it difficult to interpret the social motivation for particular linguistic devices used to distinguish doctor from nurse roles. Only when the children insisted on introducing additional puppet characters into the sessions was it possible to discriminate gender-motivated modifications from those attributable to differences in professional status. The setting for the doctor session was introduced in the following manner:

This time, how about playing doctor? We can use a doctor puppet, a nurse puppet, and this injured patient puppet. Let's pretend that the injured puppet had an accident and isn't feeling very well, okay? Now why don't you be the doctor and the nurse, and I'll be the patient. Pretend that the patient comes to the doctor's office for care. So you make that one be a doctor and that one be a nurse, right?

The Classroom Situation.   The three puppets in this session were (a) a teacher, who had gray hair and glasses; and (b) and (c) two children. There were two parts to this session. In the first part, the experimenter suggested that she and the child play school; the child could be the teacher and a student, the experimenter would be a different student. The setting was the beginning of a school day in the children's classroom. Then, halfway through the session, a somewhat different situation was set up. This time, the experimenter proposed the following:

Why don't I be the teacher now, and you can be the two children. Only this time, let's pretend that one of the children just came to this country from somewhere far away where they don't speak English. So she doesn't speak English very well. This is her first day at school, and she doesn't know what to do at school. So why don't you tell her what we do here, and maybe explain to her about a field trip we're going to go on. But remember, she only speaks a little bit of English.

The scene was set up in this way to encourage the child to speak not only *to* a "foreigner" but also *as* a foreigner, to ensure elicitation of any aspects of Foreignertalk in the child's repertoire. Indeed, some researchers have suggested that one is more likely to elicit features of Foreignertalk by asking how foreigners speak than by asking how one speaks to them:

Foreigner talk is commonly regarded in a given speech community as an imitation of the way foreigners speak the language under certain conditions and it is usually elicited more readily by asking for this kind of information than by asking the informant how he would speak to a foreigner. (Ferguson, 1975, p. 1)

Methodological Concerns

It is well known that the language people use often reflects the language of those they are speaking with; for example, if someone whispers to me, it is difficult not to whisper back. Therefore, if we as researchers want to know that this task (controlled improvisation) is actually tapping children's stored knowledge of register variation, it should be structured so as to reduce as much as possible the influence of language choices made by those with whom the children are interacting, whether that be the researcher or another child. The way I dealt with this problem was to counterbalance the order in which the settings (e.g., family and classroom) and the roles within the settings (e.g., mother, father, child) were presented to the children, so that more often than not the children were playing roles they had not already seen played by others (at least within the study).

An additional concern is to keep the settings consistent across children, so that any age or gender differences observed could be attributed to differences in the children's knowledge rather than to differences in the settings. Occasionally, however, a child would spontaneously suggest (and even insist on) slight modifications to the planned format. Examples include suggestions in the family session that they discuss a vacation (rather than the child's birthday party) and in the doctor session that the scene take place in the hospital rather than in the doctor's office or that the father come with the patient. Such slight adjustments were tolerated for the sake of naturalness of play.

One final concern is that the data collected with this technique might reflect children's stereotypes more than their actual beliefs of how a given individual (e.g., their mother) uses language in everyday, spontaneous conversation. This is not, however, necessarily a disadvantage in investigating register knowledge. One might instead argue that an additional strength of this technique is that it allows the elicitation of symbolic form choices stripped of practical compliance consequences that impact normal usage, making more explicit children's abilities to discriminate and express in their language important social relationships.

Analysis of Data

All sessions were audiotaped, and the tapes were transcribed with a modified conventional orthography. In cases of deviant pronunciation, an (IPA) phonetic transcription was made. Each transcript was checked by two researchers; in the few instances of intertranscriber disagreement, we listened to the tape again and discussed the problem until a consensus was reached.

The analysis of the speech samples coded (a) speech quantity for each "speaker" to each "addressee"; (b) function of different utterance-types used in each role (i.e., a speech-act analysis); and (c) the syntactic, lexical, and phonological devices used to mark particular registers. For 20% of the tapes, the data were coded independently by two researchers, and measures of intercoder reliability were tabulated.

SUMMARY OF
CROSS-LINGUISTIC RESULTS

Because the goal of this volume is to present a variety of methodical approaches to the study of language use and acquisition, I provide here only a brief overview of the most general results of a series of studies of the register knowledge of children acquiring English, French, and Spanish, illustrating most explicitly the use of discourse markers as indicators of register. Statistical analyses and more detailed cross-linguistic comparisons are presented elsewhere (e.g., Andersen et al., 1995).

Most generally, the findings demonstrate that there are a wide range of social relationships that young children are able to distinguish and mark linguistically. The children we have studied display their knowledge through choices of content, conversational or discourse strategies, and situationally appropriate phonological and grammatical patterns. Over developmental time they demonstrate increasing awareness of the topics appropriate for different contexts and different speaker roles; the linguistic means available for initiating and maintaining a discourse turn; and the phonological, lexical, and morphosyntactic markers used to differentiate registers in their particular language.

Among the preschool children studied, the most frequent markers of role were generally prosodic. These involved not only pitch distinctions but also differences in intonation, volume, rate, and voice quality. Thus, in the family setting, pretend fathers often had deep voices and frequently spoke louder than any other family member (sometimes yelling), with a marked tendency to back and lower vowels in a manner that produced an almost sinister "accent." In contrast, pretend mothers tended to speak with higher pitch and often used exaggerated intonation but rarely approached the volume that marked the fathers' utterances. Other phonological markings were also quite common, especially in Babytalk and Foreignertalk registers. The main developmental difference was that the older children maintained these distinctions throughout their role play, whereas the younger children used them only to contrast voices at role junctures (i.e., boundaries of roles were much more clearly marked than was more "embedded" discourse; once the younger children were into any particular role, they often reverted to their own voices). Overall, in acquiring sociolinguistic skills, there seems to be something particularly salient about prosodic modifications that makes them more available for use early on. Indeed, Crystal (1970) suggested "that the dominant perceptual component of the speech signal is non-segmental, and that some non-segmental patterns are understood and produced prior to anything conventionally syntactic" (p. 86).

A second level of register variation to which children showed early sensitivity was the distribution of different types of speech acts, especially directives. Because directives by definition place demands on the addressee, the choice of directive type can express a great deal about the social context of discourse and about the relationship of the interlocutors—for example, their age, sex, occupation, and familiarity (Ervin-Tripp, 1976; Ervin-Tripp, O'Connor, & Rosenberg, 1984). In each of the languages studied to date, the children produced more directives when they were portraying high-status roles (doctor, teacher) than they did for lower-status roles (patient, student), with the actual form of directive depending not only on the actual role being played but also to a great extent on the status of the addressee. Thus, for example, in the family setting, the pretend fathers used the highest proportion of imperatives, the mothers significantly fewer, and the pretend children still fewer. Moreover, although the pretend children often used similar numbers of directives overall to mother and father, those directed to mother were more likely to be expressed as imperatives, whereas those to father were more polite/indirect forms (e.g., fathers might be asked "Would you button me?" whereas mothers were told "Gimme Daddy's flashlight").

The other aspect of register knowledge that children seemed to acquire quite early involved choices of both topic and lexicon. Just as Berko Gleason (1975) found for real fathers, the language of fathers portrayed by children in all the languages studied clearly demarcated the father's role within the family: For example, in the American study they talked mainly about going to work, "firing the secretary," having meetings, or building a new "repartment" building; and in the French study they talked about being exhausted from working at the computer (*"Moi je suis crevé à regarder l'ordinateur"*); in contrast, mothers were more likely to be tired from doing errands (*"Oui alors heu moi tu sais j'ai travaillé dur hein. . . . Heu je suis allé faire les courses"*).

Lexical markings used fairly consistently by each group of children included endearments in the family setting, and technical terminology and the "pseudo-we" in place of first or second person singular (as in *"Maintenant nous allons te peser,"* "Now we're going to weigh you") in the doctor setting. Sometimes, however, children appeared to be aware that special vocabulary (e.g., medical terminology) was appropriate in a particular setting before they were competent in how to use it. To illustrate, both French and American role-play doctors sometimes prescribed rather unusual drugs (e.g., *"Celesthamine, plus, heu: Rinanthieu Prometozine et ce sera tout"*), and in the American study children sometimes confused the terms *temperature* and *thermometer* (e.g., in one exchange the pretend patient asked, "Do I have a temperature?" only to be told by the pretend nurse, "I'll get you one.") The example[1] that fol-

---

[1] In the role-play examples in this chapter, the role being played is indicated, followed by the person playing the role (i.e., child or experimenter) in parentheses.

lows is similar in suggesting the use of role-appropriate vocabulary before semantic mastery:

(1) Doctor (child):   Well, I think you have a hernia.
     Patient (experimenter):   What's a hernia?
     Doctor (child):   It's a sickness, like a disease.
                                  . . .
                                  Well, she's dead.

At a somewhat finer level of analysis, the data also suggest that children are sensitive to register variation even within a given role. A clear illustration of this in the French and Spanish data involves the social distribution of the two forms (familiar *tu* and distant *vous/usted*) of the second person singular pronoun; the teacher portrayed by these children would usually address individual students as *tu* but on occasion would switch to *vous/usted* after becoming angry at the student.

Surprisingly, one of the most striking register markers in children's role play turned out to be one that I had never seen discussed as such. In numerous examples such as (1), the utterances of high-status characters began with forms such as *well, now,* and *okay* in English; *alors, et bien,* and *maintenant* in French; or *bueno* and *ahora* in Spanish. When I first noticed the systematic distribution of these forms in the American data, I discussed them as placeholders or boundary markers and assumed, as did others, that they were simply sentence planning devices used to hold the floor during sentence preplanning (see also Sinclair & Coulthard, 1975, who use the term *frame*, as well as Clark, 1994).

As such, it was not entirely surprising that these forms were more common in high-status roles, as high-status individuals have more authority to hold the floor in conversation. However, as described in the next section for both my work on register and the work of other researchers on textual cohesion and coherence, these forms, now regularly referred to as discourse markers (see, e.g., Redeker, 1991; Schiffrin, 1987), are not an undifferentiated set of devices with one uniform function. Instead, different discourse markers (henceforth DMs) mark very different kinds of relations and attitudes between speech acts, between propositions, between turns, and between speakers. In the next section I discuss some of the functions particular markers can serve, how one identifies these forms in a corpus and how the analysis of such forms can inform researchers about children's awareness of social relationships.

DISCOURSE MARKERS

In her seminal work, Schiffrin (1987) defines DMs as "sequentially dependent elements which bracket units of talk" and argues that they are multifunctional, building coherence at five different planes of discourse; (a) the exchange plane (relating conversational turns), (b) the action plane (relating speech acts), (c) the ideational plane (relating propositions), (d) the participation framework (marking speaker/hearer and speaker/utterance relations), and (e) the information state (signaling relevant knowledge and meta-knowledge of the producer and recipient). For example, Schiffrin shows how a DM such as *well* (a response marker) anchors the speaker in a conversation when an upcoming contribution is not fully consonant with prior coherence options, thereby identifying the speaker with the particular participation status of respondent (as in (2), from Schiffrin, 1987, p. 109):

(2) Debby: What does your daughter-in-law
                                          call you?
       Zelda: Well that's a sore spot.

Although DMs have a primary function in one plane of discourse, they can also serve other functions, sometimes simultaneously, and the difference between these functions is not always clear (Schiffrin, 1987, p. 316, note 1). Schwenter (1996, pp. 861–862), for example, shows that a single occurrence of a DM such as *o sea* in Spanish may both play an interpersonal role and mark the relation between utterances. Sometimes when a DM performs more than one function simultaneously in a given context, it is difficult to tell which function is more prominent; at other times it is more obvious. To illustrate, consider the children's use of now/*ahora* in examples (3), (4), and (5), the first one from my original American role-play study (Andersen, 1990), the other two from the Argentinean Spanish study (Brizuela et al., 1997):

(3) Teacher (child):   Now, *tell me, how much is eight*
                                              times three.
(4) Father (child):   Ahora, *acuéstate*
                                              "Now, go to bed"
                                              Ahora, *mañana tú cumples los*
                                              tres años
                                              "Now, tomorrow you are going
                                              to be three years old."

(5)   Teacher (child):   *Bueno* ahora *hasta mañana*
                                    "Well, now, I'll see you tomorrow."

In (3), it is difficult to tell whether the prominent function of *now*, a temporal adverb, lies in the ideational plane (because the teacher is giving an order that requires an answer at that specific time—i.e., now), or whether it lies in the participation framework (because it marks the speaker of the utterance, the teacher, as having greater authority than the addressee). In contrast, it is clear in (4) and (5) that the latter function is prominent, that the DM functions as a marker of the authority of the father in (4) and the teacher in (5). The disambiguation is provided by the obvious conflict between the primary ideational meaning of *now* (at the present time) and the semantic meaning of the utterance it introduces (which refers to future time). These examples thus illustrate how DMs often lose their semantic or ideational meaning (becoming bleached; Schiffrin, 1987, p. 319) and gain another kind of meaning (in this case, a register meaning reflecting authority of the speaker in relation to the hearer). This is why, in our work, my colleagues and I have suggested that the different notions that have been discussed under the rubric of participation framework (speakers' attitudes, participant roles, and consequent linguistic changes) should be treated as matters of register: Speakers modify their use of DMs according to their position in relation to the hearer in the particular speech event. Thus, a teacher in a classroom setting speaks using the DMs that define him or her as a teacher (cf. Sinclair & Coulthard, 1975), and a child playing the role of a teacher may use the same devices if he or she has come to recognize them as register markers (Andersen, 1990).

Coding of Discourse Markers

An expression (word or set of words) was coded as a DM if it had all the following properties (see Schiffrin, 1987, p. 328):

1. a range of prosodic contours (i.e., tonic stress followed by a pause and phonological reduction);
2. the ability to operate at both local and global levels of discourse (i.e., it has both a semantic function and a discourse function, e.g., topic shift);
3. an utterance- or turn-initial location, with scope over the whole sentence;
4. its omission does not change the propositional content of the utterance.

If we again consider examples (4) and (5) in the previous section, we see that each of these criteria are clearly met and therefore *now* and *ahora* are clearly functioning as DMs; the situation in (3) is more ambiguous, as the meaning is not as clearly bleached. In cases like (3), the prosodic contour is crucially important.

In contrast, the adverb *ahorita* in example (6) is not a DM because the propositional content of *"ahorita no puedo saber"* ("now I can't tell") changes if we omit it:

(6)   Child (child):   *Hoy,* ahorita *no puedo saber pero puedo
                              llamar después.*
                              "Today, now I can't tell but I can call
                              you later."

In this case *ahorita* means "now" or "at this moment," and its meaning is stressed by the contrast to the other adverb, *después* "later"; the proposition *no puedo saber* ("I can't tell") is only true for the present time (*ahorita*), not later (*después*).

A second, more complex illustration of how we identified DMs is provided in example (7), this time with the form *Okay*:

(7)   Teacher (child 1)):   Okay, ahora *vayan todos a sus escritorios.*
                              "Okay, now, everybody to his desk."
      Student (child 2):   *Okay*
      Teacher (child 1):   Okay, ahorita *vamos a ir al lonche.*
                              Okay *vamos al lonche.*
                              "Okay, now we are going to have lunch.
                              Okay, let's go to have lunch."

In (7), the *Okay* produced in the student role is not considered a DM because it just expresses consent to what the previous speaker has said. However, the three *Okays* produced by the teacher are counted as DMs because they do not show consent as clearly.

Use of DMs in Controlled Improvisation

Although a number of studies have explored how children learn the textual coherence functions of DMs in English (Sprott, 1992) and in French (Jisa, 1985, 1987), DMs have not been studied extensively in their use as register markers indicating the social relation between participants in any speech event. One exception is the work of Hoyle (1994), who discusses the DMs *well*, *now*, and *okay* as used by three 8- and 9-year-old boys when they are participating in role play, pretending to be characters in a sportscasting event. Hoyle shows how these DMs work as initial and final bracketing devices for indicating a change in speaking role between the portrayed interviewers and interviewees, providing preliminary evidence that children of this age are aware of the linguistic rules of specialized adult roles. For example, she shows that although *now* does not occur at all in the boys' natural conversation, they do use it appropriately in pretend interviews. Furthermore, there is a very low frequency of *well* in conversations (2 per 1,000 words), but significantly more in the pretend interviews (15.6 per 1,000 words).

Our research with controlled improvisation suggests that even children as young as 4 or 5 years of age use DMs to mark differences in roles and in role realizations. Moreover, there is striking similarity in the way these forms are used cross-linguistically. To briefly summarize the findings regarding DMs, there are at least four facets to the parallel patterns we have found across the speech communities studied thus far:

- More DMs overall in high-status roles than in low-status roles;
- Greater ratio of lexical (*well, then, alors, bueno*) to nonlexical *(uh, euh)* DMs in high status roles;
- Different sets of lexical DMs for high-status versus low-status roles;
- "Stacking" of DMs to mark power asymmetry.

These patterns are illustrated in two examples from the French role-play dialogues, the first (8) from a family setting, the second (9) from a classroom setting:

(8) Mother (child): T'as fini tes devoirs?
"Have you finished your homework?"

Child (child): Oui.
"Yes."

Mother (child): Alors maintenant monte te coucher.
"Then go up to bed now."

Child (child): Ah non, ça non.
"Oh no, not that."

Mother (child): Non mais, qu'est-ce que tu fais là?
Tu veux la fessée?
"What do you think you're doing? Do you want a spanking?"

Child (child): Non, non, je veux pas la fessée.
"No, no, I don't want a spanking."

Mother (child):	Alors tu rentres maintenant te coucher, autrement quand papa il va arriver, je vais lui dire de te donner la fessée.
	"Then go right to bed, otherwise when Dad gets home, I'm going to tell him to give you a spanking."
Child (child):	Et puis je vais dormir et puis il pourra pas me donner la fessée.
	"Then I'm going to sleep and then he can't give me a spanking."
Mother (child):	Ben, oui, d'accord, alors va dormir.
	"Well, yes, alright, then go to sleep."
(9) Teacher (child):	Hum, bon, alors, maintenant, prenez vos cahiers de français.
	"Hmmh, well, then, now, take out your French notebooks."

In these examples, there is an obvious power asymmetry in the relationship of the interlocutors based on age, professional competence, or some combination of the two. And the distribution of DMs clearly reflects this asymmetry. One might be tempted to argue that the reason there are more DMs in the speech of high status individuals in these situations is simply that they are the ones who have control of the conversational floor: Perhaps, as suggested by Coulthard (1977, p. 10), DMs simply are attached to utterances that initiate new topics (or serve as coherence and cohesion devices to keep control of the topic). But this explanation does not adequately account for the data. The people with greater power or authority in these examples used not only more DMs but also different types than lower status people. Overall the data suggest that the higher the status, the greater the proportion of *well, now,* and *then,* or *bueno* and *ahora,* or *alors, maintenant,* and *bon,* often in "stacked" combination (as in "*et bon alors maintenant*"). (Although it is generally assumed that the meaning of these forms is bleached when they are used as DMs, it is certainly not an accident that forms such as *bon* and *well* are in origin evaluative and still belong to the person who has the authority to do the evaluating, whereas *now* and *ahora* are proximal-temporal and still belong to the person who has the right to set the agenda.) When the lower status individual did produce a DM in asymmetrical settings, it was most often a simple nonlexical form such as *heu* or *ah* (see Clark, 1994). However, the corpus also contains a fair number of dialogues involving equally "low status" speakers interacting with one another, and these dialogues are far from void of lexical DMs. Rather, they contain a different set of lexical forms such as *et puis* or *et ben*. This is illustrated in example (10) from the classroom context (see also the portrayal of child in (8)):

(10) Child 1:   Ah bon et puis ça va coller?
                  "Oh, well, and is that going to stick, then?"

     Child 2:   Ah peut-être ouais. Il faut que j'essaie, c'est
                  pas sûr hein?
                  "Uh, maybe, yes. I must try, it's not for sure, eh?"

     Child 1:   Ouais et ben tu sais ce que j'ai fait moi?
                  Moi, moi j'ai coloré mon ballon, j'ai coloré
                  mon ballon, je lui ai fait des yeux et un nez
                  et une bouche.
                  *"Yeh, and uh, you know what I did? Me, me,
                  I colored my ball, I colored my ball, I gave it
                  eyes and a nose and a mouth."*

     Child 2:   C'est vrai?
                  "Really?"

     Child 1:   Ouais, j'peux t' l'amener c't' après-midi.
                  "Yeh, I can bring it to you this afternoon."

     Child 2:   Ouais ce serait bien.
                  "Yeh, that would be fine."

     Child 1:   Ouais comme ça on fera un match.
                  "Yeh, that way we can have a game."

Developmentally, although the use of DMs was relatively rare among the youngest children, by age 6 or 7 children in each of the communities studied demonstrated systematic variation in their use of particular DMs, reflecting the relative status of the participants in the discourse. Moreover, the differential distribution of lexical and nonlexical DMs (and the use of stacking) was most dramatic in the classroom setting, where the status asymmetry between roles is greatest (compared to that of family and medical settings).

Strengths and Weaknesses of This Approach

Psychologists and educators, as well as most linguists, often describe skills as if they were unitary abilities: The child can read or not, the child can carry on conversations or not. Many studies, including others in this volume, demonstrate quite clearly that this is not the case: A child's competence is not a uniform thing; rather, it changes according to the context in which the child is performing. Factors that have been shown to affect developmental level include practice, familiarity, presence of other people, the setting, and the form of the task (see, e.g., Vygotsky, 1978). The child who can demonstrate an understanding of a particular social category in an imitating/pretending task, for instance, frequently cannot do so in an interview assessment (Hand, 1981). In work on the development of social cognition by Fischer and colleagues. (see, e.g., Fischer, Hand, Watson, Van Parys & Tucker, 1983), the authors suggest that the imitating/pretending task that they use is the easiest one that can be given to a child (i.e., the task in which they will demonstrate maximum social role knowledge), and certainly they see greater performance on this test than they do on an interview assessment. The reason for this, they argue, is that their context provides more support for the child. It is not clear to me, however, that having the child imitate something that the experimenter has done is more of a support than providing a general framework and allowing the child to display whatever knowledge she possesses herself and not have to remember exactly what it was that the experimenter did. (For further discussion of this issue, see Andersen, 1990, chap. 3.)

Indeed, I argue that the type of study described in this chapter provides much more accurate and complete information about the children's social knowledge. Certainly the results of these studies indicate that looking at role-play language, instead of just observing children's nonlinguistic behavior in terms of the activities that they feel are appropriate for each role, allows one to see an interaction between behaviors and roles in a more complex and intricate way. This work shows that children have knowledge of these interactions earlier than might be assumed by looking only at their nonlinguistic activities.

Many linguists, especially psycholinguists and neurolinguists, are interested in language because they believe it provides a "window into the mind." It may be that the examination of systematic language variation in children's speech can provide a better window into the social mind than other kinds of behavior that are more traditionally used by social psychologists to study developments in social cognition. Although the original motivation for my research was to learn about children's linguistic knowledge, the data are just as valuable as a measure of children's social knowledge.

On the other hand, as mentioned earlier, one concern about the use of a technique such as "controlled improvisation," or role play in general, is that it is more likely to reveal stereotypes than to show what an individual would actually do in any particular context. Children do certainly sometimes demonstrate a view of society (e.g., vis-a-vis gender roles) that is not consistent with their own experience. However, for a developmental psycholinguist or sociolinguist who wants to know what sociolinguistic markers children have come to recognize in their speech community, it can be a rich source of information, especially if one sees the same linguistic features (e.g., low pitch) showing up to mark the same social dimensions (e.g., high status) across a wide range of different roles. Certainly the data in each of our studies, across different linguistic communities and social classes, suggest that young children have much broader knowledge of situationally determined linguistic variation than could be captured in a naturalistic study.

CONCLUSIONS

In the introduction to this chapter I posed the question: Do children have passive knowledge of registers that an investigator would never have the opportunity to observe in naturalistic settings? The findings reviewed in this chapter indicate that the answer to this question is a resounding "yes." Young children are able to actively demonstrate knowledge of a wide range of register markers and subtle conditions of use if they are provided with appropriate settings for displaying this knowledge. Often in child language research we assume that children cannot do X if the data do not provide evidence of their doing X. Before conclusively accepting nonoccurrence data we should be careful to explore whether there might be other, perhaps methodological, reasons why a child does not display a certain type of knowledge in a particular setting; this is what Labov and his colleagues found in their study of standard and nonstandard English (Labov, 1972). What I have tried to demonstrate in this chapter is the usefulness of a particular research methodology, one that I have called "controlled improvisation" in eliciting evidence from children of an awareness of subtle sociolinguistic rules governing register use that would not be revealed in a naturalistic study. The findings from a set of studies (American, Spanish, Basque, and French) demonstrate the success of this technique in eliciting symbolic form choices stripped of practical compliance consequences; that is, because the child can control almost all aspects of the role play, he or she can select forms that purely reflect factors such as the status and intimacy of the pretend interlocutors, rather than worrying about whether the addressee will be more or less likely to comply if addressed in a particular way (e.g., you can address your bratty little brother the way you think he really should be addressed without worrying how he or your mom or dad will respond if you do).

Across the languages studied, children as young as 4 or 5 years of age have demonstrated an ability to discriminate and express in their language a wide range of social relationships through choices of content, discourse strategies, and situationally appropriate grammatical patterns. I have focused the discussion in most detail on the use of discourse markers because the systematic variation revealed in the use of these forms in children's role-play speech is so striking, given that researchers are only beginning to understand the social significance of these forms in adult usage. The analyses to date demonstrate striking similarities (as well as some interesting differences, discussed elsewhere (Andersen et al. 1995, Brizuela et al. 1998; Andersen, Brizuela & Gonnerman, in press) across language communities. However, before we can hope to fully understand the nature of children's communicative competence, this body of research will need to be expanded to explore not only more languages but also more registers within a given language, and more markers within any given register. Because we know that register knowledge is crucial to a child's (or adult's) chances of success in institutional settings such as school, I urge other researchers (psychologists, linguists, and educators) to help extend this area of research.

REFERENCES

Amorrortu, E. (1997). The acquisition of communicative competence: The use of Basque Vernacular/Standard in 8 and 10-year-olds. In E. Hughes, M. Hughes, & A. Greenhill (Eds.), *Proceedings of the 21st Annual Boston University Conference on Language Development* (pp. 1–12). Somerville, MA: Cascadilla Press.

Andersen, E. S. (1984). The acquisition of sociolinguistic knowledge: Some evidence from children's verbal role play. *Western Journal of Speech Communication, 48,* 125–144.

Andersen, E. S. (1990). *Speaking with style: The sociolinguistic skills of children.* New York: Routledge.

Andersen, E. S. (1996). A cross-cultural study of children's register knowledge. In D. Slobin, J. Gerhardt, A. Kyratzis, & G. Jiansheng (Eds.), *Social interaction, social context, and language: Festschrift for Susan Ervin Tripp* (pp. 125–142). Mahwah, NJ: Lawrence Erlbaum Associates.

Andersen, E. S., Brizuela, M., Dupuy, B., & Gonnerman, L. (1995). The acquisition of discourse markers as sociolinguistic variables: A cross-linguistic comparison. In Eve Clark (Ed.), *Proceedings of the Twenty-Seventh Annual Child Language Research Forum* (pp. 61–70). Stanford: Center for the Study of Language and Information.

Andersen, E., Brizuela, M., & Gonnerman, L. (In press) Cross-linguistic evidence for the early acquisition of discourse markers as register variables. *Journal of Pragmatics:* Special Issue on Discourse Markers.

Andersen, E. S., & Johnson, C. (1973). Modifications in the speech of an eight-year-old to younger children. *Stanford Occasional Papers in Linguistics, 3*, 149–160.

Atkinson, D., & Biber, D. (1994). Register: A review of empirical research. In D. Biber & E. Finegan (Eds.), *Sociolinguistic Perspectives on Register* (pp. 351–385). Oxford: Oxford University Press.

Bates, E. (1976). *Language and context: The acquisition of pragmatics.* New York: Academic Press.

Bates, E., & Silvern, L. (1977). *Sociolinguistic development in children: How much of it is social?* (Report No. 10). Boulder: University of Colorado, Institute for the Study of Intellectual Behavior, Program on Cognitive and Perceptual Factors in Human Development.

Berko Gleason, J. (1973). Code switching in children's language. In T. Moore (Ed.), *Cognitive development and the acquisition of language* (pp. 169–177). New York: Academic Press.

Berko Gleason, J. (1975). Fathers and other strangers: Men's speech to young children. In D. P. Dato (Ed.), *Georgetown University Roundtable on Languages and Linguistics* (pp. 289–297). Washington, DC: Georgetown University Press.

Berko Gleason, J., & Perlmann, R. Y. (1985) Acquiring social variation in speech. In H. Giles & R. N. St. Clair (Eds.), *Recent advances in language, communication, & social psychology* (pp. 86–111) Hillsdale, NJ: Lawrence Erlbaum Associates.

Berko Gleason, J., Perlmann, R., & Greif, R. (1984). What's the magic word? *Discourse Processes , 4*, 493–502.

Berko Gleason, J., & Weintraub, S. (1976). The acquisition of routines in child language. *Language and Society, 5*, 129–135.

Biber, D., & Finegan, E. (Eds.). (1994). *Sociolinguistic persepctives on register.* Oxford: Oxford University Press.

Brizuela, M., Andersen, E. & Stallings, L. (1999) Discourse markers as indicatros of register. *Hispania.* (pp. 128–141)

Brizuela, M., Dupuy, B., & Andersen, E. (1998, July). *Children's knowledge of the social and textual funtions of discourse markers: A cross-linguistic comparison.* Paper presented at the 6th International Pragmatics Conference, Reims, France.

Brizuela, M., Gil, M., & Andersen, E. (1997). *A discourse and social distribution of* BUENO *in the pretend-play of Argentinean children.* Paper presented at the Twenty-Eighth Annual Child Language Research Forum, Stanford, CA.

Cazden, C. (1988). *Classroom discourse: The language of teaching and learning.* Portsmouth, NH: Heinemann.

Clark, H. H. (1994). Managing problems in speaking. *Speech Communication, 15*, 243–250.

Coulthard, M. (1977). *An introduction to discourse analysis.* London: Longman.

Crystal, D. (1970). Prosodic systems and language acquisition. In P. Leon et al. (Eds.), *Prosodic feature analysis* (pp. 77–90). Montreal: Didier.

Ellis, J., & Ure, J. (1969). Language varieties: Register. In R. Meacham (Ed.), *Encyclopedia of linguistics. Information and control* (pp. 251–259). London: Pergamon.

Ervin-Tripp, S. (1976). Is Sybil there? The structure of some American English directives. *Language and Society, 5*, 25–66.

Ervin-Tripp, S., O'Connor, M., & Rosenberg, J. (1984). Language and power in the family. In M. Schulz & C. Kramerae (Eds.), *Language and power.* Belmont, CA: Sage Press.

Ferguson, C. A. (1975). Toward a characterization of English foreigner talk. *Anthropological Linguistics, 17*, 1–14.

Ferguson, C. A. (1977). Babytalk as a simplified register. In C. Snow & C. Ferguson (Eds.), *Talking to children* (pp. 209–235). Cambridge: Cambridge University Press.

Fischer, K., Hand, H., Watson, M., Van Parys, M, & Tucker, J. (1983) Putting the child into socialization: The development of social categories in preschool children. In L. Katz (Ed.), *Current topics in early childhood education* (vol. 5), Norwood, NJ: Ablex.

Greif, E. B., & Berko Gleason, J. (1980). Hi, thanks, and goodbye: More routine information. *Language in Society , 9*, 159–166.

Hand, H. H. (1981) The relation between development level and spontaneous behavior: The importance of sampling contexts. In K. W. Fischer (Ed.) *Cognitive development*, San Francisco: Jossey-Bass.

Hoyle, S. (1994). Children's use of discourse markers in the creation of imaginary participation frameworks. *Discourse Processes* , *17*, 447–464.

Jisa, H. (1985). French preschoolers' use of *et pis* ("and then"). *First Language, 5*, 169–184.

Jisa, H. (1987). Sentence connectors in French children's monologue performance. *Journal of Pragmatics, 11*, 607–621.

Labov, W. (1972). The logic of nonstandard English. In P. P. Giglioli (Ed.), *Language and social context* (pp. 179–215). New York: Penguin Books.

Ochs, E. (1988). *Culture and language development. Language acquisition and language socialization in a Samoan village.* Cambridge: Cambridge University Press.

Redeker, G. (1991). Linguistic markers of discourse structure. *Linguistics, 29*, 1139–1172.

Reid, T. B.W. (1956). Linguistics, structuralism, and philology. *Archivum Linguisticum, 8*, 28–37.

Schiffrin, D. (1987). *Discourse markers.* Cambridge: Cambridge University Press.

Schwenter, S. (1996). Some reflections on *O Sea*: A discourse marker in Spanish. *Journal of Pragmatics, 25*, 855–874.

Shatz, M., & Gelman, R. (1973). The development of communication skills: Modification in the speech of young children as a function of listener. *Monographs of the Society for Research in Child Development, 38*.

Shore, B. (1982). *Sala'ilua: A Samoan mystery.* New York: Columbia University Press.

Sinclair, J. M., & Coulthard, R. M. (1975). *Towards an analysis of discourse.* London: Oxford University Press.

Snow, C. E. (1972). Mothers' speech to children learning language. *Child Development, 43*, 549–565.

Snow, C. E., & Ferguson, C. A. (Eds.). (1977). *Talking to children: Language input and acquisition.* New York: Cambridge University Press.

Sprott, R. A. (1992). Children's use of discourse markers in disputes: Form-function relations and discourse in child language. *Discourse Processes, 15*, 423–439.

Vygotsky, L. S. (1978) *Mind in society*, Cambridge, MA: Harvard University Press.

12

The Story Behind the Story: Gathering Narrative Data From Children

Richard Ely
Boston University

Allyssa McCabe
*University of Massachusetts
—Lowell*

Anne Wolf
Harvard University

Gigliana Melzi
New York University

Narratives are an important part of human discourse. Although they can be expressed through other media (e.g., painting, dance; see papers in Mitchell, 1980), it is through language that narratives find their most explicit and most unambiguous form. Storytelling is a universal practice, found in all human cultures. For the better part of human evolutionary history, the sharing of oral stories was the primary way of preserving a sense of cultural heritage (Ong, 1982). The propensity to tell stories can be readily observed by listening carefully to ordinary conversations. In many settings, storytelling is the primary genre of talk. In these settings stories beget stories, with tellers' tales prompting listeners to tell their own stories (Georgakopoulou, 1995; Preece, 1992). As such, one would think that obtaining narrative data would be a relatively straightforward and unproblematic task, involving only the unobtrusive observations and recordings of everyday verbal interactions.

Although observation of naturalistic settings is indeed one important source of narrative data, there are a number of other equally useful and valid approaches. In this chapter we review current methods of gathering narrative data from children, including some of the ones that we have used and some that have been successfully employed by others (McCabe & Rollins, 1994). In addition, we discuss how elicitation technique, context, and culture influence the data obtained. However, before beginning our presentation, it is important to briefly define what we mean by narrative data and to describe why narrative data are important.

What constitutes a narrative, and what qualities a "good" narrative must have, are open questions. Labov (Labov, 1972; Labov & Waletzky, 1967) has defined a "minimum" narrative as consisting of two independent clauses, temporally ordered, that describe a single past event. Preece (1987), using a definition employed by Umiker-Sebeok (1979), included as narratives utterances that described a past event. In addition, Preece included as narratives any string of utterances that were labeled a "story" by her young subjects. Other scholars have been less explicit in determining what constitutes a narrative and have included utterances that do not necessarily refer to any event. For example, Sutton-Smith's (1981, p. 62) collection of folk stories of children includes some utterance strings ("verse stories") that are primarily playful and appear to make little explicit reference to any event, real or imagined (e.g., "Three ducks/quack."). Studies that employ direct elicitation techniques (e.g., "Tell a story about something that really happened to you") include a wider range of utterances, sometimes counting as narrative data much of the verbal behavior that follows the prompt (e.g., Allen, Kertoy, Sherblom, & Pettit, 1994). Finally, some researchers are interested in examining developmental and stylistic variations in different narrative genres (e.g., scripts, personal anecdotes: Nelson, 1986; online narration, news reports: Hicks, 1990). As such, these researchers are likely to include a wider range of material as data but are also more likely to be explicit as to what sorts of utterances constitute particular genres of narratives.

Numerous approaches have been used to delineate the essential constituents of "good" narratives, including high point analysis, story grammar, and stanza analysis. According to high point analysis, the classic well-formed story is structured around a high point in which the narrator emphasizes reference (what happened) and evaluation (the narrator's attitude about what happened) (Labov, 1972; Labov & Waletzky, 1967; Peterson & McCabe, 1983). Regarding story grammar, narratives are examined in terms of the structural and problem solving aspects of the story (Mandler & Johnson, 1977; Stein, 1988; Trabasso & Rodkin, 1994). Stanza analysis utilizes the notion of lines and groups of lines or stanzas in order to document coherence in narratives (Gee, 1986; Hymes, 1982).

Researchers who employ these various analytic approaches recognize that narratives are one of the most complex forms of language use. A good narrative draws on all levels of the language system. Other than the most primitive narratives produced by very young children, most narratives extend well beyond the bounds of the single sentence and often require a fairly sophisticated command of some of the more subtle features of the language system (e.g., anaphora, cohesion).

In addition to utilizing the full range of linguistic skills, narratives call on skills from other cognitive domains, including, for example, memory and counterfactual thinking. Many narratives describe events that are far removed from the current context and, as such, are considered a form of decontextualized language (Snow, 1991; Snow & Dickinson, 1991). Personal anecdotes, one of the most common types of oral narratives, refer to events that may have occurred days, weeks, or years earlier. Fantasy narratives, as well as future narratives (stories about what might someday happen) have no one-to-one real world correspondence and sometimes have only a minimal relationship to reality. In essence, telling a coherent and engaging story is likely to draw heavily on the child's linguistic and cognitive abilities. Proficiency in narration is also positively associated with competence in other linguistic and cognitive domains, the most important being literacy (Snow, Barnes, Chandler, Goodman, & Hemphill, 1991). Thus, narratives are a particularly privileged form of language data in that they are likely to represent, in a single form, a rich source of information about many aspects of the child's developmental status.

TECHNIQUES AND CONTEXTS

There are three basic approaches to collecting narrative data: naturalistic, seminaturalistic, and direct elicitation. Each approach has particular advantages and disadvantages, and each can be used profitably according to the needs of the given research project. In addition, each approach carries a number of theoretical assumptions that we attempt to make explicit in the following discussion.

Naturalistic Observations

In using this approach, the researcher primarily observes and records the ongoing "natural" discourse and extracts the narratives embedded therein. Researchers who employ this approach seek data that have ecological validity. Their goal is to capture the narratives that are characteristically generated in any given setting. Such data are best able to inform questions about how narrative practices serve a socializing function, as well as questions about how children are socialized to tell narratives (Miller, Mintz, Hoogstra, Fung, & Potts, 1992; Miller & Sperry, 1987; Miller, Wiley, Fung, & Liang, 1997; Ochs, 1982; Ochs & Schieffelin, 1984). In the following sections we focus on data collection that takes place in the home, in the car, and in school settings, although we recognize that other sites have also been employed (e.g., the neighborhood), particularly in ethnographic studies of narratives (Goodwin, 1990; Labov, 1972; Sheldon, 1989).

The Home Setting.   The home setting, especially the family dinner table, has been a frequently used site for gathering narrative data (Blum-Kulka & Snow, 1992; Ely, Berko Gleason, Narasimhan, & McCabe, 1995; Berko Gleason, Perlmann, & Greif, 1984; Snow & Dickinson, 1990; see also Pan, Perlmann, & Snow, chap. 10, this volume). In order to obtain recordings of dinnertime conversations, a common practice is to leave a tape recorder with the family and ask that a mealtime conversation be recorded. We recommend using a high quality, easy to operate tape recorder with a good built-in omni-directional microphone (e.g., Sony TCM-59V). Although 90-minute cassettes (45 minutes per side) are readily available, the 90-minute tape itself is thinner and more likely to snarl and break. We tend to use only high quality 60-minute cassettes (30 minutes per side).

For obtaining dinner-table conversations, families are encouraged to converse as they normally would. As no observer is present, it is felt that what is captured on tape is likely to represent a reasonable sample of a typical mealtime conversation. It is important to keep in mind that across cultures and social classes, there is wide variation in how talkative families are, who gets to do the talking, and what they talk about (Blum-Kulka & Snow, 1992; Jimenez Silva & McCabe, 1996). Middle-class American families are especially likely to encourage the sharing of narratives (Gee, 1992). In contrast, American working-class families produce far less narrative discourse. For example, in one study that recorded family dinner-table conversations, approximately one fifth of a sample of Euro-American and African-American working-class families (with the target child around 4 years of age) generated no narrative discourse, and the total number of narratives produced by working-class families at dinnertime was markedly lower than the total number of narratives produced by middle class families (Blum-Kulka & Snow, 1992; Snow & Dickinson, 1990). Although these differences can be explained in part by the respective differences in the average lengths of the dinnertime conversations, the differences may also be due to different conceptualizations of what constitutes appropriate dinner-table conversation (Blum-Kulka & Snow, 1992).

In terms of anticipating how much narrative data can be obtained from dinner-table conversations, the figures from Snow and Dickinson (1990) are instructive. In their sample of 10 working-class families, the range in length of mealtimes was between 8 and 47 minutes. The percentage of discourse that was coded as narrative discourse ranged from 0 to 33, with an overall average of approximately 12%. The implication these and similar findings have for researchers seeking to gather such data is that the yield or density of narrative discourse as a proportion of overall conversation is likely to vary widely. In some populations, many hours of recording and transcribing may produce only a small corpus of narratives. In addition, in settings such as dinnertime meals, many of the narratives generated by children are collaborative endeavors with elicitation, input, and support coming from a number of dinner-table participants (e.g., parents, other children).

A number of other sites have been used by researchers interested in gathering naturalistic narrative data. Within the home, the speech that accompanies play may also be a good source of data. Children engaged in play with others, or by themselves, often generate play and fantasy narratives replete with the voicing or registers of imagined characters. For example, Kuczaj and McClain (1984) collected spontaneous data from one boy (Abe) between age 2;4 and 5;1 in order to examine naturally occurring play narratives. The subject's speech (both alone and with other family members) was regularly recorded over a period of $2^1/_2$ years. A total of 118 hours of data was collected and transcribed. During this period Abe produced 58 fantasy narratives, 39 of which were initiated by Abe himself, although his parents actively contributed to all but 9 of his narratives. Clearly, collaborative narratives are relatively common and an important vehicle for socializing narrative practice; however, they may be problematic for researchers interested in focusing on the child's stand-alone narrative skills.

A final source of naturalistic home data can be found in children's presleep monologues (Kuczaj, 1983; Nelson, 1989; Weir, 1962). This "crib talk" may contain talk about the past, as it appears to be a time during which children reprocess events from the immediate and the distant past. These studies focus on children between 15 and 36 months of age (Kuczaj's subjects: 15 to 30 months; Nelson's subject: 21 to 36 months; Weir's subject: 28 to 30 months). However, the same issue regarding yield holds for both naturally occurring play narratives and crib talk, as narrative data are likely to constitute only a portion of what the child utters during play or before falling asleep.

The Car.   Moving beyond the home, the very vehicle that takes most people places—the car—has proven for one researcher to be a fruit-ful site for the collection of narrative data. When one is audiotaping in a car, the tape recorder should be insulated from the frame of the car (by placing a soft pad underneath it) in order to reduce the amount of ambi-ent noise. In addition, it is best to use a separate microphone that, again, is not directly attached to the frame of the car.

Preece (1987) recorded and transcribed 90 hours of carpooling con-versations over several months, conversations that she and her three young subjects generated while driving to and from preschool. The chil-dren were between age 5;0 and 5;6 at the onset of the study. During this time the children produced a total of 599 narratives, equivalent to nearly 7 narratives per hour. As with narratives collected at the dinner table, a proportion were collaborative (approximately 12%). More than half the narratives were personal anecdotes, stories primarily about the children themselves. Anecdotes of vicarious experience (stories about other indi-viduals) constituted 20% of the total. Also of note was the relative infre-quency of fantasy, fiction, and "what-if" narratives (constituting alto-gether approximately 10% of all narratives). Again, the yield issue arises; and in the case of the Preece study, depending on the level of detail at which the raw data were transcribed (e.g., whether pauses, overlaps, and prosody were documented), it might well have taken between 5 and 10 hours to transcribe 1 hour of recorded conversation. Thus, it may have taken between 450 and 900 hours of transcription to capture approxi-mately 600 narratives, representing a relatively labor-intensive approach when compared with other approaches (e.g., conversational prompts).

At School.   The classroom is another location where researchers have looked for narrative discourse, in part because children are some-what captive subjects in school settings. School sites have also been used because competence in narration (a form of decontextualized language) is positively associated with an important educational goal, the acquisition of literacy (Snow et al., 1991). Ironically, however, there are data that suggest that narratives occur less frequently in school than at home; and when narratives do occur in school, they are often less complex than nar-ratives told at home (Dickinson, 1991; Tizard & Hughes, 1984).

Among the range of possible sites for naturalistic observations, classroom settings present the greatest challenge to researchers interested in obtaining narrative data. Classroom observations require a large investment of time and resources. They often have to be conducted in synchrony with classroom schedules, which sometimes limit the number of hours per day during which observations can be made. Furthermore, transcribing and documenting children's classroom interactions (which may involve numerous and ever-changing interlocutors) is highly labor-intensive, with ratios running as high as 15 hours of transcription to 1 hour of classroom observation (Ely & McCabe, 1994).

Preschool and school-age children's spontaneously produced narratives have been successfully audiotaped by having subjects wear backpacks containing tiny tape recorders with small external microphones clipped to the strap of the backpack (Dickinson & Smith, 1991; Berko Gleason & Weintraub, 1976; Tabors, 1987). Alternatively, wireless microphones can be used in conjunction with a receiver and tape recorder (Ely & McCabe, 1994). Although this method requires somewhat more expensive equipment, the researcher is better able to ensure that the data are actually being recorded. Both approaches allow children to talk freely with many different interlocutors and to move easily between different activities in the classroom. Given the level of activity and the sometimes large number of interlocutors children encounter, it is important to supplement audio recordings with field notes that provide contextual information about the subjects' activities and interactions.

As we have noted, spontaneous narratives occur relatively infrequently in many classroom settings. From over 60 recorded observations averaging 2 hours in duration, only 6% of 3- and 4-year-olds' classroom speech was talk about the past (e.g., personal narratives, story retellings) or the future (e.g., planning), and only 7% represented pretend or fantasy-oriented talk (Dickinson & Smith, 1991). Recordings of teacher–student discourse during small group, free play, and mealtime activities in Head Start and private day-care centers revealed that the amount of decontextualized talk (which included talk about nonpresent actions and objects, the future, and analytical or instructional topics as well as narratives) varied considerably across classrooms, constituting as little as 1% to as much as 24% of talk during these activities (Dickinson, 1991). A more detailed examination revealed that decontextualized talk (including narratives) occurred more frequently when teachers were stationary (e.g., during small group activities or mealtimes) as opposed to moving around the classroom. In addition, teachers' classroom styles influenced narrative storytelling, with less control-oriented teachers creating more opportunities for conversations with children about their personal experiences than their more control-oriented colleagues (Dickinson, 1991).

Researchers interested in studying fantasy narratives have found preschool and early school-age play a good source of naturalistic data. Such play (termed *dramatic play*) often occurs in specially designated classroom areas that are set up along a particular theme (e.g., a spaceship, a kitchen) and are furnished with appropriate props (e.g., a control station, a toy stove). Some researchers have manipulated the dramatic play setting (e.g., housekeeping vs. trucks and dinosaurs) in order to examine how gender and setting influence children's narratives (Sheldon & Rohleder, 1996). Others have compared talk across different play sites (e.g., the dramatic play area vs. the block building area). In one such study, Pellegrini (1982) found that preschoolers used more explicit language to introduce fantasy themes and to define their roles and props in their dramatic play narratives than they did in the talk that accompanied their block building play. In this study, as well as in others (e.g., Hicks, 1991), videotapes were used to promote detailed analyses. However, videotaping is often experienced as being more intrusive and, as a result, is less frequently allowed in classrooms.

Of all the naturalistic sites, "sharing time" is one of the most fruitful sources of narrative data. Sharing time is a regularly occurring classroom activity, often taking place once a day, during which children are asked to "share" their out-of-classroom experiences with their peers and the teacher. By definition, children are asked to use decontextualized language. For example, a child might be asked to describe, in narrative form, what she did on vacation. However, we have found that when children are allowed to bring in objects to share (e.g., souvenirs, favorite toys), they produce little narrative talk, focusing instead on contextualized descriptions of the objects themselves.

During sharing time, children of all backgrounds confront most directly the demands of the dominant or mainstream language of the larger community (Heath, 1983; Michaels, 1981, 1991). Unlike the home setting, where narratives flow out of a common and shared cultural realm, narratives told in school during sharing time are subject to specific pedagogical goals. These goals include fostering children's ability to be explicit about what they are trying to communicate, and to do so in the manner accepted by the dominant culture (Dickinson, 1991; Hemphill & Snow, 1996; Michaels, 1981, 1991; Snow & Dickinson, 1990).

Researchers interested in examining how children's indigenous narrative style interacts with the narrative demands of the classroom have focused on the narratives that are generated during sharing time (Craddock-Willis & McCabe, 1996; Michaels, 1981, 1991). These researchers have found that children from different ethnic backgrounds employed distinct sharing time narratives. For example, first and second grade Euro-American children tended to tell stories that focus on a single topic. In contrast, first- and second-grade African-American children tended to tell narratives that consist of several thematically related anecdotes. Because the African-American children's narratives were not consistent with the Euro-American teacher's schema for appropriate storytelling, her pedagogical interventions were experienced as disruptive and disrespectful by the students (Michaels, 1991, pp. 321, 323).

In summary, when researchers ask questions regarding how opportunities for narrative talk unfold spontaneously or how narrative talk contributes to children's acquisition of the narrative form of their culture, gathering narrative data through naturalistic observations is necessary. By knowing when and how narrative talk is likely to occur, the researcher can focus data gathering on times (e.g., mealtimes, classroom sharing time) that are more likely to yield narrative data.

Seminaturalistic Observations

In the seminaturalistic approach the researcher manipulates the environment or context to increase the yield of useful data while maintaining as much ecological validity as possible. Within this approach we describe two distinct techniques: the Peterson and McCabe (1983) conversational prompt technique, and the requested or staged elicitation technique. The conversational prompt technique is best suited to research projects whose goals include studying children's abilities to produce minimally supported or minimally scaffolded narratives. The requested or staged elicitation technique is often used to replicate the environment in which many children share personal anecdotes with family members or generate play narratives.

Conversational Prompt Technique.   In its standard format, the conversational prompt technique involves engaging children in conversations in which the experimenter embeds a variety of narrative prompts. In order to reduce children's self-consciousness, they are often asked to perform some pleasant (but minimally demanding) task, such as drawing a picture or completing a puzzle. The prompts themselves consist of brief narratives about specific topics (e.g., doctor visits, travel experiences, bee stings) followed by a query as to whether the child had experienced a similar event. For example, the experimenter might say: "The other day I went to the doctor to get a shot. Has anything like that ever happened to you?" The subject is then prodded in a nonleading manner to describe "what happened." The interviewer expresses interest in the child's narrative by interjecting "uh-huhs" during pauses and encourages continuity and clarity by occasionally repeating what the child has just said. The following brief narrative from a 6-year-old girl exemplifies the prompting technique as well the supportive but nonleading manner in which the investigators elicited narratives (Peterson & McCabe, 1983). The investigator had preceded the following excerpt with a description of a time when she ripped a shirt.

Experimenter:	Did anything like that ever happen to you?
Child:	No-oo. Only one time when my PANTS ripped. (Giggles)
Experimenter:	Your pants ripped.
Child:	Yeah, one time my pants ripped.
Experimenter:	What happened?
Child:	Oh, just, I'm, I was, um, doing the jumping-jacks, you know?
Experimenter:	Uh-huh?
Child:	And, I, I heard something go chhh, cchhh. I go. I felt my pants. There was a gre-eat big hole and I felt my under-wear. I go, "What happened?" I didn't, I remember, when I looked down and there was a greeeat big hole there.
Experimenter:	(Laughs)
Child:	And I ripped my sides right to there.

In general, researchers who use this technique prompt children to talk about their own experiences. However, many researchers are ultimately interested in any talk about the past, whether such talk directly involves the child or not. Thus, some narratives may represent responses to specific prompts, whereas other narratives are likely to flow naturally out of the ongoing conversation. Even narratives generated by the same prompt can differ remarkably. A query about a visit to the doctor's office or the hospital might produce a story about the child's own stoic reaction to a painful shot or, alternatively, a story about a fight with a sibling that resulted in the sibling's need for medical attention (Peterson & McCabe, 1983).

In the original Peterson and McCabe (1983) study, the following prompt topics were used: spills, trips/travel, plane/train/boat trips, car wrecks, party experiences, ripped clothes, fights, doctor visits or shots, hospital experiences, pets, bee stings, future jobs, and volunteered and miscellaneous topics. Across the entire corpus of narratives generated by the 96 school-age subjects (age 4 to 9 years), volunteered and miscellaneous prompts produced more narratives than any other category. These were narratives that flowed out of the natural course of the conversation and included self-generated (volunteered) narratives as well as those elicited by nonstandard prompts, including, for example: "Do you have any brothers and sisters?" (p. 234); "Do you like to paint?" (p. 206); and "You ever seen a shark?" (p. 233).

Next in frequency after volunteered and miscellaneous prompt topics were trips, pets, car wrecks, and doctor visits or shots. The least productive prompts included fights, plane/train/boat trips, and future jobs. In terms of average length, the prompts that generated the longest narratives were car wrecks (average = 12.9 clauses), hospital experiences (11.4 clauses), volunteered and miscellaneous (10.8 clauses), and parties (10.7 clauses). In a smaller study of African-American children's narratives, three prompts were used (grandma troubles, stitches/hospital, baby sibling), with prompts about stitches and hospital experiences generating the most narratives (Champion, Seymour, & Camarata, 1995).

In the Peterson and McCabe (1983) study, it is important to stress that not every child received all prompts. A child who readily produced narratives, or a child whose narratives were largely self-generated, might have been exposed to only a few prompts. In terms of yield, subjects produced 1,124 narratives, an average of close to 12 narratives per subject.[1] This average was obtained from interview sessions that never ran longer than an hour and sometimes were significantly shorter.

The conversational prompt technique has been used successfully by a number of researchers working in a variety of cultural settings and with numerous distinct languages (Champion et al., 1995; Chang, 1994; Jimenez Silva & McCabe, 1996; Malan, 1992; Minami & McCabe, 1991; Pesco & Crago, 1996; Rodino, Gimbert, Perez, Craddock-Willis, & McCabe, 1991). It has proven to be a remarkably efficient method of gathering narrative data. By intent, the number of interlocutors is limited to two, the experimenter and the subject. The experimenter is minimally intrusive and talks only as much as is needed. The end result is narrative-rich data that are relatively easy to transcribe.

---

[1] This figure underrepresents the total number of narratives elicited. In the Peterson and McCabe (1983) study, the researchers stopped transcribing after 20 pages of text. Narratives generated after this point were not included in the analyses or in the final count.

Requested or Staged Elicitation Technique.   A second technique designed to capture naturalistic phenomena efficiently is the requested or staged elicitation technique. This is often used by researchers interested in examining how parents and children share narratives. These studies tend to focus on questions about how children are socialized to tell narratives, and although the researchers might prefer naturalistic data, they are willing to forgo some ecological validity for an increased yield. One variant of this technique is designed to obtain personal anecdotes about the past. The general format is to furnish the parent with a tape recorder and to ask the parent to talk to his or her child about the past "as they normally would" (Fivush, 1991a, 1991b; Haden, Haine, & Fivush, 1997; Hudson, 1993). Some researchers (e.g., Melzi, 1997) remain in an adjacent room while the parent and child converse. Others (e.g., McCabe & Peterson, 1991; Wolf, 1997) leave a recorder with the family and return at regular intervals to pick up recorded tapes (and often to interview the parent and child).

In general, this technique produces narrative-dense data, with most tapes containing more or less what the researcher had requested. Data from Melzi (1997) provide a sense of how effective this procedure can be. Her sample consisted of 31 working class Latino-American and Anglo-American mothers and their 4-year-old children. She asked mothers to engage their children in a conversation about four past events, two that had been shared with the mother and two that the child had experienced on his or her own. Mothers took on average 15 minutes to complete the task (in an adjacent room without the experimenter present), and most were able to comply fully with the instructions. The total number of narratives generated by the sample was 111, just shy of the targeted total of 124.

Data from a longitudinal study of parent-elicited narratives (McCabe & Peterson, 1991) are also indicative of the kinds of results that can be expected. The subjects were 10 middle class Canadian families with children (five girls, five boys) between the ages of 25 and 27 months at the outset of data collection. For the first 18 months of the study, parents were provided tape recorders and blank tapes and asked to record narratives as naturally as possible on a monthly basis. Over this period, the range in number of tapes returned to the experimenters ran from 2 to 12 ($M = 9$, $SD = 3$); the range in number of narratives elicited by parents ran from 14 to 127 ($M = 52$, $SD = 36$). Given the relatively young age of the children, these figures demonstrate how successful the technique can be.

Finally, one study (Wolf, 1997) used both the requested elicitation and the conversational prompt technique to examine how three preschool children shared personal narratives with parents, an older sibling, a preschool teacher, and the investigator. Parents were asked to tape-record conversations when narratives were likely to occur at home over a period of 4 weeks; preschool teachers were asked to do the same at school. The investigator elicited narratives from children using a version of the conversation prompt technique in which conversational support was not minimized. Each child used distinctly different narrative styles with different interlocutors. This finding emphasizes the importance of studying children's narratives, even those of the same genre, in different contexts, in order to obtain a more complete understanding of children's developing narrative abilities.

A second variant of the requested or staged elicitation technique is designed to capture children's play narratives. Here, the experimenter provides children with a standard array of toys or story-world props and asks them (with or without their parent's participation) to make up a story or to follow up on an open-ended prompt (Kruger & Wolf, 1994; Wolf & Hicks, 1989; Wolf, Moreton, & Camp, 1994). A varying degree of experimental control is maintained, ranging from merely providing the play materials to intentionally introducing specific prompts at specified intervals. The staged elicitation technique is particularly useful for studying children's overall ability to produce fantasy narratives, as well as for examining more particular features of play narratives including, for example, children's competence in enacting different speech registers to portray different characters.

Although making distinctions between seminaturalistic approaches and direct elicitation approaches can be somewhat arbitrary, the general theoretical perspective that we have used to distinguish between the two approaches rests on the degree of experimental control that we believe researchers strive to obtain. As noted earlier, one seminaturalistic technique, conversational prompts, does maintain a degree of experimental control by limiting the conversational support the investigator provides; however, the technique also preserves much of the natural informality of everyday conversation. Other seminaturalistic techniques (e.g., requested elicitation) seek data that, in the absence of logistical constraints, could be obtained through naturalistic observations. In contrast, most research that employs the direct elicitation approach aspires to uphold a relatively high degree of experimental control.

Direct Elicitation

The third approach to gathering narrative data involves direct elicitation. In this approach the researcher explicitly asks the child to tell a story by providing a prompt or stimulus, such as a story stem. A story stem is the opening line or lines of a story. The child is presented with the story stem and asked to complete the story. Other stimuli include wordless picture books, films, and videos. Researchers who use the direct elicitation approach tend to stress the importance of controlling variations in input by presenting standard stimuli. A number of different stimuli have been used, including conflict-laden story stems (e.g., Cassidy, 1988); wordless picture books, such as *Frog, Where Are You?* (Mayer, 1969) (e.g., Bamberg, 1985, 1987; Berman & Slobin, 1994); audiotaped or oral presentation of stories from various cultural traditions (e.g., Bartlett, 1932; Mandler & Johnson, 1977; Stein & Glenn, 1979); silent films, such as *The Pear Film* (Chafe, 1980); and videotapes (e.g., Özyürek, 1997).

Many researchers working within the direct elicitation paradigm believe that the structure and content of children's narratives can reveal information about underlying cognitive, social, and affective processes. For example, researchers have examined the school-oriented skills necessary for sequencing and retelling stories (e.g., Stein & Glenn, 1979). They have also analyzed the content of children's stories from a socioemotional or clinical perspective (Bretherton, Prentiss, & Ridgeway, 1990; Cassidy, 1988; Cramer, 1996; Mueller & Tingley, 1990; Oppenheim, Emde, & Warren, 1997; Slough & Greenberg, 1990). Finally, some researchers seek to elicit directly different narrative genres (Hicks, 1991; Hudson & Shapiro, 1991; Nelson, 1986) in order to examine children's knowledge of and competency with these varying genres.

Story Retellings.   In this technique, children are presented with a story and then asked to retell it. This method is rooted in Bartlett's (1932) seminal work, in which he presented a Native American folk story to subjects and had them retell the story. He found that his subjects tended to reshape the story in accordance with their own cultural standards of what a story should be. They did so by introducing words and phrases more familiar to them than those in the original story, as well as by leaving out aspects of the story that they presumably found enigmatic.

In order to elicit a retold story, some researchers have played tape-recorded versions of stories for their subjects in order to eliminate any variations that might be present in an oral presentation (e.g., Mandler & Johnson, 1977). Others have presented stories orally after finding that children's attention is more easily sustained by stories told in person than by audio-recorded ones (e.g., Stein & Glenn, 1979). As noted earlier, many researchers who employ the story retelling procedure argue that a story schema (the mental representation of the story structure) provides expectations and guidelines that facilitate the encoding and retrieval of stories (Mandler & Johnson, 1977; Stein & Glenn, 1979) The modifications that are present in the retold stories are thought to reflect the ways in which subjects alter the stimulus story in accordance with their mental schemas. By studying children's story retellings, researchers seek to uncover the organization of these mental schemas.

Wordless Picture Books.   The wordless picture book *Frog, Where Are You?* (Mayer, 1969) is a 24-plate pictorial narrative about a boy who loses his pet frog. It was first used to study how mothers and fathers narrate the story to their children, as well as to elicit narratives from preschool children after they heard the story narrated by their parents (Bamberg, 1985, 1987). Berman and Slobin (1994) adapted this technique in their cross-cultural study of narratives; specifically, they had children tell the story in response to the picture book without first having heard the story from parents or other adults. They analyzed differences in the use of a range of grammatical constructions as a function of subjects' ages and languages (English, German, Spanish, Hebrew, and Turkish). The authors argued that the use of a single set of pictures provided a shared point of departure for comparing narrative productions across different languages (Berman & Slobin, 1994, p. 42).

Film and Video Retellings.   An analogous elicitation procedure uses films or videos to present narratives. For example, *The Pear Film*, a short silent film nominally about the theft of a pear, has been employed to explore how subjects from different cultures retell a story (Chafe, 1980). Other researchers have used an abridged version of the classic French film *The Red Balloon* to explore children's knowledge of and competence in a variety of narrative genres (Hicks, 1990).

Wolf and Hicks (1989; Hicks, 1990, 1991; Wolf, 1985) used the film-retelling procedure to gather information about elementary school children's ability to make genre and voice distinctions. They showed subjects two silent films and then elicited a variety of narrative genres, including a standard story retelling, a play narrative using replica figures, a news report (like Kermit-the-News-Reporter from *Sesame Street*), and an online narration of the film (like a television sportscaster). The order of the elicitation tasks was randomly assigned, because the researchers found that the order of tasks affected the genre markings of subsequent retellings.

Concerns About Validity.   Many researchers who employ stories, films and videos, and wordless picture books as stimuli recognize that the same stimuli may not have the same interpretation for all subjects (Bornens, 1990; McCabe, 1997). For example, Berman and Slobin (1994, p. 9) acknowledge that the foreground and background of the frog story are not objectively given by the pictures themselves but are constructed by the narrator. Berman and Slobin recognize that the stimuli are filtered through subjects' unique perspectives as well through the options provided by the subjects' native language and culture. Bartlett's (1932) original findings (described earlier), as well as recent cross-cultural work, support this perspective. This recent work demonstrates that people recall stories from their own culture better than they do stories from another culture (Dube, 1982; Kintsch & Greene, 1978); they modify stories from other cultures to fit their own culturally familiar form (Harris, Lee, Hensley, & Schoen, 1988; Invernizzi & Abouzeid, 1995; Pritchard, 1990); and they retell stories in ways that are distinct to their own culture (Invernizzi & Abouzeid, 1995; John & Berney, 1968).

Limitations with film and video stimuli have also been recognized. Narrators' interpretations are likely to be influenced by the filmmaker's cinematic techniques and by subjects' previous exposure to and experiences with films and videos. As such, films and videos, like wordless picture books, cannot be expected to have a single, universal interpretation, given that the particular setting, characters, objects, and events will have different meanings for viewers from different parts of the world (Chafe, 1980).

Finally, with picture books, films, and videos, as well as with plates from projective tests like the Children's Apperception Test (a storytelling task that uses pictures; Bellak, 1993), we believe that subjects are more likely to treat the stimuli as a topic of discourse in which knowledge is already shared between subject and experimenter. This factor may explain in part some of the differences in findings across studies. For example, in a study that examined how children talked about a videotaped dialogue between two *Sesame Street* characters, approximately half the youngest children's (the 5-year-olds') quotations were unframed; that is, in recounting what they had just seen, they did not use a speech verb or explicitly identify the speaker (Özyürek, 1997). In contrast, when children of similar age shared personal anecdotes with an experimenter in a conversational context, they almost always used framed quotations by identifying the speaker and using a speech verb (Ely & McCabe, 1993). In our own work with Children's Apperception Test stories we have found that some of our youngest subjects use unframed quotations in enacting the voices of depicted figures. However, we also have noticed that they use eye contact or head nods to indicate or select out the depicted character whose voice they are enacting. The fact that these variations in the form of children's quotations can be so highly dependent on the nature of the elicitation technique suggests that particular care needs to be taken when comparing narrative data across different experimental paradigms.

CONCLUSION

In this chapter we described a range of methodological approaches that researchers interested in gathering narrative data might elect to use. In determining which approach or technique is best for any particular project, a number of factors should be considered. These include the theoretical disposition of the researcher, the goal of the project, the nature of the population under study, and the availability of resources. In addition, decisions should be guided by an understanding of the advantages and disadvantages of each technique, as well as by an understanding of the underlying theoretical assumptions associated with each technique.

In the best of worlds, researchers would employ several techniques in the same study in order to test the generalizability of findings derived from any single technique. A number of researchers (Allen et al., 1994; Berman, 1995; Hicks, 1991; Hudson & Shapiro, 1991; Wolf, 1997) have used this multimethod approach, and their findings have already greatly enhanced our understanding of narratives in general, as well as our appreciation of the similarities and differences that exist between distinct narrative genres.

REFERENCES

Allen, M., Kertoy, M. K., Sherblom, J. C., & Pettit, J. M. (1994). Children's narrative productions: A comparison of personal event and fictional stories. *Applied Psycholinguistics, 15*, 159–176.

Bamberg, M. (1985). *Form and function in the construction of narratives: Developmental perspectives.* Unpublished doctoral dissertation, University of California, Berkeley.

Bamberg, M. (1987). *The acquisition of narratives: Learning to use language.* Berlin: Mouton de Gruyter.

Bartlett, F. C. (1932). *Remembering: A study in experimental and social psychology.* Cambridge: Cambridge University Press.

Bellak, L. (1993). *The Thematic Apperception Test, the Children's Apperception Test, and the Senior Apperception Technique in clinical use.* Boston: Allyn and Bacon.

Berko Gleason, J. (1996). *The development of language* (4th ed.). Boston: Allyn and Bacon.

Berko Gleason, J., Perlmann, R. Y., & Greif, E. B. (1984). What's the magic word: Learning language through politeness routines. *Discourse Processes, 7*, 493–502.

Berko Gleason, J., & Weintraub, S. (1976). The acquisition of routines in child language. *Language in Society, 5*, 129–136.

Berman, R. A. (1995). Narrative competence and storytelling performance: How children tell stories in different contexts. *Journal of Narrative and Life History, 5*, 285–313.

Berman, R. A., & Slobin, D. I. (Eds.). (1994). *Relating events in narrative: A crosslinguistic developmental study.* Hillsdale, NJ: Lawrence Erlbaum Associates.

Blum-Kulka, S., & Snow, C. (1992). Developing autonomy for tellers, tales, and telling in family narrative events. *Journal of Narrative and Life History, 2*, 187–218.

Bornens, M.-T. (1990). Problems brought about by "reading" a sequence of pictures. *Journal of Experimental Child Psychology, 49*, 189–226.

Bretherton, I., Prentiss, C., & Ridgeway, D. (1990). Family relationships as represented in a story completion task at thirty-seven and fifty-four months of age. In I. Bretherton & M. W. Watson (Eds.), Children's perspectives on the family (pp. 85–105). *New Directions for Child Development, No. 48.*

Cassidy, J. (1988). Child–mother attachment and the self in six-year-olds. *Child Development, 59,* 121–134.

Chafe, W. L. (Ed.). (1980). *The pear stories: Cognitive, cultural, and linguistic aspects of narrative production.* Norwood, NJ: Ablex.

Champion, T., Seymour, H., & Camarata, S. (1995). Narrative discourse of African American children. *Journal of Narrative and Life History, 5,* 333–352.

Chang, C-J. (1994, April). *Chinese children's narrative structure.* Paper presented at Harvard University, Cambridge, MA.

Craddock-Willis, K., & McCabe, A. (1996). Improvising on a theme. Some African American traditions. In A. McCabe (Ed.), *Chameleon readers: Teaching children to appreciate all kinds of good stories* (pp. 98–115). New York: McGraw-Hill.

Cramer, P. (1996). *Storytelling, narrative and the Thematic Apperception Test.* New York: Guilford.

Dickinson, D. K. (1991). Teacher agenda and setting: Constraints on conversation in preschools. In A. McCabe & C. Peterson (Eds.), *Developing narrative structure* (pp. 255–301). Hillsdale, NJ: Lawrence Erlbaum Associates.

Dickinson, D. K., & Smith, M. W. (1991). Preschool talk: Patterns of teacher–child interaction in early childhood classrooms. *Journal of Research in Childhood Education, 6* (1), 20–29.

Dube, E. F. (1982). Literacy, cultural familiarity, and "intelligence" as determinants of story recall. In U. Neisser (Ed.), *Memory observed* (pp. 274–292). San Francisco: W. H. Freeman.

Ely, R., Gleason, J. B., Narasimhan, B., & McCabe, A. (1995). Family talk about talk: Mothers lead the way. *Discourse Processes, 19,* 201–218.

Ely, R., & McCabe, A. (1993). Remembered voices. *Journal of Child Language, 20,* 671–696.

Ely, R., & McCabe, A. (1994). The language play of kindergarten children. *First Language, 14,* 19–35.

Fivush, R. (1991a). Gender and emotion in mother–child conversations about the past. *Journal of Narrative and Life History, 1,* 325–341.

Fivush, R. (1991b). The social construction of personal narratives. *Merrill-Palmer Quarterly, 37,* 59–81.

Georgakopoulou, A. (1995). Narrative organization and contextual constraints: The case of modern Greek storytelling. *Journal of Narrative and Life History, 5,* 161–189.

Gee, J. P. (1986). Units in the production of narrative discourse. *Discourse Processes, 9,* 391–422.

Gee, J. P. (1992). *The social mind: Language, ideology and social practice.* New York: Bergin & Garvey.

Goodwin, M. H. (1990). *He-said-she-said: Talk as social organization among black children.* Bloomington: Indiana University Press.

Haden, C. A., Haine, R. A., & Fivush, R. (1997). Developing narrative structure in parent–child reminiscing across the preschool years. *Developmental Psychology, 33,* 295–307.

Harris, R. J., Lee, D. J., Hensley, D. L., & Schoen, L. M. (1988). The effect of cultural script knowledge on memory for stories over time. *Discourse Processes, 11,* 413–431.

Heath, S. B. (1983). *Ways with words: Language, life, and work in communities and classrooms.* New York: Cambridge University Press.

Hemphill, L., & Snow, C. (1996). Language and literacy development: Discontinuities and differences. In D. Olson & N. Torrance (Eds.), *Handbook of psychology in education* (pp. 173–201). Oxford: Blackwell.

Hicks, D. (1990). Narrative skills and genre knowledge: Ways of telling in the primary school grades. *Applied Psycholinguistics, 11,* 83–104.

Hicks, D. (1991). Kinds of narrative: Genre skills among first graders from two communities. In A. McCabe & C. Peterson (eds.), *Developing narrative structure* (pp. 55–88). Hillsdale, NJ: Lawrence Erlbaum Associates.

Hudson, J. A. (1993). Reminiscing with mothers and others: Autobiographical memory in young two-year-olds. *Journal of Narrative and Life History, 3,* 1–32.

Hudson, J. A., & Shapiro, L. R. (1991). From knowing to telling: The development of children's scripts, stories, and personal narratives. In A. McCabe & C. Peterson (Eds.), *Developing narrative structure* (pp. 89–136). Hillsdale, NJ: Lawrence Erlbaum Associates.

Hymes, D. (1982). Narrative form as a "grammar" of experience: Native Americans and a glimpse of English. *Journal of Education, 164,* 121–142.

Invernizzi, M. A., & Abouzeid, M. P. (1995). One story map does not fit all: A cross-cultural analysis of children's written story retellings. *Journal of Narrative and Life History, 5,* 1–19.

Jimenez Silva, M. J., & McCabe, A. (1996). Vignettes of the continuous and family ties: Some Latino American traditions. In A. McCabe (Ed.), *Chameleon readers: Teaching children to appreciate all kinds of good stories* (pp. 116–136). New York: McGraw-Hill.

John, V. P., & Berney, J. D. (1968). Analysis of story retelling as a measure of the effects of ethnic content in stories. In J. Helmuth (Ed.), *The disadvantaged child: Head Start and early intervention: Vol. 2* (pp. 259–287). New York: Brunner/Mazel.

Kintsch, W., & Greene, E. (1978). The role of culture-specific schemata in the comprehension and recall of stories. *Discourse Processes, 1,* 1–13.

Kruger, L., & Wolf, D. P. (1994). Play and narrative in inhibited children: A longitudinal case study. In A. Slade & D. P. Wolf (Eds.), *Children at play: Clinical and developmental approaches to meaning and representation* (pp. 261–285). New York: Oxford University Press.

Kuczaj, S. A. (1983). *Crib speech and language play.* New York: Springer-Verlag.

Kuczaj, S. A., & McClain, L. (1984). Of hawks and moozes: The fantasy narratives produced by a young child. In S. A. Kuczaj (Ed.), *Discourse development* (pp. 125–146). New York: Springer-Verlag.

Labov, W. (1972). *Language in the inner city.* Philadelphia: University of Pennsylvania Press.

Labov, W., & Waletzky, J. (1967). Narrative analysis. In J. Helm (Ed.), *Essays on the verbal and visual arts* (pp. 12–44). Seattle: University of Washington Press.

Malan, K. (1992, October). *Structure and coherence in South African children's personal narratives.* Paper presented at the 17th Annual Boston University Conference on Language Development, Boston.

Mandler, J. M., & Johnson, N. S. (1977). Remembrance of things parsed: Story structure and recall. *Cognitive Psychology, 9,* 111–151.

Mayer, M. (1969). *Frog, where are you?* New York: Dial Press.

McCabe, A. (1991). Editorial. *Journal of Narrative and Life History, 1,* 1–2.

McCabe, A. (1997). [Review of the book *Relating events in narrative: A crosslinguistic developmental study*]. *Journal of Child Language, 23,* 715–723.

McCabe, A., & Peterson, C. (1991). Getting the story: A longitudinal study of parental styles in eliciting narratives and developing narrative skill. In A. McCabe & C. Peterson (Eds.), *Developing narrative structure* (pp. 217–253). Hillsdale, NJ: Lawrence Erlbaum Associates.

McCabe, A., & Rollins, P. R. (1994). Assessment of preschool narrative skills. *American Journal of Speech Language Pathology, 3* (1), 45–56.

Melzi, G. (1997). *Developing narrative voice: A comparison of Latino and Anglo-American mothers' conversations with their preschool children.* Unpublished doctoral dissertation, Boston University.

Michaels, S. (1981). "Sharing time": Children's narrative styles and differential access to literacy. *Language in Society, 10,* 42–442.

Michaels, S. (1991). The dismantling of narrative. In A. McCabe & C. Peterson (Eds.), *Developing narrative structure* (pp. 303–351). Hillsdale, NJ: Lawrence Erlbaum Associates.

Miller, P. J., Mintz, J., Hoogstra, L., Fung, H., & Potts, R. (1992). The narrated self: Young children's construction of self in relation to others in conversational stories of personal experience. *Merrill-Palmer Quarterly, 38,* 45–67.

Miller, P. J., & Sperry, L. L. (1987). The socialization of anger and aggression. *Merrill- Palmer Quarterly, 33,* 1–31.

Miller, P. J., Wiley, A. R., Fung, H., & Liang, C-H. (1997). Personal storytelling as a medium of socialization in Chinese and American families. *Child Development, 68,* 557–568.

Minami, M., & McCabe, A. (1991). Haiku as a discourse regulation device. *Language in Society, 20,* 577–599.

Mitchell, W. J. T. (Ed.). (1980). *On narrative.* Chicago: University of Chicago Press.

Mueller, E., & Tingley, E. (1990). The bears' picnic: Children's representations of themselves and their families. In I. Bretherton & M. W. Watson (Eds.), Children's perspectives on the family (pp. 47–65). *New Directions for Child Development, No. 48.*

Nelson, K. (1986). *Event knowledge: Structure and function in development.* Hillsdale, NJ: Lawrence Erlbaum Associates.

Nelson, K. (Ed.). (1989). *Narratives from the crib.* Cambridge, MA: Harvard University Press.

Ochs, E. (1982). Talking to children in Western Samoa. *Language in Society, 11,* 77–104.

Ochs, E., & Schieffelin, B. B. (1984). Language acquisition and socialization: Three developmental stories and their implications. In R. Shweder & R. Levine, (Eds.), *Culture theory: Essays on mind, self, and emotion* (pp. 276–320). Cambridge: Cambridge University Press.

Ong, W. J. (1982) *Orality and literacy.* New York: Methuen.

Oppenheim, D., Emde, R. N., & Warren, S. (1997). Children's narrative representations of mothers: Their development and association with child and mother adaption. *Child Development, 68,* 127–138.

Özyürek, A. (1997). How children talk about a conversation. *Journal of Child Language, 23,* 693–714.

Pellegrini, A. D. (1982). The construction of cohesive text by preschoolers in two play contexts. *Discourse Processes, 5,* 101–108.

Pesco, D., & Crago, M. (1996). "We went home, told the whole story to our friends": Narratives by children in an Algonquin community. *Journal of Narrative and Life History, 6,* 293–321.

Peterson, C., & McCabe, A. (1983). *Developmental psycholinguistics: Three ways of looking at a child's narrative.* New York: Plenum.

Peterson, C. & McCabe, A. (1991). On the threshold of the storyrealm: Semantic versus pragmatic use of connectives in narratives. *Merrill-Palmer Quarterly, 17,* 45–64.

Peterson, C., & McCabe, A. (1992). Parental styles of narrative elicitation: Effect on children's narrative structure and content. *First Language, 12,* 299–321.

Peterson, C., & McCabe, A. (1994). A social interactionist account of developing decontextualized narrative skills. *Developmental Psychology, 30,* 937–948.

Preece, A. (1987). The range of narrative forms conversationally produced by young children. *Journal of Child Language, 14,* 353–373.

Preece, A. (1992). Collaborators and critics: The nature and effects of peer interaction on children's conversation narratives. *Journal of Narrative and Life History, 2,* 277–292.

Pritchard, R. (1990). The effects of cultural schemata on reading processing strategies. *Reading Research Quarterly, 25,* 273–295.

Rodino, A. M., Gimbert, C., Perez, C., Craddock-Willis, K., & McCabe, A. (1991, October). *"Getting your point across": Contrastive sequencing in low-income African-American and Latino children's personal narratives.* Paper presented at the 16th Annual Boston University Conference on Language Development, Boston.

Sheldon, A. (1989). *Sociolinguistic challenges to self-assertions and how very young girls meet them.* Paper presented at the Women in America Conference, Georgetown University.

Sheldon, A., & Rohleder, L. (1996). Sharing the same world, telling different stories: Gender differences in co-constructed pretend narratives. In D. I. Slobin, J. Gerhardt, A. Kyratzis, & J. Guo (Eds.), *Social interaction, social contest, and language: Essays in honor of Susan Ervin-Tripp* (pp. 613–632). Mahwah, NJ: Lawrence Erlbaum Associates.

Slough, N. M., & Greenberg, M. T. (1990). Five-year-olds' representations of separation from parents: Responses from the perspective of self and other. In I. Bretherton & M. W. Watson (Eds.), Children's perspectives on the family (pp. 67–84). *New Directions for Child Development, No. 48.*

Snow, C. E. (1983). Literacy and language: Relationships during the preschool years. *Harvard Educational Review, 53*, 165–189.

Snow, C. E. (1991). Diverse conversational contexts for the acquisition of various language skills. In J. F. Miller (Ed.), *Research on child language disorders: A decade of progress* (pp. 105–124). Austin, TX: Pro-Ed.

Snow, C. E., Barnes, W. S., Chandler, J., Goodman, I. F., & Hemphill, L. (1991). *Unfulfilled expectations: Home and school influences on literacy.* Cambridge, MA: Harvard University Press.

Snow, C. E., & Dickinson, D. K. (1990). Social sources of narrative skills at home and at school. *First Language, 10,* 87–103.

Snow, C. E., & Dickinson, D. K. (1991). Skills that aren't basic in a new conception of literacy. In A. Purves & E. Jennings (Eds.), *Literate systems and individual lives. Perspectives on literacy and schooling* (pp. 179–191). Albany: SUNY Press.

Stein, N. L. (1988). The development of children's storytelling skill. In M. B. Franklin & S. Barten (Eds.), *Child language: A book of readings* (pp. 282–297). New York: Oxford University Press.

Stein, N. L., & Glenn, C. G. (1979). An analysis of story comprehension in elementary school children. In R. O. Freedle (Ed.), *New directions in discourse comprehension: Vol. 2. Advances in discourse processing* (pp. 53–120). Norwood, NJ: Ablex.

Sutton-Smith, B. (1981). *The folkstories of children.* Philadelphia: University of Pennsylvania Press.

Tabors, P. O. (1987). *The development of communicative competence by second language learners in a nursery school classroom: An ethnolinguistic study.* Unpublished doctoral dissertation, Harvard Graduate School of Education, Cambridge, MA.

Tizard, B., & Hughes, M. (1984). *Young children learning.* Cambridge, MA: Harvard University Press.

Trabasso, T., & Rodkin, P. (1994). Knowledge of goal/plan: A conceptual basis for narrating *Frog, where are you?* In R. Berman & D. I. Slobin (Eds.), *Relating events in narrative: A crosslinguistic developmental study* (pp. 85–106). Hillsdale, NJ: Lawrence Erlbaum Associates.

Umiker-Sebeok, D. J. (1979). Preschool children's intra-conversational narratives. *Journal of Child Language, 6,* 91–109.

Weir, R. H. (1962). *Language in the crib.* The Hague: Mouton.

Wolf, A. (1997). *The dialogic nature of narrative interpretation: Three preschoolers conversations with different interlocutors.* Unpublished qualifying paper, Harvard University.

Wolf, D. (1985). Ways of telling: Text repertoires in elementary school children. *Journal of Education, 167,* 71–87.

Wolf, D., & Hicks, D. (1989). The voices within narratives: The development of intertextuality in young children's stories. *Discourse Processes, 12,* 329–351.

Wolf, D. P., Moreton, J., & Camp, L. (1994). Children's acquisition of different kinds of narrative discourse: Genres and lines of talk. In J. Sokolov & C. E. Snow (Eds.), *Handbook of research in language development using CHILDES* (pp. 286–323). Hillsdale, NJ: Lawrence Erlbaum Associates.

Wolf, D. P., & Push, J. (1985). The origins of autonomous texts in play boundaries. In L. Galda & A. Pellegrini (Eds.), *Play, language, and stories: The development of children's literate behavior* (pp. 63–77). Norwood, NJ: Ablex.

13

Studying Conversation: How to Get Natural Peer Interaction[1]

Susan M. Ervin-Tripp
University of California, Berkeley

Child language data collection has changed rapidly, due both to methodological innovations and to technology. Psycholinguistic child language methods began with the invention of standard comprehension and elicitation frames that could extend researchers' observations of children's knowledge beyond what they were able to produce in more natural interactional exchanges. These methods differed from traditional normative psychometrics because they were not focused on "right" or "wrong" answers but on discovering the child's linguistic constructs. Brown (1957), for example, asked children to match a picture to a nonsense word in various syntactic frames. Berko's (1958) wug study became the most widely known of the first standardized elicitations in this new vein of research.

Technological changes also led to method changes. From note-taking by linguists listening to children, which led to brilliant results, to wax cylinders, wire recording, tape recording, digital and video recording,

[1] The data reported in this chapter come from studies funded by grants from the National Institute of Mental Health (MH-26063) and the National Science Foundation (NSF-BNS-7826539), and from the University of California Committee on Research. The careful transcriptions are the work of Miriam Petruck and David Weber.

and wireless transmission, the data available for accurate transcriptions have shifted rapidly. Whereas the wax cylinder forced an artificial exchange between adult and child, the wireless transmitter allows researchers to transcribe children at play in natural environments even with no adult present. Each of these changes has made possible new views of children's talk.

Two advances in studies since the 1960s have heightened pressure to develop more situation-sensitive speech collection methods in the study of children. The first is the evidence from sociolinguistic research on adolescent and adult speech that the setting and activity context, the topics, the addressee, and the audience heavily influence the properties of language, raising issues about the type of sampling of the child's speech. The second is a new focus in child language studies on linguistic socialization, pragmatic development itself, and context of speaking as enabling and altering many aspects of language development.

CONTEXT OF SPEECH SITUATION

At the same time as changes in methods and technology were taking place in the study of child language, dialectologists and sociolinguists were going through these developments too. Hymes (1962) had a highly influential proposal concerning the variety of factors in the situation of speech that can alter speech itself, a proposal I fleshed out with examples from my own and other's research (Ervin, 1964) and Cazden (1970) connected to the study of child language. Earlier work on the naturalistic observation of children by Barker and Wright (1954) had made it clear that settings had a powerful effect on "standing behavior patterns" of children and, hence, on their speech.

Methodological changes were also coming to linguistics. Although dialectologists at first kept meticulous hand transcriptions of the lexical and phonetic features they elicited by various methods in interviews, Labov (1966) used a tape recorder and a systematic probability sample of speakers. He noticed that people do not always speak in the same way, and he argued that this was especially the case when there is a superposed variety in contact with a vernacular. He found that when people "monitor" speech they tend to move toward the superposed variety.[2] In this view, the chief factor influencing linguistic variables in a single speaker is attention paid to speech. Labov was a leader in establishing the quantitative study of linguistic variation, showing that many features of language, although perceived to be categorial, are empirically variable. This innovation allowed systematic study of subtle effects of contextual changes on linguistic features.

Labov's solution to finding the most vernacular style during a sociolinguistic interview involved two innovations. One was to build into his adult data collection new techniques for eliciting spontaneous speech that he hoped would be unmonitored, by eliciting danger-of-death narratives and childhood rhymes. He paid attention to the "channel cues" such as rapid speech that might show a reduction in monitoring, and he was attentive to serendipitous events such as phone calls and sudden visitors that might precipitate casual vernacular speech. The other innovation was the style cline. This was studied using systematic eliciting methods, with these vernacular events at one end, and interviews, reading, and specifically contrasted items to highlight the features being considered. His clines in variables such as post-vocalic r according to these contextual conditions are well known. However, it was not always easy, even with the "channel cues," to separate monitored from casual vernacular speech.

In the late 1960s, under the influence of the pioneering methodology used by Gumperz (1966), Labov (1972) changed his data collection methods while working with adolescents:

> We focus upon natural groups as the best possible solution to the *observer's paradox*: the problem of observing how people speak when they are not being observed. The natural interaction of peers can overshadow the effects of observation, and help us approach the goal of capturing the vernacular of every-day life in which the minimum of attention is paid to speech. This is the most systematic level of linguistic behavior and of greatest interest to the linguist who wants to explain the structure and evolution of language. (p. 256)

Rickford and McNair-Knox (1994) emphasized going beyond the formal–informal cline, systematically examining changes in speech with interlocutor and topic. They trace these ideas to the methods used by Labov (1972) and by Blom and Gumperz (1972), which manipulated who was present and, sometimes, what topics were taken up.

---

[2] Is adult speech a superposed variety to children? I once asked a child who had just said *he brang it* if there was another way to say that. *Yeah, adults say brought, but kids say brang.* Her reply did not privilege one or the other as a better way, but presented them as different group varieties. We know from role play that children notice such small differences.

CONVERSATIONAL
DEVELOPMENT

Why should we as researchers observe peer interaction in children? We may study conversational data from children for a wide range of goals—to examine phonetic shifts in informal speech, syntactic features brought in for different interactional functions, topical concerns, and larger issues of child pragmatics or child discourse development. Peer interaction shows us how children provide structure to talk when they are on their own. In play and in conversations, children deploy what they know about syntax and sound variation to accomplish a great variety of speech acts, and children integrate them into cohesive exchanges and larger sequences such as role play, narratives, joking, and arguing. With peers they control the timing and the topic; and if adults do not interfere, they display their own means of dealing with conflict. With studies of peer interaction, we clearly have much more access to the features of talk that are aspects of child culture transmitted from child to child.

FACTORS AFFECTING
NATURAL CONVERSATION

What is a good conversation? In our highly verbal society we think of good conversation as animated, lively, fast paced, with participation by many. We can tell when something is not working in face-to-face conversations when there are noticeably long lags between turns, rhythmic disruptions, lack of response to first turns, and little topical follow-up. The criteria of a good conversation are culturally variable after a certain age. We do know that the conversational attributes vary with setting, partner, and witnesses, as well as with activity, task, or topic, so to set the scene for a good conversation we must attend to these attributes.

A methodological handbook prepared by a Berkeley working group (Slobin, 1967) advocated collecting "100 lines of natural conversation." My colleagues and I gave no advice as to how this might be done. For many years, it was the custom to get data for child grammar or mean length of utterance (MLU) estimates by sending in a researcher with a tape recorder to talk with the child until 200 turns occurred, often in an unfamiliar setting. Another method was to instruct a parent to carry on a conversation.

What is peculiar about such data? Adult eliciting brings to bear at least four factors that can potentially alter the nature of data: (a) the familiarity of the interlocutor, (b) the adult as a social category leading to speech changes by the child, (c) the eliciting style of the adult, and (d) the model of language provided by the speaker. These factors can lead to special types of responses and alter both the formal and functional attributes of speech.

Familiarity is known to cause change in language features, as illustrated by the morphological shifts found by Fischer (1958) between -*ing* and -*in* as children got to know him.[3] Almost any form of talk that children engage in is adjusted when the partner is a child rather than an adult. Shatz and Gelman (1973) showed that children as young as age 4 were sensitive to addressee in systematic ways that affected the deployment of syntactic features such as subordination.

In studying children's discourse practices, conversations with peers give the best evidence of what children do with the features of discourse without modeling or scaffolding by adults. In naturalistic telephone conversations of preschool children, I found that in adult–child dyads the adult usually controlled topics and timing. In child–child dyads there could be long silences while one participant went off to do something else, then coming back to report, and there might be protracted misundertandings and startling topic shifts. These features would not have been apparent if only adult–child interaction was studied.

Adult eliciting of child speech can also lead to a special style, including the "elicitation question" noted by Corsaro (1977) and by Blount (1972). My students have observed similar questions in speech to animals in a zoo, although with less response. It is obvious that elicitation questions produce data that are functionally and syntactically special.

Recording Under Natural Conditions

Equipment.   Obtaining excellent data for analysis requires high quality microphones and stereo recording devices. In the analysis of conversation, loss of any segments can seriously compromise the study of continuity and conversational structure. Equipment is undergoing rapid and constant improvement. A major goal is to get a high quality

---

[3]In many languages, familiarity can cause altered speech forms. In Korean, the epistemic particle -*ci* that refers to shared knowledge is more often used with a familiar addressee by children and may be hard for a stranger to elicit.

microphone within a few inches of the child's mouth without inhibiting freedom of movement.

Research on young children's interaction usually requires radio transmitters, because they allow children to move freely yet yield a high fidelity audio record. Labov noted that even sotto voce speech could be captured by an individual lavaliere microphone attached to a transmitter. In many of my own conversational studies since 1972, each speaker carries a transmitter. I have even successfully taped children playing jumprope, so I know the equipment is versatile for use during activity (Ervin-Tripp 1986).

There is a wide range of flat and light-weight wireless microphones available for making high quality recordings. The battery pack is usually quite small, about the size of a pack of cards, and is either pinned on the child, put in a pocket of a vest or apron worn by the child, or put in a small pouch-type pack that is strapped on the child. There is typically a short stringlike antenna that must be free for the equipment to work properly. The receiver can be in another room. Each receiver is connected by line separately to the input jack of a channel of a stereo recorder. It can also be used as input to a camcorder, of course. The transmitter must have a power indicator and an on/off switch that can be taped to prevent the child from turning it off. Between uses it is desirable to disable the batteries, because a battery failure can mean loss of data.

This equipment is designed for media performers, and in some cases there are receivers that can receive input from more than two transmitters, but it is important that the receiver be configured to separate rather than mix the voices. At the time of purchase, the supplier makes sure that the transmission is on separate wave lengths and checks the wave lengths in particular regions to avoid radio interference. In some countries there are regulations regarding private use of radio transmission. The transmitters are of low strength, rather like a cordless telephone, or else they would not be safe to carry on the body.

Rampton (1991) used radio transmitters in his work on linguistically heterogeneous adolescent peer groups:

> It is often hard to know how much recordings of recreation have been affected by the wearing of radio microphones. Informants were normally given these on three or four consecutive days in the expectation that their novelty would need time to wear off, . . . and the fact that episodes were played back to informants made it easier to decide whether or not they gave a fair picture of normal practice. (p. 393)

In a pinch, in a limited space when the transmitters are in repair, high quality monophonic Electret condenser microphones can be distributed at different locations again for separate input to different channels. However, the distance from the speaker's mouth gives these lower signal-to-noise than the transmitter system does.

After the microphone-transmitter is turned on at the beginning of the episode, a way should be found for each child to give a name, so that the transcriber can identify the voice qualities and the channel for each participant. The separate channel for each voice allows either (a) the use of a balance control on the playback device, or (b) listening to the input to each ear when using earphones so as to identify the speaker for each turn by figuring out which channel is loudest.

For certain circumstances, such as telephone taping, an attachment from a phone receiver to a high quality tape recorder serves well. The recording field is changing rapidly. Many researchers find digital recorders are lightweight and provide data that can be used as input for computer sound analysis or linked to a transcript and played back at meetings from portable computers. There is a recommendation to copy to analog form for backup storage and for transcription from foot-pedal analog transcription devices, but for recording purposes DAT is superior to cassettes. At present, analog reel-to-reel or CD is the best archiving format, because digital recordings degrade in 15 to 20 years.

Video-recording is possible with young children in settings where there is a camera fixed too high for children's access or placed behind a window. Whether it is possible to do this without inhibiting talk, I have not ascertained. Video is of course necessary whenever activity is an essential component, as in Goodwin (1998) or in our work on directives of children (Ervin-Tripp & Gordon, 1985), in which we videotaped children with friends and family. In these cases, children were not alone and the researcher was noticeable.

We have found it prudent when videotaping to have a simultaneous audiotape recorder, from which we make the audio transcripts using foot-pedal transcription machines. There are multichannel courtroom transcription machines; most office transcribers are monaural, losing the advantage of the multiple voiced input from the transmitters.

Transcription. The usual estimate for time to transcribe an audiotaped conversation adequately in normal orthography rather than phonetic script is on the order of 20 times the time of the recording. Our transcription practices were described by Gumperz and Berenz (1993). Where languages other than English comprise the text, or where code switching occurs, we add for each text line (t-line) a morpheme gloss (m-line) and a free translation into English (e-line). These lines are superposed so that they can be compared—for example, to identify markers and syntactic features at codeswitches.

The reason for choosing this transcription format is that it is well designed to preserve the most important conversational interaction features on the text line in computers, including stress and intonation, overlap features, vocal and stylistic characteristics, and timing, and it is very easy to read. Normally, it is necessary to use Courier font to keep superposed lines and overlapped segments in the same position. These transcription features are present in some of the transcripts that follow in this chapter.

RESEARCH ON PEER INTERACTIONS

Observer's Paradox

Can the researcher be present at a family dinner without affecting talk? Can a person observe a couple talking and have no effect? Both adults and children can become involved in activities and forget or "background" the presence of another, but researchers too often presuppose that talk is the same with and without observation.[4] The effect of an observer on children's talk is probably different at each stage of development, because complex notions of what might be the attitude of the other to the self develop gradually. If children value privacy, the ethics of research require the child's permission to tape. The hope is that children will acclimate to the presence of the microphone, as Rampton hoped they would to the camera. Because of this problem, in working with grade school children my colleagues and I either remove all adults from the room or put them apparently out of earshot.

The familiarity of the participants in talk is likely to have many effects on interaction. In adult talk it has been found that the discourse markers

---

[4] Graves and Glick (1978) showed that American mothers in a waiting room used more baby talk with children when they believed they were being observed.

used are different, with more pragmatic markers used with friends and more semantic markers used with strangers (Redeker, 1990). It is not known how early this effect appears. The content of talk is changed by shared knowledge, including both "common knowledge" references and the use of metaphoric speech.

In the case of children, my colleagues and I have found that close friends or mutually selected dyads produce the most fluent conversations without external stimuli. This is presumably because they share the most common referential and emotional bases for talk and are well tuned to the cues given by the other.

Setting

A new setting alters the energy for talk. Settings may have strong demand characteristics or convey talk-related cultural pressures (e.g., for silence or shouting); they cannot be considered neutral. A room with toys has strong demand characteristics for a young child. Some toys lend themselves to talk, others to solitary play. In our research, we have found that minimizing objects is conducive to conversation as a time-filler and reduces the risk that all talk will be about objects. Positioning of the children can also affect talk; for example, wings on car seats reduce children's conversation.[5]

An adult comparison can be found in Soskin and John's (1963) early experiment on the radio transmission of the natural conversation of a newlywed couple at a resort. The talk in places such as rowboats and craft shops was primarily directive and explanatory; the talk while eating or in a waiting line was much more wide-ranging in topical variety.

Language

If bilingual speakers are told, or believe, that only one of their languages is appropriate to a setting or audience, they may be prevented from using the language or style most congruent with their conversational partner. For this reason, my students use a code-switching style in the introductory segments of research with bilingual children, to open up for them the option to use either language.

---

[5] Elena Escalera in our lab found that the seats accounted for reduction in talk.

Activity/Task/Topic

The activity that is ongoing during the collection of talk samples has a profound effect on the talk that occurs. In the Soskin and John study (1963), rowing was conducive to imperatives. If "pure talk" that is based on conversational interaction rather than on directives, description, narrative retellings, or other task-related genres is sought, it is necessary to discover the circumstances under which conversation is the sole activity of children.

A fertile site for the study of the activity of conversation is the waiting room. Martin Lampert, Iliana Reyes, and I used this is a strategy in several studies of elementary school children, summarized by Lampert:

> To organized groups for study, we asked the second- and fifth-grade children to nominate the friends with whom they would like to do a science project. On the basis of their nominations, we then assigned the children to groups of two and three children each, and on selected days, we invited a different group to eat lunch in an activity room located at their school, and afterwards to participate in a brief chemistry experiment. . . .
>
> On their assigned day, groups brought their lunches to the activity room where a research assistant met and invited them to eat their lunch at a table with microphones attached to a ceiling lamp overhead. The researcher . . . then left the room under the pretext of having to prepare for the science experiment and returned 20 minutes later to conduct the experiment with the children. We recorded the children's talk while they ate their lunch and while they participated in the science experiment (Lampert, 1996. p. 591).

PEER CONVERSATIONS IN DIFFERENT SETTINGS

Phone calls

Children can learn before age 2 the external conventions of telephone use and have been heard teaching these conventions to immigrant children (Ervin-Tripp, 1981). In the following example,[6] the children have no adult scaffolding to solve various problems that arise. Marko, age 3;6, and Sonia, age 3;3, are old friends.

---

[6]The notation used here is =for overlaps=, <3> for a 3 second silence, == for fast response latching, {[feature] for scope of feature}, ** for contrastive stress, * for normal stress, :: for sound prolongation, ... for silences, and (xxx) for inaudible segments.

(1) Phone conversation

```
1  M:  = you want a um = <3> what?    = i mean know what?  =
2  S:  = what are you   = doing, Marko?= what are you doing? =
3  M:  (screaming) you know what?
4  M:  you know what happened last    = night?   =
5  S:                                 = what are  = you doing now?
```

This phone conversation between friends provides many examples of telephone norms known to children. Instead of "how are you," the most common child–child initiator is "what are you doing?" Because Marko and Sonia speak simultaneously, each deploying a topic initiator, they do not hear each other even though Marko screams in line 3.

```
 6  M:  um uh y'know what happened last night? there was a
 7  M:  there was a cat. = we saw a cat =
 8  S:                   = what are you doing now? =
 9  M:  (long narrative mostly expressive meows)
10      = because = um uh th   = e  oth =
11  S:  = Marko  =               = Marko =
12  S:                 = Marko =
13  M:  our kitty hit the oth = er   ca = t and went
14  M:  {[crying tone] crying all the way home}.
15      th  = e ba-th= e       = bad  c = at.
16  S:       = Marko =         = Marko =
17  S:  Marko, don't. no no. no.
18  M:  what?
19  S:  i can't talk to you if you talk to me. Marko.
```

Marko does not listen for feedback during his long narrative composed of expressive meows, and he ignores Sonia's attempts to interrupt him. She finally tells him the conversational rules explicitly in line 19.

```
20  M:  why don't you tell your mother that, 'kay?=OK?= OK? =OK?=
21  S:                                           = no. =
22  S:  = no,  = Marko... = bye, Marko. = (hangs up)
23  M:  = OK? = ..then tell= Sally[7] that   = and tell her what I uh
24  M:  tell um your Daddy.
```

                    Ervin-Tripp Telephone Corpus (06-03-2)

---

[7]Sally is unknown to Sonia.

Until the end, Marko is oblivious to the indicators that Sonia does not like his story. A phone conversation a year later when Marko is 4;5 and Sonia is 4;2 shows far more elaborate and subtle collaboration on interaction. The contrast is a striking illustration of many dimensions of pragmatic development.

Phone conversation

```
 1   M:   {[singing] do adoodoodiiodoo} hey Sonia.
 2   S:   <l.1> hoi Marko.
 3   M:   <2> do you have a different kind of
 4   M:   do you have a different swing?
 5   S:   <1.2> again a bully ring?
 6   M:   do you have a different **si::wing?
 7   S:   <l.2> no.
 8   M:   you didn't have any swing? all right
```

In line 1, Marko uses an attention getting method, *hey* + name, showing advancement beyond *hey* alone typical of younger children (Ervin-Tripp & Gordon, 1985). In line 6 he repairs a misunderstanding by slow, stressed articulation, and in line 8 he confirms Sonia's reply.

```
 9   M:   bye by:::e. <4.2> hi Sonia.
10   S:   hi Marko.
11   M:   {[laughing] i'm just kidding}.
12        hey hey Sonia. didn't you hear me say bye-bye?
13   S:   <2.5> no, i didn't say bye-bye.
14   M:   i-i said bye-bye. i-i just **tricking you.
```

Here a playful tone that was evident in the sound play in lines 1 and 2 is taken up in a mock speech act in line 9 that was not successful, so in line 12 Marko checks on why it failed, again using an effective attention-getter. He lexicalizes what he was doing by naming his speech act in lines 11 and 14, suggesting some metapragmatic skill.

In the next section each child spins off on a separate theme, with Marko drawing in his breath as he struggles to put together a new invention. What he does is common at this age; he makes a creative permutation on shared cultural material from Mother Goose, which leads into the longer section following in which another playful permutation is presented. Sonia is as inattentive to him as he is to her and indicates her new departure with nonsense word play for the next few moments.

25 M: Miss Muffet was eating her {[laughing)] Christmas pie.}
26 M: (giggles)
27 S: {[high voice] = baba ba ba= babab = bao} =
28 M: Ja = ck and Ji- =   = here = here here here =
29 S: = Marko =
30 M: = here's = Jack and Jill. {[sings] = Jack and- hey Ja =
31 S: = ta dada ta da dao =
32 M: {[sings] hey Ja-} hey Sonia, this is Jack and Jill.
33 M: {[sings] Jack and Jill went up the hill
34 M: to get a pail of water.down he came and
35 M: {[laughing] up he came and down he came}
36 M: the ladder, {[singing] and den he's under wa::ter}.

In line 27–31 the two children overlap, until Marko grabs the floor with an attention call and succeeds in holding the floor for the next five lines with a more elaborate attempt at a new version of a familiar nursery song, with a new rhyming of *water* with *ladder,* and a new image of what happened with *water.*

40 M: ya know what (xxx)
41 S: Jack and Jill went up the hill to {[hi] fetch a pail of
42   water}. Jack fell down and Ja- and Jill was out the . . .
43   ha huh (giggles)
44 M: {[singing] Jack and Jill went up the hill to g-}
45   i'm gonna write the lines. Jack, and Jill,
46   went **up the hill, to **get a pail of **wa::**ter.
47   then down he he—then up he came
48   {[laughing] with Sonia in the pa::rlor.} hehhheehe
                                        Telephone corpus 06-10-6

By line 41 Sonia joins in to invent new variations on the Jack and Jill story, and Marko after bringing in the writing notion (he seems to have pencil and paper at hand) produces the ultimate performer ploy by including Sonia in the story.

Although it cannot be said that the children collaborate in the production of each new version, they each get pleasure out of sharing the game of invention on similar themes. What is striking in seeing the change in Marko is that even though he still tries to get the floor and perform, he displays more varied methods and more awareness of the listener in a variety of ways. This is a good demonstration of pragmatic development within the genres of natural play. It illustrates as well the kind of creative play drawn from literature read to children, which young boys and girls develop and appreciate on their own.

Role Play With Play Objects

More familiar are examples of unsolicited child role play that occurs spontaneously when children play with certain materials. In the situation that follows, a brother and sister and friend use a tennis racket as a crutch and set up roles.

(3) Doctor–patient play of 4 to 5-year-olds
1 Kit: pretend there's something wrong with my leg. my leg—
2   K: let's pretend that i tell you that my leg's—um—
3   K: let's pretend i tell you— first, you operate on it.

This is the voice of the director, setting up a narrative line for the role play. The first line contains a directive; the rest is couched (as is often found in girls' speech) as a shared suggestion.

4   K: um, but before you operate on it,
5   K: let me tell you something, okay nurse?

Here a contrastive pragmatic marker halts the action directed in line 3 for the insertion of a narrative. Stories about injuries are common, so this is a standard context for an account (Ervin-Tripp & Kuntay, 1997.) The director's voice switches either in the middle of line 3 or the beginning of line 4 to the voice of the actor enacting the role. This role includes addressing the nurse. Role names are common as address terms in role play, perhaps helping anchor the typicality of roles more than personal names would.

6   J: um, 'kay.
7   K: um, when I was walking down the street,
8   K: i saw this piece of glass and i picked it up,
9   K: then i didn't see too well, then it goes way up to here.

This is a characteristic narrative, starting with the setting of a place for the event, using a durative verb for backgrounding information in a temporal clause. This contrast in verb types is apparent from the beginning of temporal clauses before age 3 (Ervin-Tripp & Bocaz, 1989).

10 K: see now. it's—now it's over there.
11 K: can you—can you operate on it, nurse?
12 A: i can.
13 K: can you not—i said—um—
14 K: somebody has to operate on- on- on
                    Ervin-Tripp Family Transcripts: Bowyer[8]

Lines 10 to 14 illustrate children's skill by this age in mitigating requests appropriately according to addressee. In this case a mitigated conventional request is addressed to the nurse, but apparently she remains in role in making an indirect request in line 14, which does not return to her director's voice in deciding who will do the operation. Role play is particularly rich in displaying a wide variety of pragmatic skills, here unsupported by adult direction.

Waiting Room Role Play

(4) Courtroom play of 10-year-old girls
1   E: i'll be the *jury. here. i'll be the *jury.
2   L: this court will *now *come *to *order. [laugh]
3   E: yeah.. let's do that..okay?
4   E: but then you gotta think about it *okay?
5   E: you'll be the judge.. *okay?
6   L: okay.

The two girls have no problem understanding the frame for the role play, which is as familiar to them (presumably from TV) as doctor play is for the 4-year-olds. They decide on a rape theme.

37 L: you may take your seat now. [laugh]
38 L: this case will now come to order. [laugh]
39 L: you may make your opening statement.
40 E: your honor.. my first
41 E: my first defense will be the witness . . .

At this point the girls shift from legalese into a vivid and protracted description of a sexual encounter, modified by the "judge's" insistence, while laughing, on courtroom proprieties and language.

---

[8]Jill's age was 4;4. Kit and Jill's brother Andy were 5 years old.

55 E: Mary.. can you tell us what absolutely happened?
56 E: {[hi] well..um.. i was at home
57 E: and i was feeling lonely and i}...
58 L: ==what did you do.{[fast] *rape that *man?} [laugh]
59 E: {[hi] and i wanted my boyfriend to come
60 E: and i didn't think he would force me to have *sex
61 E: with him so i told him *no.}
62 L: *sshhh. *no. you cannot use that word in this court.
63 L: [laugh]
64 E: {[hi]he wanted to do the wild thing.}
65 L: [laugh]
66 E: {[hi}but i said i didn't want to.. i was married.
67 E: he slapped me and he punched me in my face.}
68 E: [mock crying]

The role-playing victim not only uses highpitched voice but a flapped /r/ in "married." The "judge" is laughing most of the time.

81 L: well.. why are you pressing charges for rape? [laugh]
82 E: <2>he.. uh.. he.. *yeah. he *forced me to.
83 L: he forced you but-
84 L: but that is called *sexual *harassment.
85 L: but did you press charges for that?
86 E: yes.
87 L: *no. you pressed charges for rape..
88 L: which he did *not *do so.. [laugh]

UC Berkeley Disclab L.5.19.5

To summarize this chapter: in school age children especially, who are more tuned to audience than are toddlers, the study of discourse development and sociolinguistic variation requires developing ways to access peer and sibling talk without adult presence. As these uncensored examples show, peer talk gives us unscaffolded and often surprising evidence of what is on the minds of young people, what types of linguistic and pragmalinguistic skills they have developed, and what their models of language are.

REFERENCES

Barker, R. G., & Wright, H. F. (1954). *Midwest and its children*. Evanston IL: Row, Peterson.

Berko (Gleason), J. (1958). The child's learning of English morphology. *Word, 14*, 150–177.

Blom, J.-P., & Gumperz, J. J. (1972). Social meaning in linguistic structures: Code-switching in Norway. In J. J. Gumperz & D. Hymes (Eds.), *Directions in sociolinguistics* (pp. 407–434). New York: Holt, Rinehart, and Winston.

Blount, B. (1972). Aspects of socialization among the Luo of Kenya. *Language in Society, 1*, 235–248.

Brown, R. (1957). Linguistic determinism and the part of speech. *Journal of Abnormal and Social Psychology, 55*, 1–5.

Cazden, C. (1970). The neglected situation in child language research and education. *Journal of Social Issues, 25*, 35–60.

Corsaro, W. (1977). The clarification request as a feature of adult-interactive styles with young children. *Language in Society, 6*, 183–207.

Ervin, S. M. (1964). An analysis of the interaction of language, topic, and listener. *American Anthropologist 66.6* (Part 2) 86–102.

Ervin-Tripp, S. M. (1981). Social process in first- and second-language learning. In H. Winitz (Ed.), *Native language and foreign language acquisition: Vol. 379*, (pp. 33–47). New York: NY Academy of Science.

Ervin-Tripp, S. M. (1986). Activity structure as scaffolding for children's second language learning. In W. Corsaro, J. Cook-Gumperz, and J. Streeck (Eds.), *Children's language and children's worlds.* (pp. 327–358). Berlin: Mouton de Gruyter.

Ervin-Tripp, S. M., & Bocaz, A. (1989). *Quickly, before a witch gets me: Children's temporal conjunctions within speech acts.* (Berkeley Cognitive Science Report 61): Institute of Cognitive Studies, Berkeley: University of California.

Ervin-Tripp, S. M., & Gordon, D. P. (1985). The development of requests. In R. L. Schiefelbusch (Ed.), *Communicative competence: Assessment and intervention* (pp. 61–95). Baltimore: University Park Press.

Ervin-Tripp, S. M., & Kuntay, A. (1997). The occasioning and structure of conversational narratives. In T. Givon (Ed.), *Conversation: Cultural, cognitive and communicative perspectives.* Amsterdam: J. Benjamins.

Fischer, J. L. (1958). Social influences in the choice of a linguistic variant. *Word, 14*, 47–56.

Goodwin, M. H. (1998). Games of stance: conflict and footing in hopscotch. In S. Hoyle & C. T. Adger (Eds.), *Kids talk: Strategic language use in later childhood* (pp. 23–46). New York: Oxford University Press.

Graves, Z., & Glick, J. (1978). The effect of context on mother–child interaction: A progress report. *Quarterly Newsletter of the Institute for Comparative Human Development, 2*, 41–46.

Gumperz, J. J. (1966) On the ethnology of linguistic change. In W. Bright (Ed.), *Sociolinguistics* (pp. 27–49). The Hague: Mouton.

Gumperz, J. J., & Berenz, N. (1993). Transcribing conversational exchanges. In J. L. Edwards, M. (Ed.), *Talking data: Transcription and coding methods for language research* (pp. 91–122). Hillsdale, NJ: Lawrence Erlbaum Associates.

Hymes, D. (1962). The ethnography of speaking. In T. Gladwin & W. Sturtevant (Eds.), *Anthropology and human behavior* (pp. 15–53). Washington DC: Anthropological Society of Washington.

Labov, W. (1966). *The social stratification of English in New York City*. Washington, DC: Center for Applied Linguistics.

Labov, W. (1972). *Language in the inner city: Studies in the Black English vernacular.* Philadelphia: University of Pennsylvania Press.

Lampert, M. D. (1996). Studying gender differences in the conversational humor of adults and children. In D. Slobin, J. Gerhardt, A. Kyratzis, & J. Guo (Eds.), *Social interaction, social context, and language* (pp. 579–596). Mahwah, NJ: Lawrence Erlbaum Associates.

Rampton, M. B. H. (1991). Interracial Panjabi in a British adolescent peer group. *Language in Society, 20,* 391–422.

Redeker, G. (1990). Ideational and pragmatic markers of discourse structure. *Journal of Pragmatics, 14,* 367–381.

Rickford, J. R., & McNair-Knox, F. (1994). Addressee- and topic-influenced style shift: A quantitative sociolinguistic study. In D. Biber & E. Finegan (Eds.), *Sociolinguistic perspectives on register.* New York: Oxford University Press.

Shatz, M., & Gelman, R. (1973). The development of communication skills: Modifications in the speech of young children as a function of listener. *Monographs of the Society for Research in Child Development, 38,* 1–37.

Slobin, D. (Ed.). (1967). *Field manual for cross-cultural study of the acquisition of communicative competence.* Berkeley, CA: ASUC Bookstore.

Soskin, W. F., & John, V. (1963). The study of spontaneous talk. In R. G. Barker (Ed.), *The stream of behavior.* New York: Appleton-Century-Crofts.

III
DEVELOPMENTAL
DISORDERS

14

Elicited Imitation and Other Methods for the Analysis of Trade-Offs Between Speech and Language Skills in Children

Nan Bernstein Ratner
University of Maryland, College Park

In studying children's speech, there are limits on what can be learned solely through the study of the child's spontaneous productions. What a child says may not be an adequate or accurate representation of what he or she knows; extrapolating control over linguistic forms from spontaneous language may over-, under- or misrepresent the degree to which a child has mastered a particular linguistic skill. Thus, to appraise the depth of children's linguistic knowledge, researchers often resort to tasks that prompt the child to process novel structures, whether they be lexical, morphological, or syntactic. Berko's (1958) elicited production paradigm was a classic first approach to this problem: By requiring children to manipulate nonsense words, she could elicit generative expression of morphological and morphophonemic knowledge.

Elicited imitation tasks used in the study of productive syntax are conceptually related: Children are challenged to reproduce the experimenter's model, which often has been selected specifically because the structure cannot easily be observed in a spontaneous language sample or because its use in some contexts may not confirm the child's ability to generate the structure in other environments.

In this chapter, I address some concerns that arise in the use of elicited imitation tasks as a measure of children's language knowledge. The use of elicited imitation to assess children's underlying knowledge of specific morphological and syntactic structures has a long history, and an extensive critique of its benefits and possible limitations when used for this purpose was recently compiled by Lust, Flynn, and Foley (1996). In the program of work I describe, my colleagues and I primarily use elicited imitation for somewhat different purposes: to explore cross-domain interactions, or trade-offs, between aspects of the child's evolving speech and language system. Specifically, we use elicited imitation and some additional approaches to explore the influences of syntactic formulation on the fluency of typically developing and stuttering children.

WHAT IS ELICITED IMITATION?

There are many forms of imitation in verbal and nonverbal behavior. This chapter addresses the use of elicited imitation, which directs the subject to repeat the examiner's model on command. Such imitation is distinct from spontaneous imitation, in which a child may repeat a conversational partner's previous utterance (or their own, self-imitation) without overt prompting to do so. The role of spontaneous imitation and interpretation of its frequency and accuracy has a well-developed history in the language acquisition literature (e.g., Bloom, Hood, & Lightbown, 1974/1991; Clark, 1977; Ervin-Tripp, 1973; Kuhl & Meltzoff, 1996; Snow, 1981). Modeling (Gordon, 1991) is an adaptation of elicited imitation in which the child is presented with a grammatical model (i.e., "The dog is barking") and is asked to generate a similar utterance with new lexical items when provided with stimuli such as a picture of a horse running.

For the purposes of this discussion, the term *elicited imitation* is also used to refer to repetitions of multiword stimuli, thereby distinguishing it from paradigms involving nonword repetition. The latter has become increasingly well known as a measure of phonological working memory (e.g., Adams & Gathercole, 1995).

History of Elicited Imitation Paradigms

Although adults have undoubtedly been asking children, "Can you say . . .?" for millennia, the first systematic examination of children's elicited imitations is credited to Brown and Fraser (1963). The researchers noted that children between 2 and 3 years of age reproduced adult models in a manner consistent with their own spontaneous, telegraphic productions. Although Fraser, Bellugi, and Brown (1963) noted cases in which children's imitation abilities appeared to exceed their comprehension and spontaneous production for identical structures, there has been general agreement by researchers working over the past 30 years that sentences constructed at a level slightly above that observed in the child's spontaneous speech are regularized in ways that reflect both the child's extraction of form and meaning and the child's productive linguistic capacity. Slobin and Welsh (1973) noted early on that the child's short-term memory was a critical factor in determining the utility of elicited imitation—if stimuli are too short, they may be imitated even in the absence of comprehension, well-formedness, or control over the target structure.

However, there is general consensus that elicited imitation, when properly utilized, provides a window into the child's competence for language. Elicited imitation tasks make clear that children are not tape recorders or parrots, nor are they even tape recorders with finite resources. In imitation, adult models do not merely get "melted down" through omission to less mature renditions; there are numerous cases in which the child's appreciation for the underlying structure of the input stimulus becomes apparent through an elaborated response that fills gaps in the original syntax (Lust, 1977; Slobin & Welsh, 1973; Thiemann, 1975). For example, the child who repeats "The owl eats candy and runs fast" as "Owl eat candy . . . and . . . he run fast" demonstrates control over coordination that would not be apparent had the sentence merely been repeated accurately. Thiemann noted a large number of such expansions: "The teacher read her children a story" → "The teacher read the story to the children"; "The boy told his mother a funny story and she laughed" → "The boy told the story to his mommy and the mommy laughed" (Thiemann, 1975). Under most circumstances elicited imitation does not exceed levels observed in spontaneous language, although it may underestimate spontaneous production ability (see subsequent discussion). While most elicited imitation studies present children with well-formed stimuli to appraise linguistic control, there is also a body of literature that has examined children's normalization of ill-formed input (e.g., Smith, 1973). Under either condition, both the accuracy of imitation and the ways that stimuli are changed shed light on the child's understanding and productive control over selected aspects of speech and language.

Aspects of Language Production Amenable to Elicited Imitation Paradigms

Elicited imitation (EI) has been used to examine children's and adult's control over a large number of linguistic and paralinguistic features. For example, Lust and her colleagues have extensively deployed EI tasks to examine children's knowledge of the principles governing anaphora and coordination cross-linguistically (see Lust, Flynn, & Foley, 1996, for extensive review), whereas Weeks (1992) examined preschoolers' control over tag question construction using the EI paradigm. Although there are numerous usages of the paradigm to examine control over narrowly specified linguistic targets, it is also impressive to observe the scope of EI investigations across the range of communicative functions. A recent sampling includes speech rate (Bosshardt, Sappok, Knipschild, & Holscher, 1997) and prosody (Bosshardt et al., 1997; Loeb & Allen, 1993; Van der Meulen, Janssen, & Den Os, 1997). EI has been used to demonstrate contrasting functional outcomes by site of hemispheric damage (Eisele & Aram, 1994) and to examine changes in syntactic processing across aging populations (Kemper, 1987). Children's understanding of metaphor has been assessed with EI (Pearson, 1990), as has children's memory for event sequences (Bauer & Thal, 1990). Beyond purely verbal production, EI has been used to study the development of children's combinatorial play behaviors (Brownell, 1988).

The Utility of Elicited Imitation Paradigms

As Lust, Flynn, and Foley (1996) note, there are innumerable advantages to the use of elicited imitation in the study of children's communicative development. In both normal and atypical development, attempts to explore and compare children's spontaneous language abilities face myriad obstacles. First, spontaneous language is notoriously unreliable in its distribution of any given syntactic structure of interest to the researcher. Complex structures of most interest to language researchers or clinicians may be rarely observed, in either the child's speech or indeed in the speech of adults in the community. If observed, structures may not be observed regularly enough or in sufficient numbers to permit statistical analysis of age or group trends. Second, a targeted structure, even if present or obligatory in the sentence being produced may show up in contexts that vary considerably in other aspects, such as length, lexical complexity, or morphological saturation. Such concerns prompt Lust, Flynn, and Foley to praise elicited imitation for its control of linguistic precision and for the statistical and scientific control that EI paradigms offer.

CONSIDERATIONS IN THE DEVELOPMENT OF ELICITED IMITATION STIMULI

A primary concern is the construction of stimuli that are appropriate for answering a given research question. For tests of the mastery of linguistic structures, it is conventional to present randomized pairs of utterances that have been balanced for length and lexical frequency, at a minimum, and that contrast only on the basis of the syntactic structure being appraised (e.g., branching direction as in "When he went home, John called the bank" vs. "John called the bank when he went home.") In the sections that follow, I discuss how to develop stimuli that are constructed to answer the question of how aspects of language production undergo "trading" relationships. For such purposes my colleagues and I have chosen to develop hierarchies of utterance difficulty, or discrete categories of utterances differing in syntactic complexity. Later in this chapter I "walk through" such stimulus development in the discussion of our research into language-fluency tradeoffs in children. However, first I address other general considerations in the development, administration, use, and interpretation of EI tasks.

Sentences in any stimulus set can potentially vary by differences in phoneme loading, lexical frequency and concreteness, length (whether measured in words, syllables, or morphemes), and grammatical structure, at a minimum. Presentation may vary in terms of presentation rate and prosodic characteristics, if stimuli are administered via live voice. Once the aspect to be manipulated has been identified, the remaining stimulus characteristics must be controlled or balanced in some fashion. In earlier work, my colleagues and I balanced lexicon by using repetitive vocabulary across sentence structures (Ratner & Sih, 1987); this can potentially be confusing to subjects. In recent work (Silverman & Ratner, 1997) we balance sentences for lexical frequency using published norms for children's texts (Carroll, Davies, & Richman, 1971). The process of controlling for lexical frequency is not at all trivial, although it is not a focus of this chapter (Ratner, 1988).

There is some debate over whether the use of picture cues affects the accuracy of elicited imitation. Madison, Roach, Santema, Akmal, and Guenzel (1989) found no changes in patterns of elicited imitation responses of typically developing and specific language impaired (SLI) preschool-kindergarten children under the contrasting conditions of sentence + visual cue / sentence – visual cue. In contrast, Haniff and Siegel (1981) did find a facilitating effect of visual context on the elicited imitation performance of SLI children. Thus, maintaining children's attention to task using visual cues runs the risk of altering study findings, particularly if typically developing children are compared to exceptional populations. For example, there is some evidence that contextual support improves imitation ability in SLI children, whereas it does not facilitate responses of their typically developing peers (Weber-Olsen, Putnam-Sims, & Gannon, 1983). Connell and Myles-Zitzer (1982) also noted that nonlinguistic contextual cues did not affect imitation accuracy in typically developing children.

CONSIDERATION IN APPLYING THE PARADIGM TO EXCEPTIONAL POPULATIONS

Age of subjects has been reported to be a concern for some investigators. Bates (1976) and Hood and Lightbown (1978) suggest that children under age 3 do not reliably participate in elicited imitation tasks. However, a number of studies have used this population successfully, and Lust et al. (1996) report successful use of the paradigm with children as young as 1 year of age. Our own experience is that children vary in their tolerance for large sets of stimuli (Ratner & Sih, 1987, required repetition of 70 utterances per child); tangible reinforcers are useful in maintaining response set, and small children are more likely to complete the task when the stimuli are randomly divided across two sessions.

There is always concern over the division between short-term memory (STM) loading and linguistic processing in EI tasks. These concerns surface when children with suspected primary impairment of STM (such as some children with SLI) are used as subjects. Smith and van Kleeck (1986) noted inverse patterns of performance by children on imitation and act-out tasks for identical structures, a phenomenon that led them to speculate that imitation tasks tap short term memory resources, which are heavily influenced by stimulus length and number of nouns and verbs in the surface structure. There is still considerable dispute about the nature or frequency of memory deficits in SLI children (e.g., cf. Gillam, Cowan, & Day, 1995; Van der Lely & Howard, 1993), as well as concerns about the directionality of any observed relationships between language impairment and memory for verbal materials. As such, the use of EI with SLI children may distinguish them from their typically developing peers, but interpretation of their behaviors remains to be resolved. Finally, Marcell, Ridgeway, Sewell, & Whelan (1995) noted that Down's syndrome adolescents and adults perform more poorly than might be expected when their performance is contrasted with that of individuals with equivalent IQ deriving from other causes of intellectual disability.

As a final note, the use of EI with children whose dialects differ from the model can be problematic. This is of particular concern when EI is used as part of diagnostic test batteries for the identification of language-disordered children.

ADMINISTRATION OF ELICITED IMITATION STIMULI

Bonvillian, Raeburn, and Horan (1979) note that the accuracy of sentence imitation in typically developing preschoolers is affected by the rate of stimulus presentation as well as its prosodic characteristics. As might be expected, retention and imitation of the original stimuli are facilitated with natural intonation contour, as opposed to a monotone. However, a less predictable finding was that accuracy was highest when stimulus presentation was at a rate similar to that of the children's own speech (2 words/sec). Rates that were faster (3 w/s) or, surprisingly, slower (1 w/s) depressed imitation accuracy scores.

Although most elicited imitation tasks are reported as "immediate," there are data to suggest that response delay significantly affects subjects' responses and that comprehension of stimuli interacts significantly with ability to imitate. McDade, Simpson, and Lamb (1982) noted that preschoolers were able to repeat stimuli they had previously shown poor comprehension of at a zero response delay. However, by 3 seconds post presentation, accuracy for structures that were not passed on a comprehension task declined significantly, whereas those the children understood could still be repeated with accuracy.

Most EI tasks used with children utilize live-voice presentation. However, in our work with older children and adolescents, we gained excellent control over rate and latency variables by having subjects respond to videotaped stimuli containing timed prompts for repetition (Silverman & Ratner, 1997).

Another reasonable question is how many trials are necessary to appraise subjects' control over the target structure or function under examination. Although few investigators have targeted this issue specifically, Fujiki and Brinton (1983) performed a post hoc analysis of SLI children's responses to a large set of syntactic structures. Even though sampling reliability was increased with multiple forms for each structure, as might be expected, the authors noted that as few as three repetitions per structure provided reliable data for each subject.

Analysis of Elicited Imitation Responses

Linguistic analyses of EI responses may be descriptive and concentrate more on the nature of children's errored responses than on numbers of errors per se. In other cases, numbers of errors per sentence type are contrasted. In trade-off analyses, it has become conventional to use either correlational analysis or ANOVA to analyze error patterns as a function of predetermined levels of complexity.

As a clinical side note, the use of EI as a component in normed tests of language development has become increasingly frequent (Newcomer & Hammill, 1997; Wiig, Secord, & Semel, 1992; Zimmerman, Steiner, & Pond, 1992). Curiously, given the historical roots of the procedure, qualitative analysis of children's responses on such measures has given way to relatively simplistic tallies of error totals over the stimulus array. Although EI has good discriminative power as a marker of delayed or disordered language ability, selection of target stimuli and test scoring procedures on some diagnostic batteries significantly diminish the potential of using children's responses to construct intervention goals. Virtually the sole diagnostic device to maintain the original premise of EI as a window into generative grammatical capacity is the Carrow Elicited Language Inventory (Carrow, 1974).

Therapeutic Applications of Elicited Imitation

Elicited imitation has often been used in therapeutic intervention with language-disordered children. Although it is an effective method for eliciting output for correction and reinforcement, its utility in promoting spontaneous gains in language use has been a matter of concern. Ezell and Goldstein (1989) noted that moderately mentally retarded children learned novel two-word combinations more efficiently when imitation was added to instruction. Connell (1987) found that imitation training produced larger gains than did modeling for SLI children. Conversely, for other children with SLI, intervention utilizing imitation produced less usage of the target in spontaneous speech than did a conversational training technique (Camarata, Nelson, & Camarata, 1994; Nelson, Camarata, Welch, Butkovsky, & Camarata, 1996). This may result from the diminished social participation of children experiencing imitation-based treatment (Haley, Camarata, & Nelson, 1994).

USE OF ELICITED IMITATION IN EXAMINING TRADE-OFFS IN LANGUAGE PRODUCTION

Elicited imitation offers enormous control when an experimenter has an a-priori desire to investigate specific linguistic structures, the primary focus of Lust et al.'s (1996) discussion. However, particularly in investigations of cross-domain interactions, there are fewer questions about what the child can imitate than there are about what toll complex language processing may take on other aspects of the communicative system (Crystal, 1987; see Camarata, 1998, for discussion of past work on cross-domain analysis). This is an area of both theoretical and practical interest, as children's language production systems are characterized by periods of dynamic change during which there may appear to be unevenness in the child's ability to realize targets. The language acquisition literature has referred to a "bucket" effect (Crystal, 1987) in which limited capacities may interact with either self- or externally imposed demands to produce cross-domain trade-offs in accuracy of production. A version of this theory, Demands and Capacities (Adams, 1990) has been applied to analysis of variations in children's fluency under varying conditions. Both theories imply that diminished capacity in a particular aspect of language functioning may become more apparent or more severe under increased demands in another domain. For example, (a) phonological performance in a child with unstable phonological skills may worsen if demanding syntactic targets must be achieved, or (b) fluency may worsen if conversational demands on the child are increased, such as syntax, pragmatic demand, or dyadic speech rate patterns. For children with developmental speech and/or language disorders, consideration of the ways in which aspects of language production may interact promotes more insightful assessment and intervention planning.

Trade-Offs in Spontaneous Language

Although one might posit interactions between levels or aspects of language production (e.g., between phonological accuracy and syntactic complexity), developing adequate operational definitions of complexity for spontaneous speech samples is quite daunting. As an example, in cases where the impact of linguistic complexity on fluency has been investigated, a number of operational definitions for defining complexity in spontaneous language samples have been tried. These include using mean length of utterance (MLU) (Logan & Conture, 1995) or Developmental Sentence Score (DSS) (Gaines, Runyan, & Meyers, 1991) calculations for fluent and disfluent utterances to examine morphological and/or syntactic complexity, and consonant cluster saturation (Throneburg, Yairi, & Paden, 1994) for phonological complexity.

Production errors have also been used as an operational definition of complexity. In normal development, phonological accuracy has been associated with a number of cross-domain performances. As sentence length increases, phonological accuracy falls for children with language disorders (Menyuk & Looney, 1972; Panagos & Prelock, 1982; Panagos, Quine, & Klich, 1979; Schmauch, Panagos, & Klich, 1978). Panagos and Prelock (1982) also noted the inverse: As children attempt to produce words that contain later-developing phonemes, the length and complexity of their utterances decrease. In normal development, accuracy of production for objects has been observed to exceed that for action words, which are presumed to have greater semantic complexity (Camarata & Leonard, 1986; Camarata & Schwartz, 1985). Again, such effects can show an inverse pattern: Schwartz & Leonard (1982) noted better lexical mapping when novel vocabulary contained phonemes comfortably within the child's phonemic inventory than when novel words contained sounds new to the child's repertoire. Finally, phonological accuracy for sequences that are monomorphemic (i.e., *buzz*) has been shown to exceed accuracy in sequences that are structurally similar but multimorphemic (i.e., *buys*; Paul & Shriberg, 1982).

Trade-Offs in the Spontaneous Speech of Children at Stuttering Onset

In our current work with children who are within 3 months of the onset of stuttering symptoms, my colleagues and I have used a similar framework to investigate trade-offs between linguistic complexity and fluency. Because stuttering typically shows an onset of between 2;6 and 3;6, children's spontaneous language samples conventionally display a mix of well-formed and developmentally ungrammatical output. We have taken this normal psycholinguistic profile and computed (a) the relative proportion of utterances that are syntactically/morphologically correct, and (b) within these proportions, for each child, the proportion of utterances that are fluent or stuttered. (A large proportion of children's spontaneous utterances are also elliptical and cannot be used in such analyses.) For all fifteen children we have studied to date (mean chronological age 34.5 months), sentences containing grammatical formulation errors (i.e., "how you do this?" and "it open") were more likely to contain stutter moments than be fluent (Wilcoxon $z = -3.0594$, $p < .0022$), whereas correctly formulated sentences did not reveal any systematic fluency patterns. Converging evidence for linguistic trade-offs with fluency were easily obtained in this sample using other spontaneous speech measures. Statistically significant differences were also found between the children's fluent and stuttered utterances for both MLU and type-token ratio (TTR) (Ratner, 1997a, 1998).

In earlier work with other young children who stutter, we attempted to create multiple complexity characterizations for children's spontaneous utterances by computing multiple length measures for each utterance in the children's output (Brundage & Ratner, 1989). A primary rationale for the study was the lack of empirical support for any single measure of utterance length in computing disfluency values in children's speech. Using the spontaneous language output of eight young children who stuttered, we evaluated the length of each utterance in words, morphemes, and syllables and computed the relationship of each length index to increases in stuttering frequency in the children's speech. For example, an utterance such as "The boys are running" would have a word count of 4, a syllable count of 5, and a morpheme count of 6. Results suggested that measuring the length of an utterance in words was the least precise predictor of fluency breakdown; morphemic and syllabic indices were almost comparable in their ability to predict stuttering, with morpheme length slightly more likely to induce fluency breakdown in the children we studied. An important implication of this study is that in evaluating language/fluency trade-offs, the issue of controlling utterance length is not trivial, nor is selection of the length index itself. Although these findings suggest caution in using number of words as a length measurement for young children's language when utterance length is a variable to be controlled, a more conservative approach might be to analyze and report results in the context of multiple length characterizations. Alternatively, for both linguistic and motoric analyses, morphemic or syllabic length is to be preferred for analysis of children's speech over words.

As noted earlier, the use of spontaneous language samples to answer questions about cross-domain trade-offs reaches its limits for a number of reasons. Error analyses become increasingly less fruitful as the children age, unless they also demonstrate clinical language delays. Further, the samples diverge greatly in the availability of structures for analysis and their relative weights across subjects' samples. Finally, because there is a wide array of structures that might be considered linguistically challenging across the developmental span, there is a need to create a continuum of complexity values rather than a unitary measure (e.g., whether a production contains an error). To some extent, computational measures such as TTR, MLU, and DSS address this concern. However, as children become more linguistically proficient, these measures tend to be less reliable in their ability to distinguish gradations in linguistic complexity.

Constructing Elicited Imitation Stimuli Using Developmental Expectations

To answer such concerns, my colleagues and I have experimented with construction of developmental hierarchies for elicited imitation. In Ratner and Sih (1987), we created a hypothetical developmental ordering for a range of sentence types of English. Using a small set of fixed vocabulary items, we constructed 7 exemplar sentences for each of 10 types and asked both stuttering and normally fluent children to imitate the sentences presented in random order for each child (Table 14.1).

Developing a hypothetical ordering by amalgamating a large number of studies that survey growth of syntactic structures in child speech is not trivial; thus, we sought to perform an initial test of the adequacy of our hierarchy by examining repetition accuracy. Our presumption was that accuracy of production should show strong correlation with our hypothetical ordering. For both stuttering and typically developing children, this was the case,

TABLE 14.1
Structures tested in Ratner & Sih (1987), Ordered From
Expectations of Least Developmental Demand to Greatest
Demand

Structure	Sample Sentence
Simple active affirmative declarative	The lady sent the man.
Negative	The lady didn't send the man.
Question	Did the lady send the man?
Passive	The lady was sent by the man.
Dative	The lady sent the man a gift.
Prepositional phrase expansion	The lady is sending the man to the backyard.
Coodinate reduction	The lady is sending the man and the boy.
Right-embedded relative clause	We later found that the lady sent the man.
Left-embedded relative clause	That the lady sent the man was not true.
Center-embedded relative clause	The book that the lady sent the man was boring.

with Spearman values ranging from .948 ($p < .0001$) for the fluent children to .994 for the children who stuttered ($p < .0001$). Reassured that our ordering had some prima facie validity, we then correlated fluency measures for each sentence type with our a priori developmental ordering. Both stuttering and normally fluent children showed strong and highly significant effects of complexity on normal disfluency behaviors and on stuttering.

Because, in general, utterances that increase in syntactic complexity might show concurrent and equally potent increases in length, stuttering and disfluency values were also correlated to stimulus length in syllables. Such correlations were non-significant, suggesting that syntactic complexity exerts a toll on utterance fluency that is independent of motor planning factors. In a later analysis (Ratner, 1997b) we reported a stronger statistical manipulation of the data, using partial correlation to separate the relative contributions of length and complexity to fluency. Such analysis further strengthened the original findings: When length is partialed from sentence complexity, the correlation between stuttering and the hypothesized developmental complexity of targets to be imitated falls only slightly and still exceeds .900; when complexity is partialed from length, associations between stuttering and stimulus length plummet to approximately .100.

Constructing Elicited Imitation Stimuli
Using Native Speaker Judgments

The problem of establishing complexity hierarchies becomes more complex as older subjects are examined for cross-domain influences on production. The growing literature on linguistic factors that exacerbate stuttering has clear clinical ramifications (Ratner, 1997b) and thus prompts concerns about how long in development such interactions can be observed. To answer this question, my colleagues and I constructed an elicited imitation study for typically fluent and stuttering children and adolescents, age 10 to 18 (Silverman & Ratner, 1997). We faced the obvious question of how to define complexity for a population beyond conventional developmental study.

As one approach to this problem, we selected seven sentence types reported as late developing by researchers who focus on older children's output (Romaine, 1984; Scott, 1988), as well as structures that have been implicated in slowed or less accurate psycholinguistic processing in adults (Fodor, Bever, & Garrett, 1974; Gleason & Ratner, 1998). Starting at a level posing the least presumed difficulty for speakers, and progressing upwards, the structures were: Simple active affirmative declarative with prepositional phrase, *wh*-questions, forward reduction coordinate constructions, right-embedded complex sentences, left-embedded complex sentences, center-embedded complex sentences (subject–subject) and center-embedded complex sentences (subject–object). For each sentence type we constructed five exemplars. Again, to reduce the influence of other factors on fluency, we kept stimulus length relatively constant in words, morphemes, and syllables and controlled frequency of lexical items in the stimulus sentences, improvements on our earlier designs. We then asked a pilot sample of typically developing adolescents to respond to the stimuli in two ways. First, we asked them to repeat the stimuli. Next, we asked them to rank order examples of the seven stimulus types by completing a worksheet on which they had to assign each sentence type a value from easiest to most difficult (Table 14.2).

Adequacy of the hierarchy was first judged by considering the correlation between fluency of repetition and subjects' perceptions of stimulus difficulty. This correlation was quite high ($r = 0.8158$). Then, to simplify the experimental design of the next portion of our investigation, we selected of the original sentence types the outliers perceived as easiest and hardest, and a type rated centrally by subjects in the pilot sample. For the sample sentences we had tested, these were *wh*-questions, right-embedded complex sentences, and center-embedded complex sentences.

TABLE 14.2
Sentence Types Used in Development of Complexity
Hierarchy for Silverman & Ratner (1997)

1. Simple active affirmative declaratives expanded with prepositional phrase

2. *Wh-* questions

3. Forward reduction coordinate constructions

4. Right-embedded complex sentences

5. Left-embedded complex sentences

6. Center-embedded complex sentences: Subject–Subject

7. Center-embedded complex sentences: Subject–Object

When this experimentally derived hierarchy was presented for the elicited imitation task, interesting patterns of behavior emerged. Because both stuttering and nonstuttering speakers produce normal disfluencies, we tabulated normal disfluencies for both groups and stutter behaviors for the stuttering adolescents. We also sought further confirmation of the adequacy of the stimulus set by computing repetition accuracy for all subjects. Accuracy of repetition fell in identical patterns for the two groups of speakers as complexity was increased, whereas the rate of normal disfluencies increased systematically. However, stuttering did not systematically increase as adolescents attempted more linguistically challenging stimuli.

Such a pattern has numerous implications, both clinical and theoretical. Because there is now strong evidence from numerous investigations that linguistic complexity affects stuttering in children (see Ratner, 1997b, Tetnowski, 1998, for recent overviews), a break in this pattern for adolescents suggests that other factors begin to exert an influence on stuttering frequency in older children and adults. A number of clinical models suggest that these factors may include learned word fears as well as situational and addressee reactions. Thus, although manipulation of linguistic complexity may be appropriate for fluency-shaping activities conducted with younger children, our results suggest a diminished role for these concerns in working with older individuals and a greater need for attention to other factors that may impact fluency. Discordance between the stuttering adolescents' normal disfluency and stuttering patterns also has theoretical ramifications, weakening the adequacy of models that place stuttering on a continuum of normal disfluency behaviors, particularly in its fully evolved form later in development.

Finally, the elicited imitation task allowed us to view patterns of language and fluency interactions that were not readily apparent on analysis of the adolescents' spontaneous language samples gathered during the same investigation. In Silverman, Ratner, and Newhoff (1997), we analyzed the relationship between utterance length in t-units (Loban, 1976) and speech fluency (whether an utterance was fluent, normally disfluent, or stuttered). Analysis of variance revealed significant differences between the length of fluent and stuttered t-units, and normally disfluent and fluent t-units (in each case, fluent t-units were shorter), with no discernable statistical difference between stuttered and normally disfluent t-units. This analysis, which was constrained by the nature of spontaneous structures available for analysis, was thus suggestive of relationships more clearly evident when the adolescents were required to produce a constrained and more tightly controlled set of utterances.

What Converging Evidence Indicates About Language and Fluency Trade-Offs in Early Stuttering

Use of converging evidence from EI and other sources has allowed my colleagues and me to better understand ways in which children's fluency evolves and changes across conditions. The fact that the stuttered utterances of children close to onset of symptoms are characterized by greater length and lexical diversity, as well as a much higher number of formulation errors, is consistent with data derived from other, more structured tasks. In EI tasks with young children who stutter, there is a strong relationship between measures of syntactic demand and fluency breakdown, a relationship that diminishes over the age span as other factors begin to impact the speaker's fluency.

The work we do with this population has been broad in scope and has involved other aspects of language production discussed elsewhere in this volume. Because stuttering is virtually unique as a communication disorder in which parental behavior is still implicated in etiology and development (despite lack of empirical support for this opinion), we have also analyzed the dynamics of parent–child interactions (Stephenson-Opsal & Ratner, 1988), the role of clinical instructions to parents on their speech behaviors (Ratner, 1992), and parental perception of stuttering children's communicative development (Ratner, 1997a). In an extension of work begun by Gleason, Greif, Weintraub, & Fardella (1977), we have compared mothers' and fathers' impressions of their stuttering and typically developing children with their observed language performance. Our results show a much higher level of agreement between (a) parents of stuttering than of nonstuttering children, and (b) highly accurate judgments of linguistic proficiency. These findings run counter to very old, usually anecdotal, reports of high levels of demand and expectation in the parents of stuttering children. Although it is possible that parents may have accurate judgments of their children's language and still impose unreasonable demands on them, our data provide an initial approach to evaluating whether parents of stuttering children have a good appreciation of their level of linguistic development. We are continuing to appraise differences in the ways in which parents of stuttering and nonstuttering children interact, but none are immediately apparent in our data.

Taken as a whole, the program of work described here suggests that the development of stuttering in children is highly influenced by co-occurring advances in language development. The use of EI has allowed us to suggest that stuttering, long thought to have a highly motoric component, does not entrain to changes in motor demand as readily as it does to language demand. Finally, our work with parents, still in progress, enables us to further discount old, prejudicial views of parental beliefs and behaviors in the development of the disorder.

SUMMARY

Few methods for the analysis of language production permit the degree of specificity and control that are provided by EI paradigms. Researchers may probe for mastery of rare or infrequent linguistic structures, or they may examine trade-offs between domains of language planning and execution that are relatively unencumbered by potential contributions of untargeted variations in other aspects of the linguistic system when spontaneous speech is analyzed. However, this increased level of power and precision comes at a cost in terms of careful design of stimuli and standard administration. To date, use of EI has shed important light on the interactions between aspects of linguistic demand in children's speech and their fluency, interactions that are confirmed by alternative methods of language analysis.

ACKNOWLEDGMENTS

I would like to thank Stacy Silverman for helpful comments on an earlier version of this chapter, and Lise Menn and Jean Berko Gleason for unlimited help with everything.

REFERENCES

Adams, A., & Gathercole, S. (1995). Phonological working memory and speech production in pre-school children. *Journal of Speech and Hearing Research, 38*, 403–414.

Adams, M. (1990). The demands and capacities model I: theoretical elaborations. *Journal of Fluency Disorders, 15*, 135–141.

Bates, E. (1976). *Language and context.* New York: Academic Press.

Bauer, P., & Thal, D. (1990). Scripts or scraps: reconsidering the development of sequential under-standing. *Journal of Experimental Child Psychology, 50*, 287–304.

Berko (Gleason), J. (1958). The child's learning of English morphology. *Word, 14*, 150–177.

Berko Gleason, J., Greif, E., Weintraub, S., & Fardella, J. (1977). *Father doesn't know best: parents' awareness of their children's linguistic, cognitive and affective development.* Paper presented at the biennial meeting of the Society for Research in Child Development, New Orleans.

Berko Gleason, J., & Ratner, N. B. (1998). *Psycholinguistics* (2nd ed.). Ft. Worth: Harcourt Brace.

Bloom, L. , Hood, L., & Lightbown, P. (1991). Imitation in language development: If, when and why. In L. Bloom (Ed.), *Language development from two to three* (pp. 399–433). Cambridge: Cambridge University Press. (Original work pulished 1974).

Bonvillian, J., Raeburn, V., & Horan, E. (1979). Talking to children: Effects of rate, intonation and length on children's sentence imitation. *Journal of Child Language, 6*, 459–468.

Bosshardt, H-G., Sappok, C., Knipschild, M., & Holscher, C. (1997). Spontaneous imitation of fun-damental frequency and speech rate by nonstutterers and stutterers. *Journal of Psycholinguistic Research, 26*, 425–448.

Brownell, C. (1988). Combinatorial skills: Converging developments over the second year. *Child Development, 59*, 675–685.

Brown, R., & Fraser, C. (1963). The acquisition of syntax. In C. Cofer & B. Musgrave (Eds.). *Verbal Behavior and Learning Problems and Processes.* (pp. 158–201). NY: McGraw-Hill.

Brundage, S., & Ratner, N. B. (1989). The measurement of stuttering frequency in children's speech. *Journal of Fluency Disorders, 14*, 351–358.

Carroll, J., Davies, P., & Richman, B. (1971). *The American Heritage Word Frequency Book.* Boston: Houghton Mifflin.

Camarata, S. (1998). Connecting speech and language: Clinical applications. In R. Paul (Ed.), *Exploring the speech-language connection* (pp. 227–252). Baltimore: Paul Brookes.

Camarata, S., & Leonard, L. (1986). Young children produce object words more accurately than action words. *Journal of Child Language, 13*, 51–65.

Camarata, S., Nelson, K. E., & Camarata, M. (1994). Comparison of conversational-recasting and imitative procedures for training grammatical structures in children with specific language impairment. *Journal of Speech and Hearing Research, 37*, 1414–1423.

Camarata, S. & Schwartz, R. (1985). Production of object words and action words: Evidence for a relationship between semantics and phonology. *Journal of Speech and Hearing Research, 28*, 323–330.

Carrow, E. (1974). *Carrow Elicited Language Inventory.* Austin: Teaching Resources Corporation.

Clark, R. (1977). What's the use of imitation? *Journal of Child Language, 4*, 341–358.

Connell, P. (1987). An effect of modeling and imitation teaching procedures on children with and without specific language impairment. *Journal of Speech and Hearing Research, 30,* 105–113.

Connell, P., & Myles-Zitzer, C. (1982). An analysis of elicited imitation as a language evaluation pro-cedure. *Journal of Speech and Hearing Research, 47*, 390–396.

Crystal, D. (1987). Toward a bucket theory of language disability: Taking account of interaction between linguistic levels. *Clinical Linguistics and Phonetics, 1*, 7–21.

Eisele, J., & Aram, D. (1994). Comprehension and imitation of syntax following early hemispheric damage. *Brain & Language, 46*, 212–231.

Ervin-Tripp, S. (1973). Imitation and structural change in children's language. In C. Ferguson & D. Slobin (Eds.). Studies of Child Language Development (pp. 391–406). NY: Holt, Rinehart, & Winston.

Ezell, H., & Goldstein, H. (1989) Effects of imitation on language comprehension and transfer to production in children with mental retardation. *Journal of Speech and Hearing Disorders, 54,* 49–56.

Fodor, J., Bever, T., & Garrett, M. (1974). *The psychology of language.* New York: McGraw-Hill.

Fraser, C., Bellugi, U., & Brown, R. (1963). Control of grammar in imitation, comprehension, and production. *Journal of Verbal Learning and Verbal Behavior, 2,* 121–135.

Fujiki, M., & Brinton, B. (1983). Sampling reliability in elicited imitation. *Journal of Speech and Hearing Disorders, 48,* 85–89.

Gaines, N., Runyan, C., & Meyers, S. (1991). A comparison of young stutterers' fluent versus stuttered utterances on measures of length and complexity. *Journal of Speech and Hearing Research, 24,* 31–42.

Gillam, R., Cowan, N., & Day, L. (1995). Sequential memory in children with and without language impairment. *Journal of Speech and Hearing Research, 38,* 393–402.

Gordon, P. (1991). Language task effects: A comparison of stuttering and nonstuttering children. *Journal of Fluency Disorders, 16,* 275–287.

Haley, K., Camarata, S., & Nelson, K. (1994). Social valence in children with specific language impairment during imitation-based and conversation-based language intervention. *Journal of Speech and Hearing Research, 37,* 378–388

Haniff, M., & Siegel, G. (1981). The effect of context on verbal elicited imitation. *Journal of Speech and Hearing Disorders, 46,* 27–30.

Hood, L., & Lightbown, P. (1978). What children do when asked to "Say what I say": Does elicited imitation measure linguistic knowledge? In P. Connell (Ed.), *Comprehension and production of speech and language: Monograph 1.* Allied Health and Behavioral Science.

Kemper, S. (1987). Syntactic complexity and elderly subjects' prose recall. *Experimental Aging Research, 13,* 47–52.

Kuhl, P., & Meltzoff, A. (1996). Infant vocalizations in response to speech: Vocal imitation and developmental change. *Journal of the Acoustical Society of America, 100,* 2425–2438.

Loban, W. (1976). *Language development: Kindergarten through grade twelve* (Research Report No. 18). Urbana, IL: National Council of Teachers of English.

Loeb, D., & Allen, G. (1993). Preschoolers' imitation of intonation contours. *Journal of Speech and Hearing Research, 36,* 4–13.

Logan, K., & Conture, E. (1995). Length, grammatical complexity, and rate differences in stuttered and fluent conversational utterances of children who stutter. *Journal of Fluency Disorders, 20,* 35–62.

Lust, B. (1977). Conjunction reduction in child language. *Journal of Child Language, 7,* 279–304.

Lust, B., Flynn, S., & Foley, C. (1996). What children know about what they say: Elicited imitation as a research method for assessing children's syntax. In D. McDaniel, C. McKee, & H. Cairns (Eds.), *Methods for assessing children's syntax* (pp. 55–76). Cambridge, MA: MIT Press.

Madison, C., Roach, M., Santema, S., Akmal, E., & Guenzel, C. (1989). The effect of pictured visual cues on elicited sentence imitation. *Journal of Communication Disorders, 22,* 81–91.

Marcell, M., Ridgeway, M., Sewell, D., & Whelan, M. (1995). Sentence imitation by adolescents and young adults with Down's syndrome and other intellectual abilities. *Journal of Intellectual Disability Research, 39,* 215–232.

McDade, H., Simpson, M., & Lamb, D. (1982). The use of elicited imitation as a measure of expressive grammar: A question of validity. *Journal of Speech and Hearing Disorders, 47,* 19–24.

Menyuk, P., & Looney, P. (1972). Relationships among components of the grammar in language disorders. *Journal of Speech and Hearing Research, 15,* 395–407.

Nelson, K., Camarata, S., Welsh, J., Butkovsky, L., & Camarata, M. (1996). Effects of imitative and conversational recasting treatment on the acquisition of grammar in children with specific language impairment and younger language-normal children. *Journal of Speech and Hearing Research, 39,* 850–859.

Newcomer, P., & Hammill, D. (1997). *Test of Language Development—Primary.* Austin: Pro-Ed.

Panagos, J., & Prelock, P. (1982). Phonological constraints on the sentence productions of language disordered children. *Journal of Speech and Hearing Research, 25,* 171–176.

Panagos, J., Quine, M., & Klich, R. (1979). Syntactic and phonological influences on children's articulation. *Journal of Speech and Hearing Research, 22,* 841–848.

Paul, R. (1992). Speech-language interactions in the talk of young children. In R. Chapman (Ed.), *Processes in language acquisition and disorders* (pp. 235–254). St. Louis: Mosby.

Paul, R., & Shriberg, L. (1982). Associations between phonology and syntax in speech delayed children. *Journal of Speech and Hearing Research, 25,* 536–546.

Pearson, B. (1990). The comprehension of metaphor by preschool children. *Journal of Child Language, 17,* 185–203.

Ratner, N. B. (1988). Patterns of parental vocabulary selection in speech to young children. *Journal of Child Language, 15,* 481–492.

Ratner, N. B. (1992). Measurable outcomes of instructions to change maternal speech style to children. *Journal of Speech and Hearing Research, 35,* 14–20.

Ratner, N. B. (1997a). *Linguistic and self-monitoring skills at the onset of stuttering.* Paper presented at the American Speech-Language Hearing Assn. Convention, Boston.

Ratner, N. B. (1997b). Stuttering: A psycholinguistic perspective. In R. Curlee & G. Siegel (Eds.), *Nature and treatment of stuttering: New directions* (2nd ed.), pp. 99–127. Boston: Allyn & Bacon.

Ratner, N. B. (1998). Linguistic and perceptual behaviors at stuttering onset. In E. C. Healey (Ed.), *Proceedings of the Second World Congress on Fluency Disorders* (pp. 3–6). Amsterdam: Elsevier.

Ratner, N. B., & Sih, C. (1987). Effects of gradual increases in sentence length and complexity on children's dysfluency. *Journal of Speech and Hearing Research, 52,* 278–287.

Romaine, S. (1984). *The language of children and adolescents.* Cambridge: Basil Blackwell.

Schmauch, V., Panagos, J., & Klich, R. (1978). Syntax influences the accuracy of consonant production in language-disordered children. *Journal of Communication Disorders, 11,* 315–323.

Schwartz, R., & Leonard, L. (1982). Do children pick and choose? Phonological selection and avoidance in early lexical acquisition. *Journal of Child Language, 9,* 319–336.

Scott, C. (1988). Spoken and written syntax. In M. Nippold (Ed.), *Later language development: Ages nine through nineteen* (pp. 49–96). Boston: College Hill Press.

Silverman, S., & Ratner, N. B. (1997). Stuttering and syntactic complexity in adolescence. *Journal of Speech and Hearing Research, 40,* 95–106.

Silverman, S., Ratner, N. B., & Newhoff, M. (1997). *Linguistic complexity in the spontaneous language of adolescents who stutter.* Paper presented at the annual convention of the American Speech-Language-Hearing Association, Boston.

Slobin, D., & Welsh, C. (1973). Elicited imitation as a research tool in developmental psycholinguistics. In C. Ferguson & D. Slobin (Eds.), *Studies of child language development* (pp. 485–496). New York: Holt Rhinehart.

Smith, N. (1973). The acquisition of phonology: A case study. London: Cambridge University Press.

Smith, C., & Van Kleeck, A. (1986). Linguistic complexity and performance. *Journal of Child Language, 13,* 389–408.

Snow, C. (1981). The uses of imitation. *Journal of Child Language, 8,* 205-212.

Stephenson-Opsal, D., & Ratner, N. B. (1988). Maternal speech rate modification and childhood stuttering. *Journal of Fluency Disorders, 13,* 49–56.

Tetnowski, J. (1998). Linguistic effects on disfluency. In R. Paul (Ed.), *Exploring the speech-language connection* (pp. 227–252). Baltimore: Paul Brookes.

Thiemann, T. (1975). Imitation and recall of optionally deletable sentences by young children. *Journal of Child Language, 2,* 261–269.

Throneburg, R., Yairi, E., & Paden, E. (1994). Relation between phonologic difficulty and the occurrence of disfluencies in the early state of stuttering. Journal of Speech and Hearing Research, 37, 504–509.

Van der Lely, H., & Howard, D. (1993). Children with specific language impairment: Linguistic impairment or short-term memory deficit? *Journal of Speech and Hearing Research, 36*, 1193–1207.

Van der Meulen, S. , Janssen, P., & Den Os, E. (1997). Prosodic abilities in children with specific language impairments. *Journal of Communication Disorders, 30*, 155–169.

Weber-Olsen, M., Putnam-Sims, P., & Gannon, J. (1983). Elicited imitation and the Oral Language Sentence Imitation Screening Test (OLSIST): Content or context? *Journal of Speech and Hearing Disorders, 48*, 368–78.

Weeks, L. (1992). Preschoolers' production of tag questions and adherence to the polarity contrast principle. *Journal of Psycholinguistic Research, 21*, 31–40.

Wiig, E., Secord, W., & Semel, E. (1992). *Clinical Evaluation of Language Fundamentals— Preschool*. San Antonio: Psychological Corporation.

Zimmerman, I., Steiner, V., & Pond, R. (1992). *Preschool Language Scale—3*. San Antonio: Psychological Corporation.

15

The Challenge of Studying Language Development in Children With Autism

Helen Tager-Flusberg
University of Massachusetts

Autism is a rare neurodevelopmental disorder of genetic origin. Among the primary characteristics of autism are impairments not only in language but also in communication. In this chapter I address the challenge of studying language development in children who lack the basic motivation to communicate with others, even when they may have acquired some linguistic competence. I begin with a description of the disorder and an overview of the kinds of language deficits that have been identified in autism. Then I take up different methodological approaches that have been used in research on language development in autism and discuss some problems encountered in using these methodologies. In the final section of the chapter I explore the possibility of using novel methods drawn from other research paradigms that may help shed further light on the mysteries of why children with autism seem to have such limited interest or ability to communicate with others.

WHAT IS AUTISM?

Over 50 years ago Leo Kanner, an eminent child psychiatrist at Johns Hopkins University, first described a set of 11 children, all of whom had in common a core set of atypical characteristics (Kanner, 1943). These children were set apart from other children, including those with emotional disturbance or mental retardation, by their social withdrawal. They appeared to have little contact with others and little interest in people, leading Kanner to view "extreme autistic aloneness" as the cardinal feature of the new syndrome he had identified. Kanner noted a number of other major features of this syndrome, including obsessive insistence on routines and lack of change in the environment; deficits in language ranging from mutism to acquiring the ability to speak but using language in a somewhat meaningless and repetitive way; excellent rote memory skills; a variety of anomalous reactions to sensory stimulation; and sleep and eating problems. Although the children Kanner described were quite different from one another, in terms of both their current levels of functioning and their developmental histories, Kanner distilled from this diversity the core similarities that warranted a new diagnostic classification.

The essence of the syndrome captured by Kanner still rings true for clinicians and researchers today. Autism is currently classified as a form of pervasive developmental disorder of early onset, usually during the infant or toddler years. The three essential criteria for diagnosing autism include (a) qualitative impairments in social interaction, (b) delays and deficits in language and communication, and (c) restricted repetitive and stereotyped behaviors, activities, or interests (American Psychiatric Association, 1994). Within this "triad" of impairments symptom expression varies, depending on the severity of the disorder, the IQ level, and the age of the child. The majority of individuals with autism are mentally retarded; these children tend to be more socially withdrawn, have more stereotyped behavior patterns, are less communicative, and may have little or no functional language. Thus, in autism the overall level of cognitive ability is closely connected to social and language functioning. However, even in high functioning children serious limitations in social interest make the study of language acquisition difficult: There is often no interest on the part of children with autism to communicate with others or respond to others' initiations, even when the children have acquired some linguistic ability. This is the challenge faced by researchers who wish to study language in autism.

COMMUNICATION AND
LANGUAGE IN AUTISM

Parents of children with autism most often report that the first sign of a problem with their child is either the absence of language or the loss of language that had begun to develop in the second year of life (Kurita,

1985; Lord & Paul, 1997). Sometimes the initial concern may be that the child is deaf because they are so unresponsive to the voice of others including parents in their environment. In retrospect, many parents recollect that even during the first 12 months their infants were unresponsive to adult contact, did not engage in turn-taking games, and failed to develop joint attention (Volkmar, Carter, Grossman, & Klin, 1997). By their first birthday, many infants who later receive the diagnosis of autism do not respond to their own name and fail to make eye contact (Osterling & Dawson, 1994). By the end of the second year, toddlers with autism still have no functional language and are extremely limited in their communication with others, perhaps only engaging another person to fulfill requests using protoimperative gestures (Stone, 1997). They also do not engage in any symbolic play. To some extent, the primary social deficits in autism set the developmental course for deficits in language and communication—there is simply no interest or "appetite" for interacting with others at any level or by any means, including language.

Nevertheless some children with autism, usually those that are less severely impaired overall, do increase the frequency of their communicative attempts and begin acquiring language before their fifth birthday. Indeed, acquiring some functional language by age 5 has been found to be the most powerful predictor of a more positive outcome in autism (Rutter, 1970; Ventner, Lord, & Schopler, 1992). This group of verbal children has been studied by researchers using a variety of methodological approaches, some with greater success than others. The findings from many studies of children with autism have provided a general picture of the patterns of relatively spared and impaired capacities, as well as clinical descriptions of the most striking characteristics of autistic language.

Characteristics of Autistic Language

Kanner (1943, 1946) was the first to note that children with autism often simply echo the words, phrases, or sentences spoken by others. This classical feature of autistic language, known as echolalia, is most typical of children who have very little productive language (McEvoy, Loveland, & Landry, 1988). Echolalic speech often retains the exact words and intonation used by others either immediately or after some time. It is now viewed as having some functional value for children. Echolalia may help children with autism to maintain some role in the ongoing discourse even when they either do not understand or have not yet acquired the pragmatic or linguistic skills needed to respond more appropriately (Prizant & Duchan, 1981; Tager-Flusberg & Calkins, 1990). Kanner (1946) also noted the autistic child's tendency to use words with special or unique meanings not shared by others. The use of idiosyncratic lexical terms, or neologisms, has been found even in higher functioning children and adults with autism (Volden & Lord, 1991), suggesting that it does not mark a developmental stage in acquisition. The source of these "words" and their function has not yet been elucidated. Another striking feature of autistic children's use of language is their reversal of pronouns—referring to themselves as "you" and their conversational partner as "I." Although reversing personal pronouns is not unique to autism, it does occur more frequently in this group than in any other population (Lee, Hobson, & Chiat, 1994) and pronoun reversals are viewed as important in the diagnosis of this disorder (American Psychiatric Association, 1994; Le Couteur et al., 1989). The reversals reflect difficulties in conceptualizing the notion of self and other as it is embedded in shifting discourse roles between speaker and listener (Lee et al., 1994; Tager-Flusberg, 1993, 1994).

Autism has been identified as a language disorder that, at its core, involves pragmatic impairments (Baltaxe, 1977; Lord & Paul, 1997; Tager-Flusberg, 1981a). Children with autism are often unresponsive to the conversational initiations of others. This has led many to question whether autism involves particular difficulties in comprehension (Paul & Cohen, 1984), although this has proven difficult to investigate using standard methods. Even when autistic children do engage and respond to others, they may offer little to the ongoing discourse, have difficulty sustaining the conversational topic, or offer irrelevant comments (Tager-Flusberg & Anderson, 1991). These discourse deficits are seen as central to the defining characteristics of autism (Tager-Flusberg, 1996); they parallel and are closely linked to the social and communicative impairments discussed earlier.

All these features of language in autism—echolalia, neologisms, pronoun reversals, and pragmatic impairment—make it difficult to investigate language acquisition in this population. Indeed, the features have led some researchers to question whether autistic children develop language following the same pathways, and using the same underlying mechanisms, as do normally developing children or other children with delayed or deficient language (e.g., Simon, 1975). Nevertheless, over the past two decades psycholinguistic approaches have led to important advances in the study of language in children with autism. In the next sections I review some of this work, focusing on the methodological challenges that stem from the particular deficits that are central to this disorder.

STUDYING LANGUAGE
DEVELOPMENT IN AUTISM

The study of language in children with autism has been limited almost exclusively to those children who do acquire some functional language, either spoken or sign (cf. Layton & Baker, 1981). Moreover, because of the behavior difficulties experienced by many autistic children, studies have been further restricted to those who are more cooperative, less aggressive, or self-injurious. Because of the rarity of the syndrome and the inherent difficulties in conducting research with autistic children, most studies have included very small samples, sometimes just single case studies. These limitations mean that research in this area has not been able to capture the full variation that is known to exist in the population. There are also so few longitudinal studies that little is known about developmental changes occurring over the course of childhood.

Collecting Natural Language Samples

In the field of child language, it is generally acknowledged that the richest source of data, especially on productive use of language, comes from spontaneous speech samples. These may be collected in different contexts as the young child interacts with some other person, either a researcher or familiar person such as the mother. This approach has been the most well utilized method for studying development in young children (cf. Brown, 1973). It is the most open-ended and least structured approach to studying language, which is often viewed as an advantage in that it allows one to view what children can do in a natural context without the external imposition of constraints or task demands that may not be understood by the child.

But what might be viewed as advantages for the normally developing child—the absence of any external constraint—operates as a distinct problem for the child with autism. The lack of structure in which natural language samples are typically collected is an especially difficult context for children with autism. Given no constraint or external demand, the autistic child enjoys his or her own isolation and does not spontaneously socially engage with others or communicate much with them. This means that very little language might be gathered using this methodological approach, thereby making the collection of meaningful data very difficult. Children with autism do not spontaneously speak that much so the methods that involve the analysis of spontaneous speech may be of limited utility with this population.

However, several studies have investigated the frequency of communicative acts in autistic children in different social contexts. These studies generally demonstrate that children with autism are sensitive to social context in ways that parallel those of very young normally developing children. Interactions with peers are the most difficult, even for high functioning older verbal children with autism. Stone and Caro-Martinez (1990) collected language samples from school-age children in their classrooms while they were engaged in free play or other informal activities. They also observed each child in their study for several hours, spread over a number of days. The average frequency of spontaneous communicative acts from the children with autism was just two or three per hour, mostly directed toward an adult. Only half their subjects ever spoke to a nonautistic peer. In other experimental settings, such as the laboratory, other studies also found that children with autism speak much less frequently and use a narrower range of speech acts when engaged in free play (Landry & Loveland, 1989; Mermelstein, 1983). The effect of social context on the frequency of communicative acts in children with autism was systematically investigated by Bernard-Opitz (1982). She found that an autistic child was most likely to talk in a highly familiar setting with a highly familiar person. Furthermore, Bernard-Opitz found that in these social settings, at home with the mother, the autistic child produced more advanced language (i.e., more complex grammatical constructions) than in other social contexts. This means that laboratory-based studies using an experimenter as the primary conversational partner will not provide the most accurate portrait of the autistic child's linguistic capacities.

Taking these concerns into consideration, my colleagues and I conducted a small-scale home-based longitudinal study of language development in six young children with autism (Tager-Flusberg et al., 1990). Using both audio- and videotape, we collected hour-long language samples from the children as they interacted with their mothers in their homes, at bimonthly intervals. Data were collected in a similar way from six young children with Down syndrome who were matched on age and language level (assessed by mean length of utterance, or MLU) to provide a comparison group. As expected, the autistic children did speak less than the children with Down syndrome, even in this context. Nevertheless, we were able to collect sufficiently large language samples from all the children most of the time (usually well over 300–400 utterances) that would allow us to conduct meaningful analyses on developmental changes in syntax, morphology, and lexical and pragmatic functioning in these children. Our success was based, in part, on the children's mothers, who knew that the focus of our research was language. The mothers worked hard at engaging their children in conversation, using many different approaches and activities to keep them talking.

New problems were encountered as we set about analyzing the transcripts we prepared from the taped language samples. The youngest children and those who were the least mature linguistically, not surprisingly, produced quite of bit of echolalia. The question we faced was how to handle these echolalic utterances in our explorations of grammatical and lexical development. We concluded that if we included echolalic speech we might overestimate the child's linguistic knowledge. Maybe these children with autism echoed words they did not know, or maybe they were able to repeat utterances that were longer or more complex than they could produce spontaneously on their own. Although in normally developing children, imitated speech may also be more advanced than nonimitated, this poses little problem because it is so infrequent in their natural language samples (e.g., Bloom, Lightbown, & Hood, 1975). We also found that the autistic children would often recite speeches, count, or sing as a way of filling "air-time." These learned segments of speech might also lead to the overestimation of the children's linguistic knowledge. At the same time, other characteristics of autistic children's language could lead us to underestimate their language abilities. In particular, we noticed that the children's mothers asked many questions to which the children often gave single-word yes/no responses rather than an extended reply. These single-word responses and the use of stock social phrases (such as "please" or "thank you") could lead us to underestimate MLU, the single most used measure of language development across a variety of populations (Brown, 1973; Miller & Chapman, 1981).

Thus, the analysis of spontaneous speech data from children with autism clearly needed to be tailored to the particular features that are characteristically found even in relatively high functioning verbal children. We chose to handle these concerns by preparing a separate corpus of 100 child utterances from each transcript for both the autistic and the comparison children with Down syndrome. These corpora excluded all echolalic utterances, defined as all full or partial imitations or repetitions within five transcript lines. They also excluded routine phrases, single-word yes/no responses, and learned speeches or songs.

Our analyses of these special corpora, that had eliminated the most problematic aspects of autistic language use, provided us with a rich and detailed picture of the development of language in this population (Tager-Flusberg et al., 1990). Contrary to claims in the literature that children with autism do not show a gradual increase in MLU or the same order for the emergence of grammatical constructions (e.g., Menyuk & Quill, 1985; Simon, 1975), we found that the developmental pathway for our autistic subjects was similar to what has been found for normally developing children. In fact, when we carefully examined echolalic utterances from the children with autism we found, surprisingly perhaps, that they were not developmentally more advanced than nonecholalic utterances from the same points in time. Echolalic utterances tended to be shorter and contain less complex constructions than spontaneously produced utterances (Tager-Flusberg & Calkins, 1990). These findings were taken as evidence that the underlying mechanisms for acquiring language were the same in children with autism, children with Down syndrome, and normally developing children. Despite the obvious surface and pragmatic differences in their speech, children with autism who do acquire language appear to depend on the same mechanisms and processes for developing language as do other children (cf. Prizant, 1983). In some, though not all, children, even the rate of development was similar to what has been found among normally developing children.

Despite these challenges in both collecting and analyzing spontaneous speech samples, they have provided the richest and most accurate source of information on the development of communicative functioning (e.g., Coggins & Carpenter, 1981; Tager-Flusberg & Anderson, 1991; Wetherby & Prizant, 1990). Natural language samples have demonstrated the restricted repertoire of speech acts, as well as deficits in communicative competence, that are characteristic of children with autism. Other methods for investigating these aspects of language and communication are not available. Indeed, it is in this context of unstructured interaction that the autistic child's communication deficits can be most clearly highlighted and explored.

Using Standardized Assessment Tools

Often it is extremely useful to assess a child's linguistic ability—in particular knowledge of structural aspects of language—using standardized instruments in order to address a number of research issues. Because these instruments tap a variety of domains, including phonology, semantics, lexical knowledge, syntax, and morphology, it is possible to explore the relation among these domains in both production and comprehension by comparing a child's performance to age-based norms. This is, perhaps, the clearest way of examining the overall language profile in autism to address a number of interesting questions about the representation and processing of linguistic information. Such questions include whether comprehension is more impaired than production (e.g., Lord, 1985), whether lexical/semantic knowledge is more impaired than computational aspects of language (e.g., Menyuk & Quill, 1985; Tager-Flusberg, 1981a), or whether language is more impaired than nonlinguistic cognitive ability (Lord & Paul, 1997; Tager-Flusberg, 1989). Answers to these kinds of questions may provide important information about the cognitive-linguistic phenotype of autism and how it compares to other groups of mentally retarded or language disordered children.

Standardized tests are also often used to provide measures by which to match children with autism to control groups in more experimental studies of language or other aspects of cognitive functioning. The most widely used measure for this purpose is the Peabody Picture Vocabulary Test (PPVT; Dunn & Dunn, 1981, 1997), which provides a norm-based measure of receptive vocabulary. Some studies might also include a measure of syntactic comprehension, particularly if the experimental task requires the child to process complex linguistic information such as stories or scripts. Examples of tests that have been used to assess syntactic comprehension include different subtests on the Test of Auditory Comprehension of Language (TACL; Carrow-Woolfolk, 1985), the Test of Language Development (TOLD; Newcomer & Hamill, 1991), and the Clinical Evaluation of Language Fundamentals (CELF; Semel, Wiig, & Secord, 1995). Finally, it is important to keep in mind that standardized tests, such as the ones listed here, are most widely used in clinical settings to provide assessment of language abilities in children in order to inform treatment and intervention planning.

These kinds of measures provide a particular set of challenges when they are used with autistic children. Psychometrically based instruments must be administered in a particular way by a trained individual if they are to provide valid and reliable data about language performance. But there may be difficulties encountered by the researcher in engaging the autistic child in the demands of a particular test. Generally, children with autism are not intentionally negative or noncompliant (Volkmar, 1987); rather, their lack of response to some standardized tests may be the result of not understanding the pragmatics of the testing situation. Typically, an unfamiliar person administers the test. As discussed earlier, the unique social deficits in autistic children might make them particularly unresponsive to the researcher in their presence. If more than one researcher is present, this might add to the autistic child's anxiety. The environment itself may also add to the distractibility of the child with autism. Even when they are able to understand the test questions and have the requisite linguistic knowledge, children with autism may be quite unresponsive in an unfamiliar testing situation.

Another concern that stems from the unique behavioral difficulties of autistic children is their tendency to perseverate, or repeat an action or response. Thus, if the answer to the first item on a task requires a child to point to a picture in a particular location—say, the first one on the left side of an array—the child with autism might continue to point to this location on all subsequent items. This kind of response may be produced not because the child does not understand the later items but because he or she is perseverating. Many tests of language comprehension involve pointing to pictures that correspond to words or sentences presented by the tester, so this kind of problem must be considered in evaluating responses given by an autistic child.

Tests of language production often have more complex pragmatic demands than do measures of comprehension. Not surprisingly, children with autism respond best to tests that require them to imitate or recall words or sentences spoken by the tester (or better still, presented on a recording), such as subtests on the TOLD. Yet these kinds of tests might not provide a particularly accurate measure on the child's knowledge. Children with autism also respond well on confrontational naming tasks, which asks them to label pictures that are usually of concrete objects. But because they have difficulty understanding the more complex instructions for other kinds of semantic tests, autistic children usually perform worse on tests that tap relational or abstract meaning. Some researchers have taken this discrepancy in performance as a sign that autistic children have particular semantic deficits, which may or may not be warranted (Menyuk & Quill, 1985; Tager-Flusberg, 1986). Sentence completion tests or sentence formulation tests (which involve asking a child to create or complete a sentence using a word or phrase given by the tester) are often not easily completed by children with autism. Examples of this kind of test include the Formulated Sentences subtest on the CELF (Semel et al., 1995) and the Grammatic Completion subtest on the TOLD (Newcomer & Hammill, 1991). Autistic children may misunderstand the instructions and imitate what they have heard, rather than ending or formulating their own utterance. It is not clear whether this kind of response reflects expressive deficits or pragmatic problems in understanding the test instructions.

All these variables, in addition to the fluctuating behavior and attention that is quite typical in autistic children, may make it particularly hard to test them in a standardized way (Sparrow, 1997). Because standardized tests typically start with easy items and progress to more difficult ones, children with autism may also begin to experience frustration as they find themselves unsure whether they have answered correctly. Frustration can lead to tantrums or other behavior difficulties, which make it impossible to continue with the testing.

On the other hand, one significant advantage of using standardized tests is that they are highly structured, which may help to maximize the performance of autistic children. Researchers can increase the likelihood that an autistic child will complete a standardized test in a relatively reliable way by making certain accommodations to the particular needs of the child. Using behavioral approaches to enhance the structure of the testing situation, including providing regular rewards (either tangible, such as food or tokens, or social praise) may be especially useful, particularly for those children who have had experience with these approaches in intervention programs or school settings. Providing frequent feedback and short breaks can also be helpful in keeping an autistic child engaged in standardized testing. Sometimes it is necessary to rephrase, simplify, or regularly repeat instructions, even though this is not strictly allowed by the standardized procedures mandated by a test. Even though these kinds of modifications might make the comparison of the child's performance to the age-based norms questionable, it may be the only way to obtain any meaningful data from an autistic child on a particular standardized test (Sparrow, 1997).

Experimental Methods for Studying Language

As is known from research on language acquisition in normally developing children, insights into the process and knowledge of children at different stages of development are best captured by experimental studies that use specially designed tasks and stimuli. Spontaneous speech data are limited by what the child actually produces; they do not reveal what the child may know but had no opportunity to use; they also provide only minimal information about the child's comprehension of language. Standardized tests are designed to capture individual variation; they typically do not include a complete set of grammatical or morphological constructions, and often their item complexity is based more on informational load than on underlying grammatical complexity. Thus, standardized tests typically increase the length of sentences to make them more difficult or add more choices of responses; these are changes that add to the memory or attentional load of the test rather than its linguistic complexity. Such tests are not applicable to the study of the development of linguistic knowledge in all its richness. Experimental studies help to fill these gaps and have provided the detailed knowledge that is now available in the field of developmental psycholinguistics.

There is no room in this chapter to cover the full range of experimental methodologies that have been used in the field of child language. Instead I cover just a few, to illustrate some of the unique issues that have to be considered by researchers who wish to employ experimental tasks with autistic children. In fact, there have been very few experimental studies of language processing published in the literature on autism (see Lord & Paul, 1997, for a recent review). Perhaps this is because the difficulties faced by researchers who wish to conduct such studies with this population have led them to seek alternative methods; this is especially true when one considers how hard it is to find a sufficiently large sample and the need to include matched control groups.

Many experimental studies of child language, which typically target young normally developing children, make use of toy props to facilitate the interchange between the child and experimenter and to enhance the child's enjoyment of the tasks. For example, many studies of language comprehension engage toy figures that the child must manipulate to demonstrate the meaning of a sentence. Studies that explore children's grammatical judgments of sentences will often employ puppets that "speak" the correct or incorrect sentences.

These methods take advantage of children's propensity to engage in symbolic and functional play, especially with a variety of fictional characters participating in different activities. But the child with autism has no such propensity. One of the primary ways in which social and communicative deficits are manifest in autism is in the absence of spontaneous symbolic play (Sigman & Ungerer, 1984; Stone, Lemanek, Fishel, Fernandez, & Altemeier, 1990). These children do not play with toy objects in conventional ways and later on show no interest or capacity for role play (Volkmar et al., 1997). At the least, these deficits in play mean that autistic children may not have the same motivation and pleasure that other children find in the experimental tasks designed to tap linguistic knowledge. Of greater concern is that fact that for some children with autism, difficulties with these tasks may confound the absence of the linguistic knowledge embedded in the task with lack of understanding the representational value of the toys. If pictures are used to replace toys, then one must beware of perseverative responses, as discussed earlier.

Stimuli for experimental tasks often depict animals as well as people, as if they were sentient beings. Researchers tend to imbue animals with human characteristics when interacting with children; story books are filled with these kinds of representations, and experimental tasks in child language research often do the same. This kind of representation assumes that young children have an implicit theory of mind: that they interpret action within a causal mentalistic framework (e.g., Wellman, 1990). There is considerable evidence that normally developing toddlers do infer that people are intentional and that their own and others' behavior and actions can be explained on the basis of desires, emotions, and beliefs. By extension, within a play context, children also accept that other animals may also have minds and that their actions can be interpreted in the same way as those of human beings.

But again, the use of these kinds of stimuli poses special problems for the child with autism. Indeed, autism is now viewed as a disorder that can be interpreted as involving core primary impairments in the acquisition of a theory of mind (Baron-Cohen, Leslie, & Frith, 1985; Baron-Cohen, Tager-Flusberg, & Cohen, 1993). Children with autism do not readily interpret their own or others' actions in terms of mental states; they have difficulty even viewing people as intentional beings. The combination of deficits in theory of mind, and in symbolic play (which are likely to be closely connected: Leslie, 1987), make the use of stimuli that treat animals as if they were people especially problematic for children with autism. Many examples can be found in the psycholinguistic literature on the comprehension of grammatical constructions by normally developing children that use stimuli of this sort. For example, studies on the comprehension of relative clauses (de Villiers, Tager-Flusberg, Hakuta, & Cohen, 1979; Tavakolian, 1981), coordination (Tager-Flusberg, de Villiers, & Hakuta, 1982), passive constructions (Maratsos, Kuczaj, Fox, & Chalkley, 1979), and anaphora (Chien & Wexler, 1990) have all included anthropomorphic animals as the prime characters in the stories or sentences that the children were asked to interpret. All these studies might be hard to replicate with autistic children because of the stimulus demands of the task.

In considering experimental methods used to elicit different kinds of linguistic constructions, some of the same concerns that were highlighted for standardized testing may also apply. Children with autism may not understand the pragmatic demands of the task or the task instructions. Gamelike contexts that work so well for other children are not appreciated or even clearly understood by autistic children. They tend to repeat what the experimenter says, rather than complete or formulate their own response. If a child with autism is asked to describe an event enacted by an experimenter or depicted in a photograph or sequence of pictures that create a story, he or she is just as likely to simply name the objects (e.g., Tager-Flusberg, 1995) as to provide a narrative description. The problem lies in how to interpret this kind of response. Does it signal deficits in language, particularly in the ability to produce sentences, or is it the result of other aspects of the autistic syndrome?

As a final example to illustrate the methodological challenges faced by researchers of children with autism, I discuss an early attempt I made to study grammatical knowledge in children with autism. As part of my dissertation research, I wanted to use Jean Berko Gleason's famous wug paradigm to explore knowledge of grammatical morphology in children with autism (1958). Using the stimuli that Berko Gleason had created, and following her exact methods, I piloted this task on three children who clearly met criteria for the diagnosis of autism. I failed miserably! The children simply did not understand what I was looking for or what I was trying to do; they clearly viewed me as somewhat bizarre. As I explored the source of the problem, it became clear that the novel stimuli (wugs, ricking, etc.) were quite incomprehensible to the children. Children with autism are concrete and literal; they have no idea how to handle the invented imaginative forms and the creative methods that Berko Gleason so successfully used on normally developing children. Perhaps, had I persevered and worked out a modified approach, I might have been able to study autistic children's knowledge of wugs with greater success. Instead, I addressed a different set of questions about sentence comprehension strategies, which turned out to be more easily implemented (cf. Tager-Flusberg, 1981b). To this day, there is no research on autism that has used the kind of elicited production methods that were pioneered by Jean Berko Gleason 40 years ago.

CONCLUSIONS AND
FUTURE DIRECTIONS

Studying language acquisition in children with autism is not an easy or straightforward task. Methodologies and stimuli have to be carefully selected, adapted, and modified to the unique set of deficits that define autism. Nevertheless, there has been some success over the past few decades in using certain approaches. Probably most has been learned about language development from the study of natural language samples, collected in different structured or unstructured settings. Standardized tests have also been used with some degree of success with higher-functioning children. But as I have already discussed, these approaches are limited and can only address certain kinds of questions. Furthermore, all the research on language development in autism has been limited to the group of children who do acquire some functional language that they use spontaneously. Half the population do not (Lord & Paul, 1997). Questions remain about whether these nonverbal children understand any language and whether they perceive speech in the same way as other children do. It is not known whether the source of their difficulties with language stems from deficits in symbolic capacity, motivation to communicate with others, mental retardation, or a combination of all these factors. Until we as researchers begin to study these children, we will not achieve a full understanding of the language deficits that are central to the diagnosis of autism.

Even verbal autistic children have been studied in only limited ways. There are too few longitudinal studies or experimental studies of either comprehension or production. Some of the reasons for the paucity of research in this area have been discussed in this chapter. But if we are to make further advances, we will need to find ways of adapting our methods to address the unique demands and challenges of working with autistic children. Very different sorts of approaches will be needed to study verbal and nonverbal children with autism—in the same way as in the field of child language, different methods are used to study prelinguistic infants compared to toddlers and preschoolers who have begun acquiring language.

One important way of addressing some of the challenges posed even by verbal children with autism would be to employ several different methodologies to investigate a particular set of research questions with the same group of autistic subjects. Using several methods simultaneously (e.g., standardized tests of language production, language samples, and elicited production methods) would help to minimize the problems found with each method used in isolation and would provide a richer set of data for analysis. The design of experimental tasks should take into consideration some of the concerns discussed in the previous section. The selection of standardized tests should also be made on the basis of which ones are best suited to this population. The multimethod approach would help to address some of the issues outlined earlier and provide researchers with a more complete picture of (a) how children with autism do acquire language, and (b) what accounts for their remaining deficits in communication, discourse, and certain aspects of language.

What about nonverbal autistic children? Little is known about this group because so few research studies have focused on them. The combination of communicative, social, and cognitive impairments that define this group make them especially difficult to study. One strategy that has not yet received as much attention would be to employ the methods that define the field of behavioral analysis—the use of operant techniques, especially computer-based technologies, to study basic research questions about the underlying mechanisms that impede the acquisition of language in this population. Behavior analysis has been extensively used with this population, especially as a primary means for intervention (e.g., Carr & Durand, 1985; Charlop & Trasowech, 1991; Harris & Ferrari, 1983). Thus, we know that operant methods can be successfully used, even as a means for assessing nonverbal autistic children (McIlvane, Deutsch, Serna, & Dube, 1988; Powers, 1988, 1997). But these kind of behavioral methods have not been used by psycholinguists in traditional research designs as a means for exploring basic questions such as whether nonverbal children perceive speech normally, or whether they understand words or grammatical constructions they do not produce. At the same time, behavior analysts who have employed these methods, usually in single case-study designs, have not used them to address the kinds of questions that psycholinguistics ask. It is time to consider integrating the methods and paradigms that have developed independently in the field of psychology, in order to address some of the fundamental questions about language and communication in autism (Wilkinson, Dube, & McIlvane, 1997; Wilkinson & Tager-Flusberg, 1998). The methods that involve traditional operant conditioning techniques, including shaping the child's response to ensure nonrandom responding, could be particularly successful because social motivation can be replaced with the use of tangible rewards and experimental presentation of materials can be accomplished via computers, thereby avoiding the social difficulties these children experience when interacting with a researcher.

The future of research on language in autism will require the development of new approaches and methods that have the potential of avoiding many of the pitfalls discussed in this chapter. It is time for researchers in this field to follow the creative pathway forged by Jean Berko Gleason 40 years ago that has made much of the work in child language as we know it today possible. Although we may not be able to use her methods exactly, we must take inspiration from her efforts if we want to come to a deep understanding about the nature of language and communicative development in this unique population.

ACKNOWLEDGMENTS

Preparation of this chapter was supported by grants from the National Institute on Deafness and Communication Disorders (RO1 DC 01234 and PO1 DC 03610).

REFERENCES

American Psychiatric Association. (1994). *Diagnostic and Statistical Manual of Mental Disorders, DSM–IV* (4th ed.). Washington, DC: Author.

Baltaxe, C. A. M. (1977). Pragmatic deficits in the language of autistic adolescents. *Journal of Pediatric Psychology, 2,* 176–180.

Baron-Cohen, S., Leslie, A.M., & Frith, U. (1985). Does the autistic child have a "theory of mind?" *Cognition,* 21, 37–46.

Baron-Cohen, S., Tager-Flusberg, H., & Cohen, D. J. (Eds.) (1993). *Understanding other minds: Perspectives from autism.* Oxford: Oxford University Press.

Berko (Gleason), J. (1958). The child's learning of English morphology. *Word, 14,* 150–177.

Bernard-Opitz, V. (1982). Pragmatic analysis of the communicative behavior of an autistic child. *Journal of Speech and Hearing Disorders, 47,* 99–109.

Bloom, L., Lightbown, P., & Hood, L. (1975). Structure and variation in child language. *Monographs of the Society for Research in Child Development, 40* (Serial No. 160).

Boehm, A. (1986). *Boehm Test of Basic Concepts.* San Antonio: Psychological Corporation, Harcourt Brace.

Brown, R. (1973). *A first language.* Cambridge, MA: Harvard University Press.

Carr, E. G., & Durand, V. M. (1985). Reducing behavior problems through functional communication training. *Journal of Applied Behavior Analysis, 18,* 111–126.

Carrow-Woolfolk, E. (1985). *Test of Auditory Comprehension of Language* (Rev.). Austin: Pro-Ed.

Charlop, M. H., & Trasowech, J. E. (1991). Increasing autistic children's daily spontaneous speech. *Journal of Applied Behavior Analysis, 24,* 747–761.

Chien, Y-C., & Wexler, K. (1990). Children's knowledge of locality conditions binding as evidence for the modularity of sytax and pragmatics. *Language Acquisition, 3,* 225–295.

Coggins, T., & Carpenter, R. (1981). The Communicative Intention Inventory: A system for observing and coding children's early internal communication. *Applied Psycholinguistics, 2,* 235–251.

de Villiers, J., Tager-Flusberg, H., Hakuta, K., & Cohen, M. (1979). Children's comprehension of relative clauses. *Journal of Psycholinguistic Research, 8,* 499–518.

Dunn, L. M., & Dunn, L. M. (1981). *Peabody Picture Vocabulary Test–Revised.* Circle Pines, MN: American Guidance Service.

Dunn, L. M., & Dunn, L. M. (1997). *Peabody Picture Vocabulary Test–III.* Circle Pines, MN: American Guidance Service.

Gardner, M. (1990). *Expressive One-Word Picture Vocabulary Test.* Los Angeles: Western Psychological Services.

Harris, S.L., & Ferrari, M. (1983). Developmental factors in child behavior therapy. *Behavior Therapy, 14,* 54–72.

Kanner, L. (1943). Autistic disturbances of affective contact. *Nervous Child, 2,* 217–250.

Kanner, L. (1946). Irrelevant and metaphorical language in early infantile autism. *American Journal of Psychiatry, 103,* 242–246.

Kurita, H. (1985). Infantile autism with speech loss before the age of 30 months. *Journal of the American Academy of Child Psychiatry, 24,* 191–196.

Landry, S. H., & Loveland, K. A. (1989). The effect of social context on the functional communication skills of autistic children. *Journal of Autism and Developmental Disorders, 19,* 283–289.

Layton, T. I., & Baker, P. S. (1981). Description of semantic-syntactic relations in an autistic child. *Journal of Autism and Developmental Disorders, 11,* 385–399.

Le Couteur, A., Rutter, M., Lord, C., Rios, P., Robertson, S., Holdgrafer, M., & McLennan, J. D. (1989). Autism Diagnostic Interview: A semi-structured interview for parents and caregivers of autistic persons. *Journal of Autism and Developmental Disorders, 19,* 363–387.

Lee, A., Hobson, R. P., & Chiat, S. (1994). I, you, me and autism: An experimental study. *Journal of Autism and Developmental Disorders, 24,* 155–176.

Leslie, A. M. (1987). Pretence and representation: The origins of "theory of mind." *Psychological Review, 94,* 412–426.

Lord, C. (1985). Autism and the comprehension of language. In E. Schopler & G. Mesibov (Eds.), *Communication problems in autism* (pp. 59–68). New York: Plenum Press.

Lord, C. & Paul, R. (1997). Language and communication in autism. In D. J. Cohen & F. R. Volkmar (Eds.), *Handbook of autism and pervasive developmental disorders* (2nd ed., pp. 195–225). New York: John Wiley & Sons.

Maratsos, M., Kuczaj, S. A., Fox, D., & Chalkley, M. (1979). Some empirical studies in the acquisition of transformational relations: Passives, negatives and the past tense. In W. A. Collins (Ed.), *Children's language and communication* (pp. 1–45). Hillsdale, NJ: Lawrence Erlbaum Associates.

McEvoy, R. E., Loveland, K. A., & Landry, S. H. (1988). The functions of immediate echolalia in autistic children: A developmental perspective. *Journal of Autism and Developmental Disorders, 18,* 657–668.

McIlvane, W., Deutsch, C. K., Serna, R. W., & Dube, W. (1998). Behavior analytic assessment of intellectual functioning and disability: An interface between research with nonhumans and humans with limited language. In S. Soraci & W. McIlvane (Eds.), *Perspectives on fundamental processes in intellectual functioning: A survey of research approaches* (pp. 215–239). Stamford, CT: Ablex.

Menyuk, P., & Quill, K. (1985). Semantic problems in autistic children. In E. Schopler & G. Mesibov (Eds.), *Communication problems in autism* (pp. 127–145). New York: Plenum Press.

Mermelstein, R. (1983, October). *The relationship between syntactic and pragmatic development in autistic, retarded, and normal children.* Paper presented at the Eighth Annual Boston University Conference on Language Development, Boston.

Miller, J., & Chapman, R. (1981). The relation between age and mean length of utterances in morphemes. *Journal of Speech and Hearing Research, 24,* 154–161.

Newcomer, P., & Hammill, D. (1991). *Test of Language Development–2: Primary and Intermediate.* Austin: Pro-Ed.

Osterling, J., & Dawson, G. (1994). Early recognition of children with autism: A study of first birthday home videotapes. *Journal of Autism and Developmental Disorders, 24,* 247–258.

Paul, R., & Cohen, D. J. (1984). Responses to contingent queries in adults with mental retardation and pervasive developmental disorders. *Applied Psycholinguistics, 5,* 349–357.

Powers, M. D. (1988). Behavioral assessment of autism. In E. Schopler & G. Mesibov (Eds.), *Diagnosis and assessment of autism* (pp. 139–165). New York: Plenum Press.

Powers, M. D. (1997). Behavioral assessment of individuals with autism. In D. J. Cohen, & F. R. Volkmar (Eds.), *Handbook of autism and pervasive developmental disorders* (2nd ed., pp. 448–459). New York: John Wiley & Sons.

Prizant, B. (1983). Echolalia in autism: Assessment and intervention. *Seminars in Speech and Language, 4,* 63–77.

Prizant, B., & Duchan, J. (1981). The functions of immediate echolalia in autistic children. *Journal of Speech and Hearing Disorders, 46,* 241–249.

Rutter, M. (1970). Autistic children: Infancy to adulthood. *Seminars in Psychiatry, 2,* 435–450.

Semel, E., Wiig, E., & Secord, W. (1995). *Clinical Evaluation of Language Fundamentals–3.* San Antonio: Psychological Corporation, Harcourt Brace.

Sigman, M. & Ungerer, J. (1984). Cognitive and language skills in autistic, mentally retarded, and normal children. *Developmental Psychology, 20,* 293-302.

Simon, N. (1975). Echolalic speech in childhood autism: Consideration of possible underlying loci of brain damage. *Archives of General Psychiatry, 32,* 1439–1446.

Sparrow, S. (1997). Developmentally based assessments. In D. J. Cohen & F. R. Volkmar (Eds.), *Handbook of Autism and Pervasive Developmental Disorders* (2nd ed., pp. 411–447). New York: John Wiley & Sons.

Stone, W. (1997). Autism in infancy and early childhood. In D. J. Cohen & F. R. Volkmar (Eds.), *Handbook of Autism and Pervasive Developmental Disorders* (2nd ed., pp. 266–282). New York: John Wiley & Sons.

Stone, W., & Caro-Martinez, L. M. (1990). Naturalistic observations of spontaneous communication in autistic children. *Journal of Autism and Developmental Disorders, 20,* 437–453.

Stone, W., Lemanek, K. L., Fishel, P. T., Fernandez, M. C., & Altemeier, W. A. (1990). Play and imitation skills in the diagnosis of autism in young children. *Pediatrics, 86,* 267–272.

Tager-Flusberg, H. (1981a). On the nature of linguistic functioning in early infantile autism. *Journal of Autism and Developmental Disorders, 11,* 45–56.

Tager-Flusberg, H. (1981b). Sentence comprehension in autistic children. *Applied Psycholinguistics, 2,* 5–24.

Tager-Flusberg, H. (1986). The semantic deficit hypothesis of autistic children's language. *Australian Journal of Human Communication Disorders, 14,* 51–58.

Tager-Flusberg, H. (1989). A psycholinguistic perspective on language development in the autistic child. In G. Dawson (Ed.), *Autism: New directions on diagnosis, nature, and treatment* (pp. 92–115). New York: Guilford.

Tager-Flusberg, H. (1993). What language reveals about the understanding of minds in children with autism. In S. Baron-Cohen, H. Tager-Flusberg, & D. J. Cohen (Eds.), *Understanding other minds: Perspectives from autism* (pp. 138–157). Oxford: Oxford University Press.

Tager-Flusberg, H. (1994). Dissociations in form and function in the acquisition of language by autistic children. In H. Tager-Flusberg (Ed.), *Constraints on language acquisition: Studies of atypical children* (pp. 175–194). Hillsdale, NJ: Lawrence Erlbaum Associates.

Tager-Flusberg, H. (1995). "Once upon a ribbit": Stories narrated by autistic children. *British Journal of Developmental Psychology, 13,* 45–59.

Tager-Flusberg, H., & Anderson, M. (1991). The development of contingent discourse ability in autistic children. *Journal of Child Psychology and Psychiatry, 32,* 1123–1134.

Tager-Flusberg, H. & Calkins, S. (1990). Does imitation facilitate the acquisition of grammar? Evidence from autistic, Down syndrome and normal children. *Journal of Child Language, 17,* 591–606.

Tager-Flusberg, H., Calkins, S., Nolin, T., Baumberger, T., Anderson, M., & Chadwick-Dias, A. (1990). A longitudinal study of language acquisition in autistic and Down syndrome children. *Journal of Autism and Developmental Disorders, 20,* 1–21.

Tager-Flusberg, H., de Villiers, J., & Hakuta, K. (1982). The development of sentence coordination. In S. A. Kuczaj (Ed.), *Language development: Vol. 1. Syntax and semantics* (pp. 201–243). Hillsdale, NJ: Lawrence Erlbaum Associates.

Tavakolian, S. (1981). The conjoined-clause analysis of relative clauses. In S. L. Tavakolian (Ed.), *Language acquisition and linguistic theory* (pp. 167–187). Cambridge, MA: MIT Press.

Ventner, A., Lord, C., & Schopler, E. (1992). A follow-up study of high-functioning autistic children. *Journal of Child Psychology and Psychiatry, 33,* 489–507.

Volden, J., & Lord, C. (1991). Neologisms and idiosyncratic language in autistic speakers. *Journal of Autism and Developmental Disorders, 21,* 109–130.

Volkmar, F. R. (1987). Social development. In D. J. Cohen & A. M. Donnellan (Eds.), *Handbook of autism and pervasive developmental disorders* (pp. 41–60). New York: John Wiley & Sons.

Volkmar, F. R., Carter, A., Grossman, J., & Klin, A. (1997). Social development in autism. In D. J. Cohen & F. R. Volkmar (Eds.), *Handbook of Autism and Pervasive Developmental Disorders* (2nd ed., pp. 173–194). New York: John Wiley & Sons.

Wellman, H. (1990). *A child's theory of mind.* Cambridge, MA: MIT Press/Bradford Books.

Wetherby, A., & Prizant, B. (1990). *Communication and Symbolic Behavior Scales.* Chicago: Riverside.

Wilkinson, K. M., Dube, W., & McIlvane, W. (1997). A cross-disciplinary perspective on studies of rapid word mapping in psycholinguistics and behavior analysis. *Developmental Review, 16,* 125–148.

Wilkinson, K. M., & Tager-Flusberg, H. (1998). Application of a lexical principles framework for studying categorization and word learning in different populations. In S. Soraci & W. McIlvane (Eds.), *Perspectives on Fundamental Processes in Intellectual Functioning: A Survey of Research Approaches* (pp. 243–263). Stanford, CT: Ablex.

16

Understanding Grammatical Deficits in Children With Specific Language Impairment: The Evaluation of Productivity

Laurence B. Leonard
Purdue University

Young children often produce forms that deviate from adult usage but nevertheless have a recognizable basis in the adult system. A child's referring to the act of sweeping as *brooming* can probably be traced to the appearance of verb forms such as "hammering" and "sawing" in the ambient language. A child's referring to the act of dropping as falling (e.g., "I'm falling the ball") might derive from having heard verbs with both a causative (e.g., "The boy is bouncing the ball") and inchoative (e.g., "The ball is bouncing") use.

Probably the most celebrated cases of errant yet sensible productions by young children are overextensions of regular past tense inflections. A child's production "the girl throwed the ball" might not conform to adult use, but the origins of this error are clear. Because productions such as "throwed" are not heard in the input but nevertheless pattern after the usual procedure for forming past tense, linguists refer to this type of use as "productive." That is, these productions indicate that at some level the child has control of a procedure or rule for forming past tense rather than a collection of stored forms to draw on when referring to events in the past.

Creative errors are not the only way that productivity can be observed. When children add appropriate inflections to familiar words that they have never heard inflected, productivity can be assumed. This probably occurs often; the problem is that it is difficult to document that a child has never heard the inflected version of the word before. Given this difficulty of documenting the originality of a production, investigators have sought other ways of evaluating productivity. The best known method was first put to use by Berko (1958). In this classic work she presented pairs of pictures to children, described the first, and prompted the children to complete a sentence that described the second. The referent characters and actions were nonsense names (e.g., *tor, spow*) that the children had not heard before. Despite the novelty of these words, the children were able to add inflections to them (*tors, spowed*) that were appropriate to the sentence context.

In this chapter I discuss the issue of productivity in children who are having great difficulty acquiring language. I concentrate on a group of children who exhibit a specific language impairment (SLI). These are children who have significant difficulties acquiring language, yet they do not show evidence of other serious conditions that frequently accompany language problems. They score at age-appropriate levels on tests of nonverbal intellectual functioning, they show normal hearing, they provide no clear evidence of neurological dysfunction, and they display none of the symptoms of impaired social interaction or restriction of activities associated with autism.

Closer study of these children's abilities reveals that problems falling outside language proper can sometimes be seen. For example, on tasks requiring the processing of brief auditory signals, or auditory signals presented at a rapid rate, these children usually perform poorly. Some also perform below the level of typical children on tasks of mental imagery. Nevertheless, there is little doubt that language represents the heart of these children's difficulties, and a great deal of investigative attention has been devoted to understanding the nature of this language learning problem.

METHODS FOR STUDYING THE LANGUAGE ABILITIES OF CHILDREN WITH SLI

The language characteristics and difficulties of children with SLI are best understood when compared to those of normally developing children. Some details of language are acquired before others in typical development; therefore, it would be improper to assume that some absent or otherwise misused detail of language reflected a problem simply because the evidence came from the mouth of a child with SLI.

Normally developing children of the same age as the children with SLI constitute the most obvious basis of comparison, and most studies of children with SLI have included such a group. However, comparisons between children with SLI and their same-age peers are not particularly illuminating when language is the focus of study. By virtue of their diagnosis, children with SLI can be expected to fall below the level of age controls on almost any developmentally appropriate measure of language. Some of these measures might assess abilities that are at the very core of a child's difficulties, but might appear as just another indicator of a general language problem if scores from age controls were the only reference point.

To isolate areas of special difficulty, investigators often recruit an additional comparison group—younger normally developing children who are matched with the children with SLI on some language measure that could otherwise obscure the details of language of greatest interest. For studies of grammatical morphology, the basis for matching is often mean length of utterance (MLU) in morphemes. Grammatical morphemes add length to an utterance (compare "Chris *is* wash*ing the* car" and "Chris wash car"). Therefore, equating children with SLI and normally developing children on the basis of MLU reduces the likelihood that any group difference in grammatical morphology favoring the normally developing children is due simply to the fact that they could produce longer utterances. Because short MLUs are among the characteristics of children with SLI, this MLU matching procedure results in a comparison group of children who are significantly younger than the children with SLI. Nevertheless, numerous studies have found that children with SLI use many grammatical morphemes with lower percentages in obligatory contexts than do their younger MLU-matched controls (see reviews in Bishop, 1992; Johnston, 1988; Leonard, 1998). This is especially noteworthy given that MLU matching is a highly conservative strategy. Precisely because grammatical morphemes contribute to utterance length, matching by MLU sets up a comparison that places odds against finding differences in degree of use of grammatical morphemes.

There are other measures on which children with SLI and younger control children can be matched. For example, the mean number of arguments per utterance or the mean number of nonnuclear predicates might be the basis for matching (Johnston & Kamhi, 1984; Kamhi & Johnston, 1992). Alternatively, children might be matched on the mean number of open-class words used per utterance (Rollins, Snow, & Willett, 1996). These measures are less influenced by function words and inflections than is MLU and consequently they represent less conservative methods for examining the use of grammatical morphemes. However, less is known about how these measures change across time in normally developing children than is true for MLU.

Measures of phonology can also be used for matching groups. For example, articles (*a*, *the*) and the past tense inflection (*-ed*) require the use of weak syllables and word-final consonants, respectively. Children might be matched on their ability to use these phonological details in monomorphemic contexts (e.g., "*ba*nana," "car*d*"). For certain experimental questions, other types of measures might be more appropriate. These include measures of lexical ability or measures of grammatical comprehension. For example, differences between two groups' use of sentences with three arguments (e.g., "She gave me the ball;" "I put the block on the table") might be difficult to interpret if it could not be established that the children were comparable in the number of verbs in their lexicons that require three arguments.

The use of younger normally developing children as a comparison group is not without controversy. Some authors (e.g., Plante, Swisher, Kiernan, & Restrepo, 1993) have argued that the age differences between the control children and the children with SLI probably introduce unwanted factors into the research designs—factors that might influence the results even though they have nothing to do with the question of interest. There appears to be no good solution to this potential problem. Statistical techniques such as the use of covariates when comparing children with SLI and age controls also require assumptions about development, and there is no evidence that these assumptions are more reasonable than those implicit in comparisons between children with SLI and younger children matched according to some measure of language. Until new techniques are developed, it appears that the design employing both age controls and younger controls matched on an appropriate measure of language represents the most suitable course of action.

In recent years, serious study of SLI from a crosslinguistic perspective has begun. In these investigations, comparisons are made between children with SLI acquiring two different languages, as well as between children with SLI and control children within the same language. How should children with SLI from two different language groups be matched? Age might seem like a sensible basis for matching; however, it is not sufficient given that within any single language, children with SLI of the same age can vary significantly in the severity of their disorder.

One useful approach to this problem was adopted by Lindner and Johnston (1992). In a crosslinguistic study of English and German, these investigators matched same-age children with SLI in the two language groups on the basis of their standard scores on tests of language ability that dealt with the same domains of language (e.g., syntax and the lexicon). This procedure increased the likelihood that the two groups' language skills relative to normally functioning compatriots were comparable. As a result, any differences observed between the English- and German-speaking children with SLI were more likely to be due to the way that SLI operates in the two different languages.

The language tasks employed in studies involving children with SLI are essentially those that have been in the child language literature for some time. Spontaneous speech samples are a mainstay in this line of work, and date back at least to the work of Menyuk (1964). The schemes of analysis applied to the speech samples also borrow heavily from the study of language development in typical children. Other frequently used tasks whose origins can be traced to research with normally developing children include carrier phrase tasks (e.g., "This is my bike, but this one is_____"), elicited imitation tasks (e.g., "Can you say this? *This is Jill's bike*"), picture identification tasks (e.g., "Does this sound OK or silly? 'Mommy walk to the store'").

More recently, treatment designs have been added to the list of methods used to explore the language abilities of children with SLI. This type of study is less dependent on normally developing children for interpretation of the data. For example, let's assume that we wish to determine whether the frequent absence of a subset of grammatical morphemes is tied to a common factor such as tense. We might teach children with SLI to use, say, past -*ed* more consistently in obligatory contexts. To ensure that the tense function of -*ed* is clear, we could employ pairs of items such as "The girls jump"–"The girls jump*ed*" in appropriate present and past contexts. Following treatment, we might then determine whether there was evidence of broader gains in tense by testing the children's use of present third singular -*s* and auxiliary *is* and *are* along with past -*ed*. Of course, even if all four morphemes were used more consistently by the children following treatment, the gains might have been due to factors unrelated to the treatment activities. For this reason, it is also important to monitor the children's use of morphemes assumed to be unrelated to tense. If the children made significant gains in the use of third singular -*s*, auxiliary *is* and *are*, and past -*ed* but not genitive '*s* and the (tenseless) infinitival complementizer *to*, we could be more confident that tense was playing a role.

Grammatical morphology seems to be among the weakest areas of language in these children. This is readily seen in studies of grammatical morpheme use in which children with SLI are compared to younger normally developing children matched according to a measure such as mean length of utterance (MLU). In these studies, the children with SLI are found to be less capable than the MLU control children in their use of a range of grammatical morphemes (see review in Leonard, 1998). The degree of deficiency seems to vary with the language being acquired. In English, children with SLI are more limited than MLU controls in many grammatical inflections as well as function words. In languages such as Italian and Hebrew, in contrast, the most obvious limitations center on function words.

WHY STUDY PRODUCTIVITY?

Productivity is a critical issue in the study of children with SLI for at least two reasons. First, these children are often enrolled in intervention to assist them in their language learning, in acquiring the linguistic principles or rules that they lack. Of course, instruction can only involve the presentation of representative exemplars. At some point it is hoped that the child will recognize the commonalities among the exemplars and establish a rule. When this occurs, instruction can be redirected to other areas in need of attention. Thus, identifying the establishment of a rule is essential to clinical management. If these children were relegated to learning language on a rote basis, piece by piece, they might require assistance indefinitely, perhaps never succeeding in mastering the input language.

Second, productivity is important because its status in children with SLI is critical to an understanding of their disorder. Different theories of SLI make different assumptions about productivity. According to some theories, children with SLI do not construct certain kinds of rules. According to other theories, rules are not only possible but probable once these children are given the extra time needed to detect and interpret the input data.

Probably the best known proposal that children with SLI do not use language productively has come from Gopnik and her colleagues (Gopnik, 1994; Gopnik & Crago, 1991; Ullman & Gopnik, 1994). This group of researchers studied a three-generational British family, many members of which were significantly language impaired. The severe limitations in the use of many grammatical morphemes by the affected individuals were interpreted as an inability to acquire implicit rules to mark tense, number, and person.

It is recognized by proponents of this account that occasional correct use is seen. However, it is assumed that this correct use is the result of either memorization—where a form such as *played* is learned by rote in the same way that *threw* is learned as the past form for *throw*—or of having learned a metalinguistic rule through instruction (e.g., "add -*ed* when talking about past events").

Clahsen and his colleagues (Clahsen, 1989; Clahsen & Hansen, 1993) proposed that the grammatical limitations of children with SLI are attributable to a selective impairment in establishing the structural relationships of agreement. That is, these children presumably lack the knowledge of asymmetrical relations between categories where one category controls the other. As a result, these children show serious problems in the use of (a) verb inflections that must agree with the subject in features such as person, number, or gender, and (b) determiners that must agree with nouns in number and gender, among others. Forms that appear to be appropriately marked are found in these children's speech; however, they are the result of memorization or fortuitous selection.

More recently, van der Lely (1994, 1996) has suggested that some children with SLI exhibit a problem best described as a representational deficit for dependent relationships. Such relationships are seen not only for grammatical agreement but also for tense and case, among others. This type of deficit is assumed to be longstanding.

REVIEWING THE EVIDENCE

Given the prominence in the literature of accounts assuming the lack of productivity in areas of language affecting grammatical morphology, it seems useful to consider the available evidence. I examine here several types of data.

Overregularizations

Productions by a child such as *deers* and *throwed* are unlikely to have been heard before; consequently, they serve as good examples of a productive noun plural and past tense system, respectively. Overregularizations of plurals by children with SLI have been reported by Albertini (1980) and Rice and Oetting (1993).

Overregularizations of past have been noted even more frequently in the literature. Studies reporting this type of use include Leonard, Bortolini, Caselli, McGregor, and Sabbadini (1992), Eyer and Leonard (1994, 1995), King, Schelletter, Sinka, Fletcher, and Ingham (1995), Smith-Lock (1995), Leonard, Eyer, Bedore, and Grela (1997), and Oetting and Horohov (1997).

The degree to which overregularizations of past occur seems to vary. Whereas Rice, Wexler, and Cleave (1995) found only rare instances of this type of use, Marchman, Wulfeck, and Ellis Weismer (1995) found that overregularizations constituted more than one third of the non-adult-like productions of verbs requiring irregular past forms.

Overregularizations have also been noted in the speech of children with SLI acquiring languages other than English. For example, Håkansson (1997) found that Swedish-speaking children with SLI overregularized past tense verb inflections. Bortolini, Caselli, and Leonard (1997) noted that Italian-speaking children with SLI frequently used the more common masculine singular article *il* with masculine singular nouns whose phonetic composition required the less common masculine singular article *lo*.

Bortolini et al. (1997) also observed a type of creative use that can best be described as stem overregularization. However, this form of use is related to grammatical morphology. For certain verbs, the present first person singular and present third person plural forms require a change in the stem. For example, for the verb "push," the stem is typically [spinʤ-]. This is true for present first person plural, second person singular and plural, third person singular, the infinitive form, all imperfect forms, and so on. However, the present first person singular is pronounced [spiŋgo]; the third person plural has the pronunciation [spiŋgono]. Bortolini et al. found that the majority of the children with SLI in their study produced at least one verb with an overregularization, as in [spinʤo] and [spinʤono]. Because these forms do not occur in the input language, they seem to be cases of systematic but creative use.

Nonsense Word Tasks

Research on children with SLI has also focused on their use of grammatical morphemes with nonsense words. The tasks most closely following the lead of Berko (1958) required the children to add inflections to novel nouns and verbs (e.g., *zecked*). However, in some cases the children were required to combine function words with the nonsense words, as in *the tiv* and *to goodge*. Because these function words had never been heard with these nonsense words, any function word–nonsense word combination is considered novel and the result of a productive process.

The evidence for these children's use of grammatical morphology with nonsense words is substantial, although investigators have disagreed on their interpretation. Gopnik and Crago (1991) administered a nonsense-word task to 20 members of the family they were studying; seven of these individuals appeared to be acquiring language normally, whereas the remaining individuals were having clear problems in the use of language. The individuals with language impairment produced instances of affixation with nonsense words. However, they produced them less frequently on the task than did the family members serving as controls. The productions observed by the affected individuals were interpreted to be the result of the application of a rule they were taught in school.

Use of the past tense with nonsense words was examined by van der Lely and Ullman (1995). The school-age children with SLI serving as subjects were compared with younger control children matched according to language test score. The children with SLI used the past inflection on approximately 5% of the nonsense-word items, well below the level of the control children. The children with SLI were also more likely than the control children to produce past tense forms that were patterned after verbs that are irregular in the past. One such example was *strank* as the past form of the nonsense word *strink*.

At least three other investigations have reported considerable use of grammatical morphemes with nonsense words. One of these, by Oetting and Horohov (1997), examined regular past inflections. Studies by Leonard et al. (1997) and Bellaire, Plante, and Swisher (1994) examined several different morphemes. For example, Leonard et al. included genitive *'s*, articles, plural *-s*, infinitival *to*, third person singular *-s*, and past *-ed* in their nonsense-word task. In each of the studies, the frequency of use of these morphemes with nonsense words was not as high among the responses of the children with SLI as among the control children. However, the use that was seen was far too frequent to be treated as a fluke.

In the study by Leonard et al. (1997), efforts were made to select as subjects only children who had not undergone instruction on grammatical morphology. Thus, it is unlikely that their use of grammatical morphemes with nonsense words reflected conscious application of a rule that they had been explicitly taught. Furthermore, naive listeners' judgments of the children's nonsense form productions revealed nothing that separated these productions from the productions of the control children.

From one perspective, the productive use shown by children with SLI on nonsense-word tasks is quite impressive, even if the frequency of this use is not especially high. These are children for whom the use of the same morphemes with real words is quite a struggle. Earlier it was noted that these children show significantly lower percentages of use of these morphemes in obligatory contexts than do younger children matched for MLU. Why, then, would one expect these children to produce grammatical morphemes as consistently as control children when the words changed to novel ones?

Nonsense Inflections and Miniature Languages

Productivity has also been studied by teaching children a nonsense affix with nonsense words and assessing the children's ability to apply the affix to new nonsense words. Children with SLI do not perform as well as age controls on this task, but they certainly show enough use of the affix with nonsense words to indicate that a rule has been acquired (Bellaire et al., 1994; Swisher, Restrepo, Plante, & Lowell, 1995; Swisher & Snow, 1994). It is interesting to note that the children with SLI performed better with a method that relied on implicit discovery of a rule than with a method in which the rule was verbalized explicitly by the experimenter.

Connell and his colleagues (Connell, 1987; Connell & Stone, 1992) found that through demonstration children with SLI can acquire novel affixes but require practice in the production of these forms before they are able to use them in their speech. Without such practice, their knowledge of these forms was demonstrated only in comprehension activities. Control children, on the other hand, produced these forms even when the teaching activity involved only observation.

Johnston, Blatchley, and Olness (1990) studied children's ability to acquire a miniature language. Two different miniature languages were employed. Each consisted of novel words with a particular (non-English) word order and a suffix attached to the noun serving as patient. The children with SLI in this study had some success in learning the language and applying it to new examples, but they seemed limited in the number of properties of the language they could process. For the language in which the affix was in sentence-final position, these children learned the affix rather well but had difficulty with word order. For the language in which the affix appeared in sentence-medial position—and hence was less salient—the children learned the word order at the expense of the affix.

Generalization in Language Intervention

It is also possible to gauge productivity through procedures designed to assist the children's learning, that is, through intervention activities. Many intervention studies evaluate progress by assessing the child's ability to apply the newly learned information to new exemplars.

One advantage of using intervention procedures is that the productivity of many different linguistic operations and forms can be examined. In these kinds of studies, children are taught not only grammatical morphemes but also syntactic frames such as subject-verb-object, complex sentences involving relativization, passive constructions, and operations such as auxiliary inversion in *wh*-questions (e.g., Camarata, Nelson, & Camarata, 1994; Warren & Kaiser, 1986; Wilcox & Leonard, 1978). Unlike overregularizations such as *throwed* and novel productions such as *vimmed*, the appearance of passive constructions or relative clauses in a child's speech following treatment might possibly be attributed to the memorization of particular sentences heard outside the treatment setting. (On the face of it, this does not seem very plausible; the likelihood that the new exemplars chosen by the experimenter are identical to sentences actually heard and memorized by the children seems rather remote.) To determine the likelihood of such rote learning effects, these studies have built-in controls. For example, children with SLI selected as subjects might initially lack both passives and relative clauses in their speech. One group might be taught passives and another group might be taught relative clauses. Throughout intervention, all children's speech would be monitored for both structures. If the first group showed gains primarily in the use of passives whereas the other's gains centered on the use of relative clauses, it seems unlikely that memorization was at work.

The results of these studies indicate that through intervention, children with SLI can acquire the productive use of a range of grammatical morphemes and syntactic structures. Furthermore, in most of the approaches used in recent years, grammatical elements are not taught explicitly. Rather, the child hears the target elements more frequently, presented in linguistically unambiguous contexts. Thus, although treatment provides the child with an idealized input, it relies on processes that are seen in everyday language learning. In addition, changes in the dependent measure—productions of the target elements—are usually measured in spontaneous speech samples. Therefore, the products of intervention efforts are not likely to be unnatural phenomena.

Summary and Implications

It is safe to conclude that the great majority of children with SLI are not restricted to rote memorization. The evidence of productive processes comes from overregularizations, use of appropriate grammatical morphemes with nonsense words, use of nonsense affixes, productions of untaught exemplars of a miniature language, and the generalization of a range of grammatical morphemes and syntactic structures to new exemplars as the result of intervention. Although it is possible that some of the creative use constitutes the application of a metalinguistic rule learned in school or in therapy, such use has also been documented in children who have not received this type of instruction.

BEHAVING BADLY WITH A PRODUCTIVE SYSTEM

Of course, the fact that many children with SLI can use grammatical morphology productively raises the question of why they lag significantly behind their peers in the use of these very morphemes. In particular, if they can use a variety of grammatical morphemes productively, why are they more likely to omit these forms than control children showing similar MLUs?

Rules of Narrow Scope

One possibility is that the productive rules of children with SLI are narrower in scope than in normally developing children. This idea was first put forth by Ingram and his colleagues (Ingram & Carr, 1994; Morehead & Ingram, 1973). Morehead and Ingram observed that children with SLI appeared to employ a narrower range of syntactic categories (e.g., Noun Phrase or NP, Verb Phrase or VP, Prepositional Phrase or PP) in their grammatical constructions than was seen for a group of MLU control children. Similarly, in a case study of one child with SLI, Ingram and Carr noted a restriction in the types of verb complements used in the child's speech.

There are hints in the literature that some of the rules formed by children with SLI are narrow in scope (see Leonard, 1998). However, the grammatical morphemes for which there is the best evidence of productivity do not yet yield clear evidence of differences between children with SLI and MLU controls in scope of application. For example, as is true for younger normally developing children, children with SLI are more likely to use past tense forms to refer to actions with clear end states (Johnson & Sutter, 1984), more likely to use contracted rather than uncontracted forms of copula and auxiliary *be* (Cleave & Rice, 1997), and less likely to use the noun plural inflection if the noun is preceded by a numerical quantifier (Leonard et al., 1997).

Bishop (1994) and Leonard et al. (1997) found that children with SLI were often inconsistent in using grammatical morphemes with the same lexical items. For example, in contexts obligating *-ed*, some children produced the verb "push" with the past inflection (*pushed*) in one instance and produced the bare stem (*push*) in another, during the same speech sample. It is not clear how a narrow scope of application of a rule would lead to such inconsistency with the same lexical material.

Extended Period of Optional Infinitive Use

Another possible explanation of productive but seemingly inconsistent use of grammatical morphology comes from Rice and her colleagues (Rice & Wexler, 1996; Rice et al., 1995). Based on work by Wexler (1994), these investigators assume that normally developing children go through a stage during which they treat tense as optional in main clauses. The children have knowledge and control of the feature of tense (as well as features of agreement); their problem is that they do not know that tense is obligatory. When tense is not selected, an infinitive form is used in its place. Thus, for a child acquiring Standard English, a production such as *Priscilla like Robert* reflects the use of the (bare stem) infinitive form rather than the deletion of *-s* from a finite form. For copula and auxiliary forms, it is assumed that when the child does not select an utterance marking tense, no overt form will appear. The reasoning here is that copula and auxiliary forms do not play a thematic role, and therefore there is no syntactic motivation for producing them if tense is not marked. Thus, Standard English–speaking children at this stage produce alternatives such as *Teresa mad* and *Teresa is mad,* but not *Teresa be mad.*

Although most children quickly develop out of this optional infinitive stage, children with SLI remain in it for an extended period. During this phase they are inconsistent in their use of tense-related morphemes such as past *-ed,* third singular *-s,* and copula and auxiliary *be* forms, among others. Compared to MLU controls, they show lower percentages of use of these morphemes in obligatory contexts. However, when grammatical morphemes appear, they usually are appropriate.

For the array of grammatical morphemes for which it is applicable, the extended optional infinitive account holds a great deal of promise. Its details are compatible with the finding that the same verb might appear appropriately inflected in one instance and as a bare stem (in a similar context) in another instance. It is important to note that because it is assumed that children with SLI have command of features of tense and agreement—they simply lack the knowledge that the features are obligatory in main clauses—the account permits productive albeit inconsistent use by these children.

Of course, there are details of this account that are yet to be worked out. Notably, it is not yet clear what factors determine when a given utterance will be generated in a finite (tense-related) or nonfinite form. This is an important question, because although children with SLI use tense-related grammatical morphemes with lower percentages in obligatory contexts than do MLU controls, even the latter group functions at levels below mastery. Differences between the groups such as 27% versus 44%, or 50% versus 64% (see Rice & Wexler, 1996), are quite typical. Given that the MLU controls, too, are treating tense-related forms as "optional," there must be some factor that determines the likelihood of a finite or nonfinite form being selected when the obligatory nature of tense is not yet established.

Prosodic Constraints on Grammatical Morphology

There is convincing evidence that production factors are responsible for some of the variability in the use of grammatical morphology by children with SLI. In a program of research with young normally developing children, Gerken (1994, 1996) found that weak syllables are especially vulnerable to omission in particular prosodic contexts. Specifically, weak syllables that cannot form prosodic units with preceding strong syllables are more likely to be omitted than are weak syllables that do enter into prosodic units with strong syllables. For a lexical word such as *banana,* for example, the final weak syllable of the word forms a metrical foot with the preceding strong syllable. The initial syllable, however, is unfooted and thus more likely to be omitted.

This prosodic factor operates for weak syllables that constitute grammatical morphemes as well. For example, the article in the sentence *Babs chases the monkey* forms a prosodic word with the following noun. But it falls outside the metrical foot represented by *monkey* and hence is vulnerable to omission. On the other hand, in the sentence *Babs chased the monkey,* the article can form a metrical foot with the preceding strong syllable and is less likely to be omitted. Thus, the same grammatical morpheme might be produced or omitted depending on the prosodic structure of the utterance.

McGregor and Leonard (1994) examined some of Gerken's assumptions with a group of children with SLI, finding that articles in subject NPs (which are unfooted) were more likely to be omitted than object articles that could be prosodically organized with preceding strong syllables. Overall, articles were more likely to be omitted by the children with SLI than by a group of MLU controls.

Bortolini and Leonard (1996) examined this issue in both English-speaking and Italian-speaking children with SLI, observing a higher degree of weak syllable omissions in contexts that barred the syllable from forming a metrical foot. The children also omitted unfooted weak syllables within lexical words (as in *banana*). However, in comparable prosodic contexts, these unfooted weak syllables were not omitted to the degree seen for unfooted weak monosyllabic grammatical morphemes. To use an Italian example, the first syllable of *Lorenzo* in *vede Lorenzo* "(he/she) sees Lorenzo" was more likely to be preserved than the article *la* in *vede la rana* "(he/she) sees the frog."

Clearly, a prosodic account such as that of Gerken (1994, 1996) might go a long way toward explaining the inconsistency in the use of grammatical morphemes by children with SLI. By assuming that children with SLI are influenced by the same prosodic factors as MLU controls, but have even greater difficulty producing unfooted material, one can arrive at a reasonable explanation of the evidence. However, this explanation seems insufficient for two reasons. First, some of the grammatical morpheme difficulties of children with SLI involve consonantal grammatical inflections, which do not seem amenable to the previously described prosodic approach. It is not clear how these children's low degree of use of, say, the consonantal allomorphs of past *-ed* relative to MLU controls can be explained by this account, or how the inconsistency of these inflections with the same verb might be handled.

Second, the prosodic account in its current form does not contain a mechanism by which unfooted weak syllables within lexical words are more likely to be preserved than unfooted weak monosyllabic grammatical morphemes. Both are problematic for children with SLI, as the account predicts; however, the latter are more likely to be omitted by children with SLI than the former.

Processing Limitations During Sentence Production

Some investigators have suggested that limitations in general processing capacity figure in the language deficits of children with SLI. Much of this work has focused on the role of processing limitations in the acquisition of grammatical morphology. For example, Leonard and his colleagues (e.g., Leonard, 1989; Leonard, McGregor, & Allen, 1992; Leonard et al., 1997) suggested that when material in the input is of relatively brief duration to begin with and requires morphological analysis as well, then in the press of dealing with the rest of the sentence that is being heard, the brief morphemes are sometimes processed incompletely by these children. Consequently, a greater number of exposures are necessary before these brief grammatical forms become established in the grammar.

If, in fact, the processing limitations are general in nature, as Leonard and his colleagues propose, they should have an effect in language production as well. More recently, Leonard (1998) specified how this might work. The approach accommodates prosodic factors while at the same time respecting the distinction between unfooted weak syllables that have morphemic status and those that do not.

Leonard's (1998) thesis is that limited processing capacity, defined in terms of reduced speed of processing, can result in lexical, morphosyntactic, and phonological errors caused by the three levels interacting in real time. Leonard adopted details of current sentence production models (Bock & Levelt, 1994; Levelt, 1989) in which it is assumed that once the lexical items appropriate for the speaker's intended message are retrieved and assigned a grammatical function, sentence fragments are retrieved. These fragments are assumed to be portions of grammatical structure. An example is seen below. The structure here is in line with the principles and parameters framework; however, more traditional structural frameworks (e.g., NP + AUX + VP) are also in keeping with the proposals.

Some investigators (e.g., Lapointe, 1985) have proposed that sentence fragments are stored in terms of morphosemantic complexity, such that the more complex fragments are less accessible and hence require more resources and more time to retrieve. From (1) it can be seen that the slot for the auxiliary form (under I) is empty. It is assumed that sentence fragments and function words are accessed from separate stores and then combined. For each function word store, entries are organized according to complexity. For example, it is assumed that the third singular form *is* is more accessible (and hence more quickly retrieved) than the third plural form *are* (Lapointe, 1985).

It is not clear that inflections are stored separately from sentence fragments. However, operationally they still have an effect on retrieval because a fragment containing one inflection (e.g., -*ed*) must be distinguished in the fragment store from one containing a different inflection or a bare stem. Fragments with bare stems are assumed to be more accessible.

According to Leonard (1998), as the child with SLI must retrieve words, assign functions, and retrieve sentence fragments and function words in real time, slow processing leads to competition between completing retrieval of an item in a less accessible position in the store and proceeding with the rest of the sentence. If proceeding with the rest of the sentence wins out, bare stems and missing function words can result.

Following the retrieval of sentence fragments and function words, phonological encoding takes place. During this phase the metrical structure of words are formed and, in parallel, the prosodic pattern of the words in combination is organized. As noted earlier, words and word combinations permitting strong syllable–weak syllable sequences are more likely to be preserved, whereas weak syllables that cannot be organized with preceding strong syllables are more likely to be omitted. Leonard (1998) points out that given the difficulty of weak syllables outside of strong–weak sequences, any faltering during sentence generation such as slower retrieval of a weak syllable morpheme in a function word store makes it even more likely that the prosodic organization of the sentence will begin without the function word.

This proposal requires empirical study. However, it has considerable face validity: (a) It permits children with SLI to be even poorer in production than in comprehension—a common profile in these children, (b) it allows inconsistency in the use of an inflection with the same lexical item, (c) it is sensitive to prosodic phenomena but assumes even greater difficulty with prosodically vulnerable syllables that have function word status, and (d) it provides an account of how morphosyntactic limitations can occur even with a productive system. Indeed, it helps explain earlier findings (Connell, 1987; Connell & Stone, 1992) that children with SLI could acquire a novel affix but were not successful in producing the affix in sentences until they had production practice.

CONCLUSIONS

There is some irony in the fact that investigators of very young typically developing children often find evidence of near-adultlike language competence in the face of extremely limited performance, whereas the highly tangible evidence of productivity from performance provided by children with SLI is viewed with a jaundiced eye. It may prove to be the case that some individuals with SLI are truly operating without a productive system. However, the evidence for productivity in many children with SLI seems quite convincing.

The finding that these children use language productively might render their language status less dramatic, but at the same time the fact that such serious limitations in language skills can occur with a productive system constitutes a puzzle that has yet to be solved. In this chapter I have considered some approaches that might constitute first steps toward a solution.

REFERENCES

Albertini, J. (1980). The acquisition of five grammatical morphemes: Deviance or delay? *Proceedings of the Symposium on Research in Child Language Disorders: Vol. 1* (pp. 94–111). Madison: University of Wisconsin, Madison.

Bellaire, S., Plante, E., & Swisher, L. (1994). Bound-morpheme skills in the oral language of school-age, language-impaired children. *Journal of Communication Disorders, 27*, 265–279.

Berko (Gleason), J. (1958). The child's learning of English morphology. *Word, 14*, 150–177.

Bishop, D. (1992). The underlying nature of specific language impairment. *Journal of Child Psychology and Psychiatry, 33*, 3–66.

Bishop, D. (1994). Grammatical errors in specific language impairment: Competence or performance limitations? *Applied Psycholinguistics, 15*, 507–550.

Bock, K., & Levelt, W. (1994). Grammatical encoding. In M. Gernsbacher (Ed.), *Handbook of psycholinguistics* (pp. 945–984). San Diego: Academic Press.

Bortolini, U., Caselli, M. C., & Leonard, L. (1997). Grammatical deficits in Italian-speaking children with specific language impairment. *Journal of Speech, Language, and Hearing Research, 40*, 809–820.

Bortolini, U., & Leonard, L. (1996). Phonology and grammatical morphology in specific language impairment: Accounting for individual variation in English and Italian. *Applied Psycholinguistics, 17*, 85–104.

Camarata, S., Nelson, K. E., & Camarata, M. (1994). Comparison of conversational-recasting and imitative procedures for training grammatical structures in children with specific language impairment. *Journal of Speech and Hearing Research, 37*, 1414–1423.

Clahsen, H. (1989). The grammatical characterization of developmental dysphasia. *Linguistics, 27*, 897–920.

Clahsen, H., & Hansen, D. (1993). The missing agreement account of specific language impairment: Evidence from therapy experiments. *Essex Research Reports in Linguistics, 2*, 1–37.

Cleave, P., & Rice, M. (1997). An examination of the morpheme BE in children with specific language impairment: The role of contractibility and grammatical morpheme class. *Journal of Speech, Language, and Hearing Research, 40*, 480–492.

Connell, P. (1987). An effect of modeling and imitation teaching procedures on children with and without specific language impairment. *Journal of Speech and Hearing Research, 30*, 105–113.

Connell, P., & Stone, C. (1992). Morpheme learning of children with specific language impairment under controlled instructional conditions. *Journal of Speech and Hearing Research, 35*, 844–852.

Eyer, J., & Leonard, L. (1994). Learning past tense morphology with specific language impairment: A case study. *Child Language Teaching and Therapy, 10*, 127–138.

Eyer, J., & Leonard, L. (1995). Functional categories and specific language impairment: A case study. *Language Acquistion, 4*, 177–203.

Gerken, L. (1994). Young children's representations of prosodic phonology: Evidence from English-speakers' weak syllable productions. *Journal of Memory and Language, 33*, 19–38.

Gerken, L. (1996). Prosodic structure in young children's language production. *Language, 72*, 683-712.

Gopnik, M. (1994). Prologue. *McGill Working Papers in Linguistics, 10*, vii–x.

Gopnik, M., & Crago, M. (1991). Familial aggregation of a developmental language disorder. *Cognition, 39*, 1–50.

Håkansson, G. (1997). Language impairment from a processing perspective. *Lund University Department of Linguistics Working Papers, 46*, 1–20.

Ingram, D., & Carr, L. (1994). When morphology ability exceeds syntactic ability: A case study. Paper presented at the Convention of the American Speech-Language-Hearing Association, New Orleans.

Johnson, C., & Sutter, J. (1984). Past time language in expressively delayed children. Paper presented at the Convention of the American Speech-Language-Hearing Association, San Francisco.

Johnston, J. (1988). Specific language disorders in the child. In N. Lass, L. McReynolds, J. Northern, & D. Yoder (Eds.), *Handbook of speech-language pathology and audiology* (pp. 685–715). Toronto: Decker.

Johnston, J., Blatchley, M., & Olness, G. (1990). Miniature language system acquisition by children with different learning proficiencies. *Journal of Speech and Hearing Research, 33*, 335–342.

Johnston, J., & Kamhi, A. (1984). Syntactic and semantic aspects of the utterances of language-impaired children. The same can be less. *Merrill-Palmer Quarterly, 30*, 65–85.

Lindner, K., & Johnston, J. (1992). Grammatical morphology in language-impaired children acquiring English or German as their first language: A functional perspective. *Applied Psycholinguistics, 13*, 115–129.

Kamhi, A., & Johnston, J. (1992). Semantic assessment: Determining propositional complexity. In W. Secord & J. Damico (Eds.), *Best practices in school speech-language pathology* (pp. 99–105). San Antonio, TX: Psychological Corporation.

King, G., Schelletter, I., Sinka, P., Fletcher, P., & Ingham, R. (1995). Are English-speaking SLI children with morpho-syntactic deficits impaired in their use of locative-contact and causative alternating verbs? *University of Reading Working Papers in Linguistics, 2*, 45–65.

Lapointe, S. (1985). A theory of verb form use in the speech of agrammatic aphasics. *Brain and Language, 24*, 100–155.

Leonard, L. (1989). Language learnability and specific language impairment. *Applied Psycholinguistics, 10*, 179–202.

Leonard, L. (1998). *Children with specific language impairment.* Cambridge, MA: MIT Press.

Leonard, L., Bortolini, U., Caselli, M. C., McGregor, K., & Sabbadini, L. (1992). Morphological deficits in children with specific language impairment: The status of features in the underlying grammar. *Language Acquisition, 2*, 151–179.

Leonard, L., Eyer, J., Bedore, L., & Grela, B. (1997). Three accounts of the grammatical morpheme difficulties of English-speaking children with specific language impairment. *Journal of Speech, Language, and Hearing Research, 40,* 741–753.

Leonard, L., McGregor, K., & Allen, G. (1992). Grammatical morphology and speech perception in children with specific language impairment. *Journal of Speech and Hearing Research, 35,* 1076–1085.

Levelt, W. (1989). *Speaking: From intention to articulation.* Cambridge, MA: MIT Press.

Marchman, V., Wulfeck, B., & Ellis Weismer, S. (1995). Productive use of English past tense morphology in children with SLI and normal language (Technical Report CND-9514). University of California at San Diego, San Diego: Center for Research in Language.

McGregor, K., & Leonard, L. (1994). Subject pronoun and article omissions in the speech of children with specific language impairment: A phonological interpretation. *Journal of Speech and Hearing Research, 37,* 171–181.

Menyuk, P. (1964). Comparison of grammar of children with functionally deviant and normal speech. *Journal of Speech and Hearing Research, 7,* 109–121.

Morehead, D., & Ingram, D. (1973). The development of base syntax in normal and linguistically deviant children. *Journal of Speech and Hearing Research, 16,* 330–352.

Oetting, J., & Horohov, J. (1997). Past tense marking by children with and without specific language impairment. *Journal of Speech, Language, and Hearing Research, 40,* 62–74.

Plante, E., Swisher, L., Kiernan, B., & Restrepo, M. A. (1993). Language matches: Illuminating or confounding? *Journal of Speech and Hearing Research, 36,* 772–776.

Rice, M., & Oetting, J. (1993). Morphological deficits in children with SLI: Evaluation of number marking and agreement. *Journal of Speech and Hearing Research, 36,* 1249–1257.

Rice, M., & Wexler, K. (1996). Toward tense as a clinical marker of specific language impairment in English-speaking children. *Journal of Speech and Hearing Research, 39,* 1239–1257.

Rice, M., Wexler, K., & Cleave, P. (1995). Specific language impairment as a period of extended optional infinitive. *Journal of Speech and Hearing Research, 38,* 850–863.

Rollins, P., Snow, C., & Willett, J. (1996). Predictors of MLU: Semantic and morphological development. *First Language, 16,* 243–259.

Smith-Lock, K. (1995). Morphological usage and awareness in children with and without specific language impairment. *Annals of Dyslexia, 45, 163–185.*

Swisher, L., Restrepo, M. A., Plante, E., & Lowell, S. (1995). Effect of implicit and explicit "rule" presentation on bound-morpheme generalization in specific language impairment. *Journal of Speech and Hearing Research, 38,* 168–173.

Swisher, L., & Snow, D. (1994). Learning and generalization components of morphological acquisition by children with specific language impairment: Is there a functional relation? *Journal of Speech and Hearing Research, 37,* 1406–1413.

Ullman, M., & Gopnik, M. (1994). Past tense production: Regular, irregular and nonsense verbs. *McGill Working Papers in Linguistics, 10,* 81–118.

van der Lely, H. (1994). Canonical linking rules: Forward versus reverse linking in normally developing and specifically language-impaired children. *Cognition, 51,* 29–72.

van der Lely, H. (1996). Specifically language impaired and normally developing children: Verbal passive vs. adjectival passive interpretation. *Lingua, 98,* 243–272.

van der Lely, H., & Ullman, M. (1995). The computation and representation of past-tense morphology in specifically language impaired and normally developing children. Paper presented at the Boston University Conference on Language Development, Boston.

Warren, S., & Kaiser, S. (1986). Generalization of treatment effects by young language-delayed children: A longitudinal analysis. *Journal of Speech and Hearing Disorders, 51,* 239–251.

Wexler, K. (1994). Optional infinitives. In D. Lightfoot & N. Hornstein (Eds.), *Verb movement* (pp. 305–350). New York: Cambridge University Press.

Wilcox, M. J., & Leonard, L. (1978). Experimental acquisition of wh- questions in language-disordered children. *Journal of Speech and Hearing Research, 21,* 220–239.

17

Influences of School-Age Children's Beliefs and Goals on Their Elicited Pragmatic Performance: Lessons Learned From Kissing the Blarney Stone

Mavis L. Donahue
University of Illinois at Chicago

Grown-ups never understand anything by themselves, and it is tiresome for children to be always and forever explaining things to them.
—Narrator, *The Little Prince*, Saint-Exupéry (1943, p. 4)

Fulfilling a life-long dream to test the mythical promise of eloquence, I recently kissed the Blarney Stone at Blarney Castle in Ireland. Later in the gift shop I selected the obligatory "I kissed the Blarney Stone!" T-shirt and took it to the cashier. After we engaged in a brief conversation, she cocked an eye at me and said "And did ye *really* kiss the Blarney Stone?" Having already acquired the Irish discourse style of answering a question with another question, I grinned and replied "Sure, and can't you tell?" Not missing a beat, she parried with "Sure, and doesn't it take a few days to kick in sometimes?"

This scrap of conversational data raises a number of thorny methodological problems in the study of pragmatic performance. The cashier had cleverly invited an unwitting participant into a pragmatic assessment task

353

by tucking it into a "real" conversation, in much the same way that child language researchers aspire to collect language data from children. If I had known that the cashier was assessing my eloquence in situ, how would this have affected my language performance? Can "blarney" and more mundane aspects of pragmatic knowledge be measured in a meaningful way? How can one identify the point at which newly acquired pragmatic skills "kick in"? When and under what contexts can authentic assessments be made? What "counts" as good data? Whose judgment is important?

Consider Bates' (1976) time-honored definition of pragmatics as "the use of language in context" (p. xi), or more specifically for this chapter, "the child's ability to select a particular type of sentence and to 'fix it up' until it will work effectively toward certain social ends" (p. 2). Does it make sense to study pragmatic knowledge through the analysis of language data for which the context and the intended social ends are deliberately manipulated for the purpose of assessment? In short, is "elicited pragmatic performance" an oxymoron?

Much of what is known about school-age children's pragmatic development is based on elicited production, in studies that have searched for an analogue to the wug in conversational interactions. The Berko (1958) task cleverly manipulated the linguistic context to elicit the child's application of his or her morphological rules to a novel lexical item. Similarly, many studies have manipulated the myriad of variables that influence pragmatic performance (e.g., purpose of the communication, listener characteristics, physical context) to prompt children to demonstrate their tacit knowledge of rules that govern socially appropriate speech.

For example, one frequently used paradigm studies the politeness of requests as a window to children's understanding of social roles enacted in language (e.g., Bates, 1976; Donahue, 1981). Children are typically asked to role-play how they would formulate particular kinds of requests (e.g., varying in imposition on the listener) to particular kinds of listeners (e.g., varying in relative social status, familiarity, and other factors.) However, given that the context is imaginary and the child's social ends are not his or her own, these tasks' resemblance to naturally occurring interactions is problematic—or at least not well understood.

One neglected dimension is that any elicited pragmatic task is nested within an interaction with a real conversational partner, that is, the experimenter. What if the child sees that very conversation as the overriding agenda, with the role playing as a subplot? What influences might expectations about the conversational contract with the experimenter have on the child's pragmatic performance? How can those influences be identified and studied? The purpose of this chapter is to highlight a methodological dilemma in using elicited data to measure pragmatic performance in school-age children (i.e., the "nested conversation" problem). It is based on the assumption that elicitation tasks for pragmatic performance are first and foremost conversation. The actual pragmatic task is thus nested within an interaction between experimenter and child, and this interaction is governed by its own set of pragmatic rules. In turn, like nesting cups, the "local" social agenda with an unfamiliar experimenter is situated within widening circles of social expectations and goals, as the familiarity of the listener and the long-term importance of the conversation increases. For example, when the child is interacting with a familiar conversational partner (e.g., a classmate), the task is embedded within a history of social interaction in which social roles and rules may be well established. Instead of treating these rules and expectations as methodological "noise," researchers should view them as an essential part of the data for understanding pragmatic knowledge.

Of course, this dilemma of the superimposed agenda applies not only to the assessment of pragmatic growth but to any human interaction that can be construed as a "language test." No phonological, syntactic, or semantic task is immune to these considerations. Consider the following example of how a difference between adult and child conversational goals may emerge when a child is questioned directly:

Adult: What's different about what you do in speech therapy and what Mrs. Michael does?

Amy: Mrs. Michael makes good "r's." I make bad "r's."

Adult: Don't you ever make good "r's," Amy?

Amy: No, I supposed to make the bad "r's."
(Spinelli & Ripich, 1985, p. 193)

This child's goal in the therapy conversation seemed to be to "sound different" from the adult, which was clearly the opposite of the speech/language pathologist's agenda. Unraveling the source of this discrepancy may be difficult but should start at the intersection of the child's beliefs about conversational rules and goals and the adult's assumptions.

Even the relatively straightforward Berko task relies on the negotiation of a complex set of pragmatic assumptions and roles by the experimenter and the child. Not the least of those assumptions is the child's willingness to believe not only that an unfamiliar adult has access to unusual labels for new concepts, but also that conversational rules obligate the child to finish a sentence with those same funny-sounding words!

An example of how ignoring the nested conversation dilemma can lead researchers astray in understanding children's lexical development is provided by Clark and Grossman (1998). Using a nonsense-word teaching paradigm in which the amount of conversational support was varied, these researchers addressed the role of adult "pragmatic directions" in young children's first stabs at the meanings of new lexical items. Even 2-year-olds relied on conversational assumptions to make inferences about word meanings, based on the discourse support in three conditions. In one condition, the experimenter introduced a new word by presenting a novel object and saying "This is a *dob*." For the next novel object, the experimenter said "This is a *ruk*. It's a kind of *dob*." This signaled that *dob* is a superordinate term; and when asked to "show me all the *dobs*," the children typically pointed to items labeled as either *dobs* or *ruks*. In the second condition, two words were presented in a repair sequence (e.g., "This is a *dob*. Oops, I made a mistake; that's a *ruk*, not a *dob*."). The same children took the experimenter at face value by interpreting the experimenter's intent as instructions to discard one word. Consequently they refused to identify any objects as *dobs* but reliably identified the *ruks*. In the condition most resembling the typical word learning task, that is, when no conversational support is provided (e.g., the experimenter labeled an object by saying only "This is a *dob*"), the children used coping strategies that have been previously used as evidence for general cognitive or semantic constraints. Instead, Clark and Grossman suggest that on this task "children are not affected by semantic constraints so much as by pragmatic constraints" (p. 16).

Of course, early research on the pragmatic domain was not concerned about children's interpretations of the methodological features of the studies (see Ninio & Snow, 1996, and Warren & McCloskey, 1993, for reviews). Initial studies typically collected data on toddlers and preschoolers, often in free play with familiar partners and settings. Later, more contrived tasks relied on younger children's generous compliance with invitations of friendly adults to engage in pretend play. Blissfully unaware that their emerging uses of communicative intentions, presuppositional rules, and conversational turn-taking were under scrutiny, the young participants probably did not expend their cognitive/linguistic resources for second-guessing (or even noticing) the experimenter. However, with increasing interest in pragmatics in children beyond the initial stages of syntactic and semantic acquisition, the possible influences of the child's beliefs about the purpose of the conversation and the agenda of the conversational partner must be considered as another dimension of pragmatic development.

DILEMMAS OF NESTED
CONVERSATIONS AND
SECOND-GUESSING

The "nested conversation" dilemma is framed in the often-overlooked notion that the conversational worlds of adults and children can be divergent (Siegal, 1991). Both the agenda or point of the conversation, and the shared assumptions that govern the process, may be interpreted by the child in ways that are reasonable but unexpected by the adult. As the philosopher Grice (1975) proposed, conversational partners are able to accomplish a cooperative exchange of information through the mutual adherence to four simple maxims. Speakers make an effort to be informative (Maxim of Quantity), truthful and sincere (Maxim of Quality), relevant (Maxim of Relation), and clear (Maxim of Manner); in turn, listeners interpret their utterances by assuming that speakers have indeed followed these maxims. However, adults understand that many contexts (e.g., classrooms, courtrooms) or conditions (e.g., when irony or politeness are the overriding goals) apparently violate these maxims, thereby triggering another interpretation of the utterance that is pragmatically derived. Grice termed these interpretations "conversational implicatures."

Although children appear to be sensitive to the conversational maxims from the very onset of language use, their reasoning processes that result in conversational implicatures may differ from those of adults. Yet tasks designed to elicit pragmatic performance are ideal examples of conversations in which typical assumptions about the purpose of the conversation, the roles of the participants, and the rules that govern the process are abandoned. In short, what may be construed as pragmatic growth on a particular task may simply reflect an emerging ability to recognize conversational implicature.

One classic example of how the child's different conversational implicatures can result in inaccurate assessments is found in the typical Piagetian number conservation task. The experimenter shows the child an array of two rows of equally spaced chips and asks "Which row has more, or do they both have the same?" After the child responds "they both have the same," the experimenter transforms one row by pushing the chips closer together and then repeats the question. Operating under the Gricean maxims, the child may think "Why would this adult ask me the same obvious question again [violating the Maxims of Quality and Quantity]? I must have given the wrong answer." The child may then change his or her answer to "more in this row" to accommodate his or her conversational interpretation. The consequence is that the adult identifies the child as a "nonconserver," still in the preoperational stage. It is interesting to note that in studies whose methodology eliminates the first question or requires the child to give the answer to the second question to a naive listener (i.e., someone who was not present to hear the first response), children show conservational thinking at significantly younger ages (Siegal, 1991).

Similarly, a number of age-related differences that have been attributed to syntactic or semantic development may instead reflect changes in children's willingness to suspend Gricean rules with unfamiliar adults. For example, in an early version of an assessment of children's acquisition of syntactic structures that violate the minimal distance principle (Chomsky, 1969), the experimenter shows a doll with a blindfold and asks "Is this doll easy to see or hard to see?" Distracted by the novelty of the blindfold, younger children may rely on their default model of conversational cooperation and give the adult the benefit of the doubt, thinking "Hmm. Why would this grown-up show me a doll with a blindfold and then ask me if I can see it? She must want me to notice that the doll can't see. So I'll say hard to see." Older children may be more skilled at recognizing that the experimental interaction may be nonsensical, not following the conversational rules of naturalistic interactions. Therefore, the age-related changes may be linked to development in social/cognitive rather than syntactic understanding.

An example of how children's overreliance on Gricean assumptions may influence their performance on semantic measures is the classic "class inclusion" task developed by Inhelder and Piaget (1964). In one typical task, children are shown an array of toy cows, three black and one white. They are then asked "Are there more black cows or more cows?" Most 5-year-olds respond with "more black cows." This confirms Piaget's belief that young children have difficulty thinking simultaneously of the entire class (the cows) and the subclasses (the black and the white), a developmental feat called "decentering" that is the foundation of operational thought. Although this task has been criticized for a variety of conceptual and methodological flaws (e.g., Hodkin, 1987; Lourenco & Machado, 1996; McGarrigle, Grieve, & Hughes, 1978), its violation of conversational rules (relevance and clarity) makes it ripe for children's generous interpretations of adults as asking worthwhile questions. Given the salient color contrast between the toys, the young child is likely to revise the adult's question to mean, "Are there more black cows or more other cows?" Fortuitously, a study by McGarrigle et al.

(1978) confirmed that providing an adjective for the superordinate class significantly improved children's performance. All toy cows were placed on their sides and described as "sleeping." When the question was altered to "Are there more black cows or more sleeping cows?" (thereby justifying why the adult would bother to ask about the superordinate category), more children responded correctly "more sleeping cows." Although McGarrigle et al. (1978) interpreted these findings as evidence for the confound of linguistic factors in assessing cognitive performance, an equally plausible explanation is that the second version supported the children's assumption that adults follow Gricean principles.

In sum, when adults seem to ask questions for which the answers are obvious, often repeatedly, or ask confusing or nonsensical questions (typical characteristics of elicited pragmatic tasks), children rely on their default model of conversational cooperation and often give adults the benefit of the doubt. Compared to the large and increasing body of research on early pragmatic development, there are few studies of how school-age children develop and refine their social uses of language. Some findings suggest that large individual differences begin to overpower age as a factor in understanding conversational development (e.g., Schley & Snow, 1992). One explanation for the large gaps may be that it is more difficult to design clever tasks that tap pragmatic knowledge in older children in unobtrusive ways. In fact, the pragmatic feat of second-guessing the experimenter may be the major developmental milestone in school-age children.

In the remainder of this chapter I describe some methodological issues that may lead to misinterpretation of elicited pragmatic data in school-age children (i.e., the effects of children's beliefs about the multiple conversational goals in an elicited pragmatic task). The range of possible effects that this "nested conversation" dilemma may have is illustrated in two series of studies whose methodologies differ along a continuum of "naturalness": a referential communication task, and role playing an interview with a peer.

LISTENER STUDIES

One early series of studies that illustrates the "nested conversation" principle focused on individual differences in children's interpretation of and responses to communicative breakdowns. Using a very structured and controlled referential communication task, children with and without learning disabilities (LD) in Grades 1 through 8 were asked to identify one of four similar pictures based on messages given by an adult experimenter behind a cardboard screen (Donahue, Pearl, & Bryan, 1980). The pictures differed in terms of distinctive features (e.g., a monkey wearing or not wearing a hat; a spaceman with and without antennae). One third of the messages gave enough information to specify just one picture; even the youngest children were capable of selecting that referent.

The other messages violated the Maxim of Quantity, that is, they did not provide enough information to rule out three of the four choices. Thus, a communication breakdown was created. On those ambiguous messages, both age and disability effects were apparent. Younger children and students with LD at all grades were less likely than comparison children to request clarification, and consequently they made more errors.

But what was the source of this pragmatic performance? Based on response latencies and a message appraisal task immediately following the communication task, my colleagues and I ruled out the explanation that these students simply did not realize that the messages were ambiguous. Further, all students had the syntactic-semantic skills to ask for more information, and each indicated in a post-task interview that the listener had been permitted to ask questions.

A second study was designed to clarify the source of these listeners' puzzling reluctance to initiate the repair of the communication breakdowns (Donahue, 1984). Students who did not request clarification on the same referential communication pretest then participated in a brief intervention in which they actively practiced asking for more needed information from another adult (i.e., they played Twenty Questions with a large array of pictures). Surprisingly, relative to a comparison group that did not have the intervention, this practice still had no effect on children's willingness to request clarification of ambiguous messages on the referential communication posttest.

The intractability of this pattern suggests that a more basic difference in the understanding of the role of the listener was guiding these listeners' performance. Finally, we analyzed which pictures students selected when they heard an ambiguous message and failed to request clarification. There was clear evidence that the inactive listeners were not choosing at random. Instead, they were using a strategy that revealed a belief that the adult was "omniscient." The listener seemed to be thinking "If this adult had meant the picture with the most distinguishing features, she would have said so! So I'll pick the one with the fewest features." Finding it implausible that an adult would violate the Gricean Maxim of Quantity, these students seemed to conclude that their inability to select just one picture must be a result of their own misunderstanding of the task.

However, the needed request for clarification may not be congruent with the social goals of many children with LD, that is, to camouflage their comprehension difficulties.

Unfortunately, the most direct route to these students' understanding of conversational rules on this task was not taken (i.e., the simple question "If you knew you were hearing ambiguous messages, and you knew you were allowed to ask questions, then why didn't you?"). A more recent study that directly assessed attitudes and beliefs about communication breakdowns in students with LD confirmed that their beliefs about the role of the listener and the speaker may underlie their conversational performance. Adapting the interview methodology of McDevitt and her colleagues (e.g., McDevitt, Spivey, Sheehan, Lennon, & Story, 1990), children were interviewed about their beliefs about how listeners should respond during communication breakdowns (Donahue, 1997). Students with and without LD between the ages of 7 and 12 were told three brief vignettes about communication breakdowns, in which a child listener becomes confused by his or her teacher's or mother's directions. Surprisingly, few age-related differences emerged. Although many students acknowledged that communication breakdowns were an interactive problem, students with LD were more likely to blame the listener. When asked to rate possible solutions to the communication breakdowns, students with LD were less likely to endorse active strategies such as "ask the teacher a question." Instead, these students preferred low-profile responses such as "listen more carefully," strategies that may be directly or inadvertently encouraged by parents and teachers.

TALK SHOW STUDIES

Data from referential communication tasks and other contrived methodologies can be criticized as not being representative of naturalistic interactions. How can the problem of "nested conversations" influence elicited tasks that more closely simulate typical conversations? Expanding the focus from the multiple agendas that may emerge between just an adult experimenter and child, it becomes clear that the large body of studies that use peer interaction as a site for assessing pragmatic performance must address a similar dilemma. Each interaction is nested within a larger history of any two conversational partners' social relationships. Therefore, the effects of children's perceptions and goals of conversation with a particular peer can not be ignored. On the contrary, they are a rich source of data concerning children's understanding of how conversation enacts social affiliations and hierarchies.

A step further on the "naturalistic" continuum are two studies that resemble role-playing tasks but offer more degrees of freedom in terms of conversational topic and strategy (Bryan, Donahue, Pearl, & Sturm, 1981; Donahue & Bryan, 1983). Both studies placed elementary-school children in the role of "talk show host." This task elicited children's script knowledge of a familiar television genre, a "talk show." Every child indicated that he or she had seen a talk show and was comfortable with enacting the roles. The experimenter not only assigned each child a role (of either talk show host or guest) but also explicitly gave each partner goals for the interaction. Guests were told "Kevin has invited you to be his guest on his show because he has heard that you have interesting things to say, so be sure to talk a lot!" The host was told to "be in charge" and "keep the show going." In addition, a broader social goal was suggested: "It will be a much better show if your guest thinks you're a nice kid. So try to get your guest to like you."

Both studies included school-age children with learning disabilities. This can be a valuable group for uncovering individual differences in responding to elicited pragmatic tasks, as they often bring less positive, or at least differing, social/communicative experiences with peers to the task. Therefore, their beliefs about the goal and agenda of the interaction may serve different purposes (Donahue, 1994). For example, on a social problem-solving task using hypothetical interaction tasks (Carlson, 1987), boys with LD knew the socially appropriate strategy when the goal of the interaction was specified by the experimenter; however, in peer conflict situations, boys with LD were more likely to select the less assertive goals of accommodating the partner or avoiding the conflict rather than compromising. This may reflect experiences in which their efforts to play assertive roles were rebuffed. In another interview study, typically developing students reported that they were much more willing to accept a student with LD as a friend or as part of a social group if the child was not in a dominant position (Miller, 1984).

For students with LD, then, the talk show host's instructions to play both an assertive and an ingratiating role may collide. First, "taking charge" of the conversation can be a challenging task for students who are often more marginal peer group members because of their oral language and social difficulties. To the degree that each student is aware of the "high-risk" nature of this assertiveness, the agenda to "get your guest to like you" is even more open to interpretation. It may be that these children were framing the social reality of the task on at least two levels simultaneously: How do I control the conversation and get my point across? How do I stay within my position in the social hierarchy that I have carefully negotiated with my classmates?

Several kinds of evidence supported the notion that students did in fact interpret these directions in multiple ways and that their pragmatic performance was influenced more by their beliefs about the conversational/social goals of the interaction than by their actual communicative skills. In the first study (including children in Grades 2 and 4: Bryan, Donahue, Pearl, & Sturm, 1981), no clear age effects on conversational performance emerged. Talk show hosts with LD contributed just as much talk as other hosts. However, their strategies for "taking charge" of the conversation were in fact less effective. Specifically, they were less likely to maintain the dialogue through questioning, and a smaller proportion of their questions was open-ended.

One compelling (and underused) indicator of the validity of elicited pragmatic performance may be the assessment of the impact on the conversational partner. It is interesting to note that even though guests were randomly assigned to talk show hosts (of the same gender), children who were interviewed by hosts with LD used conversational styles that clearly differed from those used by guests of non-disabled hosts. Classmates interviewed by a host with LD not only were less likely to elaborate on their own responses but often actually took over the interviewer role themselves. More telling, the questions directed to hosts with LD by their guests were more likely to be yes/no questions. Perhaps because of their shared conversational histories, the guests were less confident of their hosts' willingness or ability to comprehend or extend more detailed responses, or to respond to less constrained questions.

In light of the typically lower social acceptance of students with LD, it is interesting to speculate about the extent to which guests were aware that having a host with LD entailed more discourse "work." In a post–talk show interview in which children were asked what they would like to change for their next "show," guests of hosts with LD were just as likely as other guests to request the same host. However, another kind of data confirmed that hosts with LD and their guests engaged in a less smooth and satisfying dialogue. Using the same videotapes, Bryan, Bryan, and Sonnefeld (1982) showed adult raters (unaware of children's group status or the purpose of the task) the nonverbal behavior of the talk show guests only. Guests interviewed by talk show hosts with LD were rated as more hostile and less relaxed than guests of nondisabled hosts.

A second study illustrated the power of including both conversational partner performance and interview data to triangulate the interpretation of children's pragmatic strategies (Donahue & Bryan, 1983). Using the same talk show format, the study was designed to explore the source of the conversational styles of students with LD and their partners. Perhaps these students did not have the relevant conversational skills in their repertoire or did not readily recognize those contexts that call for their use. Or based on their interactional histories, they may have deliberately selected conversational strategies that served their own beliefs and goals about "fitting in." This explanation suggests an awareness of conversational norms that is more sophisticated than most students with LD are given credit for.

To test the malleability of interviewers' conversational styles, boys in Grades 2 through 8, with and without LD, listened to a brief audiotaped dialogue in which a child interviewer modeled the use of open-ended questions, conversational devices, and contingent questions and comments. (Talk show hosts in the control condition listened to a monologue presenting the responses of the interviewee, to control for topic availability.) Although selected because they differentiated groups in the Bryan et al. (1981) study, these three strategies have also been directly validated as indicators of conversational skill by Schley and Snow (1992). Two adult judges were asked to read and develop holistic ratings of the conversational skills of 99 children in Grades 2 through 5 who participated in the same "talk show" task. More open-ended questions, fewer yes/no questions, and more elaborate guest responses differentiated the highly rated talk show hosts from lower-rated hosts. High-ranked conversationalists also produced fewer topics overall and more contingent responses that followed up on their partner's remarks. It is interesting to note that these ratings were not strongly related to children's gender, age, or oral language proficiency.

In the modeling study, as predicted, boys with LD in the control condition produced fewer open-ended questions and contingent comments than did nondisabled boys. However, those who listened to the dialogue model increased their use of these strategies to the level of their nondisabled peers. An unexpected benefit was an increase in their contribution of talk to the conversation. The effectiveness of this brief modeling suggested that the boys had not acquired new skills but had been primed in terms of when to mobilize existing skills. In light of their differing social agendas, they may have been reluctant to take control of the dialogue by directing open-ended questions to their guests or to spontaneously offer their own opinions. The model may have induced the boys with LD to rethink their social goals and/or to test the appropriateness of these strategies in this context.

How did the guests of the interviewers with LD respond to these more assertive and contingent strategies? There appeared to be a social cost for changing one's conversational style, suggesting that even subtle conversational norms are enacted in delicately balanced social relationships. Guests of talk show hosts with LD in the dialogue condition actually offered fewer elaborated responses and more requests for clarification than did guests of control hosts with LD. This supports the theory that the "low profile" social goals of students with LD reflect their accurate awareness that efforts to take a dominant role in conversation will be met by subtle resistance from their classmates.

Children's beliefs about "good talk show hosts" were directly assessed and provided compelling support for this interpretation. After the videotaping, each child was asked "Now that you've been a host on a talk show, suppose you were going to give advice to another kid to help him be a good talk show host? Guest? What things would you tell him?" Children's responses were surprisingly sophisticated, indicating an awareness of the importance of the actual content or formulation of the discourse as well as the need for a natural and flowing dialogue. Boys with LD were more likely than other boys to give advice about affective state (e.g., "Don't be nervous"), suggesting that they had perceived the task as stressful. More telling was the finding that the dialogue condition enhanced the concern of boys with LD about the need to prepare for the task ("Practice ahead of time, think of good questions before you start"). Even more striking was the evidence that boys with LD were sensitive to the effects of the modeling condition on their guests' verbal and nonverbal performance. They were less likely to give advice about the quality or quantity of future guests' responses but more aware of the guests' responsibility to maintain the surface form of the conversation, that is, their affective states, fluency, and nonverbal appropriateness.

The patterns of findings of these two series of studies illustrate how elicited pragmatic performance can be influenced by children's personal theories about the multi-leveled and sometimes conflicting rules governing any particular communicative interaction—the nested conversation dilemma. The overriding question is this: How can those influences be identified and studied? These studies also illustrate how a variety of data sources can be used to enhance researchers' interpretation of elicited pragmatic findings. Of course, each of these kinds of data has its own methodological problems. However, our confidence in our interpretations is enhanced if they lie in the convergence of findings collected from different perspectives.

The influence of children's beliefs and goals may be essential in accounting for the large variability in pragmatic skills among typical school-age children. Although samples of students with LD are useful for identifying and unraveling individual contributions of social knowledge and linguistic ability to pragmatic performance, one can not assume that developmental changes can be explained by the same kinds of beliefs and goals that seem to influence the performance of students with LD. However, the assessment of children's social beliefs and goals through measures of children's temperament and social motivation (e.g., Place & Becker, 1991), through direct "de-briefing" interviews about their perceptions of the pragmatic task, and/or through observing their conversational partners' responses, may provide the missing link in understanding the development of pragmatic knowledge.

METHODOLOGICAL LESSONS LEARNED FROM KISSING THE BLARNEY STONE

To summarize, in our mission to understand pragmatic development, children's conversational beliefs and goals matter. Every attempt to elicit pragmatic performance is susceptible to the nested conversation dilemma. A description of pragmatic performance and changes during middle childhood (i.e., what behaviors develop and when) will be at best incomplete and at worst misleading if it is not interpreted within a framework that regards children, like adults, as thinking conversationalists who juggle multiple and overlapping assumptions and goals during every interaction. These reasoning processes are not simply methodological confounds or artifacts but are likely to constitute the domain that drives pragmatic growth during the school-age years.

What methodological lessons may apply to a (tongue-in-cheek) proposal to conduct an empirical test of the power of the Blarney Stone? In addition to the gift shop cashier's participant-observer ethnographic approach, how might we design an elicited pragmatic task for assessing such an experiment? Assume that school-age participants are randomly and blindly assigned to the experimental condition (kissing the real Blarney Stone) or to the control condition (kissing a placebo, a fraudulent Blarney Stone). Also assume that one excellent posttest for tapping Blarney skills is a role-playing task to persuade a classmate to donate money to an unpopular charity (e.g., Society for the Advancement of Homework). I propose at least six kinds of data sources:

1. Pretest measures of children's self-perceptions of their social status and social impact on their classmates, as well as the extent to which those in the persuader role are motivated to change the opinions of classmates;

2. Pretest measures of the classmates serving as "targets" of the persuasiveness, the "persuadees," including their ratings of the persuader's social status and social impact, and self-ratings of the malleability of their own opinions (i.e., a measure of task difficulty);

3. Posttest coding of the persuader's pragmatic strategies for engaging his or her target in the discourse event, including the quality of listener-accommodating tactics for offering arguments and rebuttals (e.g., Bryan, Donahue, & Pearl, 1981; Donahue, 1981);

4. Posttest coding of the "persuadee's" pragmatic strategies for participating in the discourse, including the quality of appeals for arguments, counterarguments, and winning moves (e.g., Donahue & Prescott, 1988);

5. A "de-briefing" interview after the persuasive task, in which both conversational partners reflect on their goals for the task, their perceptions of their own and their partner's performance, and suggestions for future participants; and

6. The most authentic and stringent measure of the power of the Blarney Stone: After the persuasive task, each persuadee will be paid for participating in the experiment and then actually offered the opportunity to contribute his or her earnings to the charity in question.

This experiment may be doomed to failure because it neglects the most important lesson: the power of individuals' beliefs and goals in influencing their pragmatic performance. Some have suggested that the Blarney Stone works only for those who have absolute faith in its magic. In this case, the performance of the skeptics in the sample may obscure any main effects of kissing the true Blarney Stone. Perhaps this is what the cashier meant by her remark "Sure, and doesn't it take a few days to kick in sometimes?"

REFERENCES

Bates, E. (1976). *Language and context: The acquisition of pragmatics.* New York: Academic Press.

Berko (Gleason), J. (1958). The child's learning of English morphology. *Word, 14,* 150–177.

Bryan, J., Bryan, T., & Sonnefeld, J. (1982). Being known by the company one keeps. The contagion of first impressions. *Learning Disability Quarterly, 5,* 288–294.

Bryan, T., Donahue, M., & Pearl, R. (1981). Learning disabled children's peer interactions during a small-group problem-solving task. *Learning Disability Quarterly, 4,* 13–22.

Bryan, T., Donahue, M., Pearl, R., & Sturm, C. (1981). Learning disabled children's conversational skills: The television talk show. *Learning Disability Quarterly, 4,* 250–259.

Carlson, C. (1987). Social interaction goals and strategies of children with learning disabilities. *Journal of Learning Disabilities, 20,* 306–311.

Chomsky, C. (1969). *The acquisition of syntax in children from 5 to 10.* Cambridge, MA: MIT Press.

Clark, E., & Grossman, J. (1998). Pragmatic directions and children's word learning. *Journal of Child Language, 25,* 1–18.

Donahue, M. (1981). Requesting strategies of learning disabled children. *Applied Psycholinguistics, 2,* 213–234.

Donahue, M. (1984). Learning disabled children's conversational competence: An attempt to activate the inactive listener. *Applied Psycholinguistics, 5,* 21–35.

Donahue, M. (1994). Differences in classroom discourse styles of students with learning disabilities. In D. Ripich & N. Creaghead (Eds.), *School discourse* (pp. 229–261). San Diego, CA: Singular Press.

Donahue, M. (1997). Beliefs about listening in students with learning disabilities: "Is the speaker always right?" *Topics in Language Disorders, 17* (3), 441–460.

Donahue, M., & Bryan, T. (1983). Conversational skills and modeling in learning disabled boys. *Applied Psycholinguistics, 44,* 251–278.

Donahue, M., Pearl, R., & Bryan, T. (1980). Learning disabled children's conversational competence: Responses to inadequate messages. *Applied Psycholinguistics, 1,* 387–403.

Donahue, M., & Prescott, B. (1988). Reading disabled children's conversational participation in dispute episodes with peers. *First Language, 8,* 247–258.

Grice, H. P. (1975). Logic and conversation. In P. Cole & J. Morgan (Eds.), *Syntax and semantics: Vol. 3. Speech acts* (pp. 41–58). New York: Academic Press.

Hodkin, B. (1987). Performance model analysis in class inclusion: An illustration with two language conditions. *Developmental Psychology, 23,* 683–689.

Inhelder, B., & Piaget, J. (1964). *The early growth of logic in the child.* New York: Harper and Row.

Lourenco, O., & Machado, A. (1996). In defense of Piaget's theory: A reply to 10 common criticisms. *Psychological Bulletin, 103,* 143–164.

McDevitt, T., Spivey, N., Sheehan, E., Lennon, R., & Story, R. (1990). Children's beliefs about listening: Is it enough to be still and quiet? *Child Development, 61,* 713–721.

McGarrigle, J., Grieve, R., & Hughes, M. (1978). Interpreting inclusion: A contribution to the study of the child's cognitive and linguistic development. *Journal of Experimental Child Psychology, 26,* 528–550.

Miller, M. (1984). Social acceptability characteristics of learning disabled students. *Journal of Learning Disabilities, 17,* 619–621.

Ninio, A., & Snow, C. (1996). *Pragmatic development.* Boulder, CO: Westview Press.

Place, K., & Becker, J. (1991). The influence of pragmatic competence on the likeability of grade-school children. *Discourse Processes, 14,* 227–241.

Saint-Exupéry, A. de (1943). *The Little Prince.* San Diego: Harcourt Brace Jovanovich.

Schley, S., & Snow, C. (1992). The conversational skills of school-aged children. *Social Development, 1,* 18–35.

Siegal, M. (1991). *Knowing children: Experiments in conversation and cognition.* Hillsdale, NJ: Lawrence Erlbaum Associates.

Spinelli, F., & Ripich, D. (1985). A comparison of classroom and clinical discourse. In D. Ripich & F. Spinelli (Eds.), *School discourse problems* (pp. 179–196). San Diego: College-Hill Press.

Warren, A., & McCloskey, L. (1993). Pragmatics: Language in social contexts. In J. Berko Gleason (Ed.), *The development of language* (pp. 196–237). New York: Macmillan.

IV
Adult
Disorders

18

Jean Berko Gleason's Contributions to Aphasia Research: Pioneering Elicitation Techniques

Harold Goodglass

Aphasia Research Center, Department of Neurology, Boston University School of Medicine

The end of World War II saw a number of nearly concurrent developments in the study of language. One was the introduction of experimental methods for analyzing the cognitive underpinnings of linguistic processing. As general modus operandi, the field of psycholinguistics had to bring a targeted operation into the laboratory by eliciting it from users of the language under experimental manipulations that were designed to reveal something about the nature of the process involved. These methods began to supplement the traditional ones of naturalistic observation and simple achievement testing in the study of both language acquisition and language breakdown.

The end of the war also saw a great explosion in the treatment and study of aphasia—the loss of language produced by injuries to the brain, such as those suffered by many soldiers. The rehabilitation of military casualties was the likely trigger for the extension of research and treatment of aphasia from veterans hospitals to civilian rehabilitation hospitals. In the period of a few years, beginning in about 1954, a cadre of pioneers were applying psycholinguistic research methods to the language of aphasics.

Aphasia presented a rich array of symptoms that invited systematic analysis with the new techniques. Among them were issues that had their counterpart in the study of child language: What does the aphasic speaker know about a target word when he or she cannot retrieve it? Are the agrammatic utterances of aphasics governed by a consistent rule system, or are they better understood as defective efforts to realize standard grammatical forms?

Problems of this type had already provoked the interest of Charles Osgood, arguably the founder of the discipline of psycholinguistics. In 1958, Osgood and Joseph Casagrande, acting on behalf of the Social Science Research Council, organized a 6-week-long summer research seminar on aphasia. They chose the Boston Veterans Administration Hospital as the venue for this multidisciplinary conference, bringing together linguists, psycholinguists, speech pathologists, and neurologists. The hospital was chosen because its aphasia program, led by the neurologists Fred Quadfasel and Norman Geschwind and the psychologist Harold Goodglass, had already accumulated a modest research track record and because it afforded a clinical population of patients for observation.

Jean Berko entered the field of research in aphasia via her participation in this meeting. Jean had just completed her doctorate at Harvard University with her landmark wug study demonstrating that children could use morphological rules generatively, even on word stems that they had never heard. Her invitation to be a participant brought to the seminar a viewpoint from the newly developing field of applied experimental psycholinguistics.

In her dissertation research Jean had confronted a problem that was to appear over and over in the study of aphasic language: how to elicit the production of a target word or morphological form, or a syntactic construction, in a way that modeled the subject's access to that form in everyday speech. The task was to devise an eliciting frame that was sufficiently constraining so that any speaker would be expected to use the target form. It could not be couched in metalinguistic terms (e.g., "What is the plural of horse?") for two reasons: The impaired or unschooled subjects might not have a formulated rule for the particular target. More important, the ability to provide the form as a metalinguistic act need not correspond to the availability of that form in a naturalistic context. Using repetition as an elicitation device would, of course, entirely evade the question as to whether the subject could retrieve the form when called for in speech.

The solution that Jean hit on was a sentence completion format in which the required vocabulary item was provided in the introductory frame but without the target morphology. The introductory sentence frame was supported by drawings—in many instances, drawings that showed the contrast between the form that was being modeled (e.g., a singular object) and the target (e.g., a plural). The sentences were designed to require a single word, inflected with the target morphology, for completion.

This model (without picture support) was used in a study by Goodglass and Berko (1960) that was aimed at examining the relative ease of access by aphasic patients to a range of inflectional morphemes. The emphasis was on comparing inflectional forms that were phonologically identical (e.g., plural -s, possessive 's, and third person singular -s) as well as on contrasting the nonsyllabic simple s form with the syllabic es following a sibilant consonant. The latter contrast had proven to be of interest in Jean's earlier work with preschool children. One of the questions raised in this study was whether there was a parallel between the partially mastered grammatical knowledge of the preschool children and the degraded grammatical ability of Broca's aphasics.

Although the one-word sentence completion task worked admirably in eliciting inflectional morphology, it was not precisely suitable for probing the availability of multiword constructions such as subject-verb-object (SVO) sentences, wh-questions, and yes/no questions. Free conversation had been and continues to be an excellent source for some of this information; but such samples rarely contain any questions or imperatives, and the presence of other constructions of interest is chancy. Moreover, free conversation affords the subject every opportunity to avoid difficult constructions by using other means or by simply not expressing anything that is difficult to formulate. The goal of the test designer is to bring the target construction under the control of a structured test that can be given repeatedly, with reasonable expectation of eliciting an attempt at the target each time and by any subject.

The solution developed by Jean with collaborators Goodglass and others was the Story Completion Test. This method preserved the principle that the nearest approach to natural speech was a completion format in which a constraining introductory frame was left hanging, awaiting completion with the target—in this case, a multiword sentence ending or an independent sentence. Jean and her collaborators developed two forms of the Story Completion technique—one without pictorial support (Goodglass, Berko Gleason, Bernholtz, & Hyde, 1972)) and others using cartoon strips (Berko Gleason, Goodglass, Ackerman, Green, & Hyde, 1975; Berko Gleason et al., 1980) leading up to the target for completion. An example of a story completion item for eliciting a yes/no question is the following: "John was working upstairs, when he thought he heard his mother call. So he went to the top of the stairs and shouted, 'Mother, . . .'"

Obviously the story format cannot be as constraining as the one-word completion task, so this technique does not completely free the examiner from the problem of dealing with evasive or off-target responses. But it comes close.

The story completion format has had considerable popularity among other aphasia researchers as a means of eliciting specific targets. At the Aphasia Research Center, a number of Jean's colleagues (Harold Goodglass, Hiram Brownell, Lise Menn, Julie Ann Christiansen) applied themselves to the development of a comprehensive Morpho-Syntax Battery for Aphasia, using both the sentence completion and the story completion techniques pioneered years earlier by Jean Berko Gleason. This instrument, in combination with free speech analysis, led to the publication of an extensive study of the expressive and receptive aspects of morphology and syntax in aphasia (Goodglass, Christiansen, & Gallagher, 1994, 1995).

Even though Jean's earliest and most unique contribution in aphasia was in the design of elicitation techniques for the study of morphology and syntax, she has left her mark on a number of other fundamental problems as well. In 1970, again with collaborators Goodglass and Hyde, Jean designed a series of procedures to examine various elementary components of receptive processing: among them, memory span for word strings and discrimination between directional prepositions, and case-marking prepositions (Goodglass, Berko Gleason, & Hyde, 1970). This became a family project, as the stimulus cards for the directional prepositions featured photographs of Pam and Cindy Gleason in various spatial configurations in relation to the family car. Among the items were "The girls going *through* the car " vs "The girls going *out of* the car." This effort gained the authors the 1970 Editor's Award of the *Journal of Speech and Hearing Research.*

Since 1985, Jean has participated in a team effort in the study of word retrieval and its aberrations based on the analysis of a corpus of errors made by aphasic patients and a parallel corpus of responses by normal subjects to a tip-of-the-tongue test created by the research team. Among the studies spun off from this project was a comparison of morphological innovations by aphasics and children (Liederman, Kohn, Wolf, & Goodglass, 1983). The initial error analysis on the aphasia data was published by Kohn and Goodglass (1985), the tip-of-the-tongue analysis was published by Kohn, Wingfield, Menn, Goodglass, Berko Gleason, and Hyde (1987), and an application of the tip-of-the-tongue analysis to the aphasia corpus was described by Goodglass, Wingfield, Berko Gleason, Hyde, and Gallagher (1996).

The story of Jean Berko Gleason's role in the understanding of aphasic language is still unfinished; her ideas are a vital force in the work of the Naming Group at the Boston Veterans Administration Medical Center, where research strategy continues to be formulated and put into practice.

REFERENCES

Berko Gleason, J., Goodglass, H., Ackerman, N., Green, E., & Hyde, M. R. (1975). Retrieval of syntax in Broca's aphasia. *Brain and Language, 2*, 451–471.

Berko Gleason, J., Goodglass, H., Obler, L., Green, E., Hyde, M. R., & Weintraub, S. (1980). Narrative strategies of aphasic and normal-speaking subjects. *Journal of Speech and Hearing Research, 23*, 370—383.

Goodglass, H., & Berko, J. (1960). Agrammatism and English inflectional morphology. *Journal of Speech and Hearing Research, 3*, 257–267.

Goodglass, H., Christiansen, J. A., & Gallagher, R. E. (1993). Comparison of morphology and syntax in structured tests and free narrative: Fluent vs. nonfluent aphasics *Cortex, 29*, 397–407.

Goodglass, H; Christiansen, J. A. & Gallagher, R. E. (1994) Syntactic constructions used by agrammatic speakers: Comparison with conduction aphasics and normals. *Neuropsychology, 8,* 598–617.

Goodglass, H., Gleason, J.B., Bernholtz, N., & Hyde, M. R. (1972). Some linguistic structures in the speech of a Broca's aphasic. *Cortex, 8*, 192–212.

Goodglass, H., Gleason, J. B., & Hyde, M. R. (1970). Some dimensions of auditory language comprehension in aphasia. *Journal of Speech and Hearing Research, 13*, 596–606.

Goodglass H., Wingfield, A., Hyde, M. R., Gleason, J. B., Bowles, N. L., & Gallagher, R. E. (1996). The primacy of word-onset phonology: Error patterns in prolonged naming efforts by aphasic patients. *Journal of the International Neuropsychological Society, 3*, 128–138.

Kohn, S., Wingfield, A., Menn, L., Goodglass, H., Berko Gleason, J., & Hyde, M. R. (1987). Lexical retrieval: The tip of the tongue phenomenon. *Applied Psycholinguistics, 8*, 245–266.

Liederman, J., Kohn, S. E., Wolf, M., & Goodglass, H. (1983). Creative morphology during instances of word-finding difficulty: Broca's vs. Wernicke's aphasia. *Brain and Language, 20*, 21–32.

19

Studying the Pragmatic Microstructure of Aphasic and Normal Speech: An Experimental Approach

Lise Menn
University of Colorado

The term *pragmatics* has been burdened with covering the enormous domain of the study of how language is used: all the choices that speakers are "free" to make—that is, those that are not fixed by the lexicon, the grammar, or the phonology. The term subsumes sociolinguistics as it applies to the behavior of individuals, intersects with diachronic linguistics in matters of style (e.g., Is it correct to split an infinitive?), collides with conversation analysis and discourse analysis, and so on.

The boundary between pragmatics and the traditional "core" areas of linguistics—those that have been (or have seemed) historically more tractable—is fuzzy, but the reason for the difference in tractability is clear enough (and it put the study of semantics outside the "core," for Leonard Bloomfield and the American structuralists): Studying pragmatics requires constant consideration of the speaker's intentions and state of mind, which are fundamentally unknowable. Yet it is this very fact that makes the study of pragmatics so enticing in the scientific era that is now dawning. The current rate of progress in being able to watch the brain in action is like the rate of change everywhere in electronic technology: Unless you've got a friend on the development team, the technology is obsolescing by the time you've heard about it. At the moment of this writing, Finland is about to have a 306-channel Magnetoencephalography (MEG) machine, giving millisecond temporal resolution of magnetic (and hence electrical) activity at 306 sites over the cortex; it uses a non-invasive, non-claustrophobia-inducing method that is sensitive enough to study individual brain activity differences in reading connected text (projected one word at a time: Helenius, 1998; Kuukka, 1998). Thus, although the speaker's state of mind will remain an intangible intermediate construct, the state of the speaker's brain is becoming quite demonstrable objectively. Indeed, intermediate constructs—say, magnetic lines of force, alertness, or noun-hood—intangible though they are, can be investigated empirically, that is, tested for their ability to render data interpretable and predictable. (As researchers we must always be prepared to abandon an intermediate construct when we find one that gives a better account of the data; but in fact, virtually every scientific concept is "intermediate," rather than tangible or directly measurable.)

The imaging of brain functions by available techniques is already relevant to two aspects of current theoretical debates about psycholinguistic language modeling and the development of language in the individual. First, if present indications of the involvement of multiple brain areas in language processing are borne out, viable theories will have to treat the brain as a system that carries out some form of distributed processing. Second, and more controversial at present, if current indications of individual differences are borne out, the only viable theories will be those that treat the brain as a self-organizing system (Elman et al., 1996; Helenius 1998; Kuukka 1998).

One can predict, then, that experimental methods for the study of pragmatics will soon be translatable into methods for studying (a) how and where the brain handles choices in the use of language, and (b) the extent to which and the ways in which these do or do not interact with choices forced by grammar. Indeed, the study of people with brain damage has already been tentatively brought to bear on this topic. Neurolinguists do not say it in print, because it is grossly simplistic; but existing studies, including those I report in this chapter, keep tempting us to say baldly that grammar is "in" the left hemisphere (of typical right-handers) and pragmatics "in" the right hemisphere; and as for the lexicon, well, that is mostly "in" the left but there are also semantic representations of, say, concrete nouns "in" the right. During the next decade, we should be able to find out whether this sketch—terribly crude, yet compatible with all the evidence available—is tenable or not.

In this chapter I set out a picture-description method for the experimental study of two aspects of pragmatics. It has been used so far with normal adults and adults with aphasia owing to left brain damage; it may soon be extended to right brain damaged adults. I hope that readers can develop it for their own needs, whether they are studying kindergartners learning to decenter, assessing and helping people with brain damage, or analyzing brain activity with a terabyte, megabuck functional Magnetic Resonance Imaging (fMRI) machine.

MACROPRAGMATICS, MICROPRAGMATICS, AND LATERALIZED BRAIN DAMAGE: RIGHT VS. LEFT

Levelt's (1989) model of language production introduces the distinction between macropragmatics (macrostructure pragmatics) and micropragmatics (microstructure pragmatics). There is some variation in the use of these terms across authors (cf. Ulatowska & Chapman, 1994), and some aspects of pragmatics do not fit gracefully into either category. However, *macrostructure* generally is used to refer to how an entire narrative or conversation or written work is organized in order to be recognized and be effective as a story, an argument, and so on, whereas *microstructure* is taken to concern the choice of words and syntax that are used to encode an idea that the speaker has decided to put into words.

Macropragmatics therefore concerns the first-pass and large-scale choices: what is to be put into words and how it is to be organized. This is where most of the study of pragmatics in people with brain damage has been focused, except for studies of the comprehension and production of intonation contour. For example, there is work on the structure of re-told stories and narratives of everyday procedures, such as how to fry an egg (Joanette & Goulet, 1990; Ulatowska, Freedman-Stern, Doyel, Macaluso-Haynes, & North, 1983); on the ability to provide summaries and morals to stories (summarized in Ulatowska & Chapman, 1994); on narrative cohesion and coherence; and on the recognition of humor and sarcasm (e.g., Gardner, Brownell, Wapner, & Michelow, 1983; Huber & Gleber, 1982; Joanette, Goulet, Ska, & Nespoulous, 1986).

The clinical study of pragmatics also includes examination of emotional prosody, an area that is given only the barest acknowledgment by experimental psychology and linguistics. It is obvious that emotion is heavily involved in a wide variety of pragmatic choices, but the academic tradition appears to be too uncomfortable with the topic to have developed effective tools for investigating it.

Macropragmatics and Emotional Expression in Aphasia Owing to Left Brain Damage

People with aphasia owing to left brain damage do relatively well on most macropragmatic tasks, making allowances for their word-finding problems. A few studies have found some primary macropragmatic deficits in aphasia. Data from Ulatowska's group (Ulatowska & Chapman 1994 and references cited there) indicate difficulty—in some but not all aphasic subjects—with the tasks of abstracting, summarizing, and recognizing the moral of a story; and Christiansen (1995) documented the production of irrelevant remarks by subjects with Wernicke's aphasia.

Outside of testing situations, exclamations of distress and surprise appear to be used appropriately by people with aphasia; the same is true for voice pitch, voice quality, and facial expressions (except in people who have pseudobulbar palsy in addition to their aphasia).

Macropragmatics and Emotional Expression in People With Right Brain Damage

Right brain damaged (RBD) patients generally show deficits in the expression of emotion: they may show "flat affect," or they may be inappropriately jovial or disinhibited (Molloy, Brownell, & Gardner, 1990). Facial expression and vocal prosody are used less by RBD subjects than by normals in responding to emotional stimuli (Borod, Koff, Lorch, & Nicholas, 1985). People with RBD also show pragmatic deficits in describing emotional stimuli (Bloom, Borod, Obler, & Gerstman, 1993), as well as in classifying and discriminating written words relating to emotions (Borod, Andelman, Obler, Tweedy, & Welkowitz, 1992).

Macropragmatic deficits are found in narratives of RBD subjects who have no discernible disorders on tests of phonology, syntax, or basic word meaning. But this does not mean complete loss of pragmatic ability; for example, in studies of narrative ability, although subjects with RBD produced less information than controls in telling cartoon stories, giving less of the "complication" part of the story (Joanette & Goulet 1990), they organized their stories according to normal story schemas. RBD patients who were asked to choose the "punch line" of stories intended to be funny (Bihrle, Brownell, Powelson, & Gardner, 1986; Wapner, Hamby, & Gardner, 1981) made more errors than normals, but their errors showed some awareness that jokes require a degree of unexpectedness because the subjects chose non sequiturs above straightforward completions.

Molloy et al. (1990) noted, in their review of work done in the Brownell/Gardner laboratory at the Boston VA Medical Center, that patients with RBD gave explanations that "reflected a reduced capacity to reason on the basis of a speaker's motivations in conversation" (p. 121). They suggest that the observed RBD pragmatic deficits might therefore result from more general underlying cognitive problems, such as the inability to integrate new information with old or "to revise initial assumptions." Lalande, Braun, Charlebois, and Whitaker (1992) suggest, along similar lines, that the pragmatic problems are the result of deficits either in some aspect of the arousal of cognitive schemata or in the ability to evaluate conflicts between aroused schemata.

Support for these ideas can be found in the results of Gardner et al. (1983), whose subjects with RBD accepted stories containing elements that were bizarre in terms of ordinary human motivations and included them in their retellings, sometimes fabricating elaborate scenarios in an attempt to integrate all of the information. In contrast, normals dropped or explained away such items in their story retellings, whereas subjects with aphasia, who were presumably less confident that they had heard the strange statement correctly, altered the information so that it made sense within the story.

In Ramsberger's laboratory at the University of Colorado (G. Ramsberger, P. K. Miller, and B. Rende, Feb. 15, 1997, unpublished data, personal communication), the same phenomenon was observed in RBD subjects using visual rather than auditory stimuli. These people were asked to describe a picture of a complex scene set in a grocery store. The scene included a display featuring an Eskimo sitting outside an igloo holding a placard with a dollar sign on it, which was interpreted by both normals and aphasic subjects as a frozen food display in the store. In contrast, subjects with RBD typically just said that there were an Eskimo and igloo in the store; they did not express surprise at this, nor did they attempt to interpret this fact by changing the context of the scene (e.g., suggesting that the store might be in Alaska).

Micropragmatic Studies of People with Lateralized Brain Damage

Micropragmatic choices include whether to use a particular syntactic form such as active or passive voice; whether to use embedding or successive clauses to convey a complex idea; which person or object to mention first;

and whether to use a complex noun phrase, a simple noun, or a pronoun to refer to someone or something. There do not seem to be any studies of micropragmatics in people with right brain damage.

In aphasiology, Bates & Wulfeck (1989) as well as Bates, Hamby, & Zurif (1983) showed that people with aphasia have appropriate reactions to the micropragmatic dimension of new versus old information: For example, if subjects are able to encode only part of the information that normal speakers would use to describe a set of pictures, what they provide is the new (and therefore most important) information rather than the old information. These studies, like ours, used minimally varied cartoon drawings for elicitation. (Greenfield & Smith, 1976, drew similar conclusions from diary studies of two very young children.)

People with aphasia do often use pragmatically inappropriate forms in (a) choosing the pronouns and articles needed to signal whether a character has appeared before in a story, and (b) in producing the conjunctions and other structures that show how statements in a story relate to one another. However, those errors may be entirely owing to the subjects' problems with lexical retrieval and morphosyntax. This ambiguity points up a recurrent methodological problem: It is not always possible to tell what level of processing has given rise to a particular error. I return to this problem in the subsequent discussion.

SPEAKER-ORIENTED VERSUS HEARER-ORIENTED PRAGMATIC FACTORS

Within a psycholinguistic approach to pragmatics (especially in a neurolinguistic context), one also must contemplate a distinction that cuts across the macro/micropragmatic division. The linguists who did the founding work in micropragmatics—notably Chafe (e.g., 1976) and Givon (1983)—took the use of real text data (as opposed to invented materials) to be essential. However, they still idealized the speakers or writers in an important way: They assumed that the speaker/writer who produced the text had fully adequate knowledge of what would be new or old information to the hearer/reader and would produce spoken or written discourse accordingly. This idealization is theoretically problematic (Brown, 1995, pp. 24–29; cf. Levinson, 1983, pp. 15ff.), although it appears to be a useful approximation of reality for many discourses between normal adults. Greenfield and Smith (1976, p. 184), observing young children, were perhaps the first to note the speaker/hearer information distinction, and Karmiloff-Smith (1979) showed experimentally that it is critical in studying children—as is borne out by one's ordinary experience of trying to decode who did what to whom from the unanchored pronouns in children's narratives of playground mayhem. Instead, one must distinguish what I have been calling hearer-oriented versus speaker-oriented discourse factors.

Hearer-oriented factors are ones that indeed take the hearer's state of knowledge into account; whereas in contrast, speaker-oriented factors are those that egocentrically reflect the speaker's impulses and needs. If a speaker presents only new information, is that indeed because she or he knows that the new information is what the hearer needs most, or is it because the novel item has aroused the speaker's interest? If a speaker uses a passive voice ("Sally got bit by a doggie!"), is it really because the speaker's empathy with the undergoer has been aroused, or is it possible that the speaker is deliberately manipulating the hearer ("Our children are being abandoned by our schools!")? In theorizing about production abilities, especially those of a child or a brain-damaged person, one should be cautious about attributing a behavior to hearer-oriented factors if it can also be accounted for by speaker-oriented factors such as arousal of the speaker's interest or attention.

EMPATHY AND EXPECTEDNESS IN APHASIC SPEECH: TWO EXPERIMENTAL STUDIES OF MICROPRAGMATICS

Empathy

Because empathy is a subjective, affective/cognitive state, it cannot be manipulated or measured directly. Rather, the experimenter manipulates properties of the stimulus that should affect the construct, if it is a valid one, and measures responses of the subject that should reflect those variables. In two studies of the expression of empathy in English and Japanese aphasic and normal speech (Menn, Kamio et al., 1999; Menn et al., 1999), my colleagues and I treated "empathy" as a psychologically primitive intermediate construct: roughly, an attitude of "identification or shared viewpoint with" a participant in an event (Kuno, 1978, 1987).

In our elicitation studies the stimuli were cartoon drawings of various events, such as a brick falling on a teddy bear, a girl winning a race and getting a prize, and a dog saving a boy from drowning. A character's (or object's) animacy and its status as protagonist in the cartoon story were the independent variables. We asked the subjects to describe the events, and we developed some measures of putative empathic language in order to analyze their narratives, working from the "shared viewpoint" definition of empathy. We came up with the following list of observable linguistic indicators of empathy to use as the dependent variables:

Partisan emotional expressions	"Hurrah!"
Direct or indirect speech taking the part of the protagonist	"Ouch!" "Sorry!"
Use of the passive voice with the protagonist as subject or topicalization with protagonist as topic	"He get hit"
Use of other forms that bring the protagonist to the beginning of an utterance	"He is drowning; dog save him"
Deixis taking the viewpoint of the protagonist	"The ball comes and hits him"
Reference to the protagonist's mental state	"Bear is dizzy"

These are all prima facie indicators of shared viewpoint with the protagonist—often quite literally, as when the narrator speaks the part of the protagonist ("Sorry!") or uses the deictic verb *come* in phrases such as *comes and hits*. We provisionally referred to the items on this list collectively as empathic expressions. In contrast, agent-first syntax (e.g., "The dog saves the boy") and sound effects ("Bang!") contain no information about the narrator's viewpoint, so they were taken to be empathically neutral.

Sometimes the entity affected by a pictured event was something that has no feelings (e.g., a truck or a toy). When it is an object that is damaged, the terms *empathy* and *shared viewpoint* do not seem appropriate as descriptors of the narrator's responses. However, we continued to use them provisionally because there is no accepted term for the narrator's emotional state in such a case, and the expressive devices, at least in our data, are the same (e.g., use of the passive in "The bag gets hit by a snowball").

The use of empathic expressions in narratives is not obligatory. A person might have an empathic reaction to an event but, like a good card player, fail to show it in any visible or audible way. Thus, a particular utterance might have no scorable empathic language because the attitude of the speaker toward the participants in a particular event did not have an overt verbal manifestation. Or there might also be no empathic language because the speaker in fact had no particular empathic reaction to the event; this degree of indeterminacy will have to be accepted until functional brain imaging makes it feasible to "look inside." Again, research results must be phrased accordingly—that is, in terms of whether subjects use (putative) empathically marked language (etc.), not in terms of whether their feelings are aroused.

In our studies of Japanese and English speakers with and without aphasia (Menn, Reilly, Hayashi, Kamio, Fujita, & Sasanuma, 1998; Menn, Kamio, Hayashi, Fujita, Sasanuma, & Boles, 1999), sketched in the subsequent discussions, we found that all four subject groups (14 English-speaking and 7 Japanese-speaking people with aphasia, plus age/language-matched normal controls) showed the same pragmatic ranges in variety of viewpoints taken, distribution of propositions encoded, and empathic marking. This was the case in spite of the patients' difficulties with syntax and lexical retrieval. The phenomena observed were found in both fluent and nonfluent patients, but the number of subjects in each diagnostic category (Broca's, mixed nonfluent, anomic, and Wernicke's) was not enough to test for possible syndrome-specific tendencies.

Although our method does yield data that reflect subjects' differing syntactic and word-finding difficulties, it has not yet been shown to be sensitive to individuals' differences in pragmatic abilities. We hope it can be developed to this end, because charting individual pragmatic gains is critical both in the clinic and in the study of development.

Empathy Study A:
The Effects of Animacy and
Agency on Pragmatic Microstructure

In this study we asked our subjects to narrate five cartoon stories; each story was presented in 3 to 5 frames, with a total of 19 frames. The cartoons showed events involving all possible combinations of animates acting on animates, inanimates acting on inanimates, animates acting on inanimates, and inanimates acting on animates, so that the animacy factor could be used in analyzing the data. An example is the 'Apple' story (Fig. 19.1).

Fig. 19.1. Apple strip.

Because all of the speakers organized their stories in terms of the events in the successive frames ("Here, the girl is putting on her running shoes"), the responses could be compared on a frame-by-frame basis; the 19 frames could be seen as depicting a total of 29 events. This turned out to be very helpful for several of the analyses that were carried out. The first analysis was a macrostructure-level comparison of the subject groups with and without aphasia as to whether they referred to each event. The English speakers with aphasia managed to encode, on average, almost 80% of the total number of events that the unimpaired English speakers mentioned. Their syntax tended to be much simpler; a speaker with aphasia might say "Ouch!" whereas an unimpaired speaker would say "The brick lands on her shoulder." More impressive, the correlation between the normal and aphasic speakers' frequency of mentioning a given proposition from the story was extremely high at 0.871.

Second, the groups were compared on the microstructure level, looking at which participants in the stories were encoded as subject; the patterns were similar for all four subject groups. This similarity was difficult to quantify but is presented graphically by Menn, Kamio, et al. (1999); the graph for the Apple story is reproduced here (Fig. 19.2).

For both speakers with aphasia and those without impaired language, three factors accounted for the choice of which participant to encode as grammatical subject/topic: Animacy, Motion/Causal Efficacy, and Affectedness. Animacy was overwhelmingly the most important: Aphasic speakers chose animates as subjects/topics in 73% of their 271 response clauses, and control speakers did so in 70% of their 296 response clauses. If an inanimate was chosen as subject/topic of a particular scene, it was most likely to be a cause and/or a freely moving object. (Sridhar, 1989, obtained similar results in a large cross-linguistic experimental study of normal speakers, using filmed stimuli.)

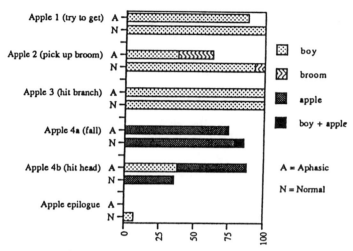

Fig. 19.2. Apple story–Choice of entity encoded as subject.

Six inanimate items were coded—mostly by unimpaired speakers—as subjects/topics of existential sentences, such as "There's a broom leaning against the tree"; these items appear to have been introduced because they were about to play roles in the story. The remaining inanimate subjects/topics were a broken window and a falling lamp, objects seriously affected by the event.

The third analysis was a comparison of the normal and aphasic speakers with respect to their use of empathic markings. Here the correlation between the normal and aphasic speakers' choice of empathically marked (as opposed to unmarked) forms for a given proposition was a highly significant 0.80.

Empathy Study B: Using Graded Undergoer-Animacy Cartoons to Study the Effect of Empathy on Microstructure

This part of the study was designed to allow isolation of a single underlying variable, namely, the putative empathic appeal of the person or object affected by the action. As has been emphasized, empathy cannot be manipulated directly; what we actually varied was how animate the undergoer was (human, teddy bear, object with no resemblance to human) and whether an inanimate undergoer was of value to a person in the picture and likely to be damaged by the action (e.g., we ranked a bag of groceries on a sled that was about to be hit by a snowball as more likely to evoke empathy than the empty sled with a snowball about to hit it).

Everything except the identity of the undergoer was held constant within a graded series. Two parallel series of single-frame cartoons were presented. One series of graded undergoer-animacy pictures showed a snowball flying into the pictured scene and landing on, respectively, a sled being pulled by a child in a snowsuit, a bag of groceries sitting on the sled, a teddy bear riding on the sled, and another child riding on it (Snowball series, Fig. 19.3). The second series (Brick series) showed a brick falling off the scaffolding at a construction site and landing on, respectively, an unoccupied truck, a wagon pulled by a little boy, a teddy bear riding in the wagon that the boy is pulling, and the shoulder of a woman passing by. (With hindsight, we see that the variables intended to affect empathy could have been more closely controlled.) The cartoons were presented in pseudo-random order, interspersed with stimuli for another study.

We introduced each pictured event separately, while the patient was looking at it, with a sentence or two that supplied the needed lexical items (e.g., "Here's a truck parked near some construction, right? A brick falls off."). We then asked the neutral question "What happens?" In Japanese, the subjects were given the neutral instruction "Please explain (this)" (*Setsumei shite kudasai*).

Fig. 19.3. Snowball series.

In this part of the study, two response modes were used: oral responses, as in Part A, and also arrangement of cards with appropriate words printed on them. I just discuss the oral response results here; the card-arrangement responses—which could only be coded for word order—gave similar results but fall somewhat outside this book's topic of language production and, of course, introduce the variable of aphasic reading ability. However, we found, serendipitously, that giving the card manipulation task before the oral response task was helpful methodologically: It got most of the subjects into the mind-set of giving the kind of basic, to-the-point responses that were relatively easy to score for syntactic structure.

We coded empathic marking in the oral responses in the following categories, most of which were also used in Part A: Undergoer Fronting, Passive/Get-Passive, Mental State, Direct Discourse, Deixis, Get-Active Voice, and Judgment/Luck (expressions evaluating the good or bad fortune of the undergoer). We introduced most of these terms in the list on page 19-9, but here are some more examples:

Example 1:   Mrs. "Kalmia" (moderate Broca's aphasia; teddy bear picture, Brick series)
"The *bear*, the bear—is [dIdi]—*dizzy*, uh, dizzy; the [bIts] (brick) fall down an' bear *gets* dizzy."
Empathy markings: Undergoer Fronting ("bear" is the first referent mentioned in this two-sentence narrative; in fact, the brick is not mentioned until the second sentence); Mental State (Teddy bear is "dizzy"); Get-Active ("gets dizzy," second sentence)

Example 2:   Mr. "Wallaby" (mild-moderate anomic aphasia with acquired stutter; grocery bag picture, Snowball series)
"*Comes* the snowball and xxx it hits—it's even possible it could even brea-break some of that mmilk that's open—could spill some of the milk out. And anyhow, it's not a good—*not a good sign*."
Empathy markings: Deixis ("comes"); Judgment/Luck ("not a good sign")

Example 3:   Mr. "Wolf" (severe anomic aphasia; lady picture, Brick series)
"*She*—looks like her hand is, hand is, it's a . . . *something's wrong* with the hand."
Empathy markings: Undergoer Fronting ("she"); Judgment/Luck ("something's wrong")

Both aphasic and normal speakers used the most overt empathic mark-ings to describe events happening to a person, and the fewest for events happening to an unoccupied sled or truck (Fig. 19.4). The linear trends were highly significant (normal speakers, $F(1) = 58.26$, $p = .0001$; apha-sic speakers, $F(1) = 19.65$, $p = .0007$). See Fig. 19.4.

Mean total number of empathic markers used by aphasic and normal speakers, at each level of presumed empathic appeal: 1 = minimal, 2 = object of value to pictured person, 3 = teddy bear belonging to pictured person, 4 = human undergoer.

We divided the empathic markings that the people in our experiment used into syntactic and nonsyntactic types. The syntactic markings were defined as those that involved undergoer-first word order: Undergoer Fronting and Passive/Get-Passive. The other empathy markings could be considered either lexical (e.g., deixis) or discourse-level (e.g., use of direct discourse). Normal speakers again showed a linear trend toward using each of the two syntactic devices more heavily as the subject increased in presumed empathic appeal: Undergoer Fronting ($F(1) = 40.36$, $p = .0002$) and Passive/Get-Passive ($F(1) = 7.48$, $p = .0257$). The speakers with aphasia, however, failed to show a significant empathy gradient in their use of the Undergoer Fronting and Passive/Get-Passive. Instead, it was their use of the nonsyntactic markers—deixis, mental state, direct discourse, and one that we called expressive locative ("right in the face")—that responded to the empathy gradient. Thus, the aphasic

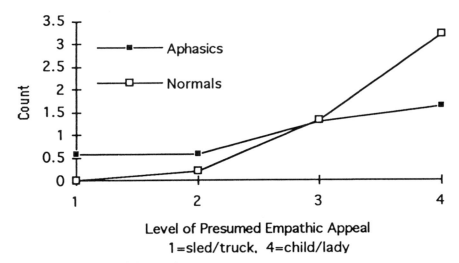

Fig. 19.4. English speakers' responses.

speakers appeared be using a strategy of relying on the syntactically less demanding methods of marking empathy, such as direct discourse (e.g., "Ow!" and its Japanese equivalent, *Itai!*).

In summary, we found that the amount of empathic language used by aphasic subjects varied in the same way as the amount used by normal subjects in both parts of this study, but that the aphasics' linguistic means for expressing empathy were constrained by their language disorders: They clearly had less access to syntactic manipulations. However, there are enough differences between the two groups to make it plausible that there might still be some macro- or micropragmatic deficit that our methods could not detect, perhaps because it could be masked by the aphasic speakers' language limitations.

Expectedness as a Pragmatic Variable.

Menn, Holland, Gottfried, and Garrett (1997) looked at the expectedness of information in a picture to be described. "Expectedness," like "empathy," refers to a psychological construct. Like empathy, therefore, it cannot be manipulated directly as an independent variable, nor can it be measured as a dependent variable. Rather, it is treated as an intermediate variable and tested for construct validity; it is valid only to the extent that it gives good explanations of the relationship between the situation to be described and the language used by the person giving the description. Expectedness can be (a) speaker oriented, considering that unexpected items are salient, or (b) hearer oriented, because unexpected items are new information. At present, we have no way of teasing these aspects apart.

As locatives are difficult for many people with aphasia to express accurately, we examined the effect of expectedness in the arena of locative description. We contrasted pictures showing culturally "counterexpected" spatial relationships (e.g., a pillow at the foot of a bed) with their "expected" counterparts (e.g., a pillow at the head of a bed). (Linguists might like to think of such pictures as constituting a pragmatic minimal pair.)

The pictures were actually photographs of Barbie-type doll furniture and household objects, taken close-up; this permitted many variations of position with uniform lighting and background. To make the pictures more realistic, we included appropriate background items (e.g., a night table with a lamp next to the bed) along with the critically oriented pair. Articles that were originally in weird colors (pink refrigerator, purple wardrobe) were repainted in conventional colors with model paints, and the results were realistic enough to satisfy most of the subjects. Fifty photographs were shown to the subjects; eleven of them—four expected/counterexpected pairs and a set of three neutral configurations—were used in the spatial relationship study.

Before we made the photographs, we polled about six staff members at the University of Arizona National Center for Neurogenic Disorders with a cloze test to make sure that our notions of expectedness were reasonable. The expected items that we used were (1) a kitchen chair facing a bare matching table, (2) the chair facing a set matching table, (3) a pillow at the head of a made bed, and (4) a small table with a table lamp on it. The corresponding counterexpected items were (1) the chair with its back to the bare table, (2) the chair with its back to the set table, (3) the pillow at the foot of the bed, and (4) the small table with the lamp on the floor next to it. The three neutral photographs contained a clothes hanger and the bed: (1) the hanger on the bed near its head, (2) the hanger on the bed near its foot, and (3) the hanger near the bed on the floor. These were considered to be neutral because it is not strange for clothes hangers to be lying around, at least briefly, in a bedroom, and because there is no particular place with respect to a bed that they "should" be. (If the picture had been of a closet, then hangers on the rod would have been expected and hangers on its floor would have been counterexpected.)

The subjects were asked to describe each photograph in such a way that it could be recognized by a listener; to liven up the task (this being during and just after the notorious O. J. Simpson trial), we asked subjects to pretend that the pictures were photographs of a crime scene and that a list of the photograph descriptions was being made in case one of the pictures was later found to be missing. To reinforce the detective game, the practice pictures included one of a hatchet on a bed. Both normal and aphasic subjects were mildly amused by these instructions, although some of the older normal speakers gave more details than we had intended; in future work, we will use fewer background items.

Our subjects were 16 people with aphasia, age range 40 to 78—anomic, 5 Broca's, 1 limited-fluency anomic, 2 with conduction aphasia, and 1 with Wernicke's aphasia, according to the Boston Diagnostic Aphasia Examination (Goodglass & Kaplan, 1983) or Western Aphasia Battery (Kertesz, 1982). Severity ranged from severe/moderate to moderate/mild; there were 10 control subjects (for some items, 9), age range 25 to 70.

Both normal and aphasic speakers gave many more explicit encodings of spatial relationships between two pictured objects when the relationship between them was counterexpected (e.g., the pillow at the foot of the bed) than when it was expected. Specifically, for counterexpected relationships,

TABLE 19.1
Attempts to Express the Figure and its Location, by
Subjects with Aphasia and by Control Subjects

	Percentage of Attempts/Opportunities			
	Encoding "Figure"		Encoding Location	
	Aphasic	Control	Aphasic	Control
Expected	73	67	13	41
Neutral	90	93	50	93
Counterexpected	97	100	78	100

Note. There were 176 total opportunities for subjects with aphasia, 106 for control subjects.

normal speakers gave explicit spatial information 100% of the time, and speakers with aphasia attempted to provide it 78% of the time (see Table 19.1, encoding location). Speakers with aphasia often made heroic efforts to communicate a counterexpected state of affairs: The most severely affected participant, a man with Wernicke's aphasia and almost no ability to name objects, responded to the picture of the bed with the pillow at the wrong end this way: "Before, nice, go sleep over here, nice over here; you know, before, now over here (makes negative facial expression) so forget about dat one." When the spatial relationships were expected (e.g., the pillow in its usual position at the head of the bed), normal speakers provided explicit spatial encodings in only 41% of the instances, whereas speakers with aphasia attempted to provide it in 13%. Indeed, for both normal and aphasic speakers, smaller objects in expected positions (e.g., pillow at head of bed, chair in usual orientation) were not even mentioned about 30% of the time (Table 19.1, columns 1 and 2); one normal speaker simply labeled the picture with the pillow at the expected end of the bed "A bedroom." Calling the pillow the "figure" in such a case is obviously incorrect; this points up the rarely acknowledged fact that the terms *figure* and *ground* are also psychological intermediate constructs, like *empathy* and *expectedness*.

When there was no expected spatial relation between two pictured objects (e.g., a clothes hanger on the bed), normal subjects still expressed the spatial relationship explicitly (93%), but speakers with aphasia in the severity range attempted to give this information only half the time (50%); for example, subject with anomic aphasia said "It's a . a . a bedder a bed an' the um hanger, ya' know." Perhaps aphasic speakers in a test situation prefer not to encode spatial configurations unless they are "newsworthy" and therefore worth the effort of coming up with the words and syntax. This way of stating the interpretation would imply that the aphasic speakers' behavior was a conscious, hearer-oriented (strategic) choice. However, the high frequency of mentioning counterexpected spatial relationships could also be preconscious (speaker-oriented): Perhaps the strange spatial configurations simply aroused the speakers more strongly.

The percentage of correct forms in encoding location was very low for all speakers with aphasia, as can be seen from Table 19.2. Indeed, normal speakers made errors in describing 4 of the 37 instances of counterexpected locations, for example, "A chair with a table turned backwards to the place setting" (intonation did not indicate that the "turned backwards" clause applied to the chair); "a pillow on the wrong side of a made bed."

The error rates in Broca's speakers were extremely high when they attempted to provide locative information—indeed, there were only two correct location responses among the total of 19 attempts made by the five speakers with Broca's aphasia, one neutral and one counterexpected. The speakers with anomic aphasia made twice as many attempts to encode location and succeeded in about half those attempts. Clearly, if a researcher needs a high yield of location errors to analyze, requesting patients to describe counterexpected arrangements of familiar objects should work quite well.

Effects of Stimulus Order.   The pilot work for the expectedness study, done with normal subjects only, produced some interesting additional information that is relevant to the design of elicitation methods

TABLE 19.2
Percentage of Attempted Encodings
That Were Correct

	Encoding "Figure"			Encoding Location		
	5 Broca's	7 Anomic	10 Control	5 Broca's	7 Anomic	10 Control
Expected	94	100	100	no attempts	40	100
Neutral	57	83	100	20	64	100
Counterex- pected	90	92	100	7	50	89

Note. There were a total of 50 figure attempts for subjects with Broca's aphasia, 64 for subjects with anomic aphasia, and 91 for control subjects; 19 location attempts for subjects with Broca's aphasia, 38 for subjects with anomic aphasia, and 81 for control subjects.)

of this general type; if ignored they would cause serious problems, but as variables to manipulate they seem intriguing. What we found was a substantial effect of the stimulus order, plus heavy effects of the phrasing of example items; these completely overrode predicted effects of item salience on word order.

The pilot work was done on about 14 normal subjects, who saw slightly differing sets of photographs as we attempted to weed out pictures that were difficult to interpret. Subjects also got slightly varying instructions as we tried to find a way of explaining the test task that would elicit approximately the desired level of detail in the responses.

As indicated, there were 39 pictures in the stimulus set in addition to the 11 analyzed for the expectedness study. Many of these pictures varied a different dimension: whether the two principal objects belonged together or not. Their relative positions were not varied. For example, expected pictures showed such item pairs as a pot on a stove-burner or ice cream in a freezer; unexpected pictures showed the pot on a couch or the ice cream on the stove-burner. Elaboration of coding was not predicted for these cases; instead the effect we were looking for was errors of naming based on arousal of expected schemata—perhaps calling an ice cream container on a stove a "pot." We wanted to pursue this because it seemed like a potential source of general aphasic naming errors. Unfortunately, only one or two such errors occurred in the whole data set, not enough to analyze.

In the pilot study, most of the subjects saw the 50 pictures in an order that had mostly expected items in the first half, and mostly unexpected or counterexpected items in the second half; but three subjects (giving 50 responses each) saw them in exactly the reverse order. (Only the normal speakers who saw the pictures in the "expected-early" condition were used as controls for the aphasic speakers, who all saw the pictures in that condition.)

We coded responses as to whether they did not mention the smaller item at all, mentioned it but did not give an explicit encoding of its location, or gave a fully elaborated location description. Subjects who saw counterexpected pictures before their expected counterparts gave twice as many elaborated encodings of the pictures as a whole than did those who saw the expected ones first. Apparently, we had created a situation-specific pragmatic bias that overrode the general effect of expectedness: Our subjects seemed to have learned that in the local context of the task, they could not rely on everyday expectations. We conclude that experiments based on description of a series of pictures are exquisitely sensitive to order of stimulus presentation; the experiment becomes a discourse world of its own. Thus, in planning semantic/pragmatic "minimal-pair picture" elicitations, stimulus order must be controlled; at least with unimpaired speakers, if one loads counter-expected items toward the beginning of a stimulus set, one can obtain explicit location encodings for expected as well as counter-expected items.

Effects of Stimulus Order and Example Wording.   In the pilot study, we gave each subject the first practice item with an example response, to try to elicit approximately the amount of speech that we wanted to analyze. About half the pilot subjects heard "There's a hatchet on a bed," and the others heard "There's a bed with a hatchet on it." We were astounded to find how strongly subjects kept to the initial pattern: 94% of the responses in the five subjects who heard figure/ground model sentences, and 71% of the responses in the three subjects who heard ground/figure models, remained in the same order as the model. Factors such as relative size and emotional import (e.g., a large kitchen knife on a living room table) did not affect the order of mention of the objects.

Clearly, if one wishes to analyze order of mention, example sentences cannot be used; as a result, in working with our aphasic speakers we changed procedure and just cued them by saying "Tell me a little more" or "That's more information than we really need," to get them to give responses of about the right length.

Toward an Experimental Functional Linguistics: A Modest Step

Consider again the issue of why the subjects with aphasia, unlike those with normal language, gave more information in the counterexpected case than in the neutral case (remember to take this result, even though statistically significant, with a grain of salt, because there was only one "family" of neutral stimuli here). Although omitting the spatial information in the hanger/bed photos gives information that is incomplete, the information that it gives is not wrong. In contrast, if a speaker omits mention of the spatial configuration in a counterexpected case, the hearer will be effectively misled; hearing a person with aphasia say simply "table, lamp," hearers are unlikely to consider the possibility that the lamp is in a strange position with respect to the table. Thus, no information is wrong information in the counter-expected case.

As pointed out previously, one cannot yet say whether the subjects— normal or aphasic speakers—are deliberately crafting their descriptions of the pictures in such a way as to avoid raising incorrect mental pictures in the mind of the hearer. To put it more formally, whether the provision of more information in the counterexpected case is a matter of the speaker's arousal or of the speaker's concern with conveying correct information to the hearer is difficult to determine.

Even with our small data set, the subtleties involved in evaluating possible cues about this issue are considerable. For example, when normal speakers described the picture of the small table with the lamp sitting on the floor next to it, they never specified that the lamp on the floor was a table lamp. Does this mean that they were not hearer oriented enough to realize that the hearer might visualize a floor lamp standing there instead? Or did they figure that saying "on the floor" would be cue enough to cause the hearer to visualize a table lamp, because if one were describing a table with a floor lamp next to it, mentioning the floor itself would be redundant? Clearly, the field of micropragmatics, even in such a mundane area as this, is full of opportunities for experimental studies of how people actually do describe things and for development of theories as to why they do so.

CONCLUSION: USING CONTROLLED-VARIATION PICTURE ELICITATION METHODS IN RESEARCH DESIGN

The empathy and expectedness study methods that my colleagues and I have used should be extendable to other areas of pragmatics. Psychologists often prefer to study comprehension, I think, just because the data analysis is so much easier: The variables are controlled by the experimenter, and the responses can be strictly defined events such as picture pointing or button pushing. But production is also amenable to controlled study and to analyses that do not become a linguistic jungle. Using pictures that vary only in one dimension, such as the animacy of the undergoer or the expectedness of a configuration of objects, allows a tightly controlled design and yields a relatively constrained and quite analyzable set of speech responses. To be sure, the responses are less natural than those one can obtain from more open-ended picture narratives, let alone free conversation; but as chapter 1 of this volume emphasizes, no single method of data collection is going to give the entire picture of production abilities for all purposes. And as chapter 17 points out, "free" conversation and elicited narratives are also affected by the speaker's agenda.

The main caveat for the use of minimally varied picture stimuli is that repeated similar stimuli readily create their own little discourse world. Stimulus order effects were discussed previously; also, in exploratory work for a study not reported here, my colleagues and I found that a kind of topicality developed rapidly. Specifically, a male character in a picture shown early in a stimulus set became "that guy" or "he" or "him again" on his second or third appearance, even though the subject had responded to a large number of intervening irrelevant picture stimuli.

The use of stimuli like ours is not restricted to the study of pragmatics. The "empathic undergoer" and "unexpected configuration" pictures can also be used as tools to study syntax and some areas of lexicon. Because people with aphasia evidently work hard to find the words and syntax needed to describe such pictures, these elicitation stimuli provide relatively natural ways to explore the limits of a person's encoding capacity. Karmiloff-Smith (1979) is the great pioneer in using complex but controlled elicitation materials for language acquisition work, and McKee (McKee, McDaniel, & Snedeker, 1998) developed it specifically for working with relative clause production. On the other hand, one cannot count on picture descriptions to give a high yield of a particular type of syntactic construction: For example, as I have shown, there are many ways to indicate empathy that can be used by normal as well as aphasic speakers. Well-designed stimuli can increase the likelihood that *some* form of elaborated description will be used, but the choice of form is still up to the speaker. If it is important for research or clinical purposes to constrain the speaker further, syntactic priming (Bock & Lobell, 1991) should be effective, at least with normal subjects; our finding that the syntactic pattern used for the example sentences percolated through most of the rest of the responses indicates that this method can be used without much additional loss of naturalness.

Implications for Cognitive Science

A more general conclusion can also be drawn from the results of the main expectedness study. People depend on real-world knowledge to supply varying but always large amounts of additional information to create the mental picture. To say, in the real world, "I see a cup and saucer on the table," is, after all, to imply that one sees a cup and saucer, of the same pattern, both concave upwards, with the cup resting, centered, on the saucer; if any of these additional unexpressed pieces of information is in fact not the case, then a well-intentioned speaker, under a fair range of circumstances, must indicate that the ordinary implication fails (e.g., "but the cup isn't on the saucer"). This well-known but frequently ignored fact has serious implications for such enterprises as getting computers to understand language; to put it bluntly, such efforts will not succeed unless the computer has an adequate model of the human's knowledge and expectations about all the domains the computer is expected to "understand." Decoding the speaker's words and syntax, as enormous a task as that will be, is only going to be the first step in figuring out what a speaker means.

ACKNOWLEDGMENTS

Many thanks to the participants in these studies; to my co-authors, Akio Kamio, Ikuyo Fujita, Sumiko Sasanuma, Kathleen F. Reilly, Makoto Hayashi, Larry Boles, Michael Gottfried, Audrey Holland, and Merrill F. Garrett; to our research assistants, Yasunori Morishima and Giulia Bencini, and our artists, Kuniko Tada and Gail Arce; and also to William Bright, who has edited more drafts of proposals and papers on this topic over the last 10 years than any of us can remember. Portions of this work were supported by NIH grant PHS-DC00730-02, the Japan Society for the Promotion of Science, and the Japan–U.S. Educational Commission (Fulbright Commission). We are grateful for the cooperation of our data collection/subject recruitment sites: the Speech-Language Clinic of the University of Colorado, the Speech-Language Clinic of the University of Hawaii, the National Institute for Rehabilitation of the Disabled in Tokorozawa, the Tokyo Metropolitan Institute of Gerontology, and the Center for Neurogenic Language Disorders at the University of Arizona.

REFERENCES

Bates, E., Hamby, S., & Zurif, E. (1983). The effects of focal brain damage on pragmatic expression. *Canadian Journal of Psychology, 37,* 59–84.

Bates, E., & Wulfeck, B. (1989). Crosslinguistic studies of aphasia. In B. MacWhinney & E. Bates (Eds.), *The Cross-Linguistic Study of Sentence Processing* (pp. 328–371). Cambridge: Cambridge University Press.

Bihrle, A. M., Brownell, H. H., Powelson, J. A., & Gardner, H. (1986). Comprehension of humorous and nonhumorous materials by left and right brain-damaged patients. *Brain and Cognition, 5,* 399–411.

Bloom, R. L., Borod, J. C., Obler, L. K., & Gerstman, L. J. (1993). Suppression and facilitation of pragmatic performance: Effects of emotional content on discourse following right and left brain damage. *Journal of Speech and Hearing Research, 36,* 1227–1235.

Bock, K., & Lobell, H. (1991). Framing sentences. *Cognition, 35*, 1–39.

Borod, J. C., Andelman, F., Obler, L. K., Tweedy, J. R., & Welkowitz, J. (1992). Right hemisphere specialization for the identification of emotional words and sentences: Evidence from stroke patients. *Neuropsychologia, 30*, 827–844.

Borod, J. C., Koff, E., Lorch, M. P., & Nicholas, M. (1985). Channels of emotional expression in patients with unilateral brain damage. *Archives of Neurology, 42*, 345–348.

Brown, G. (1995). *Speakers, listeners, and communication: Explorations in discourse analysis.* Cambridge: Cambridge University Press.

Chafe, W. (1976). Givenness, contrastiveness, definiteness, subjects, topics, and point of view. In C. Li (Ed.), *Subject and topic* (pp. 25–56). New York: Academic Press.

Christiansen, J. A. (1995). Coherence violations and propositional usage in the narratives of fluent aphasics. *Brain and Language, 21*, 9–20.

Elman, J. L., Bates, E. A., Johnson, M. H., Karmiloff-Smith, A., Parisi, D., & Plunkett, K. (1996). *Rethinking innateness: A connectionist perspective on development.* Cambridge, MA: MIT Press.

Gardner, H., Brownell, H., Wapner, W., & Michelow, D. (1983). Missing the point: The role of the right hemisphere in the processing of complex linguistic materials. In E. Perecman (Ed.), *Cognitive processing in the right hemisphere* (pp. 169–191). New York: Academic Press.

Givon, T. (Ed.). (1983) *Topic continuity in discourse.* Amsterdam: Benjamins.

Goodglass, H., & Kaplan, E. (1983). *Assessment of aphasia and related disorders.* Philadelphia: Lea & Febiger.

Greenfield, P. M., & Smith, J. H.. (1976). *The structure of communication in early language.* New York: Academic Press.

Helenius, P. (1998, June). *Studies of functional anatomy of reading in normal and dyslectic adults using MEG.* Paper presented at the Nordic research course "Languages, Minds and Brains," University of Joensuu, Finland.

Huber, W. H. & Gleber, J. (1982). Linguistic and non-linguistic processing of narratives in aphasia. *Brain and Language, 16*, 1–18.

Joanette, Y., & Goulet, P. (1990). Narrative discourse in right-brain–damaged right-handers. In Y. Joanette, & H. H. Brownell, (Eds.), *Discourse ability and brain damage: Theoretical and empirical perspectives* (pp. 131–153). New York: Springer.

Joanette, Y., Goulet, P., Ska, B., & Nespoulous, J.-L. (1986). Informative content of narrative discourse in right-brain–damaged right-handers. *Brain and Language, 29*, 217–248.

Karmiloff-Smith, A. (1979). *A functional approach to child language: A study of determiners and reference.* Cambridge: Cambridge University Press.

Kertesz, A. (1982). *The Western Aphasia Battery.* New York: Grune & Stratton.

Kuno, S. (1978). *Denwa no bumpoo* [Grammar of discourse]. Tokyo: Taishukan.

Kuno, S. (1987). Functional syntax: Anaphora, discourse, and empathy. Chicago: University of Chicago Press.

Kuukka, K. (1998, June). *Whole-head MEG and the neural processing dynamics of connected text.* Paper presented at the Nordic research course "Languages, Minds and Brains," University of Joensuu, Finland.

Lalande, S., Braun, M. J., Charlebois, N., & Whitaker, H. A. (1992). Effects of right and left hemisphere cerebrovascular lesions on discrimination of prosodic and semantic aspects of affect in sentences. *Brain and Language, 42*, 165–186.

Levelt, W. (1989). *Speaking.* Cambridge, MA: MIT Press.

Levinson, S. (1983). *Pragmatics.* Cambridge: Cambridge University Press.

McKee, C., McDaniel, D., & Snedeker, J. (1998). Relatives children say clauses produced by English-speaking children. *Journal of Psycholinguistic Research, 27*, 573–596.

Menn, L., Holland, A. L., Gottfried, M., & Garrett, M. F. (1997, January). *Pragmatic effects on locative encoding in aphasic and normal speech.* Paper presented at the Annual Meeting of the Linguistic Society of America, Chicago.

Menn, L., Kamio, A., Hayashi, M., Fujita, I., Sasanuma, S., & Boles, L. (1999). The role of empathy in sentence production: A functional analysis of aphasic and normal elicited narratives in Japanese and English. In A. Kamio and K. Takami (Eds.), *Function and structure* (pp. 317–355). Amsterdam: Benjamins.

Menn, L., Reilly, K. F., Hayashi, M., Kamio, A., Fujita, I., and Sasanuma, S. (1998). The interaction of preserved pragmatics and impaired syntax in Japanese and English aphasic speech. *Brain and Language, 61,* 183–225.

Molloy, R., Brownell, H., & Gardner, H. (1990). Discourse comprehension by right-hemisphere stroke patients: Deficits of prediction and revision. In Y. Joanette & H. H. Brownell (Eds.), *Discourse ability and brain damage: Theoretical and empirical perspectives* (pp. 113–130). New York: Springer.

Sridhar, S. N. (1989). Cognitive structures in language production. In B. MacWhinney & E. Bates (Eds.), *The cross-linguistic study of sentence processing* (pp. 209–224). Cambridge: Cambridge University Press.

Ulatowska, H. K., & Chapman, S. B. (1994). Discourse macrostructure in aphasia. In R. L. Bloom, L. K. Obler, S. De Santi, & J. Ehrlich (Eds.), Discourse analysis and applications: Studies in adult clinical populations (pp. 29–46). Hillsdale, NJ: Lawrence Erlbaum Associates.

Ulatowska, H. K., Freedman-Stern, R., Doyel, A. W., Macaluso-Haynes, S., & North, A.J. (1983). Production of narrative discourse in aphasia. *Brain and Language, 19,* 317–334.

Wapner, W., Hamby, S., & Gardner, H. (1981). The role of the right hemisphere in the apprehension of complex linguistic materials. *Brain and Language, 14,* 15–33.

20

Eliciting Language From Patients With Alzheimer's Disease

Loraine K. Obler
*City University of New York Graduate School,
Program in Speech and Hearing Sciences*

Susan De Santi
New York University Medical Center

Heidi: I came to talk to you this morning because I think you're interesting [laugh].
Elsie: Well, you're glad that you can stay as long as you want to stay a while.
Hamilton (1994, p. 52)

Working with patients with Alzheimer's disease can be a pleasure because in many patients a certain engaged charm continues until late in the disease, as the interaction recorded by Hamilton suggests.[1] The characteristic Alice-Through-the-Looking-Glass interaction with these patients can be fascinating for the researcher. For family members, by contrast, the apparent dissolution of the person they knew before the disease, and their inability to communicate with the family member, can be devastating (Mace & Robins, 1981).

---

[1] Most behavioral changes are in the direction of belligerence. Those patients who become more combative with the disease are unlikely to be studied. However, a colleague in another field once shared with LKO her distress that her mother, sharply critical through life, had become uninterestingly "nice" under the influence of dementia.

Studying the language of patients with Alzheimer's disease can be challenging. Before we consider various techniques for studying the language of patients with Alzheimer's dementia, we must mention how the disease state can be diagnosed and describe how the language patterns associated with the dementia that occurs in it typically manifest.

DIAGNOSING ALZHEIMER'S DISEASE

In the final analysis, a definitive diagnosis of Alzheimer's disease can only be made at autopsy by identifying cellular changes (senile and neurofibrillary tangles)—first reported by Alzheimer (1907, 1911)—that co-occur with a delimited set of progressive behavioral changes before death. Behavioral neurologists identify these changes as including problems in at least three of four areas: memory, language, behavior/temperament, and "the ability to manipulate acquired knowledge" (e.g., to spell the word *world* backwards or to count backwards by sevens from one hundred).

A more formal definition comes from the standard psychiatric diagnostic manual: With dementia there are "multiple cognitive deficits that include memory impairment and at least one of the following cognitive disturbances: aphasia, apraxia, agnosia or a disturbance in executive functioning" (American Psychiatric Association, 1994, p. 134). Aphasia includes the language problems we discuss in the following section. Apraxia involves difficulty carrying out even simple tasks (e.g., "Wave good-bye") when told to. Agnosia involves impairment in the ability to recognize previously known objects or people. Executive functioning includes the abilities to control cognitive abilities, as in the task of spelling *world* backwards.

THE LANGUAGE CHANGES OF
ALZHEIMER'S DISEASE

One can infer from the *Diagnostic and Statistical Manual* definition that language changes do not necessarily occur in Alzheimer's dementia. Indeed, there is a subset of patients—many with later onset of the disease, after age 70—who show little language impairment relative to impairment in memory and real world behavior (Martin, 1990). But for a large subset of patients with Alzheimer's disease (AD), a certain characteristic decline in language can be seen. Alzheimer himself gave a detailed picture of the language decline through his bedside interactions with and testing of his patients (Alzheimer, 1907, 1911; see also Bayles, Tomoeda, & Trosset, 1992 and 1993; Bayles & Kaszniak, 1993; Mathews, Obler, & Albert, 1994; Obler & Albert, 1984). In the early stages there are problems with remembering the names of objects and actions, as well as of people who are outside the immediate family, and there may be some extra repeating of conversational units (LKO remembers a friend's great grandmother who turned to me four times in the course of our hour-long first meeting to graciously ask me what brought me to her island). Comprehension in daily life does not appear impaired, although on testing with long, complex, nonredundant material, comprehension problems may be seen. Phonological structure of words and syntactic structures are not problematic. In the early stages, repetition tasks can be performed well until low frequency words or phrases or longer, more complex sentences are given.

At the mid stages of the disease, however, these patients can be mistaken for patients with florid Wernicke's aphasia. Their comprehension of sentences and low-frequency lexical items is markedly reduced, but they appear relatively unaware of this. The speech they produce is "fluent," that is, it includes all functors even if sentences may be somewhat fragmented, sometimes effusive and hard to interrupt ("logorrheic"), and quite empty of content, thereby conveying the Lewis Carroll effect. Patients' use of the wrong pronoun or of pronouns without clear referents makes conversation with them difficult to follow. At this stage, patients can still be tested on confrontation naming tasks in which they are shown pictures and asked to name them, although they make numerous errors or are unable to name particularly low-frequency items. On repetition tasks they insert neologistic nonwords into their sentences.

By the late stages, speech production is markedly reduced and limited to a few words and some social formulae. Palilalia (a spontaneous, unrequested repetition of what the interlocutor has said) may occur, and interactive communication with the patient feels distinctly one-sided.

Among the language characteristics that remain relatively spared in AD patients across the stages are the phonological shape of words, syntactic structure across sentence units used, the ability to repeat automatic sequences such as days of the week or numbers or prayers, and the ability to read aloud, albeit without comprehension. Intonation may be spared, and patients may reproduce accurate intonational patterns when words cannot be retrieved.

There are, it should be noted, other patterns of the picture in Alzheimer's dementia. As noted, there are some patients for whom language impairment is relatively minor compared to the other impairments. There are also several reported cases of primary language problems for which the atrophic brain damage is in a less usual area. Schwartz and Chawluk (1990), for example, reported on a patient who showed more of the disorders associated with frontal damage in aphasics, in particular phonemic substitutions in word choice and some breakdown of syntactic structure in production as well as on comprehension tests. We focus here, however, on the largest subgroup of patients with Alzheimer's disease whose language picture was described in the preceding discussion.

TEST BATTERIES

One standard approach to studying language in Alzheimer's disease, particularly if researchers want to focus on its relation to nonlanguage factors such as memory or visuospatial abilities, is to give patients a battery of standard tasks. Although such a research approach permits one to talk about subcategories of patient types (e.g., Martin, 1990), it is not very useful for getting a detailed picture of language performance (unless there are large numbers of language tasks included). Another approach that has been tried often is to give AD patients standard aphasia tests (e.g., Appell, Kertesz, & Fismar, 1982). This approach, too, despite giving somewhat more detailed language data, fails to pick up some of the particularly interesting characteristics of patients' interactional abilities, although it does permit one to address the question of the extent to which language in Alzheimer's dementia is in some ways similar to, and in others different from, that of the aphasias (see Au, Albert, & Obler, 1988 and responses to it in the same issue of *Aphasiology*). Test batteries that specifically address the language and cognitive problems associated with dementia are useful and necessary. The Arizona Battery for Communication Disorders of Dementia (Bayles & Tomoeda, 1993) is one such instrument for assessing functional linguistic communication skills. It provides information about mental status, memory, language comprehension, language production, and visuospatial construction. Either the entire test or subtests can be administered, as some subtests (e.g., story recall in immediate and delayed conditions) are useful as a screening device to determine whether the patient's language is indeed that of Alzheimer's dementia.

COMMENCING RESEARCH
WITH PATIENTS WITH
ALZHEIMER'S DEMENTIA

One basic principle that underlies neurolinguistic research is the subtractive principle. As researchers, we assume that looking at how certain language abilities systematically fall apart in a person with brain damage, and then contrasting those abilities with the ones that are spared, permits us to deduce patterns of language representation and processing that are operating in unimpaired individuals. Thus, in principle, the decline of cognitive abilities (i.e., memory, thinking), along with language abilities in patients with Alzheimer's disease, permits us to study how cognition underlies language use in unimpaired adults. In fact, however, it becomes quite hard to tease apart language and cognition. This is evidenced from the earliest point of any study of patients with Alzheimer's disease when one plans to obtain informed consent from the patients who will participate.

Informed Consent

Ensuring appropriate informed consent on the part of the patients is a difficult task. The legally required procedure is to have the patients sign their own consent forms unless they are found to be incompetent in a court of law. In that case a legal guardian signs for them. The more standard procedure, as many patients do not have legal guardians assigned, is to inform accompanying or visiting family members (if the patient is living outside the home) about the research and request them to co-sign. Information about the project is explained to the patients in redundant ways, and it is the researcher's responsibility to ensure that patients who express a desire to terminate testing at any point are cajoled only minimally and then permitted to stop. Informed consent forms must be written in as simple language as possible with short sentences and paragraphs. The Institutional Review Boards that oversee the ethical issues involved in researchers' projects sometimes ask for clarification on how demented patients can truly give informed consent.

Instructions

Similarly, the researcher must include instructions on the tasks to be administered that will work for all patients. Moreover, owing to the patients' forgetfulness, it is necessary to assure oneself that they continue to remember what the instructions are throughout the task. Presenting training trials and setting training performance criterion levels is one way to ensure that a given patient is appropriate for a given study. Before one of us (LKO) had turned to study of Alzheimer's disease from study of patients with aphasia, she was asked, when still a research assistant, to test a patient's ability to comprehend spatial prepositional use by moving tokens around a maplike board. One patient she believes, in retrospect, to have been demented would respond "Yes, that's very pretty" or some equivalent to each "command." Had the patient misunderstood the directions? Had they not been redundant enough? Or was this task simply beyond the capabilities of a patient with Alzheimer's disease? When appropriate, it has been useful to readminister directions at set intervals during the task to minimize forgetfulness.

There are numerous tasks that cannot be used with patients with Alzheimer's disease, others that can only be used with patients in early stages of the disease, and others that must be modified for use with patients with Alzheimer's disease. For example, lexical decision tasks using a computer usually require the participants to press *yes* for real words and *no* for nonwords. There are AD patients who can handle this task when they are required only to make the *yes* responses for real words; because researchers often do not analyze data from the *no* responses anyway, not much is lost in this modification.

Tasks

As a result of the difficulties that patients have in comprehending tasks and keeping the tasks in mind, a number of possible tasks must be ruled out altogether. In our experience, grammaticality judgment tasks are hard to use in the later stages of the disease but have been successfully used with those in the mild and moderate stages (De Santi, 1993). Other metalinguistic tasks may be problematic as well. Irigaray (1973) developed one for her work with French-speaking demented patients that one of us (LKO) has modified for English wherein the structure of the materials presents even more challenges. The task is to take a base form (such as *legal*) and create its morphological opposite (*illegal*). In French, as the words are all Romance-based, it is the rule of assimilation of the basic negating prefix *in-* in certain environments that must be respected. In English, there is as well the distinction between those base forms that take *un-* as the prefix (*unusual*) and those that take *in-* (*infrequent*) or one of its allomorphs (*irregular*). Although this task is not challenging for normal adults, even elderly ones (Obler, 1983), patients with Alzheimer's disease frequently make errors on it (such errors are, of course, interesting) but more often forget the task altogether, give synonyms instead of antonyms or other words they associate with the base forms, or otherwise evade the task.

In the spirit of searching for a key in a place where there is some light, three tasks have been most used in studying the language abilities of patients with Alzheimer's disease: confrontation naming, discourse elicitation, and repetition. A set of techniques has been used to study the lexicon in patients with Alzheimer's disease. These include (a) simple confrontation naming tasks in which patients are shown pictures of the items, and (b) word-list generation tasks in which patients are asked to generate as many animal names or items in a supermarket as they can, or words beginning with three letters, *F*, *A* and *S*. Because we have recently summarized the literature on naming and the lexicon elsewhere (Nicholas, Connor, Obler, & Albert, 1998), we focus here on the latter two tasks. The focus is on the techniques used to study sentence-level and more extended materials: discourse elicitation and repetition.

TECHNIQUES FOR STUDYING DISCOURSE IN PATIENTS WITH ALZHEIMER'S DISEASE

The two primary tasks that have been used to elicit discourse in participants with Alzheimer's dementia are picture description tasks and engaging patients in conversation (see Ehrlich, 1994). The former has the advantage that even if the patient's language is not meaningful to us as researchers, we know what the target was likely to have been; the advantage of the latter is that patients can be quite appropriately engaged in interactions until a relatively late stage of the disease, and therefore, naturalistic data are readily available. Because such techniques are relatively observational, they tend to require less preparation and more analysis of data. Needless to say, it is important that all interactions be audiotaped using high quality microphones and, if one is looking at certain pragmatic aspects of communication, videotaped as well. In one study of discourse (Nicholas, Obler, Albert, & Helm-Estabrooks, 1985) we planned to better characterize the "empty" speech that characterizes both mid-stage Alzheimer's disease and Wernicke's aphasia. We asked participants to describe what was going on in the Cookie Theft picture of the Boston Diagnostic Aphasia Exam (Goodglass & Kaplan, 1972), and then, after a pilot pass through to identify characteristics that could be counted, we operationalized our definition of these characteristics (e.g., pronouns without clearly specifying references, use of indefinite words such as *thing* and *somebody*) and counted the occurrence of each, correcting for the length of discourse of items for each individual and for each group. By comparison with paragraph-recall tasks, on which patients with dementia give markedly shorter responses than do unimpaired controls, on such tasks patients can go on at some length. Nevertheless, their responses tend to be shorter than those of the unimpaired controls (Ehrlich, 1990; Ehrlich, Obler, & Clark, 1997). By contrast, asking patients to retell fairy tales is only useful in the relatively early stages of the disease. Although one knows the target, most patients tell only sketchy stories because of the substantial memory component required by the task. Using pictures of the events in the fairy tale provides a continuous reminder to patients to include items.

One can modify the pictures used in a number of ways. Ehrlich (1990; Ehrlich et al., 1997), for example, wanted to test the extent to which ideational load and semantic-lexical load entered into patients' abilities to structure a narrative. Thus, he created four stimulus sets, two of which were high in content and two of which, although having the same overall story, were low in content. For each content condition he had one single picture or a series of three pictures that included the story units.

Among the standard items looked for in analysis of discourse, in addition to the length in words, is the amount of information conveyed, the use of nonword neologisms, the use of fragmented sentences (Hier, Hagenlocker, & Shindler, 1985), and various measures of sentence and narrative complexity. As a result of his manipulations, Ehrlich (1990) was able to conclude that problems with aspects of narrative discourse—both semantic-lexical and higher-level ideational planning—contribute to the narrative problems of patients with Alzheimer's dementia.

More and less structured types of conversational analysis can be carried out on conversations. Hamilton (1994) conducted 14 conversations with Elsie over the course of 4 years before planning her analyses of the resulting just-under-five-hours of taped data. Hutchinson and Jensen (1980), by contrast, planned three 15-minute conversations to take place on each of three different days. Moreover, whereas Hamilton let the conversations take whatever direction they might, consistent with whatever her informant, Elsie, raised, Hutchinson and Jensen planned to begin each session using a preset topic, the same for all patients. Lamar, Obler,

Knoefel, and Albert (1994) also simply approached the patients, in this instance relatively late-stage patients, and attempted as naturally as possible to see how far beyond formulaic greetings the conversation could be taken. Sometimes they used as stimuli objects in the patient's room, or meals or other simple activities that were being engaged in.

The data that result from such open-ended elicitation techniques invite description. Hamilton (1994), for example, focused on creating a communicative profile of her participant and then examined how questions and responses played out in the interactions, giving much more attention to her own contributions than many other investigators have. Hutchinson and Jensen (1980) used Searle's (1975) speech act categories, analyzing which one the patients employed, who controlled conversational tasks such as turn and topic control, and how the patients undertook them. De Santi, Koenig, Obler, and Goldberger (1994) examined both syntactic and semantic cohesion produced by two moderately demented individuals during open-ended conversation. In Lamar et al. (1994), because little actual conversation is evident in the late stages of Alzheimer's disease, focus was on pragmatic abilities that were relatively spared or impaired in these patients. Late-stage patients had been deliberately chosen, so more complex pragmatic tasks such as making inferences were not undertaken. Rather, such abilities as keeping eye contact, responding to greeting formulae, asking for clarification, and turn-taking were quantified and inter-individual comparisons were made across the 10 participants.

Some attempts at manipulation of conversation have been undertaken with patients. As mentioned previously, Hutchinson and Jensen (1980) started on a common topic for all participants. In De Santi et al. (1989, 1994), we wanted to evaluate bilingual demented patients' abilities to converse appropriately with their monolingual interlocutors, so different ones came in to engage the patients in Yiddish or English. One methodological problem was that we were unable to find a monolingual Yiddish-speaking interlocutor. Although our Yiddish-speaking examiner had been instructed to use Yiddish to bring patients back to Yiddish if they spoke in English, it would have been disingenuous for her to pretend not to comprehend their English. Laderas (1995) faced a similar problem with Dutch-German examiners of Dutch-German patients. Hyltenstam and Stroud (1985, 1989), by contrast, were able to employ monolingual examiners to preclude this complication.

In sum, conversational and narrative analysis with patients with Alzheimer's dementia can be quite revealing of the elaborate structures and abilities normal speakers have because they break down in such striking ways over the course of the disease. Although the researcher has relatively little control over the direction of the interview, much creativity is called for in analyzing the responses, and many rich analyses can be undertaken even with patients who contribute large amounts of empty speech.

REPETITION

By contrast to conversational analyses, and even narrative picture-description or story-telling tasks, repetition tasks permit the researcher much more control over the material to be elicited from the patient. As long as one can be sure the patient understands the task (doing well on easy items is an indication this is true, at least at the beginning of the task), structure and lexicon can be built in to the stimuli for testing.

For example, De Santi (1993) was interested in learning if familiar, overlearned phrases were relatively spared in Alzheimer's disease relative to novel or unfamiliar phrases. Using a repetition task to explore this, 40 phrases developed by Kempler, Van Lancker, and Read (1988) were administered. These included such phrases as "I've got a bone to pick with you" and "He's turning over a new leaf" (familiar), and "He's got a picture to show of her" and "He's chasing after a white duck" (novel). Although familiar phrases were easier for AD patients than novel phrases, errors were made. The number of errors that AD patients made in certain categories such as omission was larger than that made by unimpaired controls. Of interest was the observation that when the AD patients could not complete the phrases with words, they often completed them with the appropriate rhythm, tone, and contour. This phenomenon was seen only with familiar, overlearned phrases (e.g., for "Sticks and stones can break your bones" they might say 'duh duh 'duh duh 'duh duh 'duh).

The disadvantages of the repetition tasks are that memory can be heavily involved in materials of more than minimal length, as can attention, which tends to be disrupted in demented patients. The disadvantage is that if the patient fails, it is hard to target at what point the failure lies. Is it in taking in the information, potentially even in hearing it? (Hearing screenings are notoriously difficult to conduct with demented patients, who, moreover, tend to be older adults and therefore likely to have reduced hearing.) Or does the repetition problem lie in comprehending it, to the extent that comprehension is necessary for repetition, which is not a minimal extent for items of any length? Or do the errors arise owing to output problems?

In an attempt to tease apart some of these possibilities, we asked patients to repeat sentences spoken by speakers of Standard American English and a comparable set spoken by speakers of English with a foreign accent (Shah, Obler, & De Santi, 1998). The to-be-repeated materials consisted of all items on the repetition subtest of the Boston Diagnostic Aphasia Exam (Goodglass & Kaplan, 1972), ranging from shorter (three-word phrases in sentences) to longer (ten-word) and including phrases Goodglass and Kaplan term "high probability" (e.g., "You know how") to low probability (e.g., "Limes are sour," or "The phantom soared across the foggy heath"). To have more stimulus sentences, Shah developed a second set of comparable materials equivalent on all the afore-mentioned measures plus word frequency. Both lists were recorded by a speaker of Standard American English dialect and a speaker with a moderate degree of foreign accent. Patients and normal controls heard half of all the sentences spoken in standard dialect and the other half spoken with the accent, counterbalanced for length and probability and the list from which they originally came. Only patients with mild and moderate Alzheimer's disease were able to perform on this task, and analyses were made of transcriptions of their taped responses. Of the various levels of analyses that could be conducted, analysis of how many words were correct out of the total was most revealing of the problems patients—particularly those in moderate stages of the disease—had on the repetition task, more for accented materials than for unaccented materials. In the end, however, it was impossible to dissociate cognitive and linguistic contributions to the difficulties the seven patients displayed.

Whitaker (1976) chose to use a repetition task for analysis somewhat by chance. Her patient, who was in the relatively late stages of the disease, was palilalic. Whitaker would give her an instruction and instead of carrying it out, the patient would repeat it back. Because Whitaker was a non-native speaker of English herself, she was interested to observe that the patient would repeat back all or a substantial part of individual sentences in the patient's own dialect. Whitaker then deliberately created sentences with errors in them and was interested to note that the patient spontaneously corrected the morphosyntactic errors in repeating them.

Repetition tasks, then, can be used to create contrasting stimulus sets to answer more specific questions than narrative and conversational tasks usually address. It is possible to engage patients in them at least through the mid to late stages of the disease, and the task is relatively easy for patients to undertake; indeed, as our comments on the Whitaker task suggest, some patients cannot prevent themselves from repeating. Not all questions can be answered with such a task, of course, and crucial questions like the behavioral locus on the deficit often must remain unanswered.

CONCLUSION

In many ways, studies of patients with Alzheimer's disease should be similar to those of children in that longitudinal changes can provide insight not only into language abilities but also into their interaction with changing cognitive abilities. However, it seems that the differences in the test situation are substantial. Patients with Alzheimer's disease can be engaged, as can children, with appropriately attentive examiners and can be employed in relatively naturalistic and cognitively undemanding tasks. The discourse that results is markedly more elaborate in the early and mid stages of Alzheimer's disease than it is in young children, but it is markedly less meaningful. Moreover, the researcher becomes progressively less confident about what the patient's intentions are, particularly in more open-ended tasks. Nevertheless, the insights into pragmatic and structural abilities, as well as the interaction between memory load and linguistic structure, can be richly explored through the techniques discussed in this chapter patients with Alzheimer's disease in order to both understand the breakdown of language and cognition in Alzheimer's dementia and to shed light on human beings' abilities when they are functioning normally.

REFERENCES

Alzheimer, A. (1907). Über eine eigenartige Erkrankung der Hirnrinde. 37 Vers. südwestdeutsch. Irrenärzte in Tübingen, 1906, *Zentrallblatt für Nervenheilkunde und Psych., 63*, 146–148.

Alzheimer, A. (1911). Über eigenartige Krankheitsfälle des späteren Alters. *Zeitschrift für die gesamte Neurologie und Psychiatrie, 4*, 356–385.

American Psychiatric Association. (1994). *Diagnostic and Statistical Manual of Mental Disorders* (4th ed. [DSM–IV]). Washington, DC: Author.

Appell, J., Kertesz, A., & Fismar, M. (1982). A study of language functioning in Alzheimer patients. *Brain and Language, 17*, 73–91.

Au, R., Albert, M. L., and Obler, L. K. (1988). The relation of aphasia to dementia, *Aphasiology*.

Bayles, K., & Kaszniak, A. (1987). *Communication and cognition in normal aging and dementia.* Boston: Little, Brown.

Bayles, K., & Tomoeda, C. (1993). *Arizona Battery for Communication Disorders of Dementia (ABCD).* Tucson: Canyonlands Publishing.

Bayles, J., Tomoeda, C., & Trosset, M. (1992). Relation of linguistic communication abilities of Alzheimer's patients to stage of disease. *Brain and Language, 42*, 454–472.

Bayles, K., Tomoeda, C., & Trosset, M. (1993). Alzheimer's disease: Effects on language. *Developmental Neuropsychology, 9*, 131–160.

De Santi, S. (1993). *Formulaic language in aging and Alzheimer's disease.* Unpublished doctoral dissertation, City University of New York Graduate School.

De Santi, S., Koenig, L., Obler, L. K., & Goldberger, J. (1994). Cohesive devices and conversational discourse in Alzheimer's disease. In R. Bloom, L. K. Obler, S. De Santi, & J. Ehrlich (Eds.), *Discourse in adult clinical populations* (pp. 201–215). Hillsdale, NJ.: Lawrence Erlbaum Assocociates.

De Santi, S., Obler, L. K., Sabo-Abramson, H., & Goldberger, J. (1989). Discourse abilities and deficits in multilingual dementia. In Y. Joanette & H. Brownell (Eds.), *Discourse abilities in brain damage: Theoretical and empirical perspectives* (pp. 224–235). New York: Springer Verlag.

Ehrlich, J. (1990). *Influence of structure on the content of oral narrative in adults with dementia of the Alzheimer's type.* Unpublished doctoral dissertation, City University of New York Graduate School.

Ehrlich, J. (1994). Studies of discourse production in adults with Alzheimer's disease. In R. Bloom, L. K. Obler, S. De Santi, & J. Ehrlich (Eds.), *Discourse analysis and applications: Studies in adult clinical populations* (pp. 149–160). Hillsdale: N.J.: Lawrence Erlbaum Associates.

Ehrlich, J., Obler, L., & Clark, L., (1997). Ideational and semantic contributions to narrative production in adults with dementia of the Alzheimer's type. *Journal of Communication Disorders, 19,* 79–100.

Goodglass, H., & Kaplan, E. (1972). *Assessment of aphasia and related disorders.* Philadelphia: Lea and Febiger.

Hamilton, H. (1994). *Conversations with an Alzheimer's patient: An interactional sociolinguistic study.* Cambridge: Cambridge University Press.

Hier, D., Hagenlocker, K., & Shindler, A. (1985). Language disintegration in dementia: Effects of etiology and severity. *Brain and Language, 25,* 117–133.

Hutchinson, J., & Jensen, M. (1980). A pragmatic evaluation of discourse communication in normal and senile elderly in a nursing home. In L. K. Obler & M. L. Albert (Eds.), *Language and communication in the elderly: Clinical, therapeutic and experimental issues* (pp. 59–73). Lexington, MA: Lexington Books/D.C. Heath and Company.

Hyltenstam, K., & Stroud, C. (1985). The psycholinguistics of language choice and code-switching in Alzheimer's dementia: Some hypotheses. *Scandinavian Working Papers in Bilingualism, 4,* 26–44.

Hyltenstam, K., & Stroud, C. (1989). Bilingualism in Alzheimer's disease: Two case studies. In K. Hyltenstam & L. K. Obler (Eds.), *Bilingualism across the lifespan: Aspects of acquisition, maturity and loss* (pp. 202–226). Cambridge: Cambridge University Press.

Irigaray, L. (1973). *Le langage des déments* [The Langage of patients with dementia]. The Hague: Mouton.

Kempler, D., Van Lancker, D., & Read, S. (1988). Proverb and idiom comprehension in Alzheimer's disease. *Alzheimer Disease and Associated Disorders, 2,* 38–40.

Laderas, S. (1995). *Language choice and language separation in bilingual Alzheimer patients.* Amsterdam: Uitgave IFOTT.

Lamar, M. A., Obler, L. K., Knoefel, J., & Albert, M. L. (1994). Communication patterns in end-stage Alzheimer's disease: Pragmatic analyses. In R. Bloom, L. K. Obler, S. De Santi, & J. Ehrlich (Eds.), *Discourse analysis and applications: Studies in adult clinical populations* (pp. 217–235). Hillsdale, NJ: Lawrence Erlbaum Associates.

Mace, N., & Robins, P. (1981). *36-Hour day: A family guide to caring for persons with Alzheimer's disease, related dementing illnesses and memory loss in later life.* Baltimore: John Hopkins University Press.

Martin, A. (1990). Neuropsychology of Alzheimer's disease: The case for subgroups. In M. Schwartz (Ed.), *Modular deficits in Alzheimer-type dementia* (pp. 143–175). Cambridge, MA: MIT Press.

Mathews, P., Obler, L., & Albert, M. (1994). Wernicke and Alzheimer on the language disturbances of aphasia and dementia. *Brain and Language, 46,* 439–462.

Nicholas, M., Connor, L. T., Obler, L. K., & Albert, M. L. (1998). Aging, language and language disorders. In M. T. Sarno (Ed.), *Acquired aphasia* (3rd ed., pp. 413–449). Orlando: Academic Press.

Nicholas, M., Obler, L., Albert, M., & Helm-Estabrooks, N. (1985). Empty speech in Alzheimer's disease and fluent aphasia. *Journal of Speech and Hearing Research, 28,* 405–410.

Obler, L. (1983). Language and brain function in dementia. In S. Segalowitz (Ed.), *Language Functions and Brain Organization* (pp. 267–282). NY: Academic Press.

Obler, L. (1984). Language through the life-span. In J. Berko-Gleason (Ed.), *Language development* (pp. 275–299). Columbus, OH: Charles Merrill.

Obler, L., & Albert, M. L. (1984). Language in aging. In M. L. Albert (Ed.), *Neurology of aging* (pp. 245–253). New York: Oxford University Press.

Schwartz, M., & Chawluk, J. (1990). Deterioration of language in progressive aphasia: A case study. In M. Schwartz (Ed.), *Modular deficits in Alzheimer-type dementia* (pp. 245–296). Cambridge, MA: MIT Press.

Searle, J. (1975). A taxonomy of illocutionary acts. In K.Gunderson (Ed.), *Minnesota studies in the philosophy of language* (pp. 344–369). Minneapolis: University of Minnesota Press.

Shah, A., Obler, L. K., & De Santi, S. (1998, April). Processing accented English: Alzheimer's disease vs. normal elderly. Paper presented at New York Speech, Hearing, and Language Association, New York.

Whitaker, H. (1976). A case of isolation of the language function. In H. Whitaker & H. Whitaker (Eds.), *Studies in Neurolinguistics: vol. 2* (pp. 1–58). New York: Academic Press.

Index

Siegler, R. S., 141, 147
Sigman, M., 324, 331
Sign language, 127, 317
Sih, C., 295–96, 303, 310
Silverman, S., 295, 298, 304–6, 310
Silvern, L., 226, 246
Simon, N., 316, 320, 331
Simplified registers, 227
Simpson, M., 297, 309
Simpson, T., 42
Simulated Oral Proficiency Interview, 151
Sinclair, J. M., 227, 237, 239, 248
Single-word responses, 319
Sinka, P., 340, 351
Situations, 226, 272–74
Ska, B., 379, 400
SLA: see Second language acquisition
Sleep problems, 314
SLI: see Specific language impairment
Slobin, D., 1–3, 21, 23, 70, 88, 91–92, 98, 114,
    141, 147, 194, 203, 262–63, 264, 265,
    274, 288, 292, 310
Slough, N. M., 262, 268
Smedts, W., 60, 67
Smith Cairns, H., 1, 22
Smith, C., 296, 310
Smith, J. H., 382, 400
Smith, L. B., 135, 147
Smith, M., 184–85, 203, 255, 266
Smith, N., 293, 310
Smith, R., 206, 224
Smith-Lock, K., 340, 352
Snedeker, J., 398, 400
Snow, C., 2, 16, 23, 28–29, 31–32, 36, 41, 43,
    54, 67, 109, 122, 139, 147, 182–83,
    192, 200–01, 203, 227, 248, 251–54,
    256, 265–66, 269, 310, 336, 342, 352,
    356, 359, 364, 368; (co-author) 205–24
Snowling, M. J., 129, 147
Snyder, L., 38, 42, 139, 142
Social agendas, 10
Social beliefs, 366
Social categories, 229
Social class, 214, 226
Social cognition, 244
Social context, 28, 318
Social deficits, 315, 328
Social development, 35
Social factors, 227
Social formulae, 405
Social goals, 361, 365–66
Social interaction, 314, 355

Social knowledge, 244
Social meaning, 226
Social perspectives, 35
Social processes, 262
Social relations, 41, 235, 361
Social Science Research Council, 372
Social situations, 228
Social variation, 228
Social withdrawal, 314
Socialization, 211, 214, 216, 219, 221–22, 226,
    272
Socializing functions, 252
Sociolinguistics, 272, 377
Soderman, T., 151, 153, 176
Sokolov, J., 2, 23, 75, 92, 182, 203
Sonnefeld, J., 363, 368
Soskin, W. F., 279–80, 288
Sound effects, 384
Spadaro, K., 153, 176
Spanish, 3, 165, 230, 234, 236–38, 263
Sparrow, S., 322–23, 331
Spatial configurations, 391–94, 396
Spatial distinctions, 88–89
Speaker-oriented pragmatics, 382–83
Specific Language Impairment (SLI), 4, 14, 18,
    127–29, 132, 134, 136–38, 140,
    296–97, 299, 333–52
Speech acts, 234–35, 274, 320, 411
Speech communities, 229
Speech elicitations procedures, 149–77
Speech events, 221
Speech rate, 294, 300
Speech verbs, 264
Speech/language trade-offs, 291–311
Speed of processing, 348
Sperry, L. L., 252, 267
Spielmann, G., 153, 174
Spinelli, F., 355, 368
Spivey, N., 361, 368
Spontaneous speech, 1–57, 69–93, 151, 221, 291
Sportscasting, 241
Sprott, R. A., 240, 248
Sridhar, S. N., 386, 401
Stacked DM's, 241–43
Staged elicitation technique, 257, 260–61
Stallings, 230
Standardization, 182
Standardized tests, 320–23
Standing behavior patterns, 272
Stanford University, 225
Stanowicz, L., 128, 142
Stanza analysis, 250